My Petersburg/Myself

Mental Architecture and Imaginative Space in Modern Russian Letters

My Petersburg/Myself

MENTAL ARCHITECTURE AND IMAGINATIVE SPACE IN
MODERN RUSSIAN LETTERS

Anna Lisa Crone & Jennifer Jean Day

Bloomington, Indiana, 2004

© 2004 by the authors. All rights reserved.

Excerpts from THE WORKS OF JOSEPH BRODSKY, published by *Komarov-Gordin* as *"Sochineniia Iosifa Brodskogo."* Copyright 1992, 1998 by Joseph Brodsky. Reprinted by permission of Farrar, Straus and Giroux, LLC, on behalf of the Estate of Joseph Brodsky.

"Dlja stranstvija nočnogo mne ne nado..." by Vladimir Nabokov is reprinted and translated by Jennifer J. Day and Anna Lisa Crone by arrangement with the Estate of Vladimir Nabokov. All rights reserved.

Library of Congress Cataloging-in-Publication Data

Crone, Anna Lisa.
  My Petersburg/myself : mental architecture and imaginative space in modern Russian letters / Anna Lisa Crone & Jennifer Jean Day.
     p. cm.
  Includes bibliographical references and index.
  ISBN: 0-89357-313-2
  1. St. Petersburg (Russia)--In literature. 2. Russian literature--20th century--History and criticism. 3. Self in literature. 4. Space and time in literature. 5. Authors, Russian--Russia (Federation)--Saint Petersburg. I. Day, Jennifer Jean, 1973- II. Title.

PG2988..L4c76 2004
891.709'384--dc22

2004009946

Slavica Publishers
Indiana University
2611 E. 10th St.
Bloomington, IN 47408-2603
USA

[Tel.] 1-812-856-4186
[Toll-free] 1-877-SLAVICA
[Fax] 1-812-856-4187
[Email] slavica@indiana.edu
[www] http://www.slavica.com/

To Philip C. Hoffman, M.D.

TABLE OF CONTENTS

PART I. TOWARDS A THEORY OF IDENTIFICATION WITH PETERSBURG SPACE 1

1. The Uses of Space in Petersburg Poetry: From Neutral Description to Identification 11
2. Embattled Spirits-Selves: Elegy and Identification with Petersburg Spaces 37

PART II. "HISTORICAL" TREATMENTS OF PETERSBURG SPACE 57

3. Rushing Back to Nothingness: Historical Treatments of Self and Space before and during the Revolution 61
4. Identification with Petersburg, Dead or Dying 91
5. Attempts to Reverse Time: Traveling in Space in Quest of the Integral Self 145

PART III. PETERSBURG AND THE IDYLLIC CHRONOTOPE: "AHISTORICAL" TREATMENTS OF SPACE 203

6. The Visible Petersburg and the Dominance of Space 209
7. The Buried Sun and the Invisible Petersburg: A Reconstructed Writer's Idyll 239
8. Changing, Mastering, and Amazing Spaces 269

PART IV. MIXED MODELS OF PETERSBURG SPACE AND SELF 297

9. Petersburg Space as Creative and Destructive Memory: Recovered Health and Tragic Sickness in Mandel'štam and Nabokov 301
10. Poem without a Hero: The Complexity of the Creative Self in Twentieth-Century Russia 323
11. Conclusion: The Russification of Petersburg 359

Index 371

Acknowledgments

First and foremost, we wish to thank Prof. George Fowler of Slavica, who took this project on faith, and inspired us to overhaul and rewrite a long-abandoned manuscript; and our patient editor, Dr. Vicki Polansky, who cheerfully helped us through every stage of shaping this project. The astute and detailed criticism of Prof. Nina Perlina (Indiana University) helped us improve the book, and the last-minute reading of the work by Prof. Roman Timenchik (University of Jerusalem) is also gratefully acknowledged.

[A.L.C.] I thank my wonderful co-author, Jennifer Day of Bard College. I dedicated this book to my oncologist, who has taught me to tread gingerly through life in treatment. I wish also to thank my husband, Vladimir Donchik, and my daughter, Liliana Donchik, who have been my constant support and solace. I have a debt of gratitude to my friend and colleague, Sidney Monas (University of Texas at Austin), who first inspired me to study *Petersburg* and who has been a wonderful mentor to me over a quarter of a century. I thank Chicago artist Aleksej Klimov, who did such a fine job executing my husband's cover design.

[J.J.D.] I would like to express my deepest thanks to *my* co-author, Lisa Crone, who has been a scholarly inspiration as well as a wise and caring mentor to me. I treasure her optimism and her laughter. Much gratitude is due as well to my husband, Robert Schott, who, with his enthusiastic support and valued advice, has been an anchor for me.

Anna Lisa Crone *Jennifer Jean Day*
Chicago, Illinois *Annandale-on-Hudson, New York*

August, 2004

Part 1

Towards a Theory of Identification with Petersburg Space

In the St. Petersburg carnivals of recent years, maskers were costumed as the buildings, monuments, and other landmarks of their city.[1] For all the manifold colors of the Venetian *carnivale*, one would look in vain for a person masquerading as the Rialto bridge or the Cathedral della Salute. No, it is Petersburgers who are especially prone to act out or literalize the metaphor of Petersburg space as self in this particular way and in so doing participate in a tradition associated with Russia's northern capital since the late nineteenth century.

This book is a study of that important strain of Petersburg poetry and prose in which the poet identifies himself powerfully with a space, be it a private room, an imperial square or *prospekt* (avenue), or an architectural monument. The phenomenon of the writer's identification of his "self"—individuality, body, psyche—with urban spaces, while not exclusive to Petersburg literature, is one of its salient characteristics in the twentieth century, and one that pervades more than one poetic "school." The importance of Petersburg architecture and space in this tradition has been noted before the Silver Age, to be sure. But the intimate quality and the dynamics of this poetic dialogue with space at the beginning of the new century and beyond have never been studied in adequate detail. Our book is a first attempt to do just that. *My Petersburg / Myself* is not then a general poetics of space à la Bachelard's *La poétique de l'espace*,[2] but the peculiar identification with space at the end of the imperial Petersburg tradition in Russian letters, a phenomenon whose complexity and intensity may be unique in world literature.

The spatialization (spatial treatment) of the struggles of modern man and the human individuality in difficult, even apocalyptic times, is so important

---

[1] These costumes, when not in use during the Petersburg carnivals, are displayed at the Interior Theater on Nevskij Prospekt. They were designed by Nikolaj Beljak, Mark Bornštejn, and Fuat Samigullin.

[2] Gaston Bachelard, *The Poetics of Space*, trans. Maria Jolas (Boston: Beacon Press, 1969).

because in a tradition without a Proust or an existentialist literature the complexity of the human psyche and experience, so prominent in the novels of the great "psychologist" Dostoevskij, moved directly from the garrulous prose of the underground man to these highly personalized visual treatments of the poetic or creative biography in space. Thus the typology of spatial treatments we present in these pages encompasses the psychological complexity of twentieth-century man in perhaps its most compelling Russian version—as "othered" into or onto urban space.

PETERSBURG AND THE IDENTITY OF THE RUSSIAN ARTISTIC INTELLIGENTSIA

The Rumanian philosopher Emil Cioran has written humorously about the Russians' penchant for pondering the problem of their own national identity, both collectively and as individuals. What does it mean to be Russian? Is one Eastern, Western, a curious Eurasian mix? Orthodox or cosmopolitan? He remarks that it is impossible to imagine an Englishman or Frenchman (or their respective literatures) obsessed with this question the way Russian literature has been for 150 years.[3]

In 1836 the Russian philosopher Petr Čaadaev asked "Who are we?" and "When are we?", and concluded that the incompleteness of the answer and of Russian historical experience was probably a result of *where they were*, their geographical location.[4] Čaadaev, denied after his "First Letter" the right to publish in Russia for the rest of his life, did not have the opportunity to solve these problems, and they have been thrashed out in Russian literature, philosophy, and political thought ever since. The problem became especially acute in the Silver Age (1890–1920 circa), when most of the writers in this study entered the literary arena. This was so because the Russians of their generation shared an apocalyptic sense that history, and particularly the Petersburg period of Russian history, was about to end, and that the time remaining for Russia to make her mark in world history and culture was severely limited. After the Bol'ševik Revolution of 1917, attempts to impose a Soviet supranationality (albeit with a largely "Russian" content) and to create a Soviet cultural monopoly further clouded the problems of what was "Russian" in Russian literature and culture. In that framework of Soviet-Russian culture, Petersburg was severely debunked from its erstwhile central importance. In

---

[3] E. M. Cioran, *The Temptation to Exist*, trans. Richard Howard (Chicago: Quadrangle Books, 1968), 311.

[4] Peter Yakovlevich Chaadayev, *Philosophical Letters and Apology of a Madman*, trans. Mary-Barbara Zeldin (Knoxville: University of Tennessee Press, 1969), 165 ff.

Soviet parlance and ideology there was a renewed attempt to make Petersburg "peripheral."

For very long periods Petersburg had not been considered sufficiently Russian in the national consciousness. Gogol' had called Petersburg an "*akkuratnyj nemec*" (a fastidious German) and a "foreigner in its native land," and many Petersburgers are viewed similarly by their compatriots. In reaction Petersburgers, writers and artists in particular, appear to bolster their sense of identity by affixing it to place: in so doing they unwittingly invert the Slavophile attachment to the Russian earth. For there was no solid earth under Petersburg. Given its swampy location and the turbulent waters under it, the Petersburger chose to identify with the man-made buildings and squares of the northern capital instead of the barren landscape.

As in many other things, it is Dostoevskij who first understands this ploy, putting it into the mind of the ultra-Westernizer Karmazinov in *The Possessed*: "Holy Russia is a poor, wooden, and—and dangerous country.... In Europe ... there are stone structures there and people have something to hold onto."[5] Hence it is no wonder that studies concerning a Russian poetics of space have dealt more often with Petersburg's European spaces than with Moscow. Petersburg, with its Western Neoclassical buildings, statuary, and strict urban layout, is a strikingly organized space, emblematic of the Western education and mentality of its sophisticated citizenry and intelligentsia. The architecture and "foreign" look of Petersburg space is the surface manifestation of its differences from the rest of Russia, differences which in the mythology of the city and the minds of its writers are not skin deep. Differing form implies a different, or differently shaped, content. A Petersburger's "Russianness" is delineated in a way unlike that of a Muscovite or a Pskovian.

In our definition, Petersburg poets and writers are those who explicitly associate their creative lives and their *oeuvres* with the Northern capital, and who are emphatic about their "city sense," be that sense positive, negative, or essentially mixed. We speak of such writers as Dmitrij Merežkovskij, Aleksandr Blok, Innokentij Annenskij, Anna Axmatova, Osip Mandel'štam, Nikolaj Gumilev, Georgij Ivanov, Vladimir Sirin-Nabokov, and Iosif Brodskij, to mention the main ones treated on these pages. The list could be vastly lengthened to include Vaginov, Sosnora, Kušner, Rejn, Krivulin, and, of course, Andrej Bitov.[6] Of major poets more associated with Moscow, two can be said to have experienced very important "Petersburg periods," Vladislav Xodasevič

---

[5] Fyodor Dostoyevsky, *The Possessed*, trans. Andrew R. MacAndrew (New York: Signet Classic, 1962), 353.

[6] Viktor Krivulin and Andrej Bitov, while they engage Petersburg, do so somewhat differently than the older writers and Brodskij, upon whose works the present study is based.

and Andrej Belyj. The latter, in his great novel *Petersburg*, used the presentation of Petersburg man in architectural space he inherited from Puškin's *The Bronze Horseman* through Gogol''s Petersburg tales to Dostoevskij's "White Nights" and "The Double" and his post-exilic novels. In joining this great tradition, however, Belyj infused notions of modern psychology, Nietzschean and Neo-Kantian philosophy, and Anthroposophy into his treatment of characters in space. His novel is a kind of compendium of the themes and motifs of the Petersburg tradition up to 1910. Yet Belyj initiates imaginative structures or models of identification of self with space that were subsequently adopted and modified by others throughout the first third of the twentieth century and beyond. The images of Belyj's great novel, like those of Dostoevskij and Gogol' before him, left an indelible impression on the writers and, seemingly, on the space itself, imbuing it with unavoidable literary and cultural associations.

The inclusion here of Annenskij, and to a lesser extent, Axmatova, who in addition to Petersburg wrote many poems about Carskoe Selo (as had Puškin), is deliberate. For a long period Carskoe Selo represented an idyllic alternative to the darker urban Petersburg environment in Russian letters. In the period we treat, however, we shall see certain of the idyllic traits of Carskoe Selo being incorporated into the greater Petersburg poetics.

This book will present a virtual typology of imaginative structures in which Petersburg writers present their own existential/biographical experience in spatial, visual terms. We will see a pattern of intimate identification with spaces—parks, gardens, urban planning, buildings, houses, rooms, corridors, ensembles—indeed, with architecture in the broadest sense of the word. In Petersburg poetry and prose this is hardly the only use that space has been put to over the last 200 years. But it is striking in the modernist tradition. We concentrate on these varied and complex treatments of space because they convey the tragedy and psychological richness of the human creative personality in time. In the texts and passages chosen they constitute a dominant in the Jakobsonian sense.

SHUTTLING BETWEEN TRAGEDY AND IDYLL: A NEW TRADITION IN THE PETERSBURG MYTHOLOGY

The intimate identification of the writer with Petersburg space in the period of which we speak represents a new turn in the 200-year mythology of the city, a mythology totally inscribed in literary art. When historical events are incorporated they are mythologized as literature, as verbal art, as specific additions to what Vladimir Toporov has called the global *peterburgskij tekst* (Petersburg text).⁷ Toporov and Jurij Lotman have mapped the semiotic markers of this "text" over the first two hundred years of its existence.⁸ We are dealing with a particular period when treating the human self and its vicissitudes in terms of Petersburg spaces became a dominant. This period begins in the Silver Age around 1890 and continues in the works of writers whose identification with Petersburg began at that time; it further continues, with marked interruptions, in the Soviet period and in the emigration. Iosif Brodskij is the exception treated here, a writer born in the Soviet period (1940) who consciously embraces and embodies the Petersburg attitudes of his literary forebears. He is important for our subject as his articulation of the identification with Petersburg space is often stronger and more blatant than that of his predecessors. He not only carries the same tradition forward, but contributes substantially to its development in the latter half of the twentieth century.

As mentioned above, the positive and negative literary mythologies of Petersburg arose very early and have been treated descriptively and ideologically by Nikolaj Anciferov in several books, by Ettore Lo Gatto, and by Leonid Dolgopolov.⁹ Lotman and Toporov have covered much of the same material in structuralist, semiotic terms. Critical histories such as Solomon Volkov's and Katerina Clark's embrace much more than contributions of great writers to a discrete artistic trend; they treat culture, and largely political culture.¹⁰ Interesting recent work on the metaphysics and memories of Petersburg space has been conducted by Renate Lachmann and Svetlana Boym, and by the Petersburg writer Viktor Krivulin,¹¹ and recent volumes of conference

---

[7] V. N. Toporov, "Peterburg i peterburgskij tekst russkoj literatury," *Semiotika goroda i gorodskoj kul'tury: Trudy po znakovym sistemam XVIII* (Tartu: Tartu University Press, 1984), 4–29.

[8] Jurij M. Lotman, "Simvolika Peterburga i problemy semiotiki goroda," *Semiotika goroda i gorodskoj kul'tury*, 30–45.

[9] Nikolaj Anciferov, *Duša Peterburga*, in *"Nepostižimyj gorod..."* (Leningrad: Lenizdat, 1991); Ettore Lo Gatto, *Il mito di San Pietroburgo* (Milan: Feltrinelli Editori, 1960). On Leonid Dolgopolov's many works on Petersburg writers, see especially *Andrej Belyj i ego roman Peterburg* (Leningrad: Sovetskij pisatel', 1988).

[10] Solomon Volkov, *Petersburg: A Cultural History*, trans. Antonina W. Bouis (New York: The Free Press, 1995); Katerina Clark, *Petersburg, Crucible of Cultural Revolution* (Cambridge: Harvard University Press, 1995).

[11] Renate Lachmann, *Memory and Literature: Intertextuality in Russian Modernism*, trans. Roy Sellars and Anthony Wall (Minneapolis: University of Minnesota Press, 1997); Svetlana Boym, *The Future of Nostalgia* (New York: Basic Books, 2001); Viktor Krivulin, *Oxota na Mamonta* (St. Petersburg: BLIC, 1998). See also the edited volume *Metafizika Peterburga*, Peterburgskie čtenija po teorii, istorii i filosofii kul'tury 1 (Sankt-Peterburg: "Eidos," 1993).

proceedings and anthologies offer eclectic approaches to the question of what one collection terms "the phenomenon of Petersburg."[12]

We highlight here the artistic trend we call "intimate identification with space" because it interfaces in interesting ways with the aspects these scholars have treated, and requires separate and detailed treatment. The "fantastic and intentional" Petersburg of these imaginative spaces is the modern Petersburg, a Petersburg where Yeats' "terrible beauty" often dominates, where modern self-reflective European man with his sophisticated preoccupations posits himself as Russian man, and Petersburg finally achieves a degree of "Russianness" before being re-peripheralized and re-cosmopolitanized (with a clear negative and elitist connotation) in Soviet propaganda. It goes without saying that the literary texts in which this trend is embodied are among the greatest monuments of prose and poetry in the entirety of Russian literature.

Almost all great cities, for example Rome, have origins steeped in myth. In this Petersburg is no exception. Yet most cities arose in a period when oral tradition dominated, and the literary codification of the founding myths occurred centuries later, when those myths had solidified. In Petersburg's case, the simultaneous formation of and interpenetration between orally-based urban folklore and written responses to the city meant that myth has not been merely a latent subtext of its literature. Literary versions of the city have always had the peculiar power to define it, to continue shaping it in an ongoing reprise of its foundations in myth. The character of the Petersburg myth itself can be related to the archetypal image of the city in Western civilization, which, as Burton Pike notes, is a highly ambivalent one.[13] Sometimes it has been seen as the earthly "contact point" with the divine, a sacred incarnation of the heavenly on earth; early, and for the most part state-commissioned, celebratory odes stress Petersburg's miraculous appearance, amazing beauty, and precedence over all other earthly cities. Peter himself referred to the Summer Garden as "*moj paradiz*" (my paradise), thus appropriating the role of liaison to the divine for himself. Yet often some sin or sins are associated with the founding of cities (as in the archetypal myth of Cain), a transgression against the rural countryside and its way of life amidst and against which the city arose. In idylls and pastorals the rural setting is often portrayed nostalgically and sympathetically as a contrast to "evil urbanism." In founding St. Peters-

---

[12] See, for example, *Fenomen Peterburga*, ed. Jurij N. Bespjatyx (St. Petersburg: BLIC, 2001); *Moskva-Peterburg, pro et contra: Dialog kul'tur v istorii nacional'nogo samosoznanija. Antologija* (St. Petersburg: Izdatel'stvo russkogo xristianskogo gumanitarnogo instituta, 2000).

[13] Burton Pike, *The Image of the City in Modern Literature* (Princeton: Princeton University Press, 1981). See chap. 1 in particular. See also Jurij Lotman's classification of Petersburg as an "excentric city" in "Simvolika Peterburga."

burg, a modern city as a new capital, Peter's sin exceeded that of most founders. It was a sin against rural Russian folkways, but it also went against the cultural tradition of all of Russia as embodied in Muscovy and the Orthodox religion—a more powerful betrayal in the negative mythology. Moreover, calling it *Saint* Petersburg after the founder of the Christian Church, while the tsar was far from a saint, added a note of blasphemy that the religious Moscow boyar opposition and the Old Believers could not help but exploit. The impostor, Peter, was vilifying the name of St. Peter, founding an anti-Orthodox city, both secular and foreign, a European and godless accretion on the body politic. This led to the association of the new capital and the European secularization of Russia with the reign of Antichrist, which the actual limitation of the Orthodox Church's erstwhile authority (debunked to one of Peter's ministries, or Collegia) only exacerbated. The curse of Petersburg's emptiness was laid upon it at the very outset, in its lack of Russian Orthodox content, and over time, in history, with the words pronounced, according to legend, by Peter the Great's first wife, Evdokija Lopuxina, *"Peterburgu byt' pustu!"* (May this place be emptied out!) Emptiness, "the abomination which devastates," was proclaimed both as the city's essence and its inexorable tragic destiny.

The Russian word for fate or destiny, *rok*, is a Slavic root associated with time intervals, with the words *srok, urok, priuročit'*, which in Russian all denote time-bound concepts. (The Polish word *rok* means "year," as does the Ukrainian *rik, roku*.) Petersburg was inaugurated as a new historical beginning for Russia with all the Enlightenment optimism and expectations of progress on its new historical path. Yet with the European look of its built environment and the prominence of its statuary in a culture where even two-dimensional representation in icons had been opposed (as in the *ikonoborčestvo* of the seventeenth century), Petersburg was a space beset from its inception with charges of foreignness and imitation, and threatened with tragic retribution to be visited upon it in time.

The emptiness and emptying-out of the city space over time led us to formulate the notion of Petersburg's *negative kenosis*, which we shall refer to repeatedly in these pages. *Kenosis*, an Orthodox concept characteristic of many Russian saints (including Boris and Gleb), derives from the belief in the complete, literal incarnation of Jesus Christ. The kenotic Christ descended literally and fully to the conditions of humanity (pain, physical frailty, death), pouring his divinity out of himself as a gift to the wayward world which he endeavored to bring back to God the Father. He became *syn čelovečeskij* (the Son of Man) with all that that entails, and this pouring-out of oneself, which may appear as excessive passivity in the eyes of the secular world, is a gift actively given and an aspect of *imitatio Christi*.

With Petersburg, an impostor city with no "divine content" to pour forth, a perverse *negative kenosis* occurs. The city pours out its own chaotic version of emptiness onto its spaces and inhabitants, often appropriating and negating any positive content therein. It is emptied out as a punishment, and that process has no redeeming features nor beneficence for Russia or Russians for much of the city's history. In the Silver Age texts to be considered here we shall observe the slow transformation of this perverse negative *kenosis* into something positive. *Writers in their texts*, through their verbal art, begin to bring about the expiation over time of Peter's sins. Time is perceived as accelerated at the end of the Petersburg period, which Anciferov hailed as a period of the "renaissance of love and sympathy for the Northern capital."[14] Artists and art historians such as Benois and Grabar′ began to see Petersburg as beautiful and, more importantly, as representing a special form of *Russian* beauty. Ironically, love for and acceptance of Petersburg grows strong in a period of apocalyptic premonitions when it and imperial Russia are threatened with total emptiness, destruction, and loss. Identification, acceptance, and love come, moreover, as an acknowledgment or result of Petersburg's accumulated and present suffering, in which these writers and artists actively participate. Suffering in time "Russianizes" Petersburg.

In such a seminal text as Puškin's *The Bronze Horseman*, the "Petersburg tale" which Toporov sees as inaugurating a generic subtype in Russian literature, the positive Enlightenment myth in the "Introduction," with the author's proclaimed love for the young capital and pointed odic praise for its architectural beauty, coexists in sharp contradiction with the suffering inflicted on the space—the destruction by the flood and the ruination of the lives of Petersburg's inhabitants, emblematized in the total destruction of Paraša's house (and her death), which represents the life and hopes of the little man, Evgenij. The built environment is the force of the new order, and chaos is embodied in the revenge of nature, the vengeful elements, "the malice of the Finnish waves," which resent the straightjacket of the embankments in the flood of 1824 so dramatically presented in the *poèma*. The elements, in their revolt against the tsar's historical will, lead to Evgenij's derangement, madness, and his eventual death. Sixty years later Petersburg writers would still identify themselves with Petersburg creatures like Evgenij, and their creative lives and aspirations would still be associated with tragedy-ridden Petersburg spaces, but their attitudes towards the founder and the space would undergo a material change. The forces of chaos leading to the destabilization and dissociation of the personality, schizophrenia, doubling and multiple personalities—

---

[14] Anciferov, *Duša Peterburga*, 123. This and all further translations from the Russian, unless otherwise indicated, are our own.

associated in the nineteenth century with the terrible weather, floods, fogs, cold, and reflections in the mirror of the Neva—would be combined with the chaos of historical events. Goljadkin's madness and Svidrigajlov's suicides are preceded and seem precipitated by atmospheric, climatic events.[15] In Nekrasov's "O pogode" ("About the Weather"), climatic conditions stand both for historical rebellion, destructive blows against order, and the *creative destruction* of art and artist.[16] In the Silver Age the rage of the elements against Petersburg is compounded by historical events. Thus in Blok's *The Twelve*, the winds of *history* combine with nature as a force of chaos and destabilization of the artist's personality: "Black wind. / White snow. / The wind, the wind! / A man can no longer stay on his feet."[17] These are the snows and winds of history, of *historical vengeance* (Blok's term) wrought on Petersburg in time and on the writer who feels himself inexplicably bound with and permeated by that weather and space.

> Желтый пар петербургской зимы,
> Желтый снег, облипающий плиты…
> Я не знаю, где вы и где мы,
> Только знаю, что крепко мы слиты.
>
> Yellow steam of Petersburg winter,
> Yellow snow clinging to stone slabs,
> I don't know where you are and where *we* are,
> All I know is that we are inextricably bound.[18]

As we shall see, the "Mongol chaos" underlying Belyj's Petersburg and the "Judaic chaos" underlying Mandel'štam's are imbibed in the bacilli-infested waters of the Neva; they are within the Petersburg creature as much as they are outside him.

Representations of Petersburg in which weather and events destabilize and empty the city/self are called herein historical treatments, representing mythologization of historical events. Those where the city/self remains whole, unperturbed, and triumphant in the face of time and climate are called ahistorical or anti-historical treatments, denying the destabilizing force of events and the eerie "noise of time." To present the besieged Petersburg and the

---

[15] These are characters in Dostoevskij's *The Double* and *Crime and Punishment*, respectively.

[16] Such a relationship between weather and artist is seen especially in the death of Italian soprano Angiolina Bosio (who died in Petersburg of pneumonia in 1859) in part 4 of the cycle.

[17] Aleksandr Blok, "Dvenadcat'," *Sočinenija v odnom tome* (Moscow: GIXL, 1946) 257.

[18] Innokentij Annenskij, "Peterburg," *Stixotvorenija i tragedii* (Leningrad: Sovetskij pisatel', 1959), 199.

Petersburg writer as stable and indestructible, writers take the unexpected tack of resorting to urban Petersburg idyll and the closely related urban elegy (a generic category to be discussed in chapter 2). Tragedy-ridden Petersburg is one of the least likely sites in Russia for Baxtin's idyllic chronotope, yet it is seen repeatedly in the art of modern writers who identify with Petersburg. It is as if they are following Lermontov's dictum "*Kak budto v bure est' pokoj*" ("As if there were tranquility in a storm").[19] This is an *as if* that is possible in imaginative Petersburg space, in the realm of art.

---

[19] This is the final line of Lermontov's 1832 poem "A lone sail whitens" («Белеет парус одинокий»).

1 THE USES OF SPACE IN PETERSBURG POETRY: FROM NEUTRAL DESCRIPTION TO IDENTIFICATION

Because of Petersburg's striking and "un-Russian" appearance, emphasis in poetry about Petersburg since the eighteenth century has been on visual aspects of the city, and poets therefore often make reference to its spatial configuration and presence. Evocations of the geographical site—the Neva and its swampy delta, the Gulf of Finland, the Baltic landscape—as well as of the architectural adornments of the city have been a constant in this poetry. Yet the uses or functions of poetic allusion to these spaces have varied over the last two centuries. Our subject, the identification by the poet of his psyche-self-personal spirit with the space, is particularly characteristic of twentieth-century poetry.

In his well-known study *Duša Peterburga*, Nikolaj Anciferov has traced in great detail the general attitudes towards Petersburg in Russian literature. He demonstrates that the literary attitude towards the Northern capital was generally positive throughout the eighteenth century and up to the Decembrist rebellion in 1825. As noted above, it became markedly negative for the national psyche throughout the reigns of Nicholas I, Alexander II, and much of the reign of Alexander III. A renewed appreciation for and positive feeling towards Petersburg arose in the 1890s, at the dawn of Symbolism. It is then, in a period of historical turmoil and uncertainty, when the future of the Empire seems perilous and Petersburg seems vulnerable, that our study of intimate identification with Petersburg spaces in modern, and even modernist, Russian letters begins.[1]

The sense of identification we speak of can be noted in Annenskij's poem published in 1910 (quoted in chapter 1), where the snow and the slabs of (cemetery) stone are evoked as one with the self, as inextricably inseparable. To paraphrase the poet, one cannot draw a boundary between the fog, the snow, the slabs, and the "self"; the space and the self are powerfully bound together. Mandel'štam's *The Egyptian Stamp* contains one among many echoing variations of this sentiment, as we shall see in the course of our study: «… держусь я одним Петербургом—концертным, желтым, зловещим …

---

[1] Coverage of the same material by Ettore Lo Gatto and by Leonid Dolgopolov is inspired by Anciferov, and yields very similar conclusions.

зимним» [2: 25] ("... I am sustained [held together] by Petersburg alone—the Petersburg of concerts, yellow, ominous ... and wintry").[2] Such a strong binding of self with space is found in Tjutčev's nineteenth-century celebrations of rural nature: «Все во мне и я во всем» ("Everything [I behold] is in me and I am in everything [I behold]"), and is especially common in the Romantic elegy (see chapter 2). In his chapters on the "darkening of Petersburg" in the national consciousness in the post-Decembrist part of Nicholas I's reign and up to the dawn of the Silver Age, Anciferov examines the same sense of powerful identification, but this time with traditionally negative urban spaces—an intriguing development indeed!

In this chapter we shall first trace five common literary functions of Petersburg space in the Russian tradition that lead up to such a firm bonding of self with urban space at the turn of the century, in Axmatova, and in several émigré poets who wrote well beyond the Silver Age. Some of these uses of spatiality often accompany identification and may be easily confused with it. The five non-identificatory functions are:

1. neutral
2. encomiastic
3. historiosophic
4. metapoetic (metapoetry being a clearly modernist focus in Russia)
5. decorative-virtuoso (a function which is an emphatic objectivization rather than subjectivization of space).

As distinct from the other functions we trace, our subject—the *identification* between self and Petersburg space—clearly derives from the elegy (discussed in more detail in chapter 2).

Although the five functions of allusion to Petersburg spaces and architecture in the Russian literary tradition are distinct from our main subject, they at times impinge importantly upon it. They have been encoded in literature virtually since the founding of the Northern capital by Tsar Peter I in 1703. The first we shall call *neutral*. This usage merely registers Petersburg as the scene of the action and goes no further. The second, which we call *encomiastic*, uses Petersburg architecture to convince the reader of the city's beauty and importance to Russia. Since there was considerable opposition to the transfer of the capital from Moscow to Petersburg in Peter's day, the tsar himself commissioned positive "odes to Petersburg," a genre which clearly influenced

---

[2] Osip Mandel'štam, *The Noise of Time: The Prose of Osip Mandel'štam*, trans. Clarence Brown (San Francisco: North Point Press, 1986), 149. All references to the English translation of *The Egyptian Stamp* are from this edition.

and perhaps reached its apogee in the *Vstuplenie* (Introduction) to Puškin's *The Bronze Horseman*:

> Отсель грозить мы будем шведу,
> Здесь будет город заложен
> Назло надменному соседу.
> Природой здесь нам суждено
> В Европу прорубить окно…
> Прошло сто лет, и юный град
> Полнощных стран краса и диво,
> Из тьмы лесов, из топи блат
> Вознесся пышно, горделиво…
> Люблю тебя, Петра творенье,
> Люблю твой строгий, стройный вид,
> Невы державное теченье,
> Береговой ее гранит,
> Твоих оград узор чугунный,
> Твоих задумчивых ночей
> Прозрачный сумрак, блеск безлунный,
> Когда я в комнате моей
> Пишу, читаю без лампады,
> И ясны спящие громады
> Пустынных улиц, и светла
> Адмиралтейская игла…

> Hence shall we strike fear in the Swede,
> Here a city shall be built
> To spite our haughty neighbor.
> Nature has decreed that here we
> Should break a window through to Europe…
> A hundred years have passed, and the young city,
> The beauty and wonder of the northern countries,
> From the darkness of forests and marshy swamps
> Has arisen sumptuous and proud…
> I love you, Peter's creation,
> I love your severe, graceful look,
> The powerful current of the Neva,
> Its granite shores,
> The wrought-iron tracery of your fences,
> The transparent twilight, the moonless shine
> Of your pensive nights,

When in my room
I write and read without a lamp,
And the sleepy hulks
Of the deserted streets are clear, and
The needle of the Admiralty is bright...[3]

In Puškin's paean to the city, he not only stresses its miraculous appearance, its might, and its beauty (motifs seen in earlier odes by poets such as Tred'jakovskij, Bogdanovič, and Deržavin), but he also introduces an introspective note which clearly ties the spaces of the city and its white nights to poetic inspiration.[4]

A third common function of Petersburg space in literary texts can be termed *historiosophic*. Here city artifacts and architecture are used to assert the historical continuity of (1) Petersburg with the rest of Western culture, and (2) Petersburg culture over the more than two hundred years of the city's existence. The most striking example of this historiosophic function is found in the *ekphrasis* in Merežkovskij's novel *Peter and Alexis*.[5] There an ancient Greek statue of Aphrodite, unearthed after being buried in Renaissance Florence, is found by one of Peter the Great's emissaries and transported to Petersburg. In the Summer Garden Peter "implants" it into the Petersburg soil. The planting of the "Venus of Petersburg" symbolizes the implantation of and imminent resurgence of world culture in the Hyperborean North, and in Hegelian fashion signifies that Russia under Peter has finally and dramatically obtained a connection with ancient Greece, Rome, and Renaissance Europe—in other words, that it has entered the arena of world culture and universal history. The Absolute Spirit arrives, and Russia becomes linked with everything significant in preceding world history. This linkage with the "great Western tradition" occurs late, but earlier history is treated as a preparation for Russia's all-important entrance into that tradition. The lateness is not allowed to mitigate the greatness of Russia's Westernization and her imminent future.

A very similar historiosophic usage is seen in Blok's poem "The Snow Maiden":

---

[3] Aleksandr Puškin, "Mednyj vsadnik," *Polnoe sobranie sočinenij* (Leningrad: Akademija nauk, 1937–59), 5: 131.

[4] A similar image is seen at the end of Mixail Murav'ev's 1794 poem "To the Goddess of the Neva."

[5] Dmitrij Merežkovskij, *Antixrist: Petr i Aleksej*, in *Izbrannoe* (Kišinev: Literatura artistike, 1989).

Она пришла из дикой дали—
Ночная дочь иных времен.
Ее родные не встречали,
Не просиял ей небосклон.

Но сфинкса с выщербленным ликом
Над исполинскою Невой
Она встречала легким вскриком
Под бурей ночи снеговой.

Бывало, вьюга ей осыпет
Звездами плечи, грудь и стан,—
Все снится ей родной Египет
Сквозь тусклый северный туман.

И город мой железно-серый,
Где ветер, дождь, и зыбь, и мгла,
С какой-то непонятной верой
Она, как царство, приняла.

Ей стали нравиться громады,
Уснувшие в ночной глуши,
И в окнах тихие лампады
Слились с мечтой ее души.

Она узнала зыбь и дымы,
Огни, и мраки, и дома—
Весь город мой непостижимый—
Непостижимая сама.…

She came from afar,
Nocturnal daughter of other times.
Relatives did not greet her,
Nor did the firmament shine for her.

But she greeted the sphinx with a pockmarked face
Above the giant Neva
With a light cry
Under the snowstorm of night.

It would happen that the snowstorm would sprinkle
Her shoulders, torso and chest with stars—
She ever dreams of her native Egypt
Through the dim northern fog.

And my iron-gray city
Of wind and rain and swells and haze
With a mysterious faith
She accepted as her kingdom.

She began to like the hulks of buildings
Which slumbered in the hush of night,
And the quiet lanterns in the windows
Became one with her soul's reverie.

She recognized the swell and smoke,
The fires, and darkness, and the houses—
My whole unfathomable city—
She who was herself unfathomable....[6]

Here an Egyptian sphinx destined to be placed in front of the Academy of Arts is personified. She arrives in Petersburg, like the statue of Venus in Merežkovskij's novel, and in time grows to realize that this is her home in the present, that the vanguard of world art and history is in Petersburg as nowhere else, and she adopts the city as her home.

Both these statues bring with them the immanence of world historical culture, and by their arrival confer that past heritage upon Petersburg, which, as a new city built on a swampy, deserted site, it had lacked. Through their arrival Petersburg symbolically achieves a non-Russian cultural past belatedly, but it is Petersburg's connection to that largely European heritage that explains its Westernized, internationalist present. Merežkovskij's novel and Blok's poem present interesting instances of the cultural ideology of Peter as it was understood by Petr Jakovlevič Čaadaev. According to this seminal thinker, Peter had a very specific cultural imperative to Russia:

> See that civilization over there, the fruit of so many labors, those sciences, those arts which cost so much sweat to so many generations; all that is yours if only you will cast off your superstitions ... if only you will not pride yourselves on your barbarous past ... [and] aspire only to appropriate the achievements of all peoples, the riches acquired by the human spirit in all the latitudes of the globe.[7]

Another very important historiosophic symbol of the continuity of Peter's project and his spirit in the city is Falconet's statue on Senate Square, the Bronze Horseman. From the writing of Puškin's great *poèma* to the present

---

[6] Blok, "Snežnaja deva," 122.

[7] Chaadayev, *Philosophical Letters*, 166.

day, the unity and continuity of Petersburg history is guaranteed by the tsar's perennial presence, as a state on the one hand and as a literary character on the other, who gallops about protecting and defending his capital against the many attempts of others to betray his Westernization project and destroy the city which symbolizes it. "He will protect his city," wrote Blok emphatically in his 1914 poem "Petr" ("Peter").[8] Indeed, Peter the Great appears in some texts to be waging a losing battle against anti-Petersburg forces, or to be partially destroying his creation himself; yet his spirit as the Bronze Horseman courses through the pages of Petersburg literature, a permanent reminder of Peter's Europeanizing cultural projects, of his aim to integrate Russia into Europe and make his country a military, political, and cultural force of world historical stature. Russia's modern identity in these works is defined as the results of a Petrine project very close to what Čaadaev described.

THE METAPOETIC FUNCTION

There are two functions of architecture and statuary in twentieth-century Petersburg poetry which, while quite distinct from identification, impinge upon it very often indeed. These are the *metapoetic* and *decorative* functions (the fourth and fifth listed in our inventory above). Their importance for our subject compels us to dwell on them in considerable detail here. The *metapoetic* function, as we define it, entails the equation by poets of their artistic works (poems) with Petersburg buildings and statues. Starting in his first collection *Stone*, Mandel′štam treats words metaphorically as *stones*, and poems, consequently, are stone edifices. Mandel′štam is not alone in his use of architectural metaphors and special interest in architecture. Iosif Brodskij shares it completely. Mandel′štam and Brodskij are the two Petersburg poets most sensitive to the architecture of Petersburg and to architecture in general. Poem titles such as "Notre Dame," "Hagia Sophia," and "Einem alten Architekten in Rom" bear witness to this orientation. Sometimes Mandel′štam speaks of himself as an architect building an edifice of words, a monument such as Puškin had built:

> Я памятник себе воздвиг нерукотворный,
> К нему не зарастет народная тропа,
> Вознесся выше он главою непокорной
> Александрийского столпа....[9]

> I erected to myself a monument not made by human hands,
> The people's path to it will not be overgrown,

---

[8] Blok, "Petr," 152.
[9] Puškin, "Exegi monumentum," 3: 424.

> It [my monument] has grown higher, with its indomitable head,
> Than the Alexander Column....

Mandel′štam likewise aims to build a monument like Puškin's that will be less destructible than a monument in stone, more durable even than the angel column in Petersburg's Palace Square commemorating Alexander I's defeat of Napoleon. Brodskij, who senses this architectural attitude in Mandel′štam's poetry very keenly, reads the older poet's celebrated 1913 architectural poem "The Admiralty" metapoetically as a work about the mode of existence of a poem or work of art. We cite the poem in its entirety and then discuss what we feel to be a "Brodskijan" reading of it:

Адмиралтейство

В столице северной томится пыльный тополь,
Запутался в листве прозрачный циферблат,
И в темной зелени фрегат или акрополь
Сияет издали, воде и небу брат.

Ладья воздушная и мачта-недотрога,
Служа линейкою преемникам Петра,
Он учит: красота—не прихоть полубога,
А хищный глазомер простого столяра.

Нам четырех стихий приязненно господство,
Но создал пятую свободный человек.
Не отрицает ли пространства превосходство
Сей целомудренно построенный ковчег?

Сердито лепятся капризные медузы,
Как плуги брошены, ржавеют якоря;
И вот разорваны трех измерений узы,
И открываются всемирные моря.   [1: 29][10]

The Admiralty

Weary is the dusty poplar in the northern capital,
The transparent sundial is mixed up in foliage,
And in the dark greenery a frigate or an acropolis

---

[10] All references to poems and prose of Mandel′štam herein are to the edition *Sobranie sočinenij v trex tomax*, ed. Gleb Struve and Boris Filippov (Munich: Interlanguage Library Associates, 1966–69), and will be referenced by volume number followed by page number in the body of the text. Translations, except for *The Noise of Time* and *The Egyptian Stamp*, are rendered by Anna Lisa Crone.

Shines from afar, brother to sea and sky.

An airy bark and an untouchable mast
Which served as a yardstick to Peter's successors,
It [He] teaches that beauty is not the whim of a demigod
But the shrewd eye-measurement ["eyeballing"] of a simple carpenter.

The dominance of four elements is agreeable to us,
But free man created a fifth element.
Doesn't this chastely-constructed ark
Deny the dominance of space?

Angrily weave the capricious Medusae,
The anchors rust like abandoned ploughs;
And lo, the bonds of three dimensions are broken,
And universal seas are opened up.

The following metapoetic analogy is implicit in this work:

Peter creates his Petersburg	*as*
Architects create the Admiralty	*as*
Poets create their poetry / their Petersburg.	

This three-tiered analogy is used again and again: a Petersburg poet, like Peter, creates a European-Russian creation, and his heart is his Petersburg. In the poem Mandel'štam alludes to many of the concrete details of the Admiralty—the sundial, the poplars on the grounds, the Medusae on the window keystones, and the anchor in front of the north façade. He further alludes to the fact that the Admiralty was planned by Peter to be the focal point of three major streets: Nevskij Prospekt, Goroxovaja, and Voznesenskij Prospekt. The apparently "Acmeistic" inclusion of such concrete details helps anyone familiar with the building conjure it up visually. The shining of the Admiralty spire, Puškin's «адмиралтейская игла», a traditional symbol of Petersburg, is also present. But this Acmeistic conjuring of the Admiralty as a building comprises only one aspect of its characterization in the poem. It also serves as a symbol of Petersburg and as the creation of the "artisan tsar"[11] who was, among other things, a notable ship-builder. The Admiralty-as-ship here further alludes to the ship of the Russian state with Peter at its helm, a metaphor as old as Alcaeus' "the ship of state," and as a winged "ship-poem." In the poem the Admiralty is shown to be particularly at home in two elements—air and water. Built at the water's edge, it is at once a ship and a fortress: «фрегат или

---

[11] Peter was dubbed the "artisan tsar" by the historian Vasilij Ključevskij.

акрополь» ("a frigate or an acropolis"). It is both, but treated ultimately as a winged ship: «воде и небу брат» ("brother to sea and sky"). In stanza 2 it becomes an airy, elevated ship, one free of its moorings and the earthly attributes of bulk and weight: «ладья воздушная и мачта-недотрога» ("an airy bark and an untouchable mast"). Its beauty, like Petersburg's, is shown to be the product of the conscious craftsmanship and planning of the carpenter and shipbuilder Peter. Furthermore, in stanzas 3 and 4 this boat takes on characteristics that transcend its concrete, material construction. Crafted by an artisan's careful calculation, «хищный глазомер простого столяра» ("the cunning eye-measurement of a simple cabinetmaker"), the final product exceeds and transcends all the elements that went into it. The whole is more than the sum of the parts and has a magic, unexpected autonomy: weighty, it becomes light; spatial and architectural, it magically denies space, seeming to fly. Called an ark, like Noah's, it transports man from one historical period to the next, and thus becomes a bridge between the old pre-Petrine Russia and the New World, as well as between Russia and the rest of the European world.

The fifth element freely created by man appears to be poetic language. In his essays Mandel′štam treats the Russian language as a sea of words on which poem-boats float about. These boats have three dimensions—height, length, volume—and they also exist in time. The denial of space's predominance is accompanied by language: air, fire, water, and soil are spatial concepts; poetic language is not. The answer to the question "Doesn't this chastely-constructed ark / Deny the dominance of space?" presupposes an affirmative response. One looks at the graceful edifice and the equally beautiful poem—a flying bark composed of words—and it seems to break loose from the shore where it sits to float upwards and away: «И вот разорваны трех измерений узы, / И открываются всемирные моря» ("And lo, the bonds of three dimensions are broken, / And universal seas are opened up"). In *The Bronze Horseman* Peter predicts for his capital: «Сюда по новым им волнам / Все флаги в гости будут к нам» ("Hither, along waves that are new to them, / All flags of the world will visit us"). Mandel′štam's declaration completes Peter's (Puškin's) prediction as the opposite movement of the ship of Russian culture, Russian language, and Russian beauty. At the end of Mandel′štam's poem the Russian ship goes out to conquer the "seas" of Europe and the rest of the world. In so doing it overcomes the bonds of three dimensions. The building, flying and floating, will deny the structure's own material nature.

It was probably with this poem in mind that Brodskij chose "the strictly classical portico of the ... Admiralty" as the best symbol of Mandel′štam's

Petersburg.[12] A great example of man-made beauty, the Admiralty is a worthy brother to God's "sea and sky." It is a bastion of Russian culture, one that received additions and improvements from several generations of architects. In his essay "On the Nature of the Word" Mandel'štam speaks of the poem as an Egyptian ship of the dead afloat on a sea of language, outfitted with all that it needs to survive on that sea. In the same essay Mandel'štam writes, "That stream [the Russian language] will take with it the fragile boat of the human word into the wide open sea of the future" [2: 287–88]. This is exactly what the Admiralty performs; by its formal beauty it instructs future generations of architects, giving them a lesson in craftsmanship and aesthetics. The bridging quality derived from its connection with Noah refers to the preservation of elements of the earlier creation/culture. The bursting out of the here-and-now Russian culture and the conquest of the new, universal open seas reflects the perennial struggle of Petersburg culture against the wild, chaotic, and formless elements of Russian nature—a chaotic sea which threatens the ship from all sides: "Our every word is a little Kremlin, outfitted [the maritime word оснащенный is used] for an untiring struggle with the formless element, with non-being which threatens our history from all sides" [2: 248].

Brodskij emphasizes that, unlike most Russians (who are not Petersburgers), Peter I had been in love with the sea and with open spaces. For most Russians, "the idea of the sea is ... alien.... The notions of freedom, open space, of getting the hell out of here, are instinctively suppressed and consequently surface in the reverse forms of fear of water...."[13] Brodskij associates the Petrine love for the sea and open space with being "born free." People like his father, a naval officer, carry this Petrine free spirit. The free ship of poetry or art has been equipped to conquer other seas, other languages and literatures. Russian beauty in Mandel'štam's poem will make its contribution to world art and culture. Brodskij's very description of language's functioning in poetry reminds us of this image of the Admiralty: "... for language [poetry] is the highest form of its existence. In purely technical terms, of course, poetry amounts to arranging words with the greatest specific gravity in the most effective and externally inevitable sequence."[14] Thus poetic creation and artisanship (shipbuilding) are equated. Once built, however, the three-dimensional creature acquires other dimensions, as does the Admiralty in the poem. It escapes the limitations imposed by the material: "Ideally, however, [poetry] is language [man's fifth element] negating its own mass and the laws

---

[12] Joseph Brodsky, "The Child of Civilization," *Less than One* (New York: Farrar Straus Giroux, 1986), 130.

[13] Brodsky, "A Guide to a Renamed City," *Less than One*, 75.

[14] Brodsky, "A Poet and Prose," *Less than One*, 186.

of gravity; it is language's striving upwards—or sideways—to that beginning where the Word was. In any case [poetry] is movement of language into … the spheres from which it sprang."[15] Just as Mandel'štam's "Admiralty" is not a stationary structure but a dynamic flying one, so the great poem, composed of down-to-earth everyday words and phrases, morphemes, and phonemes, *strains upwards*, denying the mere materials of its make-up.

The above is but one example of a Petersburg landmark becoming "a winged edifice of the word," a metaphor for verbal art and analogon of its mode of existence. Many such examples of modern Petersburg metapoetry could be adduced. But for all its importance (particularly for the Acmeists), the metapoetic function of space in Petersburg works is, in our opinion, still not the most central in twentieth-century Russian letters. Poets creating their Petersburg amounts to only one part of the more complex function of identification, as we shall see below.

Differentiating the Decorative Function

The last important function which is easily confused with identification is what we term the decorative or virtuoso function of space. Given the plethora of poems dealing with and describing the architectural or external aspects of Petersburg, we must delineate this function which, despite the frequent presence of minute architectural detail in it, involves minimal identification with the city's spaces, ethos, or citizens, and oftentimes involves an ironic or even parodic distancing of the poet from them. The latter ironic distancing is particularly to be felt when Muscovite Futurists disassociate themselves from traditional Neoclassical Petersburg and its traditional classical rhymes and meters. This parodic stance towards Petersburg is another way of "throwing Puškin from the steamship of modernity." But for all this, the decorative function is the most easily confused with identification by the poet of himself, his *oeuvre*, or both with Petersburg.

When Petersburg is used in the purely decorative function in artistic texts, architecture is almost always involved. A clearly identifiable Petersburg monument, avenue, street, or building is depicted in a highly unusual or atypical manner. *Ostranenie* (defamiliarization or "making strange"), usually of the most familiar aspects of the Northern capital, is the hallmark of this function. The inner or intimate meaning of the space is not exploited. These treatments are highly visual, and the visual aspect of the space may be rendered totally unrecognizable, like a difficult riddle. As in architectural or interior decoration, the visual depiction of the space may take on Cubist or abstractionist contours. What was colored may become black-on-black, or white-on-white à

---

[15] Ibid.

la Malevič; it may be visually and/or logically surreal; or it may be embellished or skewed beyond recognition in accordance with some other visual or literary style. It is a decorative (stylistic) statement by the artist, and often at the same time a demonstration of his virtuosity in the style. Language and rhetorical figures (metaphors, similes, metonymies, etc.) play a prominent role in the decorative function. The reason confusion may occur between a poem with decorative function and one where there is maximal identification of the poet with the space is that defamiliarization is an important factor in both.

Thus in Axmatova's "Second Northern Elegy" the poet pours strange inner experiences out onto the city and "makes Petersburg strange" indeed. But the complex cityscape that results from this process, though it may seem surreal at first perusal, is not a mere stylistic exercise, a demonstration of the tenets of a manifesto, or a virtuoso performance, but an attempt to portray the complex reality of her psyche in spatial terms. This reality is the result of the complex interaction over time of the locale in Petersburg where she finds herself with events in her biography and her psyche. Thus Axmatova's defamiliarized depiction of Petersburg in that poem is far from merely decorative, and is the proper subject of our study. It is a space with which, for better or worse, the author is deeply identified.

In true decorative treatments of Petersburg architecture and space, Petersburg is fully objectivized in the alteration. The poet/writer *performs an action upon* Petersburg in a way analogous to that in which an interior decorator redecorates a room. Just as he is forced to work with some of the existing aspects of the room such as the location of the walls and doors or the placement of windows, so the "redecorating" poet is unable to do away with the Nevskij Prospekt, the Admiralty, the Baltic Sea, or the Fontanka Canal. He defamiliarizes these spatial aspects of Petersburg, using reality or photographs of it or the artistic rendering of other poets and writers as his point of departure. Sometimes it is clear in a poetic treatment that he is "making strange" the Petersburg of Puškin's *The Bronze Horseman*. At other times, one feels that the poet has made an actual visit to the locale which he is depicting with such originality or so iconoclastically.

Symbolist poets, under the influence of Baudelaire and Verhaeren, were avid describers of city streets and city life, but they personalized it profoundly in their Symbolism. Likewise, it was a subject that affected them deeply. They were creatures of the city, as are the characters of Dostoevskij's works. This is the case with the defamiliarization of the Petersburg Symbolists as well as of the Acmeists. The kind of objectivization of the cityscape which we put in the decorative and virtuoso category is associated most prominently with Futurist poetry, and certainly not solely with St. Petersburg. The Cubo-Futurists not only metaphorically deform the thing they are describing, but treat the word itself in the same way a Cubist or abstractionist painter treats a geometrical form. To take the street (*ulica*) and see faces (*lica*), as in Vladimir Majakovskij's 1913 poem «Из улицы в улицу» ("From Street into Street"), is similar to the skewing or distending of a rhombus or a square. Just as the poet here reveals and highlights the *lica* (faces) both in the morphology of the words and in the semantic message of the poem, so a Cubist painter emphasizes or reveals the geometric shapes that underlie a human face or a still life. Let us quote this poem on a generic modern city street in its entirety because it is a virtuoso performance in its genre:

У-
лица.
Лица
у
догов
годов
рез-
че.
Че-
рез
железных коней
с окон бегущих домов
прыгнули первые кубы.
Лебеди шей колокольных,
гнитесь в силках проводов!
В небе жирафий рисунок готов
выпестрить ржавые чубы.
Пестр, как форель,
сын
безузорной пашни.
Фокусник
рельсы
тянет из пасти трамвая,
скрыт циферблатами башни.
Мы завоеваны!
Ванны.
Души.
Лифт.
Лиф души расстегнули.
Тело жгут руки.
Кричи, не кричи:

«Я не хотела!»—
резок
жгут
муки.
Ветер колючий
трубе
вырывает
дымчатой шерсти клок.
Лысый фонарь
сладострастно снимает
с улицы
черный чулок.[16]

A street has faces.
Bulldogs have faces sharper than years.
Through iron horses from the
windows of running houses the first
cubes jumped.
Swans of bell necks,
bend in the power of wires!
The giraffe's drawing is ready to make
the sky motley with rusty clumps of hair.
Motley, like a trout,
is the son
of an unpatterned ploughed field.
A magician pulls the rails
from the maw of the tram car,
hidden by the clock faces of the tower.
We are conquered!
Bathrooms.
Showers/souls.
Elevator.
They've unbuttoned the bodice of our soul.
Hands burn our body.
Shout, why not:
"I didn't want to!"
sharp is the

---

[16] Vladimir Majakovskij, "Iz ulicy v ulicu," *Izbrannye proizvedenija* (Moscow: Sovetskij pisatel′, 1963), 1: 71. On closer consideration, a sense of identification can be seen in this poem of the self and the ravished street, but this is not readily apparent to most readers, even sophisticated ones.

tourniquet
of torment.
A piercing wind
tears a smoking clump of wool out
of the chimney.
The bald lantern voluptuously
removes the street's black stocking.

Majakovskij is often very specific in his treatment of architectural monuments and city streets (cf. "The Brooklyn Bridge," "Broadway," and his many poems about Paris). In "From Street into Street" we have a generic turn-of-the-century street with its streetlights and trams being conquered by modern technology. The treatment of the "personae" of the street may be a distant echo of the treatment of the houses at the opening of Dostoevskij's "White Nights," but Majakovskij would prefer that we not see such a connection.[17] It is not only Futurists who were wont to treat cities and spaces this way. Even Mandel'štam, who was against Futurist word games and riddles, seems to have been influenced by them in this 1935 poem to Voronež, the city of his exile:

Пусти меня, отдай меня, Воронеж:
Уронишь ты меня иль проворонишь,
Ты выронишь меня или вернешь—
Воронеж—блажь, Воронеж—ворон, нож…   [1: 211]

Let me go, give me back, Voronež:
Will you drop me or haphazardly let me free,
Will you drop me out or return me—
Voronež—a whimsy, Voronež—a crow, a knife…

Here there is a virtuoso performance in the plays on the root *ron*, the stressed syllable of the city's name, and with *neš', niš', noš'* and the pronunciation of the city's last syllable, as well as with *vor* and *vo, ve, vy*. There can be no question of a deep identification in this poem with the place of exile. Voronež is a big unreliable character that has stolen the poet from his true city and should return him, although he is very unsure that it is willing to do so. The treatment of Voronež, after all the city of Kol'cov, is one-sided; there is very little penetration into its essences and character, and virtually no identification with its spaces.

From Mandel'štam Voronež gets a milder version of the one-sided "selfish" treatment Petersburg receives when the decorative function is exer-

---

[17] In the first few pages of "White Nights," Dostoevskij's *flâneur*-hero befriends houses, speaking to them as to people. See chap. 6, p. 226.

cised. Let us look for examples in one of Majakovskij's several poems on St. Petersburg:

Кое-что про Петербург

Слезают слезы с крыши в трубы,
к руке реки чертя полоски;
а в неба свисшиеся губы
воткнули каменные соски.
И небу—стихши—ясно стало:
туда, где моря блещет блюдо,
сырой погонщик гнал устало
Невы двугорбого верблюда.[18]

A Thing or Two about Petersburg

Tears slide down from the roof into pipes
drawing stripes to the river's hand;
and lips hanging down have thrust
their stone nipples into the skies.
And the sky has understood, having grown quiet,
that the saucer of the sea shines towards the place
where the raw driver wearily chased
the two-humped camel of the Neva.

It can be argued that there is less in this 1916 poem about Petersburg than there is about the wit and imagination and strange points of view that Majakovskij, himself a painter, can adopt. As we saw in "From Street into Street" above, the city space becomes a huge animal chased by a personified rainstorm. This is a constant device in Majakovskij, who treated the Brooklyn Bridge as a large animal with paws pulling Brooklyn and Manhattan together, and who often deals with creatures and himself in such hyperbolic terms as to be as big as a metropolis himself. This is not Petersburg viewed from an airplane or high tower, as in Blok's poem «Вися над городом всемирным» ("Hanging over the Universal City"), or in «Петербург с Адмиралтейской башни» ("Petersburg from the Admiralty Tower") by the minor poet V. Romanovskij;[19] however, as always with Majakovskij, the sweep of his vision is enormous, as well as his ability to divine a pursuer and a camel (the underly-

---

[18] Majakovskij, "Koe-čto pro Peterburg," 1: 73.

[19] Both texts are given in M. V. Otradin, ed., *Peterburg v russkoj poèzii: XVIII–načalo XX veka* (Leningrad: Izdatel'stvo Leningradskogo universiteta, 1988), 117.

ing forms) in the topography of the city during the rain.[20] While this poem represents a "making strange" of an actual Petersburg on a rainy day, which sidesteps the Petersburg of the Word entirely, in Majakovskij's best known Petersburg poem, «Последняя петербургская сказка»[21] ("The Last Petersburg Tale"), he engages *The Bronze Horseman* only to satirize and reject Puškin. In it the Bronze Horseman and his steed leave their pedestal and go for a repast and drink to the Astoria Hotel, a scene which represents a humorous and satiric debunking of the entire mythology of Petersburg. The untoward behavior of horse and Horseman in the restaurant results in their return to the pedestal in Senate Square, and in the rather melancholy mood of the Bronze Horseman:

> Унынье у лошади на морде.
> И никто не поймет тоски Петра—узника,
> закованного в собственном городе.

> Despondency is all over the horse's muzzle [face].
> And no one can understand the melancholy of Peter—a prisoner trapped in his own city.

Thus Majakovskij throws Puškin from the "ship of modernity." This then is a defamiliarization of the literary myth, especially as set forth in Puškin and then refracted through Belyj. But it is more decorative and lightly humorous than anything else. It does not engage Puškin or Belyj seriously. It has none of the deep and tragic significance of the Bronze Horseman's visit to Dudkin's garret, no matter how much satire and caricature some critics are inclined to find in Belyj's treatment of the Bronze Horseman in his novel *Petersburg*. Of course, much humor is present in Belyj's treatment of the Bronze (Metallic) Horseman, but it is almost always "laughter through tears."

It is precisely the decorative and virtuoso treatments of Petersburg, particularly of Petersburg architecture and urban spaces, or attacks on the "Petersburg" of leading nineteenth-century poets, that can be confusing for the reader who cannot decide whether such treatments distance and objectify the city from the poet or represent a very personal identification with it. Sometimes poems that are part of the strong tradition of identification with Petersburg and its spaces—our subject—have a surface appearance that differs very little from others which do not belong to that tradition, while naming

---

[20] Indeed, the image of the Neva as a "two-humped camel" is entirely accurate when one examines the river's curves around Stone Island and Petrovskij Island (the first "hump") and around the eastern spit of the southern bank near Smol'nyj Cathedral (the second "hump").

[21] Majakovskij, "Poslednjaja peterburgskaja skazka," 1: 118.

and treating the same places and buildings. Identification with the actual city or literary evocations of urban locales (or both) must be dominant in the texts of our typology. Strong identification with Petersburg spaces is a permanent characteristic of the poetics of Blok, Axmatova, Mandel'štam, Georgij Ivanov, Nabokov, and Brodskij, and in certain periods in the *oeuvres* of Belyj and Xodasevič, as we have indicated. For some poets, such as Innokentij Annenskij, a single poem—his "Petersburg"—is so important for the tradition, so identified with that space, that it is a major contribution, despite the fact that a larger part of his *oeuvre* is probably more important for the sense of place of Carskoe Selo. Other poets and poems engage Petersburg, its architecture, and its spaces much more superficially and much more occasionally, and are minimally identified with the space, if at all. Our subject, *identification*, inevitably involves what we might call dialogue with the actual Petersburg spaces and often with the "word-made" spaces which Brodskij has called the "second Petersburg."[22] Such dialogue involves a very deliberate communion between self and the space-text of the city, where each takes on features of the other, and where each may even come to depend upon the other. Petersburg affecting the self or the poet affecting Petersburg space, in our formulation of the function of identification, is an essentially sympathetic gesture, one that under duress can become a way of coping with assaults to the integrity of a self or a building.

In both Majakovskij poems cited above there is little involvement with the space or the representations of it in the literary tradition—with the "second Petersburg." Majakovskij alters and revamps the space in his treatment, showing his power as an artist to change or affect something else, something alien to himself. It is like an unusual Cubist or abstractionist portrait of *someone else*, or of *something external to the self*. It is not a deformed, unusual self-portrait, which is what the poems we concentrate on here are. The poet's exertion of his creative powers over the spaces and architectural monuments remains of course an expression of his ego—Petersburg, like Venice or Paris or any other city, is subjected to the formative influence of his art. In "From Street into Street" it is passivized, raped, confused by the tram's *fokusnik* (magician). The influence and formative force moves in one direction only. The space described merely passively receives the remodeling that is done to it, and has no reciprocal effects on the remodeler.

---

[22] In "A Guide to a Renamed City" Brodskij writes, "For there is the second Petersburg, the one made of verse and of Russian prose. That prose is read and reread and the verses are learned by heart.... And it's this memorization which secures the city's status and place in the future—as long as this language exists...." (93–94).

Not many cases are as clear as those in Majakovskij or Xlebnikov. Poets such as the Futurist Benedikt Livšic, who wrote over twenty-five poems to Petersburg, give us some poems that belong to our subject and others that do not. We will look at the interesting and often borderline cases of Livšic to illustrate the problems of deciding whether the decorative-virtuoso function is dominant in Petersburg poems or whether identification and/or the metapoetic function are actually dominant in the work. For this purpose we will compare Mandel′štam's poem on the Kazan Cathedral with Livšic's poem on the very same building (both written in 1914).

Mandel′štam:

На площадь выбежав, свободен
Стал колоннады полукруг,—
И распластался храм Господень,
Как легкий крестовик-паук.

А зодчий не был итальянец,
Но русский в Риме,—ну, так что ж!
Ты каждый раз, как иностранец,
Сквозь рощу портиков идешь.

И храма маленькое тело
Одушевленнее стократ
Гиганта, что скалою целой
К земле, беспомощный, прижат!   [1: 38]

Having run out onto the square,
The semicircle of the colonnade stopped, free,
And God's temple spread out
Like a light cross-spider.

But the architect was not an Italian,
But a Russian in Rome, so what do you expect?
Each time you pass through
The groves of these porticoes like a foreigner.

And the small body of the temple
Is a hundred times more animate
Than the giant who is attached helplessly
To the ground by a whole boulder!

Livšic:

Казанский собор

И полукруг, и крест латинский,
И своенравца римский сон
Ты перерос по-исполински—
Удвоенной дугой колонн.

И вздыбленной клавиатуре
Удары звезд и лет копыт
Равны, когда вдыхатель бури
Жемчужным воздухом не сыт.

В потоке легком небоската
Ты луч отвергнешь ли один,
Коль зодчий тратил, точно злато,
Гиперборейский травертин?

Не тленным камнем—светопада
Опоясался ты кольцом,
И куполу дана отрада
Стоять колумбовым яйцом. [23]

The Kazan Cathedral

You [Kazan Cathedral] overgrew
The half-circle and the Latin cross
And the Roman dream of that maverick
With your doubled arc of columns.

The strokes of stars and the flight of hooves
Are equal to a reared-up keyboard
When he who breathes storms
Is not sated by the pearly air.

Will you turn away a single ray
In the light stream from the sky's cascade,
When the architect spent so much
Hyperborean travertine like gold?

You have belted yourself in a ring

---

[23] Benedikt Livšic, "Kazanskij sobor," *Polutoraglazyj strelec* (Leningrad: Sovetskij pisatel', 1989) 69–70.

Of falling light,
And it gives your cupola the joy
Of standing like a Columbus egg.

In the first place, and very important for both poems, is the fact that the poets celebrate the Kazan Cathedral as designed by the architect Voronixin, *not as it was built*. The original design called for a semicircle of columns from the front *and* the back.

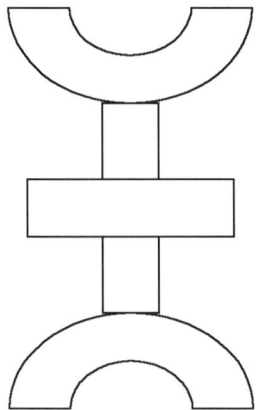

Only in this sense could it, as a plan, be said to "overgrow" the plan of St. Peter's, which has only one arcade of frontal columns. The "cross-spider" (крестовик-паук) spread on the ground makes sense only if we consider the original plan drawn above. The uneven Latin cross of St. Peter's is replaced here by the four equal sides of a Greek cross.

Livšic's poem on the Kazan Cathedral is much more intimate than his poem on the Admiralty, yet despite his address of the church as *ty* (you), his poem is an ingenious riddle and *not* an identification with the cathedral or with the architect's activity. Livsič, unlike Mandel'štam, describes a passive object praisefully and even beautifully, but the building does not shape or deeply affect the perceiving poet.

The lightness of the building is much more clear in Mandel'štam's poem; in the last lines it is described as lighter and more animate than St. Peter's: «Гиганта, что скалою целой / К земле, беспомощный, прижат!» ("Than the giant who is attached helplessly / To the ground by a whole boulder!"). The heaviness of Carlo Maderno's façade of St. Peter's is helplessly earthbound for Mandel'štam, the lover of mobile and even flying stone edifices, of the Gothic and airborne.

The double set of columns in Livšič's poem are likened to a keyboard reared up, the black and white keys being represented by the chiaroscuro of the colonnade under different lighting. In stanza 2 we see the cathedral on a stormy night, where the "flight of hooves" may refer to lightning and thunder "breathed" by the storm-creator, who may be a night rider, distantly recalling the racing Bronze Horseman clanging through his capital. Stanza 3 depicts the cathedral during a beautiful sunset, when not a single pouring ray of light is refused by the grey limestone (the local building material), which becomes like bestrewn gold in that sunlight. The sun's light so affects the perishable limestone that the building is surrounded by a ring of falling light (a "lightfall," on the model of the word *vodopad* "waterfall"). This ring of light gives joy and makes the cupola and building like a Columbus egg—suspended still as no natural egg can be. A "Columbus egg" in Russian is a resourceful and successful solution for a difficult problem (in this case, an architectural one), and the visual aspect of the cathedral here described is just such an architectural solution. So the poem itself is a "Columbus egg," representing a very resourceful, original, and quite elegant and light solution to the problem of how to describe it. We feel that the poet has been very creative and successful, and that he has some inkling of the problems of the architects, but we do not feel that he is very much influenced or shaped by the Kazan Cathedral as we do in the poem of Mandel'štam. Livšic, like his Voronixin, is a *svoenravec* (a "maverick-creator").

Although Livšic's cathedral has some animated characteristics and the architect is mentioned, Mandel'štam's treatment of the same building betrays a much greater involvement on the part of Mandel'štam with the building, the architect Voronixin, and the solution. First of all, the tremendous dynamism with which the building, a free agent, runs out onto the square and suddenly halts is so lively that the reader unwittingly feels that in response the poet, Mandel'štam, has run out onto the square in virtually the same way to observe and describe it. There is a familiarity with the fact that Voronixin was in Rome and brought some of Rome back to Petersburg with him, a kind of superimposition of Rome and St. Peter's in the second stanza: «Ну, так что ж!» ("Well, what did you expect?"). The *ty* (you) then addressed—who walks through the thicket of those columns, turned by the place into a foreigner, a "Russian in Rome" or an "Italian in Russia" as he does so—is Voronixin, but he is also very importantly Mandel'štam as he is affected by the building, and his reader as he is affected by the poem and would be affected by a visit to the cathedral. Then, in the last stanza, the image of the cathedral's small body, like that of the man running through the portico, by its smallness turns the cathedral into a man—not an animal, as is common for the Futurists—and a man who is as light and free as Mandel'štam wishes to be. And the Russian architect, who also so freely dealt with St. Peter's (making it smaller and lighter), is like Mandel'štam, a poet dealing more lightly and gracefully perhaps with some ponderous monument of world—even Italian—literary culture. Thus the poem has more personal involvement of Mandel'štam, the man and poet, with the space. The work has a more metapoetic manifesto value for the Acmeist attitude towards culture than Livšic's poem, which emphasizes the architect's and Livšic's virtuoso performance, a manipulation of the "egg"-object that affects the building much more than the architect or the poet himself—a relationship which lacks the two-way movement of dialogue.

The way in which the Kazan Cathedral is acted upon in Livšic's poem is duplicated in his "Admiralty," from the 1925 collection «Из топи блат» (*From the Marshy Swamps*). Ronald Vroon has discussed how this collection, later grouped with other poems on Petersburg in «Болотная медуза» (*Swamp Medusa*), appears to contradict Livšic's brilliantly articulated Futurist positions, and to exemplify the very "passéism" Livšic so condemned.[24] Ètkind has come closest to giving this Livšic the title of traditional and Acmeist, which the poet, of course, eschewed: "These images, if they sometimes seem enigmatic to the point of non-comprehensibility, are not futuristic—they are, if you will, closest of all to Acmeism."[25] Gasparov's notion that the Petersburg poems represent "the poetics of the riddle," implying that the familiar becomes riddle-like in Livšic's *oeuvre*, is also very much to the point: a riddle presents something familiar from a fresh, and often strange, perspective. Vroon characterizes the poems of *Swamp Medusa*, which include those of *From the Marshy Swamps*, as poems which "downplay the lyrical subject, concentrating instead upon objects—mostly paintings and architectural monuments…."[26] Livšic himself felt that in this collection he effected "a deformation of the semantic and emotional aspects of the word."[27] Markov has called this trait "the loosening of traditional semantics," and feels that it disqualifies Livšic once and for all from the charge of Acmeism and makes him a true representative of the Avant-garde.[28] The Acmeists, rather than loosening traditional semantics, could be seen as having culturally (and perhaps personally) over-loaded the word. In the same collection, however, Livšic does have some poems that treat Petersburg space in a manner much closer to our subject, a usage betraying intimate identification with the space. Thus the lyri-

---

[24] Ronald Vroon, "The Citadel of the Revolutionary Word," *RCSCSPL* 27: 4 (1990), 533–56.

[25] Efim Ètkind, "Master poètičeskoj kompozicii," quoted in Vroon, "Citadel of the Revolutionary Word," 533.

[26] Vroon, "Citadel of the Revolutionary Word," 539.

[27] Ibid.

[28] Vladimir Markov, *Russian Futurism: A History* (London: Macgibbon and Kee, 1969), 189.

cal ego in "Fontanka" not only *acts upon* the famous canal, but is subject very much to being *acted upon* by it:

Асфальтовая дрожь и пена
Под мостом—двести лет назад
Ты, по-змеиному надменна,
Вползла в новорожденный град.

И днесь не могут коноводы
Сдержать ужаленных коней:
Твои мучительные воды
Звериных мускулов сильней.

Что—венетийское потомство
И трубачей фронтонных ложь,
Когда, как хрия вероломства,
Ты от дворцов переползешь

Под плоскогорьем Клодта Невский
И сквозь рябые черныши
Дотянешься, как Достоевский,
До дна простуженной души?..[29]   (1914)

Asphalt trembling and foam
Under the bridge—200 years ago
You, haughty in a serpent-like way,
Crawled into the newborn city.

And today the drivers cannot
Restrain the horses you sting:
Your tormenting waters are
Stronger than a beast's muscles.

What of the fact that you are descended from Venice
And what of the falsehood of trumpeters on a façade
When, like the chreia[30] of perfidy,
You crawl across the Nevskij

---

[29] Livšic, "Fontanka," 68–69.

[30] A *chreia* is an exercise meant to develop rhetorical skills (originally used in Greco-Roman schools for writing and oratorical practice). It is formally composed of eight steps, and for this reason here may suggest the image of a "crawling" and venomous spider (which has Dostoevskian echoes, especially in the context of the Underground Man).

> From the palaces and under Klodt's plateau
> And across the black keys of swells
> Will you reach, like Dostoevskij,
> Into the very depths of a chilled soul?..

Here the past passive participle *prostužennyj* (chilled) passivizes the soul of the lyrical ego, or any onlooker. He is in the same position as the Petersburg he describes, penetrated by the Fontanka now just as the young capital was two hundred years before. The overarching theme of the collection *From the Marshy Swamps* is the unresolved tension of cosmos and chaos inherent in Petersburg, and dominant in it is the tension associated with the "swamp Medusa." This monster, used as a shipping canal throughout most of the eighteenth and nineteenth centuries, is held in check by the embankments and architecture of the capital at present, but not indefinitely. The power of the Fontanka ("haughty in a serpent-like way"), so powerful that horses stung by it are driven wild, is partly associated with the power of the chaotic forces of the swamp Medusa, visited upon the city so many times in the form of flood. This snake-like finger of the Neva penetrates and drives wild both Petersburg and the onlooker. His sense of being affected by the Fontanka willy-nilly is parallel to the passive infant Petersburg, permeated by the "penetrated word" (Baxtin's «проникновенное слово») of Fedor Dostoevskij.[31] The inexorability of his prose left a permanent imprint on Russians' concept of Petersburg in his time, and has likewise affected the poet, Livšic. His Fontanka is "devilish and Dostoevskian," like Axmatova's city in *Poem without a Hero*: here, in the "person" of the Fontanka, Petersburg both acts on the poet and writer and is acted upon by Dostoevskij and Livšic. And the poem engages, is influenced by, and participates in the modern tradition of identification with Petersburg.

---

[31] Mikhail Bakhtin, *Problems of Dostoevsky's Poetics*, trans. and ed. Caryl Emerson (Minneapolis: University of Minnesota Press, 1984), 242, 249–50.

2   EMBATTLED SPIRITS-SELVES: ELEGY AND IDENTIFICATION WITH PETERSBURG SPACES

The identification of self, individuality, and the creative personality with urban spaces in the modern Petersburg tradition has deep roots in Russian pre-Romanticism and Romanticism. In particular, the projection of the lyric ego and the human psychology in the traditional elegy continued to exert a strong influence on poets who felt themselves bound to Petersburg. Blok, Mandel'štam, Axmatova, and Brodskij wrote elegies in the Silver Age and beyond. Axmatova even inaugurated a genre called the "Leningrad" or "Northern" elegy in her well-known cycle spanning the twenties to the forties, and her *Requiem* cycle has been treated in scholarship as an "elegy for [all of] Russia."[1]

In the anticipation and, later, the wake of great historical changes, Petersburg poets reassumed the elegiac tradition, which hinges (1) on mourning and loss (the death of a friend or loved one, lost love or friendship, lost youth, loss of poetic creativity), or (2) on the absence, the non-givenness of love, creative genius, or some highly desirable alternative state. In the elegy all these losses and absences are blows inflicted on the poet's selfhood or lacks which diminish the sense of self. The first, more common, type of elegy takes very overt cognizance of events occurring in biographical time, and thus explicitly acknowledges the self's changes in and over time. The second type posits a hypothetical other life and occurs in the subjunctive mood, in a species of ahistorical "dream-time."[2]

Despite the elegiac cast[3] of the modern Petersburg tradition in poetry and the prominent presence of the generic type with its rather elegiac hero, this connection to elegiac space has been overlooked in the scholarship. This is largely because Romantic elegies are set amidst nature, either in idyllic, peaceful rural locales (what Russian scholar Mixail Epštejn has termed the *ideal'nyj/idilličeskij pejzaž*), or markedly crepuscular or eventime settings (in

---

[1] Sharon M. Bailey, "An Elegy for Russia: Anna Axmatova's *Requiem*," *SEEJ* 43: 2 (1999): 324–46.

[2] Anna Lisa Crone, "Towards a Grammar of the Elegy," lecture, University of Chicago Slavic Department, May 2001.

[3] We employ the terms "elegiac cast" or "elegiac mode" because not all the poetic and prose texts dealt with here belong to the genre of elegy.

Epštejn's terminology, the "despondent landscape" [*unylyj pejzaž*]).[4] In both these cases the natural landscape is closely connected to the inner states of the elegiac speaker. Such a connection is self-evident in Blok's 1910 "To Jurij Verxovskij (Upon Receipt of *Idylls and Elegies*)":

> Мы посмеялись, пошутили,
> И всем придется, может быть,
> *Сквозь резвость томную идиллий*
> *В ночь скорбную элегий плыть.*
>
> We have laughed and joked a bit,
> And perhaps we shall all be forced
> *To swim through the langorous playfulness of idylls*
> *Into the mournful night of elegies.*[5] [italics ours]

The italicized section of this poem of gratitude to another poet, Jurij Verxovskij, shows Blok's powerful sense of the deep connection of idyll to elegy and, we believe, to the spatial-temporal settings in both genres. The happy days of idyll and its "ideal" landscape are powerfully present in elegies because they are what is desired, and usually lost, destroyed, or being dismantled. In Blok's time-bound expression, the "swimming" is uni-directional (*plyt'*) and it is forced by time—from happy, diurnal personal idylls to sad, nocturnal elegies. In his treatment of chronotopes in the novel, Baxtin speaks a good deal of the dismantling of the idyllic chronotope in urban novels. The elegy is the locus of the disturbed idyllic chronotope, or one that is hopelessly lost but still fervently sought.

In the case of Petersburg, the dramatic switch to the urban landscape and the man-made built environment was not, however, totally novel in an elegy, though the first important such uses did not involve Petersburg space. Petersburg, in Russian attitudes towards the city and in the literary tradition so powerfully associated with the space was, as Anciferov has amply demonstrated, a very poor candidate for the Romantic elegy, or idyll for that matter. This was not only because it was urban but because it was traditionally presented in Russian letters as a "stormy landscape" [*burnyj pejzaž*], Epštejn's markedly non-elegiac third spatial category of the function of nature in Russian poetry. This "stormy landscape," so brilliantly inaugurated in the raging assault of the flood of 1724 and in the flood of 1824 in Puškin's *The Bronze Horseman*, is indelibly imprinted on Petersburg space, as both verbal

---

[4] Mixail Epštejn, *Priroda, mir, tajnik vselennoj: Sistema pejzažnyx obrazov v russkoj poèzii* (Moscow: Vysšaja škola, 1990), 142 ff.

[5] Blok, "Juriju Verxovskomu (Pri polučenii *Idillij i èlegij*)," 198.

art and historical fact. Wild, stormy, inclement weather presents a threat to the very existence of Petersburg. Puškin's Finnish waves "do not forget" their vengeance towards the man-made city; rather, elemental threats from snow, wind, fog, and water are ever-present in Petersburg space, able to sally forth and wreak destruction at any moment. The space is marked in literature and the national mentality as inhospitable to man and his architectural creations, enacting its peculiar "negative *kenosis*" in the unleashing of its own inner emptiness and devouring the creative selfhoods of its inhabitants.

In the stormy (*burnyj*) Petersburg cityscape of nineteenth-century Russian literature, nature (i.e., weather) acts on the space in a manner clearly adversarial to man; the terrible weather of Nekrasov's classic four-poem cycle "About the Weather" is shown destroying man, his buildings, and other arts, as exemplified in its destruction of the operatic art and life of the great Italian diva Angiolina Bosio in part 4.[6] Petersburg nature is inhospitable and threatening and, as pointed out above, as the literary tradition moves towards the twentieth century, climatic phenomena are increasingly associated with historical events, revolutions, wars, and the like. A historical flood or a storm symbolizing revolution is equally destructive of man's creations and man himself, as in the adage "*staryj gorod Piter, čto narodu boka povyter*" ("the old city Piter that stripped off people's sides"). Despite the built-in threat of such a stormy landscape, the hero's/poet's identification, intimate interaction, and interpenetration with Petersburg spaces are of virtually the same kind that occurred with natural settings in the traditional Romantic elegy. Hence, in modern Russian letters, a "Petersburg elegy" ceased to be a contradiction in terms. In the modern treatment of Petersburg space as self, the ideal/idyllic and despondent natural landscapes described by Epštejn become Petersburg cityspace, and the stormy landscape becomes a possible condition for creative introspection: "*Kak budto v bure est' pokoj*" ("As if there could be tranquillity in a storm").[7]

THE URBAN ELEGY

Perhaps the most remarkable early identification with an urban setting in the Golden Age was Batjuškov's "To Daškov," cited by Frizman for its innovative inclusion of personalized patriotic themes.[8] In this poem, Batjuškov depicts the horrendous scenes he sees during three strolls through burned and wartorn Moscow in 1813. The cityscape could not be more "despondent."

---

[6] See p. 9, n. 16.
[7] See p. 10, n. 19.
[8] Leonid G. Frizman, *Russkaja èlegija XVIII–načala XX veka* (Leningrad: Sovietskij pisatel', 1991).

Moscow had been identified by Batjuškov with his carefree, happy, and artistically creative youth in "Separation" ("*Razluka*"),[9] and in "To Daškov," he refers to this previous association: "I newly visited the ruins of Moscow, Moscow where I used to breathe complete freedom."[10] In this great elegy, the devastation of Moscow and its ruined spaces are intimately associated with the poet's inner state, in the same way that natural settings are in other elegies, for example, in Žukovskij's sunset- and death-bound "Evening."[11] Moscow in "To Daškov" is no longer its former, full self, and the poet proclaims to his friend that he is no longer the man or poet he had once been, the singer of Anacreontics and milder, more meditative elegies. Distress and dramatic change in the city and the poet is caused here by historical misfortune.

Mixail Epštejn's 1990 monograph covers the functions of nature in Russian poetry from the eighteenth century to the present day. He divides the natural landscape settings in poetry into the three types we have indicated: ideal, despondent, and stormy. Urban landscape does not enter into his deliberations at all. Nevertheless, destroyed or disrupted cityscapes become very common in Petersburg poetry of the twentieth century, especially given the several revolutions, Civil War, the purges and transport of the arrested masses to camps and prisons, the 900-day German siege, and the post-war vengeance of Ždanovism.

The ideal and the despondent elegiac natural landscapes, especially when described against the background of or inscribed cozily within a "stormy landscape," are most pertinent to our discussion and categorization of Petersburg spaces with which the poet identifies in the twentieth century. The ideal natural landscape is a *locus amoenus* (pleasing or charming place) from classical Latin through Renaissance to modern European poetry. It is an aesthetically or literarily predetermined nature, including a catalogue of fixed natural items that occur with limited variation, including trees, flowers, and water for reflection. The recognizable architectural landmarks and locations in Petersburg by the Silver Age are limited, and come imbued with the baggage of literary tradition in the same way. They are already part of the greater "Petersburg text," as Toporov defines it. In the Romantic elegy the despondent landscape is likewise predetermined by literary precedent; it is thus idealized rather than directly reproductive of actual space. According to Epštejn, the despondent landscape entered poetry in the epoch of Sentimentalism; it can alternatively

---

[9] Konstantin Batjuškov, "Razluka," *Polnoe sobranie stixotvorenij* (Leningrad: Sovetskij pisatel', 1964), 145.

[10] Batjuškov, "K Daškovu," 153.

[11] Vasilij Žukovskij, "Večer," *Sočinenija V. A. Žukovskogo* (St. Petersburg: Glazunov Publishers, 1855), 1: 50–53.

be termed the "elegiac landscape," as it is closely linked with the complex of sad, meditative motifs which comprise the generic specificity of the elegy.[12]

The ideal or idyllic landscape and the despondent landscape are semantically loaded and emotionally nuanced, the first as neutral, serene, and peaceful or positive, the second replete with elegiac themes of loss, death, waning power, illness, absence, loneliness, and isolation. Both types are, needless to say, connected with the hero's mood and sense of bereftness. In terms of identification between self and space, what Epštejn writes of the ideal/idyllic landscape is equally applicable to the despondent/elegiac one; in fact, he draws his examples for both types from elegies.

Citing Lermontov's "When a yellowing meadow becomes agitated" ("*Kogda volnuetsja želtejuščaja niva*"), Epštejn remarks that the setting "is enlivened by being transferred from a purely spatial plane to a temporal one, as well as from a spatial to a temporal mode of perception," and "it ceases to be a static given [what we have called in chapter 1 "neutral background," merely a description in verse] and becomes a harmonious expression by the lyric hero, as the state of his soul."[13] Epštejn further characterizes the landscape: "in Lermontov the ideal landscape is structured in temporal terms—*when* instead of *where* … and by this very fact it is sharply subjectivized." It is dependent on how and when the lyric hero experiences it, and may represent the composite sense of multiple visits to one locale. For Epštejn, "… in essence Lermontov gives us not a landscape, but rather the process of creating an ideal landscape out of the elements of his spiritual being." In Tjutčev, Epštejn observes that "the ideal landscape is even more sharply denatured [rendered unnatural, that is, rendered human, psychologized], it becomes the 'landscape of the poet's soul.'"[14] Here, of course, Petersburg space has something in common with ideal and elegiac space as analyzed by Epštejn. In his Introduction to *The Bronze Horseman*, Puškin presents a barren natural landscape onto which Peter the Great maps his great ideas (*velikie dumy*). The Petersburg which arises from the swamps is Peter's mental space, the projection of the tsar's mind. Petersburg's French formal gardens are the transposition of the landscape architect's concepts, his creative visions, onto the forest primeval.

The Moscow in Batjuškov's "To Daškov" must be characterized as highly despondent, or even tragic—a destroyed space analogous to the destroyed self-sense and sadness of the elegiac speaker. But it has in common with the ideal landscape the fact of its extreme psychologization. For Epštejn, "the transformation of a space into a temporal concept and the collapsing of differ-

---

[12] Epštejn, *Priroda, mir, tajnik vselennoj*, 132–34.

[13] Ibid., 134.

[14] Ibid., 135.

ent periods of time into a simultaneous, spatially represented moment when the soul or lyric subjectivity could touch the ideal, perceive it in nature" is the essence of elegiac space.[15] As we shall see, this identification with space holds equally well in an urban setting. This sympathetic function of nature is not the only one in Romantic poetry; another is the contrastive use of nature which highlights opposition to the internal states of the subject's soul, that is, nature's indifference. The similarity, even equation, of the internal state of the hero to the state of external space is more characteristic of the elegy.

The Petersburg tradition of identification of self with space has a great deal in common with the elegiac one from which it is largely derived. The Petersburg poet-speaker, who has expressed his psychology or psychological dilemma in or through urban spaces, interior and exterior, can be divided into two basic types which can be determined by the way he treats the passage of time and how events in time affect his selfhood. The second type, as we shall see, presupposes the prior existence of the first. The first type of elegiac lyric ego is the sensitive, emotional "beautiful soul" of Sentimentalism and early Romanticism, who continues to "feel" in the face of every manner of loss. He evinces a dismissive attitude towards time and therefore towards history. This type is perhaps most clearly represented in the poetry of Vasilij Žukovskij. Dreadful events and losses doled out by time do not significantly change him. He retains his warm sensibilities and finds consolation in religious faith or in creativity; through his verbal expressions he "entrusts himself to language," which provides enough mitigation of despair or partial recompense for his losses. He does not admit that tragic events have rendered him "less himself."

The second type of elegiac lyric ego can be called disappointed or embittered. He has been irrevocably altered by losses that the passage of time has inflicted, and admits that they have caused a "loss of self." When he laments his lost youth, he often laments a better, more sensitive self and integral man of the first elegiac type, which he can no longer be. Baratynskij's cry "*Mertva duša moja*" ("My soul is dead") or Tat'jana Larina's "*Onegin, ja togda molože, lučše, kažetsja, byla*" ["Onegin, I was a younger, and it seems, a better person then"] are virtual signature tunes of the hero who has lost parts of, or has actually survived his better, more feeling or life-affirming self. In "To Daškov," Batjuškov exemplifies this latter type of hero very well. The lyric self who experienced the positive feelings and creative energies subsumed under the notion of "direct freedom" in his Moscow youth is changed utterly and rendered disappointed and embittered by his experiences and losses. The ruined and ravaged Moscow streets emblematize the blows to the poet's selfhood. He is no longer the man or the poet he formerly had been. This type of embittered

---

[15] Ibid., 136.

lyric ego can and does change; his losses lead to the psychological sense of "loss of self."

How do the two types of elegiac hero and their differing stances correlate with the lyric speakers and treatments of space in our Petersburg urban texts? Since we have moved towards the equation "space=self," do we find it borne out in two overarching types of spatial treatment corresponding to two types of poet-speaker? The answer is resoundingly affirmative, except that the lyric speaker can almost never be equated with the poet/author, as most Petersburg writers adopt both types of voices and stances, and there are mixed types. In the historical stance, Petersburg spaces are emptied, destroyed, degenerated, not what they had once been, due to losses and displacements caused by historical and biographical events (in time), as in the case of Batjuškov's elegy. When the second, ahistorical stance is adopted, there is a refusal to admit change or a straining attempt to "write back" the former ideal or idyllic Petersburg space that would correspond to the wholeness or integrality of the lyric speaker (his ability to withstand the assaults of time), that is, what Batjuškov called his "inner freedom."

Most elegiac Petersburg poems and heroes deal with the loss of Petersburg in some sense, the loss of that which was formerly actually possessed. Of course, in elegies the temporal remove from the past self and the past possession may lead to their embellishment in memory and acquire an overly idyllic evocation. Thus in "Separation," Batjuškov's "direct freedom" in the Moscow of his happier youth is especially idealized. There is, as pointed out above, a second, less common type of elegy, in which there is not loss as such, but the abiding absence (non-givenness) or non-attainment of some desirable alternative state or possession, or the presence of some person. These hypothetical elegies lie in the area of a wish-fulfillment or reverie, and deal with "might have beens" and "would have beens." They usually reflect the desire for a more fulfilled life or potential.

The hypothetical wish-fulfillment type of elegy, often called "reverie" (*mečta*), which we identified as somewhat less frequent in the tradition, is exemplified in Batjuškov's "Tauris" ("Tavrida"):

> … сокроемся туда,
> ……………………………
> В прохладе ясеней, шумящих над лугами,
> Где кони дикие стремятся табунами
> На шум студеных струй, кипящих под землей,
> ……………………………………………………
> Под говором древес, пустынных птиц и вод:

Там, там нас хижина простая ожидает[16]

... let us [run away] and hide ourselves there,

....

In the coolness of aspens, rustling o'er the meadows,
Where wild horses gallop in herds
To the sound of icy streams boiling beneath the earth,

....

With the speech of trees, and desert birds and waters:
There, there is where a simple hut awaits us

Such wish fulfillments occur in the twentieth-century Petersburg tradition both when the poet is in Leningrad (exile *in situ*), and even more so when he is in actual exile and unable to return to the physical city.[17]

When the poet is abroad, as in "Tauris," the alternative reality and the more fulfilled self it implies is represented in an idyllic space. Unlike "Tauris," where the poet wishes to leave the cold, inhospitable North of Russia for Southern Crimean climes, in the Petersburg poem of the modern exile one wishes to execute a mental return to the places of youth and happiness. When the poet is still in Russia, the place he wishes to depart from is called "Leningrad," and the idyllic destination is called "Petersburg," where he will be "one's self" and "at home." This is a Petersburg of the spirit, possible in emotion, in memory, and in art.

EMBATTLED SPIRITS: PETERSBURG SPACES FROM SYMBOLISM TO ACMEISM

Все во мне, и я во всем!...

Everything is in me, and I am in everything!...

Tjutčev[18]

Epštejn's stormy landscape (*burnyj pejzaž*) is ever potential in Petersburg space, and part and parcel of the literary tradition of the city, as mentioned above. It is juxtaposed with the overall elegiac cast of modern Petersburg texts; a stormy, hostile nature representing historical "storms" and "winds of

---

[16] Batjuškov, "Tavrida," 194.

[17] The role of memory and manipulation in memory in the latter case, particularly in Brodskij and Nabokov, is the subject of the doctoral dissertation by Jennifer J. Day, *Memory as Space: The Created Petersburg of Vladimir Nabokov and Iosif Brodskij* (Ph.D. diss., Indiana University, 2001).

[18] Fedor Tjutčev, "Teni sizye smesilis'," *Stixotvorenija* (Moscow: Xudožestvennaja literatura, 1972), 107.

change" are assaulting buildings, man-made spaces, and human beings, especially in those poems which take historical events of the twentieth century very strongly into account. Therefore we call such poems *historical* treatments of Petersburg space as self (discussed in part 2). The ever-present threat, the potential for history to wreak its vengeance on Petersburg space at any moment underlies all modern Petersburg space, but it and the historical cataclysms that represent it are discounted as unimportant or meaningless in a large body of texts in the modern tradition which we term *ahistorical* treatments of Petersburg space as self (in part 3 of this study). In these treatments, the buildings and spaces which deny history's/time's power over them are what Brodskij has called "embattled spirits,"[19] creatures nobly withstanding losses inflicted by floods, winds, blizzards, and erosion. In "Vladimir Solov'ev and the Present Day," Blok describes the mode of existence of the great religious thinker as "a man standing in a window open to the winds of the current apocalyptically accelerated time" who, unlike the average person, is *not* being ground down and eroded away like a stone edifice. If he were part of the built environment, he would be an edifice that survives the assaults of time unscathed.[20]

Yet the assaulted human individuality is often presented as clinging for substance and sustenance to the stones, to the solid, tangible, and material space as a way to survive in such historical turbulence. In this tradition the measure of man's (the poet's) coping and surviving is the state of the built environment, to which myriad humanizing epithets and metaphors are attributed. The weather often parallels the psychological confusion or dismay of the lyric ego—or his Dionysian frenzy/creativity—but the embattled buildings and monuments still "stand as a measure" of his failure or success in remaining his strong self and remaining active as a poet. The state of the space is also indicative of how he exists as an individual or creator. His Petersburg is, in a very important sense, his creative or higher self.

Symbolic Space in Belyj's *Petersburg*

The spatialization of self in modern Petersburg letters owes a tremendous debt to the complicated self-presentations of the major characters in Andrej Belyj's novel *Petersburg*. More than anyone else, even Blok, it is Belyj who unabashedly treats spaces as human selves, and his influence as a Symbolist novelist extends to Acmeism and to most Petersburg texts after 1913. Acmeism presents selves and Petersburg as impervious to historical onslaughts in some texts, and in others it gives continuations and evolutions of the

---

[19] Brodskij, "Guide to a Renamed City," 83.
[20] Blok, "Vladimir Solov'ev i naši dni," 490–92.

threatened self of Belyj's and Blok's Petersburg texts. The nervous, tragedy-ridden Petersburg self about to explode and cease to exist at every moment in Belyj's novel (the building-city on the verge of explosion and utter destruction) is typically counteracted in Acmeism by the sterner, stiller, quieter image of the embattled building-self as dignifiedly receiving the assaults of time and circumstance and withstanding them. The most architecture-obsessed poets of the twentieth century, Osip Mandel'štam and Iosif Brodskij, maintain both the Symbolist model and the Acmeist reaction. These are two versions of heroic, creative selfhood and maintenance of self-in-time. As we shall see, imaginative literature is not the sole province where the enormous metaphor of Petersburg as the human self functions. Even architectural historians and critics, such as the artist-critic Aleksandr Benois, are infected with it.

In Belyj's novel (written in 1912 and successively reworked until 1928), not only are human persons characterized as buildings (in the case of Apollon Apollonovič and Nikolaj Apollonovič) or as large topographical sites (Aleksandr Dudkin as Vasilievskij Island, with its Tučkov factories), but more dynamic models are also presented. Sof'ja Petrovna Lixutina is represented as a stone road being destroyed as she moves down it, a road which is beset by the racing of apocalyptic time (parallel to the situation in Gumilev's "The Tram That Lost Its Way" [1921])[21] or which accompanies her total amnesia and loss of self-sense (thus becoming the road of life). This road imagery makes her a modern Evgenij pursued by the Bronze Horseman, but one who finally regains some sense of self by coming back to her house on the Mojka. In the detailed breakdown of types of self-presentation below, we shall present some of the more complicated versions of spatialized human individuality.

In Belyj's novel, Petersburg is presented as an entire, enclosed but threatened world, just as its characters are very solipsistic, but not quite hermetic selves. Petersburg is a whole world, an enormous *individuum*, surrounded by a nothingness (the abyss of times, the abyss before birth and after death[22]), an abyss of eons, a post-Einsteinian time-space continuum lurking everywhere, like the void before the creation in Genesis. Loss of self—totally ceasing to exist as a human individual—is represented spatially in various ways: as falling into the void, disappearing into it, or being sucked up by it. The so-called void is a formless chaos of non-being, like Berdjaev's *Ungrund*, and yet seems often to have unstructured chaotic "content." It is not empty, but in each individual, like the unconscious or id, it has a wild, unknown, and therefore undiffer-

---

[21] Nikolaj Gumilev, "Zabludivšijsja tramvaj," *Stixotvorenija i poèmy* (Leningrad: Sovetskij pisatel', 1988), 311.

[22] As Nabokov describes it (Vladimir Nabokov, *Speak, Memory* [New York: G. P. Putnam's Sons, 1966], 19).

entiated content. It is frightening as a threat to individual existence. Belyj, and Rozanov after him in "The Apocalypse of Our Time,"[23] present the void as inner holes in the human subject (city), a chaos both within and without. In Belyj's characters, the Ableuxovs, it is sometimes characterized as a non-Petersburgian "Mongol chaos"; in Mandel'štam's Parnok (in *The Egyptian Stamp*), as a non-Petersburgian "Judaic chaos" inside the city self as well as threatening from without.

The paradox of voids or chaos with "content" is clear: they represent the irrational element in man, the *thanatos* drive, the often self-destructive forces connected with the noise of time (an eerie opposite of the "music of the spheres," that is, the deeper tragedy of Nietzsche's "spirit of music/cacophony" in his *The Birth of Tragedy*). They are connected in Belyj and Mandel'štam with the tragic Dionysian music of creativity and with Dostoevskij's "most advantageous advantage," the one element without which the personality will be effaced, cease to exist as a human individual, and become an "organ stop."[24]

In order to remain in existence, Nikolaj Ableuxov, like the unsuccessful Parnok in Mandel'štam's *The Egyptian Stamp*, must negotiate—as must Petersburg as a whole enormous humanized character/hero—the difficult path between chaotic disorder, unformed being, and some reason-controlled, structured ego forces. This is presented by Belyj in Nietzschean terms together with concepts adapted from Tjutčev's poetry:[25] the Apollonian *stroj* must subdue the Dionysian *roj* (the "swarm" or disorder) that even the word *stroj* contains within itself as a morpheme.

Thus being oneself as a creative personality is not a total rejection of one's unconscious and emotional self, be that self associated with Mongol or Hebrew ancestry, but rather the artful mastery of that *roj* and channeling of it in intentional intellectual or imaginative artistic creativity. The situation described in Nietzsche's *Birth of Tragedy*, in which too much Apollonian control or too much Dionysian chaos make the embodiment of great art impossible, is clearly mirrored in Belyj's text. Belyj equates both extreme reaction, associated with the character Apollon, and extreme revolution, associated with the terrorist Lippančenko and Nikolaj, with "nothing," and both are equally deadening to Petersburg and every Petersburger in the novel:

---

[23] Vasilij Rozanov, *Apokalipsis našego vremeni*, in *Izbrannoe*, ed. Evgenij Ziglevič (Munich: A. Neimanis, 1970), 444.

[24] In his *Notes from Underground.*.

[25] Fedor Tjutčev, "Den' i noč'," 137..

... the Mongol cause [revolution] came through everywhere.... the mission that had been entrusted to him [Nikolaj Ableuxov] before he was born.... And Nikolaj Apollonovič rushed to the guest (one Turanian to another), a notebook in hand:
"Kant (Kant too was a Turanian).
"Value as a metaphysical nothing!
"Social relations based on values.
"The destruction of the Aryan world by means of a system of values.
"Conclusion: the Mongol cause."
The Turanian [representing the father Apollon's extreme conservatism] replied:
"The task has not been understood. Paragraph one—the Prospect.
"Instead of value, numeration: by houses, floors and rooms for time everlasting.
"Instead of a new order, the record of the circulation of the citizens of the Prospect.
"Not the destruction of Europe [Petersburg] but its immutability....
"The Mongol cause...."[26]

Here extreme revolution and extreme reaction are both revealed to be the same Mongol Cause.

The vertical spatialization of the self, where the unconscious, collective past is an "underground," is associated by Belyj with the primordial Petersburg swamp and the bacilli-infested waters of the Neva, as is the Petersburgian text *Notes from Underground*, a work we know made a great impression on Nietzsche when he read it in Nice in 1884:[27]

> And there was no center of consciousness.... In his soul was an empty hole. And over this hole Nikolai fell to thinking.... he had stood in exactly the same way in the gusts of Neva wind, leaning over the railing of a bridge, and looking into germ-infested water (all that had happened before, and had happened a great many times).[28]

---

[26] Andrei Bely, *Petersburg*, trans. Robert A. Maguire and John E. Malmstad (Bloomington, IN: Indiana University Press, 1978), 166. Our references to Belyj are from this excellent translation, which is based on the 1922 edition of the novel. In those cases where we elected to use longer versions from Belyj or parts of the 1912 version edited by Dolgopolov (passages that were subsequently truncated or excluded from the later version), they will appear in A. L. Crone's English rendering with reference to the Dolgopolov Academy edition (Andrej Belyj, *Peterburg* [Leningrad: Akademija nauk, 1981]).

[27] Anna Lisa Crone, "Nietzschean, All Too Nietzschean," *Nietzsche in Russia*, ed. Bernice Glatzer Rosenthal (Princeton: Princeton University Press, 1986), 95–112.

[28] Bely, *Petersburg*, 127.

These frightening waters are constantly rotting through the foundations of the elegant buildings on the embankments, and the latter stand refusing to crumble, yet are eaten away slowly all the same.

The Nietzschean Apollonian-Dionysian dichotomy has a more horizontal spatialization in Belyj's *Petersburg* as the linear, organized city center and the spherical, disorganized periphery (the islands, hotbed of revolutionary activity). The centripetal and centrifugal forces must be balanced in order to avoid destruction of the identity of the center (the self). Here again the centripetal, center-maintaining forces are *both* salubrious *and* destructive; they have the potential both to maintain the heart (the central squares) of Petersburg and to destroy them utterly. The centripetal-centrifugal model of personality was used by Vjačeslav Ivanov, but the Petersburg *locus classicus* of it is Mandel'štam's 1925 "The End of the Novel," an essay in which the biographical novel is clearly used as a metaphor for the structure of the human self. There is no doubt that this essay, which explains the disappearance of Parnok's self in *The Egyptian Stamp*, a work which does not materialize as a novel, is as much about being and remaining one's self as it is about genre. Mandel'štam states in no uncertain terms the jeopardy of the individual in this period, in which "we will see the end of individual biography as a mode of existence," in other words, the end of the human person as known up to that time:

> The measure of the novel is human biography or a system of biographies. From the very first the contemporary novelist sensed that individual fates no longer exist.... Therefore the novel always offers a system of phenomena directed by a biographical link, measurable in biographical terms, and a novel holds together compositionally only insofar as the centrifugal force of its planetary system ... the force pulling from the center to the periphery, does not overwhelm the centripetal force [towards the biographical center]. [2: 310]
>
> The further fate of the novel will be nothing other than the history of its atomization as a form of personal existence, even more than its atomization—the catastrophic death of biography....
>
> Today Europeans are thrown out of their biographies like balls from a billiard table.... A man without a biography cannot be the pivot of a novel.... [2: 311]

The center-periphery image of the self is seen in Belyj's *Petersburg* as the metaphorization of the self as a house in central Petersburg, on the English Embankment or elsewhere. The house's location varies in the text, not only because of the forgetfulness of the author, but because it is more than a mere house. Space is portrayed more intimately as "a room of one's own" inside the neo-Classical mansion. In his own room, Nikolaj Ableuxov can be his complete self—a Europeanized student of Kantian philosophy who is comfortable with his Mongol inner self, wearing his ancestral caftan, feeling at one with his Tatar antecedents in the steppes: in a word, being his whole self. Sitting there, he concentrates and goes deeply within himself to become, in Belyj's words, a "truly creative man" (in his case, as a scholar or philosopher.) Here the inner-directed, centripetal vector is self-affirming, as in Brodskij's attempt to reach the central city squares (the center of the authentic self) in his 1962 poem "From the Outskirts to the Center" (see chapter 5).

Paradoxically, at the same time that the revolutionary forces threatening the wholeness of Petersburg and its characters are centripetal—they enter the city from the islands, cross the bridges with spherical bombs, and circulate in the streets with these bombs—Dudkin brings the bomb inward to explode that very center, after which, as Yeats noted, "things fall apart; the centre cannot hold."[29] The revolutionary, dynamic forces must come into the center to bring about heightened vitalization, illumination, activity, and yet they must be handled, used, and channeled in such a way that the thinking, creative energies remain intact. Creativity in this model is always the managing of the frightening and life-threatening, the management of tragedy—which must be actively mastered and foisted back onto the peripheral spaces, "amazing" and altering those spaces in the image the creator wants (see chapter 8 below).

In Belyj's novel, Nikolaj, the most autobiographical character, manages to be this creative man successfully, if intermittently. But it is important that his father, Apollon, has a parallel ambition of controlling and dominating more and more space with his project of rendering it immutable. In his case he wants to encompass, to overpower the round and spherical with lines and parallelipipeds. This is a parodic re-evocation of Peter the Great's obsession with the linear and angularly geometrical, of Peter who drew lines over the round islands on maps, and had Leblond and other French formal architects impose order on wild nature in the lines and squares of the city's gardens. Here an excessively Apollonian image of creativity is seen in Senator Ableuxov's desire and in the reminder that the Petrine lines have lapsed since the Petrine period; Peter's lines have "gotten rounder" under later tsars and have not totally controlled the elements and natural environment. There is still in the novel a sense of temporary, fragile existence although Petersburg's built environment, its buildings and streets, are above the floodwaters and intact.

---

[29] W. B. Yeats, "The Second Coming," *The Collected Poems of W. B. Yeats* (New York: MacMillan, 1979), 184.

Belyj's novel is shot through with neo-Kantian concepts, as he was a serious student of neo-Kantianism. Hence the emphasis on mental activity—*mozgovaja igra* ("brain play"), both successful and abortive—and the unusual presentation of the brain bloodlessly opening up, with a spatialized site virtually emanating out of it:

> Apollon Apollonovič ... would notice that the bubbling vortex suddenly formed into a corridor stretching off into an immeasurable expanse. What was most surprising was that the corridor began from his head, i.e., it was an endless continuation of his head, the sinciput of which suddenly opened up into an immeasurable expanse.[30]

Thought acting on a space—filling an empty space—is the reason Mandel'štam gives in "The Morning of Acmeism" as to why architects build and creators create. The brain is acting on emptiness, creating and filling a space—its own.

This is a variation of the Kantian notion that actual reality/space, the phenomenon in itself, cannot be known, that all space is representation, and that the world is human will and representation. Katerina Clark quite correctly accuses the Russian avant-garde of treating all space and empirical reality as material for reshaping, for creation, imposing their own formations as reality. Space in Petersburg is the mental product of the perceiving mind, the projection of each character and of the authorial self, space as extension of self and as self. It is a simplification of Kant that this generation abused, as Clark points out, for their own purposes.[31]

The rotund, spherical, circular forms are used by Belyj to symbolize the revolutionary forces, and the bomb threatening destruction of the self by explosion represents the peripheral forces overwhelming the centripetal ones. These forces, as seen in the quotations above, are as much within that self as without. Thus Nikolaj and Dudkin, the most intellectual characters, are characterized as filled with the chaotic dynamism of the Petersburg streets. In multiple instances in the novel, it is made clear that they bring the outside street life (the Revolution) into their inner spaces. The outer spaces are projections of the characters' minds; material and spiritual spaces are identified with individualities, and self is equated with space in a striking multiplicity of concrete cases. This equation can be seen when the characters come in from the street to the protection of a Neo-classical mansion and their own room, in Nikolaj's case; and in Dudkin's case to the seclusion of his garret, described directly as Dudkin's body or Dudkin's attic (later invaded by the

---

[30] Belyj, *Peterburg*, 93.
[31] Clark, *Petersburg, Crucible of Cultural Revolution*, 33.

Metallic Guest and the Persian/Mongol Enfranšiš). To remain whole, Nikolaj and Dudkin must negotiate the difficult path of maintaining a balance, of being invigorated by the outside, not deadened by the static, nor overwhelmed by the dynamic.

The Preservationists

There is something of Apollon Ableuxov's mania for order and geometric symmetries in the Acmeists' Apollonism. As a group, the Acmeists are inordinately fond of Neoclassical Petersburg, and this unites them in their aesthetic tastes with Benois and the group of Petersburg architects and critics known as the Preservationists. Benois called his idealized Petersburg a "painterly Petersburg" in his 1902 article, where he enjoined artists to paint the city, and attempted to convince Russian artists that it was indeed beautiful.[32] This Petersburg is often painted by those who answered his call (including Dobužinskij, Ostroumova-Lebedeva, and Benois himself) as virtually devoid of people, with empty Chirico-like squares with a few dwarfed figures—that is to say, with none of the clutter of the actual teeming life of the capital. What could represent more of an opposite to the visual aspect of Belyj's Petersburg with its crowded prospects and the unruly human myriapod circulating through it *ad nauseum*? Belyj's chaotic Petersburg virtually pulsates with the same kind of frenzied life that Pasternak saw in Blok's personality and his Petersburg.[33]

On the surface it cannot be denied that the Preservationists' desires for Petersburg have something in common with the desires of Apollon Ableuxov. They wanted an apparently more static and streamlined, ordered beauty. Clark has emphasized that the order they admired bespeaks a more static aesthetic. Their solution was to remove the surface chaos of people, of shops (*lavočki*), the presence of the lower classes, the unwashed, the Gogolian, Dostoevskian, and Belyjan aspects of the northern capital, and restore its cold, clear, rational lines and contours: a somewhat deadening aestheticization, but, to borrow a surrealist metaphor, "an exquisite corpse."[34]

Closely associated, as were the Acmeists, with the journal *Apollon*, the depopulated, Neoclassical idealized environment was nevertheless also an extension for the human self, identified with the selves of the architect-creators who designed it, as well as its poet-creators. They wanted to emphasize the European aspect of Russianness, not the Mongol. Attacking Belyj not terribly obliquely, they shunned the "Asiatic-daring gaudiness" of contemporary

---

[32] A. Benua, "Živopisnyj Peterburg," *Mir isskustva* 1 (1902): 2 ff.

[33] See the introduction to part 2, pp. 58–59.

[34] Clark, *Petersburg, Crucible of Cultural Revolution*, 59.

Petersburg.³⁵ Lukomskij, one of the leaders of the Preservationist movement, wrote in 1913 that Petersburg's architectural essence reflected "an overall harmonious interconnectedness of all its component parts."³⁶ A self, a human individual organized in this way would call forth the integral personality (*cel'najaличnost'*) of the Slavophiles, reborn here in a secular version. The utopian dream of a perfectly harmonized personality that was part of Kireevskij's Christian *sobornoe soznanie* (collective ecclesiastical consciousness) as an almost totally harmonic instrument has as its counterpart a totally harmonized space. Benois stressed that he wanted no disorder in the architectural environment in Petersburg: "Disorder ... was anathema to his ideals. He contrasted the 'elemental force of the old lady (Moscow)' with Petersburg's 'Roman severe ... spirit.'"³⁷

Yet, surprisingly, this retrospectivist, seemingly conservative group equates the built environment with man as much as Belyj does. Benois' descriptions of the buildings as *strogie, surovyje, vyderžannyje* (strict, severe, restrained) are identical to his descriptions of the architects who built them. The men are depicted to be as strict, restrained, and simple as their buildings had been, a similarity that Clark calls an "isomorphy in the depiction of the architects and their building."³⁸ For our purposes here, they are equated to them. The architectural critic Rudnickij, who wrote a long discursive review of the Preservationists' exhibition in 1912, in particular characterized those architects as having "sacrificed themselves in the supreme effort of designing and overseeing construction of their genial buildings so that they are totally spent thereafter."³⁹ Such effort clearly represents a pouring-out of one's life force, one's self-center, from the body into the artistic product, parallel to but somewhat differently from the characters who "other" themselves into a building or space directly presented as the character's body. The life force of the architect and its dynamism is displaced from his body into the architectural creation. The architects and their creative struggle become deposited into the buildings in which they go on living. Rudnickij's description of this pouring the self into the creative product has an uncanny similarity to positive Christian *kenosis* and to the kenotic notion of the artist pouring out blood in Dante's *Inferno*. Similarly, in Mandel'štam's 1931 poem "Preserve My Speech," the tree/poet emits sap/ink and transforms his tree/body into paper,

---

³⁵ Quoted in Clark, *Petersburg, Crucible of Cultural Revolution*, 61.
³⁶ Quoted in ibid., 62.
³⁷ Ibid., 61.
³⁸ Ibid.
³⁹ Paraphrased by Clark, *Petersburg, Crucible of Cultural Revolution*, 61.

logs, skittles, and finally a wooden axe handle for his own beheading, thus pouring himself into his creative work.[40]

For Mandel′štam, in the same way, Voronixin, a "Russian in Rome" (*russkij v Rime*), *is* his Kazan Cathedral, and the cathedral is vitally alive. Clark is only wrong in that she overemphasizes the static qualities of the Acmeists' poem-buildings and of their view of architecture. Mandel′štam's Admiralty, as we observed in chapter 1, is a ship about to weigh anchor and become airborne, and his Kazan cathedral almost jumps out to meet the poet as he approaches it. The humanization of these Neoclassical buildings in the post-war Petersburg of Brodskij's childhood is even greater. They are large "embattled spirits" educating the little boy who walks through them more than any Soviet textbook; they are not only aesthetic, but ethical presences, teachers and mentors, the formers of his Petersburgian character and artistic proclivities, of his selfhood; moreover, they are "selves," like him and his generation. Like the suffering male caryatid in Belyj's novel (discussed in detail in chapters 3 and 4), they are humanized in the extreme, struggling in difficult times to maintain their identity and succeeding. There may be a Museum of Atheism in the Kazan Cathedral, but it stands there bearing this degradation with dignity and grace, telling the passerby that it is still who it always was, that it has not succumbed to the pseudo-identity the Soviet state has foisted upon it. Brodskij describes the built environment in the same humanizing terms in which he describes Anna Axmatova in his essay "The Keening Muse."[41] The poetess, given a pseudo-, and very negative, identity by the Soviet state, bears up, true to herself. A regal building is Axmatova, a monument to the true Petersburg, as she had said, in her turn, of Blok:

Он прав, опять фонарь, аптека,
Нева, безмолвие, гранит,
Как памятник началу века
Там этот человек стоит.[42]

He is right. Again the streetlight and the druggist's shop,
The Neva, silence and granite,
Like a monument to the beginning of the century,

---

[40] Anna Lisa Crone, "Wood and Trees: Mandel′štam's Use of Dante's *Inferno* in 'Preserve My Speech,'" *Studies in Russian Literature in Honor of Vsevolod Setchkarev*, ed. Julian Connolly and Sonia Ketchian (Columbus, OH: Slavica Publishers, 1986), 87–101.

[41] Brodsky, "The Keening Muse," *Less than One*, 34–52.

[42] Anna Axmatova, *Sočinenija*, ed. Gleb Struve and Boris Filippov (Munich: Meždunarodnoe literaturnoe sodružestvo, 1967–68): 1: 317. Further references to Axmatova's poems will be cited in the text by volume and page number.

There stands that man.

Not only Brodskij, but Evgenij Evtušenko also sees Axmatova as a monument:

> ... не убий
> ту связь времен—она еще поможет.[43]

> ... do not kill
> That linkage of times—she/it [a person/ the link] will help yet

To the point of incredulity she is un-Soviet; she is both one harmonized self and the unbroken link of times, the proof that there is one integral and continuous Russia. She who said of herself in 1944, "I myself was made of granite," is but another Brodskijan noble building.

ଓ ଃ

We have posed the question of how Petersburg spaces and selves respond to assaults to their integrity, both from within and without, in the context of Silver Age intellectual history. We have also framed the question by a consideration of generic provenance. As in the case of Blok's enforced poetic "swimming" from the daytime playfulness of idylls to the mournful night of elegies, the few scholars who have thought penetratingly about lyric landscapes in the idyll versus the elegy (most recently M. Epštejn) have realized that the "despondent" landscape represents the lyric ego's present sense of bereftness, and that the "ideal/idyllic" landscape in elegy represents what has been lost, what is disturbed or being dismantled, as well as the object of elegiac quest—what might be regained or even attained for the first time. Even Baxtin, with his minimal emphasis on lyric poetry, recognizes Blok's linkage of idyll and elegy, with their respective subjectivized spaces. In his writing on types of chronotope in the novel, he discusses the intensified sense of time's passage in the eighteenth century idyll as leading to a change in the idyll and ultimately to "a special form of the elegy ... an elegy of the meditative type with a strong idyllic component.... The problem of time is elevated to the level of philosophy in several eighteenth-century idylls. The real organic time of idyllic life [and space] is opposed [in these idylls or elegies] to the frivolous, fragmented time of city life or even to historical time...."[44] It is this pressure of time/history on space that is the subject of part 2, "'Historical' Treatments of Petersburg Space."

---

[43] Evgenij Evtušenko, "Pamjati A. A. Axmatovoj," *Stolen Apples* (Garden City, NJ: Doubleday, 1973), 246–48.

[44] Mikhail Bakhtin, "Forms of Time and Chronotope in the Novel," *The Dialogic Imagination*, trans. Caryl Emerson and Michael Holquist (Austin: University of Texas Press, 1981), 228.

Part II

"Historical" Treatments of Petersburg Space

The tradition of the poet's treatment of Petersburg space as self includes, very prominently, those examples in which historical events have decisive effects on the poet's selfhood. Historical events are often treated as elemental—as storms, floods, blizzards—in which climatic metaphors are associated with a historical time that is accelerated in an apocalyptic age. So bound are historical time and the elements that the usual question about the weather was rephrased by Pasternak: "What millenium is it outside today?"[1]

These history-ridden treatments of space at the close of the Petersburg period—with the debacles of Port Arthur and Tsushima, the Revolution of 1905, important political assassinations, disaster in the first World War, the two revolutions of 1917, the Civil War, War Communism, the purges beginning in Leningrad with the murder of Kirov, the 900-day siege, Ždanov's attack on Petersburg/Leningrad writers (Axmatova and Zoščenko) in 1946—are basic to our study. What is happening to the writer identified with the city and its culture is that he is, in parallel fashion, constantly besieged, and yet proclaims, "I ... am sustained [held together] by Petersburg alone."[2] We also see many metaphors of Petersburg during this tragedy-ridden period as an illness (influenza, for example), often one contracted in childhood and paradoxically linked to the highest moments of creative inspiration. Both images—that of the city being attacked by storms of history from without and that of a disease eating away the organism from the inside—are derived from the notion of a time-bound sense of fate, of the prophecy of Petersburg's complete emptying-out coming to fulfillment.

Historical treatments of Petersburg space are divided in chapters 3, 4, and 5 below into (1) pre-1917 and 1917 and (2) post-revolutionary responses. The

---

[1] Boris Pasternak, "Ne vremja li pticam pet'?" *Stixotvorenija i poèmy* (Moscow and Leningrad: Sovetskij pisatel', 1965), 694.
[2] Mandel'štam, *The Egyptian Stamp*, 149.

first type expresses anxiety and foreboding about Petersburg's impending end—like the expectation of imminent death in the individual—and simultaneously it involves attempts by the poet to stave off the final catastrophe that is visualized as encroaching in space-time. Such responses are numerous in Blok's poetry and Belyj's *Petersburg*, where the road of life and the Neva as the river of time are prominent.

The second type, post-revolutionary responses, shows the poet accepting Petersburg's recent death—its having ceased to be what it formerly was and represented—and thereby the cessation of the sustenance that "held the self together," the sustenance to the writer's creativity. At other times this death is presented as an ongoing, gradual process, with which the poet identifies himself and his generation; he fears that he will be unable to cross over into a post-Petersburg future. The city, already renamed and deprived of its position as capital, is being debunked, and alien forces are assaulting the poet in a similar manner, pigeonholing him as a "has-been" (*byvšij čelovek*) or as baggage of the past, a holdover from a superceded epoch. These forces attempt to regiment him and his art, to "Sovietize" him, in a word, to turn him into someone else. Hence the repeated metaphors of destroyed and crumbling roads; rivers off their course or diverted to alien riverbeds; trains and trams off their tracks, lost in "abysses"; and frequent falling, out of time and into gaping holes. These are all spatial metaphors of a biography or creative life sundered, broken into parts, or destroyed. "Today Europeans are plucked out of their biographies," as Mandel'štam wrote in "The End of the Novel" [2: 269].

The identity and inextricable tragic bond with a Petersburg in crisis humanizes the city space almost by definition, and that suffering space becomes a kind of tragic hero. Its negative *kenosis* and negative aspects in general are gradually rewritten as positive in a collective attempt to change the city's fate in the consciousness of the nation. No one sensed this powerful identification of poet with place or expressed it more eloquently than Moscow poet Boris Pasternak in reference to the poetic greatness and achievements of Aleksandr Blok: "Blok had everything that makes a poet great—fire, tenderness, a penetrating mind, his own personal image of the world, the gift of being able to transform everything he touched—a personal fate, which took everything into itself...."[3] Pasternak emphasizes the incredible dynamism of Blokovian space, its *stremitel'nost'* (its force straining, dashing somewhere), and he associates this dynamism with the spatialization of Blok's poetic self:

> How well his straining style fit the *Zeitgeist*, with his language, secretive, an inner treasure, underground, barely peeking out of cellars, the

---

[3] Boris Pasternak, "Paul Marie Verlaine," *Literatura i iskusstvo*, 1 April 1944, 694.

language of conspirators, *whose main hero was the city, whose main event was—the street....* [italics ours] The combined bearer of Blok's world, his soul, was the city of Blok's verse, it was the main hero of his tale, of his biography. That city, that Blokovian Petersburg, is the most real of the Petersburgs of artists of the modern world. That city exists equally in life and in the imagination.... At the same time the image of this Petersburg is composed of traits chosen by a hand so very nervous, yet subjected to such a spiritualization [by the poet] that it is transformed into the gripping phenomenon of a very unique inner world.[4]

The angst, ambivalence, and tragedy of Blok's personal life are here seen imprinted by the author on the city-space. The deeply *personal Petersburg* of each of the modern poets covered in our book differs from Blok's in its particulars, but each example in this "historical" section personalizes and mythologizes the self in time-space. Moreover, the "unique inner world" of each poet humanizes the space, opening the way for a dialogic interaction between self and space. In their recognition of the effects of history, these examples of spatialization correspond to those elegies that treat losses or absences caused by events in time.

In the three chapters below, we aim to show in greater detail the variety of models of personalized Petersburgs in the *oeuvres* of Blok, Belyj, Mandel'štam, Axmatova, Xodasevič, Nabokov, and Brodskij, among others. These models include static, resultative images (comparable to a resultative perfective emphasizing the changes and effects brought about by history) such as a house finally emptied out as the result of a tortuous life's path and the devastation or other "unnatural" alteration of that life. They also include more dynamic visualizations of the process of change (comparable to an imperfective verb, repetitive and having long duration), "being Petersburg to utter death." In the latter, the complex disruptions of a multiply-broken life are presented as the interaction of numerous Petersburg buildings and locales, where lost parts of the self (bits of biographical time) lurk or are thought to be lodged. This search to recapture lost aspects of a divided self and the attempt to reintegrate them is geographically presented, and has an undeniable Proustian quality. While the methods and models of spatialization of self differ from Blok's in the *oeuvres* of other poets, they all reaffirm the central correctness of Pasternak's assessment of Blok's cityscape as Blok's own inner world, a world where the streets are the "events": each of our poets in a very important sense is *his Petersburg.*

---

[4] Ibid.

3 RUSHING BACK TO NOTHINGNESS: HISTORICAL TREATMENTS OF SELF AND SPACE BEFORE AND DURING THE REVOLUTION

The idea that Petersburg's fate in the twentieth century represents the result of the linear unreeling of history over time is often conceived of spatially as horizontal movement. Events in time are viewed as a pre-scripted pageantry, a procession towards an inevitable goal. This horizontal movement in time (*Chronos*) is represented instead of a vertical flight upwards, out of linear time into *Kairos* (Berdjaev's eternal, transcendental time). Of course, a movement downward and below the earth would be a negative sinking-below history, perhaps the most fearful consummation of destiny for this city—"Petersburg will sink." Yet in these instances the image of a forward progression is a function of Russia's having chosen (through Peter the Great) to be a modern historical nation. In this chapter we examine four major works which present Petersburg and the self who dwells there as bound up in a horizontal progression towards the cataclysm of 1917 (even if the work itself was written after 1917). Here we will see preliminary evidence of the "stormy landscape" as a condition for elegiac reflection on loss of self and city, and the projection of self onto the similarly threatened Petersburg architecture.

The first two works we will consider, Belyj's *Petersburg* and Blok's *poèma Retribution*,[1] are very closely related in their position of *anticipating* the conclusion (goal) of history's horizontal movement. By contrast, Blok's *The Twelve* is a poetic attempt to represent the end at the very moment of its arrival. The fourth work, Axmatova's *Poem without a Hero*, although influenced by the three earlier ones, is more complex in its positional perspectives on the cataclysmic period, and thus includes more types of identification with space. It operates on at least two important horizontal temporal planes, one corresponding to 1914 and the other to the 1930s–40s, a time when Petersburg once again sustained devastating historical and cultural blows. Such multidimensional, even theatrical, treatment of *Poem without a Hero* is suggested by the author herself, who visualized it as a ballet and even planned a libretto for it.

Towards the end of the nineteenth century, faith in Russia's fulfillment of her great historical destiny—a positive sense of horizontal movement which

---

[1] Blok, *Vozmezdie*, 239–56.

had before now been opposed to the negative, "cursed" Petersburgian variety of temporal progression—was on the wane. Some seventy years before, Puškin had asked of Russia and Peter the Great:

> Куда ты скачешь, гордый конь,
> И где опустишь ты копыта?

> Whither do you gallop, proud steed,
> And where will you set down your hooves?

In *The Bronze Horseman*, he was filled with optimism that great things lay in his nation's future. So was Gogol', who ended *Dead Souls* with all and sundry making way for the Russian troika as it rushes down the road of history, full of exhilarating if uncontrolled potential. By the turn of the century, however, this sense of unchecked Russian flight began to resonate with a particularly Petersburgian destiny. Wildly careering, Petersburg and Russia seemed to be headed back to the abyss of non-history. For its writers, this eventuality foreshadowed the end of Russia as an ongoing cultural and historical force, the loss of its art and even of Puškin:

> And who knows, contemporary literary Russia may finally become unworthy of its great past.... Puškin will become alien in a literature that has grown savage, and his genius, it is frightening to say this, may be lost to the people. *Caveunt consules!* What is it that lies before us in the dark future? The death of the nation's literature is the greatest of misfortunes—the reduction to dumbness of a whole nation is the wordless death of its creative genius![2]

Kol'cov uses the notion of ensavagement (*odičanie*) in his famous poem on the death of Puškin, in which Petersburg is a forest once more, now missing a heroic tree. Merežkovskij and Blok use the word to refer to the coming era. Brjusov compared the new age to a "return of the Huns," and Belyj saw it as a new period of Mongol (Tatar) domination. Rozanov spoke of a "sudden closing down of Russia" in terms reminiscent of the swift fall of Babylon, while Mandel'štam spoke of the "wing of approaching night" and the black velvet of "universal emptiness," as well as of a Petersburg newly engulfed in grass and weeds. Such images point to the imminent death of the city, and threaten the Petersburger with a loss of his sense of self. Ensavagement—a return to the savage state—is the idea here which corresponds to our formulation of Petersburg's negative *kenosis*, the destructive process which had been

---

[2] Dmitrij Merežkovskij, "O pričinax upadka i o novyx tečenijax sovremennoj russkoj literatury," *Sobranie sočinenij* (St. Petersburg: Marks, 1914), 28: 210.

felt in that city well before the apocalyptic age under discussion here. The force of negative *kenosis*, as explained above, is the opposite of the Petrine civilizing process, in which the city's chaotic content, alternately visualized as its inner emptiness, is poured forth upon its spaces and those who inhabit it. In another, differently-directed sense of negativity, this force is also the "dumbness" occasioned by Petersburg's violent and intrusive appropriation of the vital energies of its inhabitants—from "little men" like Gogol'ʹs Akakij Akakijevič to its major creative personalities.

Earlier Konstantin Leont'ev had declared Petersburgian Russia to be on a path of self-destruction. The Petrine period for him had been a flowering epoch in the national history, when a maximal differentiation of elements had all functioned in unified harmony. Consonant with his treatment of states as organisms, he sees late nineteenth-century Russia as rushing to its death: it exhibits a blurring of functions and organic resimplification which mark its weakness and decline. Decomposition would lead to death and the undifferentiated primordial state that pre-existed Petersburg.[3]

In Belyj's *Petersburg* and Blok's *Retribution*, the first works to be examined in this chapter, the re-ensavagement of Petersburg is underway, but not yet complete. Both works deal with the Revolution of 1905 and its aftermath, but stop short of the city's actual demise. If one takes these works as wholes, both authors evince considerable identification with the Petersburg project, and treat themselves and their creations as microcosms of a rapidly disappearing Petrine Russia. Their characters are not prepared for the end of the old, familiar world, and fear that the new world will arrive before they have completed their paths of development or can prepare themselves to "cross over" into the new. The experiences of the characters in Belyj's novel, in particular, for all its extremes of parody, reflect the tribulations and tragic lostness of the writer-self in a transitional period. In no other representation does the Petersburg world teeter so dangerously over the abyss without actually falling in. The same sensation of a frightening abyss and the unstable foundation of the self in Petersburg space occurs in the other two major works presented here. In *The Twelve*, which depicts the moment of transition between old and new when the Revolution arrives, the author figure seems to remain, paralyzed, at the crossroads while history marches forward. In Axmatova's *Poem without a Hero*, the progression of events leading up to the dawn of the "real twentieth century" is made even more inescapable rather than less so by the complex layering of anticipatory and retrospective views which constitute its structure.

---

[3] Konstantin Leontiev, *Against the Current*, ed. and trans. George Ivask (New York: Weybright and Talley, 1969). See in particular "The Triune Process of Development," 147–69.

In the atmosphere of frightening uncertainty and instability leading up to and including the October 1917 revolution, these authors, through their characters or lyric persona, appear to cling to Petersburg as if trying to create for themselves a solid assurance that elements of the city, if not they themselves as creatures of Petersburg, will be able to cross over into the future. Identifying with the city's spaces is an attempt to weather history's forward progression by forging a certain solidarity with an embodied *other* who understands these frightening events in the same way. Clinging to Petersburg buildings and locales, the self bolsters its sense of connection with the city and a Westernized Russia. In this identification, not only do manifestations of history's movement in buildings, streets, squares, and water affect the self as an integral being and as a writer, but at the same time the self's intense feelings of fear and suffering are projected onto the city. In this way, Petersburg experiences the same threatening forces as the poet-self, and in so doing, doubles and imprints the self into its spaces. Significantly, if earlier the appropriation of personality involved in the city's negative *kenosis* had been invasive and malevolent, now its writers share of themselves with Petersburg as a gesture of solidarity and in hopes of survival—in an effort to combat the historical forces which threaten to rip both them and the city out of existence altogether.

In our analysis of each of the Petersburg works below, our concern will be with the effects of the "noise of speeding time" and with the visible symbols of the movement of history—be they equestrian statues, trains, carriages, automobiles, boats, or climatic episodes—on the figure or figures representing the author or his generation. Where on the stage of history does the author place his figure, if he does so at all? Does the figure hear or see the future approaching? How does he react? Does he move, and does his vantage point change? Or does he appear to be like a cameraman shooting a film of events in which he is not an active participant? Is he rushing through space-time himself, or does he stand stationary while others do so? Finally, how does he interact with Petersburg architecture (or its lack)? We will use these questions to guide our inquiry into the creative relationship between self and Petersburg space from a historical perspective.

BELYJ'S *PETERSBURG*

Some may object to our use of Belyj's novel *Petersburg* on several grounds: (1) that he is predominantly a Muscovite writer; (2) that his Petersburg is cerebral and somewhat outside of the spirit of the tradition; and (3) that many Petersburg writers, such as Axmatova (and particularly Mandel'štam) opposed

Belyj's brand of Symbolism and his attitude toward the word.[4] Belyj's novel nevertheless plays a major and still underestimated role in the treatment of Petersburg in the rest of the century, particularly where our subject, Petersburg man in his spaces, is concerned. In fact, in a very important sense Belyj definitively codifies the relationship between mental and physical space suggested by Peter the Great's original projection of self into the structures of his new city. Without denying the great influence of *The Bronze Horseman*, Gogol''s Petersburg tales, and Dostoevskij's great novels, tales, and even feuilletons on Belyj and his novel, we hope to show through myriad examples that what happens to Belyj's characters in Petersburg space, both interior and exterior, is repeated with variations by the Petersburg poets of the twentieth century from Blok to Brodskij.

Belyj's novel, like his earlier "Symphonies," is famous for its elaborate wordplay and its significant repetitions of sound and its rhythms. Musical symbolism, however, does not overshadow completely the importance of the novel's visual and spatial elements, its color symbolism, and the symbolic meaning of lines, spirals, and other geometric shapes and forms. Belyj's *Petersburg*, for all its undeniable musical qualities, is one of the most visual novels ever written, and one of the main goals of Symbolism, which Belyj pointed out as early as 1902 in his «Символизм как мировоззрение» ("Symbolism as a Worldview"), was the visualization of the spirit.[5] Visions, eyes, and the spatial look or configuration of things is extremely important in the novel. By associating the spaces, ensembles, and buildings of Petersburg with individual characters and their psychology, Belyj psychologizes and personalizes this Petersburg and these spaces. In contrast, however, to Dostoevskij's metaphoric and somewhat static approach to this same device, Belyj introduces a dynamic, metapoetic element into the relationship between internal self and exterior space. Just as the city has engendered its "Petersburg creatures," the characters may alter the "objective" Petersburg by their psychological effects on it. In this novel, Petersburg space is "visualized" psychological space, and the reader perceives not only verbal music in it, but also a sense of highly personalized visions. Despite the Acmeist attacks on Belyj's musical experimentation, as in Mandel'štam's essay "The Morning of Acmeism," the experiences of Dudkin and Nikolaj on the streets of Petersburg are repeated in

---

[4] Mandel'štam's attack on Belyj and Symbolism can be found in "O prirode slova" ("On the Nature of the Word" [2: 246]), where he says, "Andrej Belyj, for instance, is a morbid and negative phenomenon in the life of the Russian language only because … he unmercifully and without ceremony chases the word, making it conform to his speculative thought." See also "Utro akmeizma" ("The Morning of Acmeism" [2: 32–34]).
[5] Belyj, "Simvolizm kak mirovozzrenie," *Mir isskustva* 12 (1904).

various Acmeist poetry and prose works such as Mandel'štam's *The Egyptian Stamp*. It is not Belyj's theories and intellectual position that are so important for later generations of Petersburg poets, but the visions and psychological experiences of his distraught and harried characters. Dudkin, Sof'ja, Apollon, and Nikolaj live in the imagination of Petersburg poets and others writing about Petersburg after this novel. It is here that the twentieth-century type of identification of a character/poet/Petersburg creature with his city spaces crystallizes, and its influence is pervasive.

ଔ ଓ

Peter I's personal fascination with straight lines and linear geometrical figures is well documented, and in Belyj the lines of the city's original urban layout and the original Petrine wooden buildings, insofar as they survive, become spatial representations of Peter's project. These lines are treated as man-made order and control, and are opposed by spherical, rounded contours which represent disorder, irrationality, and the betrayal of the Petrine conception, as well as the possibility of explosion and destruction. In Belyj's novel this opposition is best exemplified in Apollon Ableuxov, and is here represented by the narrator as the Senator's inner thoughts:

> Lines!
>
> Only in you has the memory of Petrine Petersburg remained. Peter once drew parallel lines upon the swamps.... Those lines became overgrown with granite and stone and wooden fences. Not a trace of the straight Petrine lines remains. Peter's line has turned into the line of a later epoch, into a rounded Catherinian line, into the Alexandrine order of white stone columns [Voronixin's Kazan Cathedral]....
>
> ... Only here amidst the large buildings have small Petrine houses remained. There's a green one. And a blue one, one-storied with a hanging sign "Dining Room." It's just as it was when these houses were all over the place in olden days....
>
> Lines!
>
> How they have changed. How these severe days have changed them![6]

Here the true Petersburg project is still present, hidden in the straight linear contours of the city.

---

[6] Belyj, *Peterburg*, 13–14.

In the same section of the novel there is a subchapter entitled "The Caryatid."[7] The male caryatid referred to is a bearded, sculpted figure of stone, an architectural element perched on Senator Ableuxov's Ministry building and therefore related, in accordance with the identification of spaces we are treating here, to the Senator himself. The epithet "stony" (*kamennyj*) is used elsewhere for Apollon without reference to the caryatid. This stone figure is given a consciousness of the whole trajectory of Petersburg history. Like the lines, Apollon himself, and the narrator, the caryatid is a receptacle of that history, a solid but impressionable substance which not only records the past in general, but preserves the marks of individual humans who have "touched" it, either mentally or physically. Gazing for over 200 years at the street below, the caryatid meditates upon the pivotal events in the life of the capital that it has witnessed—the murder of Tsar Paul I, the Decembrist uprising, the 1905 revolution. Coming alive as much more than a mere sculpture, he enlivens the Ministry building. The Bronze Horseman, Falconet's statue, plays a similar role as a meditator upon and actor in Russian history in this novel. He does so most notably in a long historiosophical passage where he is presented as contemplating several alternative historical courses Russia might take. While the passage in Belyj's novel has general historiosophical interest as a meditation on Russia's future, it is also presented as the personal preoccupation of Aleksandr Dudkin. Dudkin had been out about Petersburg during the day, and remarks, "You bring back home with you what you have experienced in the streets, in squalid restaurants and tearooms."[8] Throughout the course of this study we will see Belyj's sense of internalizing the outside world and externalizing the inner world onto the Petersburg cityscape many times and in many contexts.

In a famous passage, as in the one about the caryatid, Belyj personifies the statue and projects Dudkin's inner thoughts onto it, displacing his intellect and historical consciousness into an architectural detail. The considerable permanence of stone and bronze gives Belyj's characters a sense of the abiding presence or immanence of Petersburg's past in its sculpted figures and buildings as well as in the less permanent, human characters, Apollon and Dudkin. The fact that the caryatid was not only a Russian architectural detail, but one derived from ancient Hellas, confers upon it even more ancient knowledge and a deeper sense of cultural continuity. As long as the Ministry building stands, lines remain straight, and the Bronze Horseman stands in Senate Square, the sense of the past and of Peter's perennial guardianship of the city

---

[7] While a caryatid is a female sculpture in Greek statuary, Belyj treats his caryatid as a male personified element on a façade.

[8] Belyj, *Peterburg*, 98.

through the ages is maintained. Thus in his 1904 poem "Peter," Blok said of the statue-tsar: «Он будет город свой беречь» ("He will protect his city"). From Dudkin's point of view,

> Farther down beyond the bridge, against the background of St. Isaac's Cathedral, there appeared before him the same boulder, and the same enigmatic Horseman stretching his weighty, patina-covered arm over the Neva...[9]

A certain repetitiveness ("the same," etc.) is used to invoke the situation in Puškin's *poèma*, in which the Petersburg "little man" Evgenij confronts the same statue. Belyj's passage continues:

> A vacillating half-shadow covered the Horseman's face, and the metal of his face doubled in an ambiguous expression; his palm cut into the turquoise air.
> From that pregnant time when the metallic Horseman rushed here to the shores of the Neva, from that time pregnant with days when he threw his steed onto the grey Finnish granite—Russia has been divided in twain.... And the very fates of the fatherland have been divided....[10]

> You, Russia, are like a steed! Your two front hooves strike out into darkness, into emptiness, but the two back ones are firmly implanted in the granite soil.[11]

After having the revolutionary Aleksandr Dudkin, his latter-day Evgenij, reformulate Puškin's question, Belyj has him propose four possible answers to it, some positive and some involving the frightening flight of Russia-Petersburg and all European civilization into a void. Here is Dudkin's most frightening vision of the outcome of Russian history:

> Once he has reared up and measures the air with his eyes, the bronze steed will not set down his hooves; there will be a leap over history; a great agitation will occur. The earth will be split and the very mountains will crumble from a great earthquake.... Petersburg will sink.[12]

---

[9] Ibid., 99.
[10] Ibid.
[11] Ibid., 98.
[12] Ibid., 99.

Russia, the last country to join European history, will be the first to fall from history, but Europe itself will not lag far behind: "Under the heavy Mongol heel the shores of Europe will sink and foam will curl over them."[13]

This apocalyptic vision depicts the end of Petersburg as the Bronze Horseman's dash into nothingness. Blok uses a closely related image of Russia as a wild "mare of the steppes" (*stepnaja kobylica*) in his cycle on Kulikovo Field.[14] A horse, train, fire brigade, or automobile racing out of control, off the path of history, is particularly frequent in the Petersburg texts of the period, though it is found elsewhere as well. Wild dashing at an accelerated apocalyptic pace is found very notably in Gumilev's "The Tram That Lost Its Way."[15] There, too, Petersburg is the take-off point, and the destination appears to be a void. The speed of the tram is so great that it seems to be in three places at virtually the same time: «Через Неву, через Нил и Сену / Мы прогремели по трем мостам» ("Across the Neva, the Nile, and the Seine / We thundered across three bridges"). The sense of simultaneity is reinforced by the perfective verb, which tends to unify the three crossings. The tram is ultimately in the abyss of time, of non-history: «Он заблудился в бездне времен» ("It was lost in the abyss of times"). In straying from the path of history, Petersburg in fact remains true to its own, doomed course as preordained by nature and the cyclical configuration of the unique mythology upon which it was based. It races forward back into the past, into the void of non-history from which it emerged virtually ready-made. It is at the same time both a rushing figure itself and a portal to an experience of time so layered and multi-dimensional that it devolves into a void filled with chaos.

What effect does such a sense of rushing time have on the people of Petersburg? It is important, as we have noted, that the "emptying-out" experienced by the characters/personae in Belyj and Blok is basically of the same type as that repeated by Petersburg poets for the rest of the century. In the essay "Solov'ev and the Present Day," as we have seen, Blok discusses again, in architectural terms, the effect of such fast-moving time on man. He points out that the very apocalyptically-oriented Solov'ev was a man ahead of his time, already living partly in the future into which his generation was being so violently propelled. Solov'ev could stand this agitation, whereas most men could not: "A perfectly … well-balanced individual would never hold up, standing in the wind from a window opened wide to the future … a normal

---

[13] Ibid.
[14] Blok, *Na pole Kulikovom*, in the poem "Reka raskinulas', tečet lenivo," 225. See especially the line «Покоя нет! Степная кобылица / Несется вскачь!»
[15] Gumilev, see p. 46, n. 21.

man would be worn down too quickly, go mad or perish."[16] In the prose introduction to *Retribution*, a poem he says "is filled with revolutionary premonitions," Blok speaks at greater length of the effect of rushing time on man:

> In a word, the universal maelstrom sucks almost the whole man into its funnel. Not a trace of his personality remains; if it does remain in existence, it becomes unrecognizable, uglified, maimed. There had been a man—and he exists no longer; all that remains is flabby flesh and a rotting little soul.[17]

Here again we see the effects of negative *kenosis*, the enforced gathering-up of man's vital forces into Petersburg's great void and the redirection of his historical identity into the raging course of the city's mythic chaos.

In a striking scene in *Petersburg*, a fire brigade dashes by Sof'ja Petrovna Lixutina, who experiences a loss of personality that is presented as her life crumbling like a stone edifice. This flighty character, with whom Nikolaj Ableuxov is in love, is on one level a parody of Blok's "Beautiful Lady," and the attempts of Nikolaj to steal the wife of Lixutin, his best friend, are not without allusion to the relations of Belyj himself with Blok's wife, Ljubov' Mendeleeva-Blok. The name Sof'ja associates the character with God's wisdom in a hopelessly fallen state, as in the Gnostic beliefs of Simon Magus, as well as with Vladimir Solov'ev's related Divine Sofia. Clearly she has gone so much astray as to be unrecognizable as we find her here; in fact, she has the comical alternate name of "Angel Peri." In a similar way, the "Beautiful Lady" of Blok's early poetry was unrecognizable in his "terrible world" phase. In *Petersburg*, in the subchapter "She Forgot What Had Been," Sof'ja is pushed off her path very seriously indeed. Her name, Sof'ja Petrovna, means "wisdom, fathered by Peter," and her confusion and suffering from the Russian disease of a lack of historical sense (comparable to the lack of a sense of identity or continuity of life) makes her parallel to Peter's brainchild, the city itself. This parallel is made explicit by the textual comparison of Sof'ja's biography to a Petersburg building or house.

Sof'ja, then, very lost and disoriented on a Petersburg street and thrown into a total panic, stands for Petersburg-Russia lost in time. Čaadaev's diagnosis of the sickness of Russian "history" as a whole was that Russians do not know who they are because they do not know "when" they exist, i.e., they have no coherent historical development. Russia, and especially Petersburg, is thus flawed from within, and is threatened both by the chaotic forces welling up inside it and by the historical storms which rage without. Personifying histori-

---

[16] Blok, "Vladimir Solov'ev i naši dni," 490.

[17] Blok, "Predislovie" (to *Vozmezdie*), 240.

cal memory (память) and Petersburg, Sof'ja has lost not only her path, but also her Orthodox religion, embodied in the text by a silent and mysterious Christ figure.

In "The White Domino," the subchapter immediately preceding "She Forgot What Had Been," the Christ figure confronts Sof'ja. He is called "the tall and sad one." Shortly after this event, the caryatid, already familiar to us as a receptacle of Petersburg's historical consciousness, crumbles and begins to fall from his building:

> Sof'ja Petrovna saw how … the caryatid of the entryway fell down and how it was hanging, how a piece of the neighboring building with semicircular windows and with small carved wooden statues stuck out into the spot.[18]

Apparently what is crumbling is a Petrine house, and Sof'ja feels that she, as a result, is plunged into hellish chaos. The Christ figure accuses the Petersburg populace in the person of Sof'ja Lixutina: "I go after you all. You abjure me and then summon me later…."[19] She takes a cab and sets out on a disturbing ride across the city, apparently trying to reach "home," a home that would be, in our context, a sense of self:

> Sof'ja Petrovna forgot what had been. Her future had fallen into a blackish night. Into the blackish-grey night behind her a piece of her recent past fell off … after the piece of her recent past the whole of yesterday fell off. Hardly had she moved farther [in the cab], seeking support for consciousness [in a solid building], hardly had she conceived a desire to call forth the impressions of yesterday—when again they fell away like a chunk of a huge granite paved road … they fell away from memory and a loud sound broke out, a sound of crushing stones.… What an emptiness was ripping off, pieces hurtling off one after another. And metallic strokes were heard.… The love of this unhappy summer … her spring conversations with Nikolaj Ableuxov, flitting by, fell away: the years of her marriage, the wedding … everything fell from her memory and again a sound of crushing stones was heard….[20]

All the events of her personal past are chipped off the edifice of her biography:

---

[18] Belyj, *Peterburg*, 173.

[19] Ibid., 172.

[20] Ibid., 174 ff.

Her life flitted by, her whole life fell, as if it had never existed.... Some sort of void began directly behind her back (because everything was falling through a hole there, crashing into a bottom of some sort), the void continued into the ages.... That which was flying off into some sort of bottom was the pieces of her life falling.[21]

During this cab ride, Sof'ja Petrovna felt that she was being pursued by the Bronze Horseman, and that he was stomping on the broken-off chunks of her life. Later, when the cab finally brings her to her house on the Mojka, she manages to come to her senses and recall who she is. Nevertheless, the reader is left with the devastating impression that her "recalling everything" is the illusion, and that her amnesia and sense that her life is crumbling is the more genuine experience. Her life/house in this metaphor is depicted as a stone structure of events which crumble and fall off when forgotten. The crashing pieces during the ride are precipitated by the fall of the caryatid. Remembering that the caryatids are receptacles of the memory of the past, the reader is not surprised when its destruction has amnesiac effects on Sof'ja, a Petersburg creature whose existence is intimately bound up with that stone. It falls from its place and hangs suspended, the objective correlative for her amnesiac experience. It is the catalyst and accompaniment to her bewilderment. It effectively joins her personal identification with a building and her existential preoccupations with the overarching question of Petersburg-Russia's place in or out of world history. Sof'ja is like Petrine Russia, and her wild cab ride shows the misguided trajectory of a Russia unconscious of and at odds with itself. Her sensations of breaking apart and crashing down in pieces is literally spatialized as "chunks of life." In this, her image prefigures many examples in later Petersburg poetry, analyzed below, of lives compartmentalized into numerous architectural chunks. Belyj's use of the abyss which swallows up the pieces of Sof'ja's life was borrowed a few years later by Vasilij Rozanov, in two passages that have become better known than "She Forgot What Had Been." However, Sof'ja's apocalyptic experience has no finality, whereas Rozanov depicts an unequivocal end.

The more an author attempts to depict the actual end and its coming in such spatial models, the more devastating and destructive the effect on the individual, and the more Petersburg space, in turn, becomes identified with that individual's profound sense of disorientation and suffering. Rozanov's *The Apocalypse of Our Time* (1918–19) is the book of a dying man. Employing the image of the stage of history, he sets his vignette in a theater in revolutionary Petrograd, a frequent setting of Mandel'štam's poems in *Tristia*,

---

[21] Ibid., 174.

which date to the same years. Rozanov includes in his book the first coinage, to our knowledge, of an expression later made famous, or recreated, by Winston Churchill in a slightly different context—"the iron curtain." Churchill could have read it in the Kotelianskij translation of Rozanov's book published in London in the late 1920s:

> La Divina Comeddia
>
> With clanging, creaking and shrieking an iron curtain is lowering over Russian history.
> The show is over.
> The audience rose. It's time to put on our fur coats and go home.
> They looked behind them.
> But there were no fur coats and no houses either.[22]

The audience, like Sof'ja Petrovna, is on the edge of a gaping abyss that is swallowing everything, although they hardly suspect it. In a brief introduction at the beginning of his *Apocalypse*, Rozanov speaks of the death of God (loss of religion) and the loss of a prevailing philosophy, and he attributes the abysses and voids in the universe to these inner losses in men's psychology. His mode of expressing the external losses is, appropriately, architectural, given the tendency in the Book of Revelation toward urban-destruction metaphors and metaphors of devastation ("Babylon was laid waste / fell in a single day"):

> There is no doubt that the deep foundation of everything that is happening now lies in the fact that in European humanity (and in it, Russian humanity, of course) there have formed colossal voids from former Christianity, and everything falls into these voids … thrones, classes, estates, labor, wealth. But all this falls into the emptiness of a soul which has lost its ancient content.[23]

An image of everything falling without and emphasis on people of the Old World is found in Blok's *The Twelve*, written about the revolution in January 1918 (see below). There the representatives of that world are falling and being knocked down, assaulted by the terrible Petersburg winds and snow in a historical and apocalyptic storm. Sergei Hackel has discussed the influence of

---

[22] Vasilij Rozanov, *Solitaria*, trans. S. S. Koteliansky (London: Mandrake Press, 1929).
[23] Rozanov, *Apokalipsis našego vremeni*, 444.

Rozanov's *Apocalypse* on Blok's revolutionary cycle. They were written virtually simultaneously.[24]

In Sof'ja Petrovna Lixutina's case, an abortive mini-apocalypse, there is, seemingly, an interaction of factors. The fall of the caryatid and the Bronze Horseman's pursuit, as well as the mysterious appearance of the Christ figure, are related to the consumption of the pieces of her dispersed life by the gaping void. The emptying-out of the place and the soul go hand in hand, as they do later in Rozanov. Even the road down which Sof'ja is coursing is crumbling. It is not only the wrong road, but a disintegrating one. In both excerpts from Rozanov above, a gaping abyss is devouring Russia, its people, and their houses. In the second excerpt, collapse and falling into voids rather than inundation is the generalized metaphor for apocalypse. The abysses metaphorized spatially and geographically are then revealed to be the emptiness inside the human soul, which has lost its former, pre-Petrine Christian content. The abyss said to lurk under and around Petersburg is the objective correlative of an inner spiritual emptiness. It was partly Peter's debunking of Orthodoxy that led to the Church's and the Old Believers' contention that the city lacked content and was spiritually void. Sof'ja Petrovna's emptiness manifests itself in a total ignorance of who she was and a sense that she had never been born. Indeed, Rozanov's description of a lost and emptied soul could have been based on this image from Belyj, or another from Blok's famous poem to Zinaida Gippius about their generation:

Рожденные в года глухие
Пути не помнят своего.
Мы—дети страшных лет России—
Забыть не в силах ничего.[25]

Those born in deafened years
Have lost their path.
We are the children of Russia's terrible years,
We can forget nothing.

This last line may appear paradoxical in view of our argument. That generation was able to remember the traumatizing events that caused them to lose their path, and they are disturbed because they are conscious of forgetting or "losing themselves." Their amnesiac moments are painful because of the sense

---

[24] Blok wrote his *poèma* in January of 1918, when Rozanov was also at work on his *Apocalypse*. See Sergei Hackel, *The Poet and the Revolution: Alexander Blok's 'The Twelve'* (Oxford: Oxford University Press, 1975).

[25] Blok, "Roždennye v goda gluxie," 232.

of losing hold, losing the self. They have not reached the painless state of total amnesia or oblivion. Blok's poem continues, blaming time for their sufferings:

> Испепеляющие годы!
> В сердцах, восторженных когда-то,
> Есть роковая пустота.[26]
>
> Incinerating years!
> In hearts once in ecstasy
> There is now a fateful emptiness.

In Rozanov's "Divine Comedy," the parts of the theater, along with the whole of Petersburg, are seriously falling into the abyss. In his preface, people and buildings are being engulfed by external voids which are at the same time voids in the human soul—the falling-off of the "home" which had previously been the receptacle of the self. In people in general, as in Sof'ja Petrovna, these souls are empty, disoriented, off their path. People may collapse into the outer void immediately at their backs, or be consumed by the inner emptiness inside them.

In Nikolaj Ableuxov, one of the main and most autobiographical characters in Belyj's *Petersburg*, the same problem of inner-outer correlation is found in his fear that he will open the door of the family house and, instead of a vestibule, find a gaping abyss and fall into it. It is the expression or translation into space of an anxiety that does not come to pass in this work. Sof'ja has the experience that Nikolaj fears, but only temporarily.

BLOK'S *RETRIBUTION*

Blok's *Retribution*, begun roughly at the same time and written in part concomitantly with *Petersburg*, is an unfinished work which presents a fictionalized, but realistic chronicle of several generations in the life of a St. Petersburg intelligentsia family of noble origin. Covered from the 1860s through the Revolution of 1905 and up to circa 1910–11, this family is clearly modeled on Blok's own. The *poèma* is poised "on the boundary between the centuries" (*na rubeže vekov*), a phrase made famous as the title of Belyj's memoir, and, as the other works analyzed here, treats the passage of time on a horizontal plane. The work begins with a contrastive comparison of the nineteenth and twentieth centuries and the idea of crossing into the twentieth century, being propelled into it by time. Time here is marching forth to the inexorable beat of iambs, a variation of Belyj's Bronze Horseman dashing forward from his pedestal. Again, as in Belyj's novel, it is not clear where time is rushing. There

---

[26] Ibid.

is considerable anxiety that the wrong path has been taken, or that the scions of this noble family have only been emptied out and worn down by time. They cannot stay in step with it, making it impossible for them to fulfill their destiny as poet-leaders or poet-heroes for Petersburg-Russia.

Nevertheless, Blok did project some hope, both in the text and in the prose description of its genesis added in 1919. While the figure representing Blok who attends his father's funeral in Warsaw cannot be the future leader of Russia, there is hope that his son, who is born to a simple Polish girl, may be able to be the future hero who will put Russia back on the right path:

> Yet the seed is thrown out, and the next generation produces something more obstinate ... and this characteristic finally begins to act upon the surrounding world; in this way the family that had experienced the vengeance of history [seen in the fates of its own members related in the successive chapters of the work] ... begins in its turn to wreak its own vengeance; the last scion of the family ... is ready to grab onto the wheel that moves human history, and perhaps he will.[27]

The hope expressed here is admittedly very vague, and Blok never wrote the life of the young Pole who might be the future poet-hero of Russia.

The general disposition of the historical scene is virtually the same in Blok's *Retribution* and in *The Twelve*. Both represent the movement of history horizontally, and both allude to a crossroads from one century into the next. Yet the differences are instructive. In *The Twelve*, the crossroads from the Old World to the New is physically delineated. The boundary is much vaguer in *Retribution*; it is spoken of but not spatialized, and there are only meditations about who might cross and what the crossing might be like. Another striking difference is the absence of a clear representative of Blok in the New World of *The Twelve* and the clear presence of the Blok figure in the third part of *Retribution*. The poet, a lover returning from a tryst on a white night, walks through a Petersburg that spans 1900–05. Standing on the shore of the Neva, he sees the future coming towards him from the Baltic Sea, the farthest reaches of which are the years 1904 (Russia's defeat in the Russo-Japanese War) and 1905, with its revolution and general strikes. His evocation of the city, Peter's creation, shows it to be passive and in need of protection, just as the men of his generation were shown in his prose introduction to be considerably worn down by age and morally weaker than their predecessors: "There had been a [whole] man—and he exists no longer; all that remains is flabby flesh and a rotting little soul." Whether one envisions the sea on one side of the stage or at the backstage with the hero standing upstage and looking to-

---

[27] Blok, *Vozmezdie*, 241.

wards it, the movement of time is horizontal in this important passage. He apostrophizes Petersburg, the nocturnal city, and himself simultaneously, which tends to turn the place into a kind of *alter ego*:

О, город мой неуловимый,
Зачем над бездной ты возник?…
Ты помнишь: выйдя ночью белой
Туда, где в море сфинкс глядит,
И на обтесанный гранит
Склонясь главой отяжелелой,
Ты слышать мог: вдали, вдали,
Как будто с моря, звук тревожный,
Для божьей тверди невозможный
И необычной для земли…
Провидел ты всю даль, как ангел
На шпиле крепостном; и вот—
(Сон, или явь): чудесный флот,
Широко развернувши фланги,
Внезапно заградил Неву…
И Сам Державный Основатель
Стоит на головном фрегате…
Так снилось многим наяву…
Какие ж сны тебе, Россия,
Какие бури суждены?..
....
Да и народу не бывало
На площади в сей дивный миг
(Один любовник запоздалый
Спешил, поднявши воротник…)
Но в алых струйках за кормами
Уже грядущий день сиял,
И дремлющими вымпелами
Уж ветер утренний играл,
Раскинулась необозримо
Уже кровавая заря,
Грозя Артуром и Цусимой,
Грозя Девятым января…[28]

---

[28] Ibid., 252.

Oh my unfathomable city,
Why did you appear above the abyss?...
Do you remember coming out on a white night
To where the sphinx gazes into the sea,
And reclining your heavy head
On the hewn granite,
You could hear, far, far away
As if from the sea, an alarming sound
Impossible in God's heaven
And unusual on earth...
You saw the whole distance, like the
Angel on the fortress spire, and there—
(Am I awake or dreaming?) a miraculous fleet,
Spreading its flanks wide,
Suddenly blocked off the Neva...
And the Autocratic Founder himself
Was standing on the first frigate...
Many dreamed this in a waking state...
What dreams, what snowstorms
Are in store for you, Oh Russia...
....
But there were no people on the
Square at that amazing moment
(Only a lover, late,
Was rushing, his collar turned up...)
But in the crimson streaming beyond the ships
Future days already shone,
And their sleepy flags
Were played with by the morning breezes,
Already a bloody sunrise
Spread itself, enormous,
Threatening us with Port Arthur and Tsushima,
Threatening us with January 9th ["Bloody Sunday"]...

    Blok first sees Peter return as a sea captain. Peter at the helm of the ship of state, in his second most frequent hypostasis (after the Bronze Horseman), appeared very similarly to Dudkin and Nikolaj in a Petersburg restaurant in Belyj's novel, where he is called the Flying Dutchman. In that scene, Peter on the restaurant mural-wallpaper comes alive (both hypostases are relevant in Belyj's novel). Here in *Retribution*, the poet, standing on the shore, sees the great tsar again active. Peter interposes himself in between his city and the frightening debacles at Port Arthur and Tsushima. With his navy he blocks the city, protecting it from the advancing events, stalling or staving off the coming cataclysm of the twentieth century. Both *Petersburg* and *Retribution* present the active involvement of Peter the Great in the fate of his city in the apocalyptic age. In both, this intervention can be seen as a supernatural event or as a hallucination or vision of one of the characters ("am I awake or dreaming?"). Dudkin only takes decisive action when he feels he has become the great tsar, and the murder of Lippančenko, like blockading his city from a threatening future in *Retribution,* is an action that protects Petersburg and its inhabitants from their inevitable fate only for a while longer.

If the circumstances of Peter's original founding act had created an insurmountable antagonism between city and individual, reflected and perpetuated in the "little man" dramas of nineteenth-century Petersburg literature, then the tsar's protective gestures in these works of the twentieth century implicate both city and inhabitant-self as a single unit in their vulnerability and need for shelter. In the poet's lament, "O my unfathomable city, / Why did you arise above an abyss?" Petersburg has become "mine" in a very literal and empathetic sense. The rising wind and icy drops of water in the poem serve as evidence of the real presence of this chaotic abyss which physically and psychically threatens both the city and the man himself: «А с крыши холодная капель / Уже за воротник мой тупо / Сползает, спину холодя… / Куда ни повернись, все ветер…» ("And from the roof already a cold drop / dully slips past my collar, chilling my back… / Wherever you turn, there is wind…"). This is the same wind that would totally engulf the city in *The Twelve.*

Like Belyj, Blok shows how his wandering figure interacts with specific Petersburg architectural figures which, along with him, witness the horizontal march of the future toward the city. The notion of memory and history congealed, as it were, in such figures is introduced by the question "Do you remember…", and the lone wanderer lays his head on the granite with the carved sphinx in a gesture of "becoming" the statue. He, like the sphinx, "gazes at the sea" so that he projects his own animated sense of approaching doom onto the stone figure at the same time that the sphinx imparts its equally portentous "memory," its preserved history, to the human Petersburg creature. In a similar fashion, the wanderer is compared to "the angel on the fortress spire" (on the Peter-Paul cathedral) who sees "the whole distance." What the angel and the poet figure can make out, past Peter's navy, is the approaching future, envisioned as history/time "catching up" with Petersburg— a "vengeance" glimpsed from afar, much like the avenging horseman in the Carpathians miraculously seen all the way from Kiev in Gogol'′s "A Terrible Vengeance": «вдруг стало видимо далеко во все концы света» ("suddenly one could see far, to all the ends of the earth").²⁹ And both the city and those who live there, no matter where they turn, are led against their will toward a gaping abyss, the end of its history and the beginning of a new era for a qualitatively new place.

BLOK'S *THE TWELVE*

Another treatment of future time approaching horizontally can be found in Blok's *The Twelve*. This twelve-poem cycle-*poèma* deals, as did Rozanov's *Apocalypse*, with the actual arrival of the revolution, the end of the Petersburg world. Rozanov evinced less interest than Blok in the world that was to come, and emphasized, as we have seen, that everything was collapsing and falling into voids. Rozanov, as a dying man, has no vision of himself in the New World. Blok shows more interest in the twelve Red Guardsmen who march through the work as the movement of history, a movement that can easily be conceived as moving horizontally across a stage, left to right, from the past into the future.

Blok attempted to hear the music of the revolution. His work is full of the rhythms of revolutionary hymns, such as "Varšavjanka," with its refrain, «Марш, марш вперед, / Рабочий народ» ("March, forward march, / Working people"). The apocalyptic forces that accompany the march are the black wind and the white snow that knock down almost all of the representatives of the Old World, who are thus rendered incapable of crossing into the New World-Time. Falling down and out of step, these people cannot cross the stage, despite the constant revolutionary imperatives: «Смело, товарищи, в ногу / Революционный держите шаг» ("Bravely, comrades, march in step / Keep a revolutionary step").³⁰

This work can easily be visualized as a ballet. The wind, snow, and storm stop virtually everyone except the Red Guardsmen: they are in their element, though the narrative story of the work does slow their progress towards the future. At this point the whirling snow obscures the specific features of this new future, as it does the city itself. The love triangle (which we will see again in *Poem without a Hero*) between Van'ka, a bourgeois, Kat'ka, a prostitute, and Petka, a Red Guardsman, does force a temporary halt in their march. Kat'ka, a symbolic Christ figure standing for long-suffering Russia, is the object of a struggle between her two suitors, and she ends up murdered in a useless sacrifice.

The question of Blok's own place in the poem is moot. He is certainly not in the vanguard of history. This puzzling question may be answered through

---

[29] N. V. Gogol', "Strašnaja mest'," *Sobranie sočinenij* (Moscow: Russkaja kniga, 1994), 1: 157.
[30] Blok, *The Twelve*, 258–59.

reference to the passage in *Retribution* (treated at length above) in which the poet, wandering on a white night, sees Peter I's return with his fleet, and Peter's act of temporarily blocking off his capital from frightening future events. In that scene, except for the observing poet and his exalted vision of the tsar and the future, the only figure on the landscape is described as a "lover … with his collar turned up." This figure clearly has an affinity with the biographical Blok, given his general reputation and the fact that in *Retribution* itself he is the "lover" who in Warsaw engenders the child who may become Russia's great future poet and who may "take hold of the wheel of history." The time depicted in the scene is circa 1900–05, a "crossroads" of times.

Reading *The Twelve*, set at an even more crucial crossroads of times, 1917, one involuntarily recalls the lover with his collar turned up. In *The Twelve*, a bourgeois with an upturned collar is strategically placed at center stage, at the very crossroads of the old and new worlds. He is not rushing home here, but hesitating:

Ветер хлесткий!
Не отстанет и мороз!
....
Стоит буржуй на перекрестке
И в воротник упрятал нос.
А рядом жмется шерстью жесткой
Поджавши хвост паршивый пес.

Стоит буржуй, как пес голодный,
Стоит безмолвный, как вопрос…[31]

The wind is ripping!
The frost does not abate!
....
The bourgeois stands at the crossroads
And has hidden his nose in his collar.
And next to him, with rough fur,
A mangy dog tucks his tail between his legs,

The bourgeois stands like a hungry dog,
Stands silent like a question…

Still moving in 1900–03, the bourgeois is paralyzed along with his partner, the mongrel cur, during 1917 and the Bolševik Revolution. In the story line of *The Twelve*, he is associated with Van'ka, another lover who steals Petka's girl

---

[31] Ibid., 260.

Katja and ends up causing her tragic death. Blok, the poet-lover, would again be the culprit in the love triangle of *Poem without a Hero*.

The bourgeois is related to the cur first by a simile ("like a hungry dog"), and later the dog becomes a metaphor for the man. The ambiguity of the bourgeois' situation is like Blok's. In *Retribution* there is the ambiguity of a return from a late-night tryst; he is cold, rushing semi-incognito. In *The Twelve* he is brought to a halt, hiding his face in his collar from a reality that frightens him and is actually pursuing him. He hopes to avoid being recognized by the hostile Red Guardsmen. He is attacked by the "stinging wind," as are other ambiguous characters from the old Petersburg who make their way in a narrative "procession" through the street: in addition to the poet, in the first chapter an old woman, a priest, and two aristocratic ladies (*baryni*) bemoan their fate, envisioned spatially as a treacherous, slippery path filled with obstacles and beclouded by whirling snow. It is significant that, on this stage set of driving snow and black night, the physical structures of Petersburg itself are not visible. The buildings seem dwarfed and obscured not only by the snow, but by large banners with Bolševik slogans which have been stretched between the buildings on ropes: "All power to the Constituent Assembly!" The identity of Petersburg's structures is thus appropriated by the new, yet still undefined order, as are the lives of its inhabitants; the old woman exclaims, «Ох, большевики загонят в гроб!» ("Oh, the Bolševiks will put us in our grave!") Only occasionally is a streetlight visible («электрический фонарик / На оглобельках» ["an electric lamp / On poles"]), and the only clear spatial configuration in the city is the crossroads at which the bourgeois and the mongrel eventually come to stand. It is as if the entire city has been reduced to this cross-shaped emblem, the remnants of the old Petrine mental map *and* the beginnings of an entirely new and uncertain landscape. In this *poèma* there are no spatial masses to which Petersburgers of the old order can cling, no "remembering" architectural figures to anchor their own memory. Petersburg is on the verge of effectively vanishing, evaporating into the wind and snow in a variation on what Dostoevskij had predicted in his 1861 "Peterburgskie snovidenija v stixax i v proze" ("Petersburg Dreams in Verse and Prose"):

> The compressed air trembled with the slightest sound, and like giants, columns of smoke from all the roofs on both banks rose and were carried upward in the cold sky, weaving in and out of each other on the way; thus it seemed as though new buildings had arisen above the old ones, as though a new city had formed in the air.... It seemed, actually, as if this whole world, with all its inhabitants, strong and weak, with all its dwelling-places, the shelters of those in poverty or gilded palaces, in this twilit hour resembled a fantastic, magical vision, a

dream which in its turn would immediately disappear and burn itself out like steam into the dark blue sky.[32]

In *The Twelve*, Blok is not the «писатель-вития» ("writer-orator") who Sergei Hackel has identified as someone like Rozanov or a Rozanovian prophet of doom.[33] Blok is, rather, associated with the figure paralyzed at the crossroads, the anxious observer of a history being enacted on the very streets where he stands. The otherworldly vision of Peter's "second coming" in *Retribution* is paralleled in *The Twelve* by the poet's vision of the ethereal Christ at the end of the work (part 12), stepping gracefully above the marching Red Guardsmen and interpretable as their leader, or, conversely, as a leader on a higher plane.

Both these visions (transcendent realms), Peter and Christ, have much in common with the two figures in Belyj's *Petersburg*. First, in the novel, Peter is very active in his city as the Flying Dutchman, who drinks and carouses with the Bronze Metallic Horseman, his equestrian hypostasis. This odd couple goes from bar to bar along the embankments, appearing in visions and hallucinations to both Dudkin and Nikolaj Apollonovič. Miša, the ethereal Christ figure (also known as the White Domino), appears several times in *Petersburg* on the streets of the capital to Dudkin and, most notably, to Sof'ja Petrovna. His radiance (white and shining are sacred and very positive for Belyj) is associated with the fire that will rise over Russia on the final day of victory in the passage "Rise, O Sun."[34] Miša is very reminiscent of the Christ who appears above and in front of the Twelve Red Guardsmen at the end of *The Twelve*, snow-covered and besplattered, at whom they shoot:

От пулей невредим
В красном веничке из роз
Впереди Иисус Христос.

Impervious to bullets
In a red crown of roses
Ahead walks Jesus Christ.

---

[32] Fedor Mixajlovič Dostoevskij, *Polnoe sobranie sočinenij v tridcati tomax* (Leningrad: "Nauka," 1972–85), 19: 69. Dostoevskij was not the first to notice this quality of doubling smoke in Petersburg. Mickiewicz described something very similar in the famous "Digression" (*Ustęp*) to his *Dziady* (1832).

[33] See Hackel on Rozanov's influence on Blok's *The Twelve*, 166–71.

[34] Belyj treats the Sun-Christ in his novel on pp. 99 ff.

Christ as the leader of Russia in the final days is common to both works as the ultimate leader after the Petrine period has ended.[35]

Belyj put his famous historiosophical vision of a Russian armageddon, at which a Sun-Christ will be the final victor, into the mind of Dudkin. Dudkin is a character who totally sacrifices himself for what he feels is right—first undergoing privations and isolation for the revolutionary movement, and then, learning of its evils (the plot to have Nikolaj kill his own father), joins forces with Peter the Great as the Bronze Horseman to kill Lippančenko. He could be seen as misguided or sacrificing, in the way Petka is, to the revolution, a tragic victim of events in which he is an active participant. It is not clear whether the Metallic Horseman under whose sway Dudkin falls is good or evil—he is ambiguous, as both pro-Petersburg and anti-Petersburg (revolutionary). The Christ in Blok's *poèma* is equally ambiguous, if not more so. The Christ figures of Blok and Belyj are figures of historical inevitability who must come, must act, and human figures such as Dudkin and the Red Guardsmen are implicated in the actions of these Christ figures. The inevitable second coming of Christ is played out simultaneously with the equally inevitable destruction of Petersburg: both are mythically-ordained prefigurements of the end of time and history. Belyj and Blok, however, are ambiguous in their assignment of positive and negative signs to the reactionary old world and to the bloody revolutionary new world. Both worlds pose multiple questions. Both are fraught with evil.

In Belyj's novel, the negation of that evil—the reduction of Apollon's position and the murder of Lippančenko—may help bring about a better world. Dudkin, the twentieth-century Eugene, the Petersburg underground man, and Raskol'nikov rolled into one, is the last rider in Petersburg, astride the slain Lippančenko. He is shown in the famous subchapter "The Guest" to be not the antagonist of the Petrine guest (the Metallic Rider), but his grandson and disciple. Peter, the first revolutionary, created Petersburg, which is perishing in the novel's present. Apollon Ableuxov represents the total ossification and deadening of the order and love for beautiful classical lines, parallelipipeds, and geometric shapes and configurations of the historical Peter, carried to caricaturish extremes. Dudkin, in a sense, represents the martyr-like dedication of Peter to a goal no matter the personal cost. But neither the conservative fossilizing protectionism of Apollon nor the revolutionary violence of Dudkin represents the true spirit of the Petrine project. Rather, it is embodied in the tragic figure of the Bronze Horseman (the Metallic Rider), who is very active in the novel. His eyes are sad with years of meaningless circulating

---

[35] Hackel discusses the revolutionary Christ of nineteenth-century proletarian movements on 103–09.

on land, like the perorations of the Flying Dutchman at sea, and with the tragedy of the full consciousness of the failure and death of his project, of which he is both creator and destroyer («я гублю без возврата» ["I doom irrevocably"]) despite himself. It is only when he feels that the Bronze Horseman's metal has poured into his veins and that they have become identified that Dudkin undertakes to murder Lippančenko, an unambiguously evil figure. He does it on moral grounds, because Lippančenko has betrayed the high principles Dudkin believed were part of the revolution. Dudkin is the only figure in the novel who, in his destructive and constructive actions, to both of which he totally sacrifices himself, comes close to the Horseman himself in intelligence, zeal, and tragic qualities. The saintly Sergej Lixutin, a good character whom his wife compares with Miša the Christ figure, though excessively selfless is also portrayed as excessively conservative and as having a certain Vronskij-like shallowness of character. He, too, shows himself to be quite brave in his confrontation with Nikolaj. Both the murder of Lippančenko and the sound whipping of Nikolaj by Lixutin serve to impede the murder of Apollon Apollonovič, the would-be central and constantly expected event of the novel. It is aborted, but Apollon is debunked and discredited, and he loses his position anyway. Dudkin ends as a mentally incapacitated idiot, not unlike Evgenij himself, or the other ineffectual Petersburg Christ figure and victim, Dostoevskij's Prince Lev N. Myškin.

Still, the brave, self-sacrificing Dudkin is a heroic actor dedicated to his goals and willing to die for them. He is an ill-fated "hero" of the type Axmatova is calling for in her *Poem without a Hero*. He is a hero. In *Poem without a Hero*, which spans 1913–1960s, the death of the poet, who should have been the hero of the new age, and his totally abortive life are the central plot elements. Life in Petersburg in the apocalyptic age leads to death, martyrdom, madness, and hallucination. The Petersburg poet should show not the inability to act, but the underground courage, guts, dedication, and zeal of a Dudkin. He should not, as Blok's poet-heroes do, passively accept the destruction, debunking, murder, or even death of his city or himself.

AXMATOVA'S *POEM WITHOUT A HERO*

Axmatova's *Poem without a Hero* (hereafter *PWH*) is a work written from the 1940s to the 1960s, and one even more complicated than Blok's in the spatial treatment of time and the identification of the poetic self with Petersburg places. Nevertheless, it was influenced by Belyj's *Petersburg* and was conceived by Axmatova herself as a kind of polemic with Blok. As Sam Driver has shown, *PWH* polemicizes with both *Retribution* and *The Twelve*.[36] The parts of *PWH* which deal with the crossing from the nineteenth century into the "real twentieth," a crossing which Axmatova feels takes place on the New Year's Eve between 1913 and 1914, again present the same horizontal depiction of time's inexorable movement that we have seen throughout this chapter. The figure associated with this movement is the prophetic Dostoevskij, whose shade advances towards the female poetic persona down the Petersburg embankments as time advances towards Blok. Just as in *Retribution*, the poetess standing there hears Blok's "noise of time" and the same historical storms of *The Twelve*:

> Были святки кострами согреты,
> И валились с мостов кареты,
> И весь траурный город плыл
> По неведомому назначенью,
> По Неве иль против теченья,—
> Только прочь от своих могил.   [2: 117]

> The holidays were warmed by bonfires,
> And carriages fell from the bridges,
> And the whole mournful city floated
> In an uncharted direction,
> Down the Neva or against the current—
> Only away from its graves.

Forgetting graves is a very negative image for Axmatova, who exhibits a veritable Antigone complex in *PWH*, the work in which she tries to render proper burial to so many poets and cultural figures of her generation. If the city is floating away from its graves, it is on the wrong course. It appears to be retreating in the face of advancing time:

Оттого, что по всем дорогам,	Because along all roads,
Оттого, что ко всем порогам	Because toward all thresholds
Приближалась медленно тень	A shade was coming slowly

It is made clear that the final stages of Petersburg's disappearance and the fulfillment of its negative *kenosis*, its being emptied of a hero who was himself emptied, predicted by Evdokija Lopuxina, is about to take place:

---

[36] Sam Driver, "Axmatova's *Poèma bez geroja* and Blok's *Vozmezdie*," *Aleksandr Blok Centennial Conference*, ed. Walter N. Vickery and Bogdan B. Sagatov (Columbus, OH: Slavica Publishers, 1984), 61–72.

И, царицей Авдотьей заклятый,
Достоевский и бесноватый,
Город в свой уходил туман

And cursed by Tsarina Avdot′ja [Evdokija],
Dostoevskij-like [Dostoevskij] and bedeviled,
The city was withdrawing into its own fog

The city appears to be retreating as the future advances upon it in its Dostoevskian hypostasis. The anticipation of personal cataclysm is conveyed by the depiction of Dostoevskij at the moment before his scheduled execution on Semenovskij Square, something Axmatova alludes to similarly in her "First Northern Elegy":

И выглядывал вновь из мрака
Старый питерщик и гуляка,
Как пред казнью бил барабан…
И всегда в духоте морозной,
Предвоенной, блудной и грозной,
Непонятный таился гул…
Но тогда он был слышен глухо,
Он почти не касался слуха
И в сугробах невских тонул.
Словно в зеркале страшной ночи
И беснуется и не хочет
Узнавать себя человек,—
А по набережной легендарной
Приближается не календарный—
Настоящий Двадцатый Век.   [2: 117–18]

And once again out of the darkness gazed
An old denizen of Petersburg, a drunkard,
As the drum beat for the execution…
And always in a freezing breathlessness,
Pre-war, debauched and threatening,
An incomprehensible din was hidden…
But then it was barely audible,
It hardly reached our ears
And died out in the Neva snowdrifts.
As if in the mirror of a terrible night
A man impishly doesn't want
To recognize himself—

But down the legendary embankment
Approaches not the calendar version—
But the real Twentieth Century.

The death by suicide of the young poet Knjazev, the central event of the story of *PWH*, is portrayed as a death on the road of the difficult history of Petersburg-Russia. He is berated for choosing the first death when a series of many more heroic deaths lay before him in the apocalyptic and tragic life of his city:

> Сколько гибелей шло к поэту,
> Глупый мальчик, он выбрал эту…
> Он не знал на каком пороге
> Он стоит и какой дороги
> Перед ним откроется вид. [2: 120]

> So many deaths there were for the poet,
> Stupid boy, he chose his own…
> He knew not on what threshold he stood
> And what road
> Was about to open before him.

Knjazev's self-imposed death is the kind of collapse of a hero that is endemic in apocalyptic times—like the falling of the figures in *The Twelve* («на ногах не стоит человек» ["man can't stand on his feet"]) and the cardboard emptiness of heroes in *Balagančik*—but Axmatova does not condone it. The effect of the whirlwind of time and revolution has been the death and disappearance of almost all the people presented in part 1, entitled "A Petersburg Tale. 1913." She alludes to Blok's notion of their being worn down by time:

> А вокруг старый город Питер,
> Что народу бока повытер. [2: 112]

> And around stood the old city "Piter,"
> That rubbed off men's sides.

This is a clear allusion to the winds of Blok's storm in *The Twelve* by means of the literalization of a folk proverb. The events take place to the noise of time that is again Blok's "winds of history":

> Под музыку дивного мэтра,
> Ленинградского дикого ветра [2: 115]

> To the music of the wondrous maestro,
> The wild Leningrad wind

There is no single work in the Petersburg tradition in which the identification of the poet-self with the city and its spaces is as intense and varied as *PWH*. We will keep returning to this work because almost every type of identification with space that occurs in the Petersburg poetry examined here is exemplified in it. In chapter 10 we will analyze *PWH*'s imagery of Petersburg spaces and structures as they relate to the self in more detail; as we shall see, its presentation of such motifs and themes is structured by a much more complex relationship between memory, time, self, and space than we see in the examples given in this chapter. Here we have limited ourselves to the sense of the city and its people being attacked by the imminent future approaching on a spatial plane, an image which we saw in *Retribution*.

03 80

In this chapter we have seen how the identification between self and Petersburg space—the sense that both the self and Petersburg are undergoing the same experience and are being affected in the same way—allows the self to cling to, or at least seek, an external support. It also allows spaces and sculpted figures, in their threatened and/or protective incarnations, to coincide with humans in their emotional and mental being. This is an important new development in the history of relations between Petersburg and the selves that dwell there. Even if this identification does not result in the reversal of history's trajectory, it makes the Petersburg man (such as Dudkin) stronger in his futile fight against spreading chaos, and repairs to some degree the traditionally negative mythology of the city even while its cataclysmic fate is being played out. Ironically, it is precisely this condition of the imminent loss of both Petersburg and self which occasions a new sense of intimacy between them, and it is the wild, stormy conditions threatening both that serve as the urban setting for the elegiac treatment of such loss (of which we shall see more evidence in succeeding chapters).

In the next chapter, which treats the post-revolutionary period in Petersburg, we shall see that the anguished poet who is aware of the city's history and of the *fait accompli* of Petersburg's death must struggle, in many cases even more futilely, against such situations, and may often experience the same sorts of schizophrenia, hallucination, and dissociation of the self that Dudkin did. Nonetheless, resistance of whatever kind, even if it is futile and ineffectual, and even if it is moral rather than physical, is preferable to suicide and succumbing. Identification between self and space, once again, is the main enabler for such attempts at resistance.

4 IDENTIFICATION WITH PETERSBURG, DEAD OR DYING

Dynamic Diachronic Identification with Space: The Linkage of Space and Biographical Time

In this chapter we will see examples of a post-revolutionary Petersburg in the process of dying or already dead. For the most part we shall deal with "imperfective" selves (as in the Russian grammatical category of verbal aspect), that is, the self-as-ongoing-process. Identification with buildings and the built environment in general confers a sense of who they are on a series of Petersburg poets as well as fictional Petersburgers. They are often identified with a native house, room, square, or other place where they have spent a protracted period. The historical catastrophes befalling the city in the Silver Age and beyond are ever implicit in the spatialization of selves.

This chapter, then, is devoted to cases in which Petersburg spaces and the historical tragedy of Petersburg-Petrograd-Leningrad in the twentieth century are most intimately intertwined with *personal biographical time*. Such treatments appear to reflect the direct influence of Proust's *À la recherche du temps perdu*, and scholarship on time-space relations in Proust, such as the work of Georges Poulet and studies of the chronotope by Mixail Baxtin, will become important critical tools here.[1] The spatialization of time is a concept common to most Western (and Slavic) languages. Our common prepositions *in*, *out*, etc., can be used equally for spatial and temporal relations. Man feels the need to divide and delineate time no less than space. The spatialization of time in twentieth-century Petersburg poetry and prose, however, goes far beyond this general linguistic phenomenon.

Sof'ja Petrovna's amnesiac predicament, discussed in detail in chapter 3 above, is reminiscent of, and perhaps was influenced by, a passage in Goncourt's *La fille Elissa*; in both scenes, time is spatialized by lumping it in "chunks": "In this memory, day by day, whole chunks of her existence of long ago were sinking into dark holes of night, and her entire past, as if amputated and torn away … was removed and lost in empty space."[2] Here Elissa's past is

---

[1] Georges Poulet, *Studies in Human Time*, trans. Elliott Coleman (Baltimore: The Johns Hopkins Press, 1956); Bakhtin, "Forms of Time and Chronotope in the Novel."

[2] Goncourt, quoted in Poulet, *Studies in Human Time*, 33.

visualized as spatial chunks, not as clear pieces of a building as in Belyj's case. Many of our types of imaginative space represent strategies for coping with a tragedy of the kind Sof'ja's temporary hellish amnesia represents. The threat of a total loss of one's sense of self is constantly present. Russians in the twentieth century, as we have indicated, are anxious about an unstable sense of self. The philosopher Vasilij Rozanov, for most of his literary career, rejoiced in the endless diversity of his ego, and therefore his late works *Solitaria* and *Fallen Leaves* have been compared to the writings of Michel Montaigne. As we shall see, Rozanov came to share the anxiety of his contemporaries only in *The Apocalypse of Our Time*, a work written as he was dying (1918–19). Montaigne views multiple successive selves in time as the richness of the ego; in his self-revelatory *Essais*, he had revealed many "selves" in the constant diversity of his ego, unfolding in time, as if he were a series of many different people unified only by the use of the shifter "I": "Every day I escape or steal away from myself;"[3] "*I* now and *I* anon are indeed two persons."[4] Instead of the self there appears "an infinite diversity of faces;"[5] Poulet explains that "the feelings of the past self become as enigmatic to the present self as those of a stranger,"[6] and that present self "[doesn't] know what [he] had wanted to say."[7] The difference between Montaigne's observation and that of Petersburg writers in the post-revolutionary period is that the rich multiplicity and pliability of the human personality is extremely positive for the Frenchman, at times exhilarating. His self is manifested in a series of appearances and disappearances. Poulet says it is "as if an interminable procession of strangers walked the same corridor, separated each from the other by an interval...."[8] This is a self who is ultimately *more* than one single being in its joyful diversity, in contrast to what Brodskij would call the defensive posture of existing as "less than one" (see chapter 7).

The Petersburg writers we treat here, who lived through historical events such as the Revolution of 1905, the First World War, the two revolutions of 1917, the Civil War, and War Communism into the Soviet era, were traumatized by external historical changes and the new views of themselves that the new society with its political changes forced upon them. They are too familiar with new and different "selves" imposed by external forces. Because of these outside pressures they are more desirous of maintaining a sense of unity of

---

[3] Montaigne, quoted in ibid., 41.

[4] Montaigne, quoted in ibid., 44.

[5] Montaigne, quoted in ibid.

[6] Poulet, *Studies in Human Time*, 44.

[7] Montaigne, quoted in ibid.

[8] Poulet, *Studies in Human Time*, 44.

self, of collecting the dispersed self or selves they have relinquished involuntarily and putting it back together, rather than reveling in incessant diversity. Thus they—especially, but not exclusively, émigrés—tend to associate a certain part of themselves or their whole lives with a place or places in Petersburg, to anchor their life/being in a place which they have, in accordance with Montaigne's *prise*, taken and made their own. *La prise* is the operation of the human mind that takes something *into the self* in the moment (which is all one has). It makes the object, house, place, or square pass from the category of having to that of being.

Incessant flux and political upheaval make them want to treat parts of themselves as settled and anchored in a place—at least in retrospect—so that they might someday "return to Petersburg," to the places, at least in art, where those lost selves are still lurking. This sort of Romantic, nostalgic myth represents an idyllic dream of personal integrality, of an integrated biography, and even émigrés known for cynicism, like Georgij Ivanov, who sometimes made fun of this myth, cherished it at the same time: «Если где-то плещется Нева…» ("If there is somewhere a Neva splashing…"). It was he who wrote in a 1950s poem that made fun of this sort of nostalgia:

> Четверть века прошло за границей,
> И надеяться стало смешным.
> Лучезарное небо над Ниццей
> Навсегда стало небом родным.
>
> ....
>
> Но поет петербургская вьюга
> В занесенное снегом окно,
> Что пророчество мертвого друга
> Обязательно сбыться должно.⁹
>
> A quarter-century has passed abroad
> And it's become silly to hope.
> The resplendent sky above Nice
> Has become once and for all our native sky.
>
> ....
>
> But the Petersburg snowstorm sings
> In a snow-covered window
> That our dead friend's prophecy
> Will have to come true.

---

⁹ Georgij Ivanov, "Četvert' veka prošlo za granicej," *Sobranie stixotvorenij*, ed. Vsevolod Setchkarev and Margaret Dalton (Würzburg: Jal-Verlag, 1958), 23.

The deceased friend is, of course, Osip Mandel'štam, who in his most famous Petersburg poem had written: «В Петербурге мы сойдемся снова, / Словно солнце мы похоронили в нем» ("We will gather again in Petersburg, / As if we had buried the sun there"). In this poem Mandel'štam is probably contemplating, as Ivanov is, a return to a spiritual, inner Petersburg for poets ("one's own" Petersburg), a return in art, in his creative powers. This is especially clear in that he wrote the poem while living in revolutionary Petrograd, so there was no need for a physical return. Thus he speaks of a return to an idealized place-time, rather than an empirical one, or to a series of such time-places which are regarded as the components of a dispersed ideal self. Those who will "return to Petersburg" are in search of "Puškin, the buried sun" who is buried there in a figurative sense, but for them as creative artists this means finding "the Puškin that has not yet been," the best poet in themselves. They are also returning in search of lost parts of themselves. These "returns" vary greatly in terms of the complexity of the poetic persona portrayed and in the relative success of the attempt.

The general tendency to feel that the "self" is embedded in or attached to architectural spaces or monuments has much in common with the antique genre of the idyll.[10] The idyllic strategy denies history, and will therefore be treated in part 3 of this book. It is nevertheless necessary at this juncture to recall that an idyll is a picturesque, peaceful tale of undisturbed, usually rural, life. It is the opposite of the revolution- and civil-war-torn lives of most of our poets and writers, and thus functions for them as an idealistic possible biography that they never experienced—a wish fulfillment of a desirable alternative fate. It stands in contrast to the other pole, i.e., their actual lives. In this connection Vladimir Nabokov is interesting because he presents his life as having begun idyllically, and he makes the maintenance or sustaining of that idealized past the goal of his idyllic quest in his memoir-autobiography *Speak, Memory* (*Другие берега* [*Other Shores*] in its Russian version). He quickly points out at the outset that the "place" of his truly idyllic childhood depicted in that work (a rival to Oblomov's) no longer exists: "that world is now gone," *unfindable* in actual space. His is not a dummy idyll, erected to be disqualified (like some of the examples to be treated herein), and may be the more unique and interesting for that reason. Dogged attempts such as Nabokov's to present a time-space "chronotopic paradise," despite practical and every other kind of obstacle and impossibility, represent a unique strategy on the part of what we call the "controlling elegist" to willfully resist or overcome history. We treat it as a transition between historical and ahistorical examples of identification

---

[10] See Baxtin, "Forms of Time and Chronotope in the Novel," on the idyllic chronotope, 224–36.

between self and space, and we return to it in detail at the end of chapter 5 below.

What urges so many Petersburg writers to pursue the irretrievable golden fleece of self-reintegration? The example of Proust, with his emphasis on memory and self as presented in his multi-volume masterwork *À la recherche du temps perdu*, seems to have provided one stimulus. It is what helps the narrator to become a writer. Many of the personal "instabilities" we have observed in Belyj and other examples here are found in Proust's great novel. Proust shows very clearly how the being who is uncertain of himself wants to lean on the stability of things (buildings, in Belyj). These things may provide what Charles Isenberg calls in his book on Mandel′štam's prose "substantial proofs of being."[11] Such proofs become especially important given the prevailing sense that Petersburg and the self are on the verge of dying out completely. Existence as a flickering and momentary candle between two abysses of darkness is the hallmark of Petersburg life in Mandel′štam's *Tristia*:

Чуть мерцает призрачная сцена…	[1: 82]
The ghost-like stage barely flickers…	
На страшной высоте блуждающий огонь…	[1: 70]
A wandering fire at a terrible height…	

It is also the opening image of Nabokov's memoirs: "The cradle rocks above an abyss, and common sense tells us that our existence is but a brief crack of light between two eternities of darkness. Although the two are identical twins, man, as a rule, views the prenatal abyss with more calm than the one he is heading for…."[12]

The Proustian world is one of chaos and dispersion, of personal emptiness and lack of self-content, in which the character must will his own order: "a world anachronistic in itself, without a home, wandering in duration as well as in extent, *a world to which the mind must precisely assign a certain place in duration and space*, by imposing its own certitude upon it, by realizing oneself in the face of it" (our italics).[13] To impose these certainties the subject must find them in himself. One strategy to aid in this search—used, for example, by Mandel′štam in his *The Egyptian Stamp*—is to make time move backwards. Poulet describes this movement as "A journey backwards, as if at the very moment the being discovers his existence, he experiences as well the need of

---

[11] Charles Isenberg, *Substantial Proofs of Being: Osip Mandelstam's Literary Prose* (Columbus, OH: Slavica Publishers, 1987).

[12] Nabokov, *Speak, Memory*, 19.

[13] Proust, quoted in Poulet, *Studies in Human Time*, 293.

sustaining rather than fulfilling it, of giving himself reasons for being rather than reasons for acting."[14] Proust's question then becomes, "How then, seeking for one's mind, one's personality, as one seeks for a thing that is lost, does one recover *one's own self* rather than any other?" (italics ours).[15] He treats the loss of the self as a death, and the remembrance as a resurrection. Proustian memory is often associated with the affective memory of psychologists, a revival in us of a forgotten state of mind. In experiences such as these in Proust's novel, "what [is] lost and what [is] found is not just time, but a fragment of time to which clings a fragment of space; and in the interior of this small universe, the self, the individual is individually bound by its faith and its desire to this moment of time and this point in space."[16] We read the following in *Guermante's Way*:

> The scent of hawthorn ... a sound of footsteps followed by no echo, upon the gravel path ... my exaltation of mind has borne them with it, and has succeeded in making them traverse all these successive years, while all around them the once-trodden ways have vanished, while those who trod them, and even the memory of those who trod them, are dead. Sometimes the fragment of landscape thus transported into the present will detach itself in such isolation from all associations that it floats uncertainly upon my mind, like a flowering isle of Delos [mental imaginary space], and I am unable to say from what place, from what time—perhaps, quite simply, from which of my dreams—it comes. But it exists pre-eminently as the deepest layer of my mental soil, as a firm site on which I still may build....[17]

Sometimes these pieces of landscape were not appreciated at the time of the original experience there. According to Proust, this is not necessary. Nabokov appears to be inspired by Proust in his project to return to time-space, to the Petersburg spaces—the city, the house, the nearby country estate of his family—upon which his childhood self/selves had become grafted. He says of this in the foreword to *Speak, Memory*, "the present work is a systematically correlated assemblage of personal recollections *ranging geographically* from St. Petersburg to St. Nazaire and covering thirty-seven years, from August 1903 to May 1940, with only a few sallies into later *space-time*" (italics ours).[18] The sense of a self dispersed in "time" and connected with particular

---

[14] Poulet, *Studies in Human Time*, 297.
[15] Proust, quoted in Poulet, *Studies in Human Time*, 297.
[16] Ibid., 301–02.
[17] Proust, quoted in ibid., 303.
[18] Nabokov, *Speak, Memory*, 9.

spaces could hardly be clearer. While memory does not always serve Proust well, Nabokov is particularly happy with what he finds when he probes into his childhood:

> How small the cosmos ... how paltry and puny in comparison to human consciousness, to a single individual recollection, and its expression in words! I may be inordinately fond of my earliest impressions, but then I have reason to be grateful to them. They led the way to a veritable Eden of visual and tactile sensations.... Nothing is sweeter or stranger than to ponder those first thrills. They belong to the harmonious world of a perfect childhood and, as such, possess a naturally plastic form in one's memory, which can be set down with hardly any effort....[19]

However, Nabokov admits that there is a price to pay for such an unusually powerful interpenetration of memory and experience—one that, for the writers in this chapter, guarantees no creative triumph over time. He sets forth a theory of the "geniuses of memory" among the Russian children of his generation, whose lives were destined soon to be broken apart into many pieces:

> I would ... submit that, in regard to the power of hoarding up impressions, Russian children of my generation passed through a period of genius, as if destiny were loyally trying [to do] what it could for them by giving them more than their share, in view of the cataclysm that was to remove completely the world they had known.[20]

Proust's stance and type of search is valid for the elegiac quest of the majority of the authors treated here. They wish to go back to the deepest layers of mental soil, Proust's "*terrains résistants sur lesquels on s'appuie*" (the resistant terrains on which one supports oneself).[21] They thus re-embody this mental soil in language, as Proust did, in order to be able to build the future upon them. The shaky, swampy Petersburg earth appears to be the firmest of soils for Nabokov in this Proustian sense, but it is a bit of a quagmire for some of our less sanguine poets. This leads us to a series of poetic space-time representations of biographies, some of which can be thought of as "disturbed idylls," and others as non-idylls. They differ from each other both in terms of the spatial disposition of the parts of the "lost self" and in the number of components of that self.

---

[19] Ibid. 24–25.

[20] Ibid., 25.

[21] Proust, quoted in Poulet, *Studies in Human Time*, 305.

INNER AND OUTER GEOGRAPHY

> В Петербурге жить—словно спать в гробу.
> Living in Petersburg is like sleeping in a coffin.
> Mandel'štam [1: 160]

Almost all the well-known Petersburg poets of the Silver Age—Mandel'štam, Axmatova, Blok, Nabokov, and later Iosif Brodskij—wrote poems exemplifying the identification of self with a Petersburg space assaulted by historical "storms." As we have mentioned, such storms, wearing down the city and the individual, were presented either as an ongoing process of destruction (imperfectively, as it were), or as the completed achieved result: "*Petersburg tott ist.*" In the second case, death then was treated as a sickness unto death and as an accomplished fact.

In these identifications the poet, sick and compromised, likens himself to his city, itself ill and compromised, at times moribund, if not already dead. The protracted death agony and the repeated deadly blows inflicted upon the city space are absorbed simultaneously by the poet as its part, or as the city's externalized spirit; both experience the agony as one. In such poetic scenarios, attempts to destroy buildings, to change or deface them, to change their function, to house institutions within edifices intended for a markedly different purpose originally, to rename streets and locales—all these become tantamount to the substitution of authentic being by the inauthentic. Such processes, very characteristic of the early Soviet period, are paralleled with and analogized to similar phenomena in the lives of defamed, ostracized, and persecuted poets.

Brodskij, in his peculiar Petersburg braggadoccio, said that his city "derives pride and almost a sensual pleasure from being 'unrecognized,' rejected."[22] To a man, the Petersburg poets (including Brodskij, of course) evince a distinct pride in the nobility and tragedy of their struggle and resistance, even their end—to paraphrase Heidegger, in "being Petersburg to utter death." A bold move in the direction of equating the city with the dying poet was made by Vladislav Xodasevič at the 1921 Puškin Celebration. In his speech "The Shaken Tripod," he characterized the present period as the "second eclipse of Puškin in the Russian national consciousness."[23] In this speech, the dawn of the Soviet period is envisaged as dark, like the reign of Nicholas the First, when the Third Section persecuted great poets. Puškin was brought down in an intrigue, and the ignominious official handling of his fu-

---

[22] Brodskij, "A Guide to a Renamed City," 93.
[23] Vladislav Xodasevič, "Koleblemyj trenožnik," *Koleblemyj trenožnik* (Moscow: Sovetskij pisatel', 1991), 201–04.

neral was fraught with political overtones, with the political persecution of high culture and the free, independent poetic spirit—Puškin's "peace and freedom" («покой и воля»). A similar equation of the dead Puškin with the dead city in Xodasevič's memoirs is striking indeed:

> In this period [1920–22] Petersburg itself became as uncommonly beautiful as it had not been for a long time, perhaps even ever.... [Anyone] possessing feeling, intelligence, and understanding could not help but see to what extent misfortune was becoming to Petersburg. Moscow, deprived of its commercial and administrative bustle, would have been, most likely, pathetic. Petersburg became majestic. It was as if, together with all the signs, all excess coloration fell away. Buildings, even the most ordinary, took on that proportion and severity which previously only palaces possessed. Petersburg became unpeopled, trams stopped moving through the streets, only rarely did hooves clatter or an automobile blow its horn—it happened that immobility was more becoming to Petersburg than motion. Of course, nothing was added to the city. It acquired nothing new, but lost all that was unbecoming. There are people who grow more attractive in their coffins: such was the case, it seems, with Puškin. Undoubtedly, this was the case with Petersburg.
>
> This [type of beauty] is temporary, momentary. The terrible ugliness of decomposition follows after it. But in the contemplation of such beauty there is an inexpressible painful delight. Before our eyes the decay had already begun to touch Petersburg: here some beams had collapsed; here some plaster had crumbled; here a wall was shaky; here an arm on a statue had broken off. But even this barely apparent decay was beautiful, and the grass, which here and there had forced its way through the cracks of the sidewalk, did not yet disfigure, but only beautified, the wonderful city, as ivy beautifies classical ruins.[24]

This beautiful evocation of a Petersburg newly deceased was preceded and paralleled in the literary tradition by a series of descriptions of a beautiful Petersburg about to die. The most famous of these is Dostoevskij's evocation in his story "White Nights" of the northern capital as a consumptive maiden, rendered beautiful by the last blush in her cheeks before a deathly pallor set in.

These anxious premonitions that the patient was about to die, or had died already, were punctuated by the statements of the most apocalyptic seer of the

---

[24] Vladislav Xodasevič, *Nekropol'* (Brussels: Éditions Petropolis, 1939; reprint, Paris: YMCA-Press, 1976). This passage is from David Bethea, *Khodasevich, His Life and Art* (Princeton: Princeton University Press, 1983), 188–89.

period, the very Dostoevskij-identified Vasilij Rozanov, in his *The Apocalypse of Our Time*.[25] There he states unequivocally that Russia/Petersburg has died and been emptied, and also that his contemporary generation of Russians was too uncomprehending to appreciate the fact. In Rozanov's formulation, the death, the sudden and total "closing down of Petersburg/Russia," to the general perplexity of men who tried foolishly to continue as though nothing had happened, sounds like a paraphrase of Nietzsche's famous proclamation of the "death of God."

While some authors viewed the death of Petersburg as imminent and others as a tragic and perplexing occurrence of the recent past, there was a frightening and overwhelming sense that the prophecy of Peter's first wife, Evdokija Lopuxina—"May Petersburg be emptied out"—had indeed come true. This fulfillment, the effective undoing of the creative act of Peter, was particularly disturbing. Peter had created a great city and culture on the empty "shore of desolate waves," calling it forth *ex nihilo* as Jehovah had created the world in Genesis. And just 200 years later, it was returning or had returned to the wild, savage place it had been before Peter's coming: it was virtually emptied out.

Identifications by poets with a Petersburg assaulted by historical cataclysms are the most numerous in our study and the most varied. We will begin below with rather static examples of identification with Petersburg locales and buildings. In the first ones, emptied Petersburg houses are equated to an emptied-out self or psyche, the static end result of an emptying process. In another slightly more complex, but still static, type, Petersburgers identify with a house and/or place, and the relations between individuals are conveyed in terms of the interrelations of buildings. The first type is like a traditional metaphor, while the second involves a willful, extended displacement of self into the building, in which it becomes virtually impossible to decide where the man ends and the building begins. These types of identification are, as it were, the basic building blocks of identification with space, the simple components of which all more complex, dynamic, and multileveled historical identifications are comprised. They represent the physically and temporally static (referring to one point in time) self. In this connection it is interesting to note that in the period from 1918–22 numerous Petersburg writers became virtual chroniclers of the "lives" of individual city buildings. In his prose and poetry

---

[25] Though he wrote *The Apocalypse of Our Time* in Sergiev Posad (Zagorsk), Rozanov lived for much of his adult life in St. Petersburg, near Znamenskaja Square, and his urban images, including that of the theater, are associable with Petersburg/Petrograd more than with any other Russian city. Rozanov's tendency to treat himself as a living Dostoevskian character, be it the Underground Man or Fedor Karamazov, is another reason to treat this great Dostoevskian "irrationalist" as a "Petersburg creature."

Konstantin Vaginov covered the islands, Šklovskij the University, and Ol′ga Forš the House of the Arts and Carskoe Selo. Perhaps this trend was set by Blok's poem "To Puškin House."[26]

Emptied Space

The use of the empty (emptied) house for the dispossessed or devastated self is, as Bachelard points out, found in almost all European literatures. The first famous example in the Russian tradition is found in Puškin's treatment of the pointlessly slain Romantic poet Vladimir Lenskij in his great novel-in-verse *Eugene Onegin*:

Недвижим он лежал, и странен
Был томный взор его чела
....
Тому назад одно мгновенье
В сем сердце билось вдохновенье,
....
Теперь, как в доме опустелом,
Все в нем и тихо и темно;
Замолкло навсегда оно.
Закрыты ставни, окна мелом
Забелены. Хозяйки нет.
А где—Бог весть. Пропал и след.[27]

He lay immobile. Strange
Was the weary gaze of his brow
....
One moment ago
Inspiration beat in this heart,
....
Now as in an emptied house
Everything in him is quiet and dark.
It has grown silent forever.
The shutters are closed, the windows
Whitened with chalk. The mistress is not at home.
Where she is, God knows. There's not a trace.

---

[26] Blok, "Puškinskomu domu," 199. The authors are grateful to Professor Nina Perlina of Indiana University for pointing this out.

[27] Puškin, *Evgenij Onegin*, 6: 730–31.

The tragic fate of Eugene in *The Bronze Horseman* is also associated with an empty and devastated house, the one where his beloved had lived: "Byl on pust i ves' rasrušen" ("It was empty and completely destroyed").

A similar treatment by the poet of himself as an empty house is found in Blok, where it refers to spiritual/emotional emptiness:

К чему спускать на окнах шторы?
День догорел в душе уже давно.²⁸

Why lower the shades on the windows?
The day burnt out in my soul long ago.

As we pointed out above, in Belyj's *Petersburg* Nikolaj Apollonovič Ableuxov, in moments of upset, has the distinct sense that he will return to the yellow house where he and his father reside, open the door and find, instead of the vestibule, a gaping abyss into which he will fall. The abyss is the metaphor of his own inner world.

In *Requiem*, Axmatova uses an empty house as a metaphor for the woman in the poem "The Sentence," often associated with Lidija Čukovskaja and Axmatova herself. In it a woman, upon receiving news of her husband's or son's death sentence, decides she must start life over again from the very beginning. She *wills* herself to forget the past, her past life and identity—something that Belyj's Sof'ja Petrovna did not want to happen at all. Her summary statement (quoted below) of her situation at the end of the poem refers not to a concrete apartment or house that has had its master or the son removed, as in two other poems of the cycle, "They took you away at dawn" or "Quietly flows the quiet Don." It refers, rather, to her whole biography as a house:

Я давно предчувствовала этот
Светлый день и опустелый дом.   [1: 366]²⁹

I long ago had a premonition of
This bright day and emptied house.

We can interpret these lines to mean "I have long feared that this life/house would be devastated in this way, and now it has." We can see Axmatova's poem as a fulfillment of what young Ableuxov fears in Belyj's novel. In his case it is an architectural expression or translation of an anxiety, and does not

---

²⁸ Blok, "Vesennij den' prošel bez dela," 183.
²⁹ Unless otherwise noted, we provide references for Axmatova texts quoted in this study, in the English rendering of Anna Lisa Crone, from the edition Anna Axmatova, *Sobranie sočinenij v trex tomax*, eds. Gleb Struve and Boris Filippov (Munich: Interlanguage Library Associates, 1968).

come to pass. In Axmatova's case it actually happens, as she feared it would. Čukovskaja, a Petersburger who lived much of her life in Moscow, adapted this house imagery into her novella *The Deserted House (Sof'ja Petrovna)*—perhaps the most famous Russian use of this image.

Whereas Bachelard and others discuss identification with houses and other nooks, shells, and protective spaces as a fairly universal phenomenon, the employing of houses as selves is not as statistically frequent in French poetry as it is in the Petersburg tradition. Emptying and collapse because of voids and abysses within is perhaps so frequent because of the prediction that Petersburg would be emptied out, the strange negative *kenosis* the city was expected to undergo. In addition to those examples where a house is used as the analogon of the self, in many cases we see the entire city presented or implied as an enormous house whose various locales are so many rooms. This huge house is assaulted from without by storms, floods, and historical catastrophes, and from within by its own inhabitants and their inner voids.

Macrocosm and Microcosm

In a second type of identification between self and house, rather than a traditional metaphor, we have a more complex identification of the building and the man. The complexity of the metaphor has a Gogolian quality in that we forget what is the main thing, what is substituting for what: the man, building, or both. In Belyj's *Petersburg*, as we saw in chapter 3, both Ableuxovs, father and son, are so intimately identified with buildings that a merging occurs, and Dudkin is identified with Vasil'evskij Island in the same way. For both, moments of particularly powerful identification occur at the same junctures, and thus the merging gains a synchronic intensity. At these moments the characters are under duress and feel they are losing their grip on their mental health. At the ball in chapter 4, both Ableuxovs receive shocking news, and both try to keep from being devastated by clinging for support to something spatial and external in order to avoid the experience of things falling totally apart that we saw during Sof'ja Petrovna's cab ride.

At the ball, Nikolaj Ableuxov receives news, by letter and from the double agent Morkovin, that the party wants him to hurry up and assassinate his father as he had promised to do. Nikolaj denies and does all he can *not* to face the meaning of the promise they extracted from him. At the same ball and from the same Morkovin, the elder Ableuxov first finds out that his son is the infamous "red domino" that is scandalizing Petersburg. Then he learns that he himself is the target of a revolutionary assassination plot. At this point he is directly faced with the prospective parricide that he has been trying not to see for much of the novel. Apollon's reaction to it shows his desire to "other himself" into a building rather than handle the shock straight on: "Apollon caught sight of the caryatid of the entryway, quite some caryatid."[30] But the architectural element is not neutral and cannot be an innocent inanimate object: "No! no! no! It is not such a caryatid. Never had he ever seen anything similar in his whole life. There's the side of the house. Quite a side. A side like any other, of stone. No! no! It's not simply a side, just as nothing is simply what it seems."[31] Then comes the most important and ambiguous phrase: «Все сместилось в нем. Сорвался сам с себя. Он сорвался и бормотал в полуночную темь» [«Everything was displaced in him/it. He/it was torn off from himself/itself. He/it was torn off and muttered in the midnight darkness."] Until the last sentence it is totally ambiguous whether the masculine subject (*on*) is Apollon or the side of the house. Displacement seems to happen in him and the house, as well as a *sryv*—a falling-apart through the stripping-off of one's mask or self. The building's façade is stripped off. The man is unmasked, revealed, exposed. The last sentence lessens the ambiguity of the passage somewhat because we are more inclined to associate the "muttering" with a man.

In a closely parallel passage concerning Nikolaj Ableuxov, the situation is even more ambiguous: "Nikolaj ... was always trying to cling to externals. There was the caryatid of the entryway.... And over there was a little house, quite a nice little house ... a black one, no! It's not simply a house, just as nothing is simply what it seems."[32] This notion that nothing in the outer world is what it seems has a clear Symbolist ring to it. Objects point to, hint at other, deeper realities whose existence Nikolaj suspects, and in his case these frightening, but more real, things (*realiora*) are also within him. The reader feels that his attempt to seek support in externals is a futile gesture. The passage continues with extreme ambiguity: "Everything was displaced in him, ripped off. He was ripped off from himself and from somewhere (it is not known where) where he had never been he was looking."[33] Did everything become displaced in the house or in Nikolaj? Is he or the house looking from a strange vantage point? Have they changed places? As in the previous passage, the verb *gljadet'* (look) would more likely refer to a man, but in this novel it is used repeatedly for buildings and architectural elements, such as the caryatids or windows. The sense the reader gets here is that the essential Nikolaj, his spiritual self (which often separates from the body in Anthroposophic belief), has left his body and is now enclosed or located in the black house, and that the spirit of the black house (about which we have less information), in its

---

[30] See chap. 3, p. 67.
[31] Belyj, *Peterburg*, 189. The epithet "of stone" is several times used for Apollon.
[32] Ibid., 183.
[33] Ibid.

turn, has gone into Nikolaj's body. As a simultaneous unification-identification with a building, this is much stronger than the case of Sof'ja Petrovna Lixutina treated above. When she heard mental sounds of Petersburg buildings crashing, they had the looser, accompanying function of a simile. Here we see a flush joining of man and house as a metaphor. Belyj makes the reader very conscious of this type of metaphor in the novel.

In the first chapter of *Petersburg*, Apollon rides along the prospects in his carriage and feels for the first time the hate-filled gaze of the revolutionary Aleksandr Dudkin upon him, with its murderous intentions. We are told that before the invasion of that homicidal gaze, Apollon had been riding along at peace, "gazing in reverie into the endlessness of fogs" which is Vasil'evskij Island, the source of disorder and chaos. Not only do Ableuxov and Dudkin have an eye-to-eye confrontation, but Ableuxov, as he gazes into Dudkin's eyes, sees Vasil'evskij Island enclosed in them, "that very endlessness of chaos." Dudkin contains within him the geographical locale whence the disgruntled workers come into Petersburg via bridges. He is in his space and he bears it within him.

But Dudkin, who had been exiled in Jakutija Province and had voluntarily lived in the icy expanses of Russia (non-Petersburg) for the good of the revolutionary cause, also exhibits a schizoid division not unlike the sense of feeling that one is partly or wholly a building. He says of himself, "I am not an 'I'—but a sort of 'We,'" expressing what the Party told him and the division he himself experiences. He further says, "My usefulness for society brought me into an icy space, here while they mentioned me, they had forgotten me completely, that I was there in a void, and the more I went into that void ... all categories fell away from me."[34] He claims that the spatial category of ice and the wide-open expanses of Russia are inside him: "This is the ice of Jakutija Province. I carry it in my heart, you know, I carry ice with me ... ice separates me and even when I am amongst people, I am thrown into immeasurability."[35] No wonder Apollon sees these geographical locales inside Dudkin when he gazes into his eyes, the windows of the revolutionary's soul.

Thus Dudkin's inner geography as viewed by the elder Ableuxov includes the specifically frightening (for Ableuxov) cold immensity of Russian expanses, which are inimical to Petersburg, as well as the nearer danger of cloud-covered Vasil'evskij Island, which bears a revolutionary threat to the capital. On the level of microcosm, Dudkin bears the bomb that is destined to destroy Apollon. Dudkin's gaze invades Apollon's inner peace, and he invades Petersburg with a bomb, taking it right into Apollon's house, to his son's

---

[34] Ibid., 86.
[35] Ibid.

room. Invasive gazes enter people's consciousness and invasive people enter buildings, their protective spaces.

After Apollon and Dudkin mutually exchange hostile gazes, their microcosmic exchange is projected onto the macrocosm of the cityscape, the Petersburg topography *en gros*. Apollon is metaphorized, represented by his yellow mansion, and Dudkin by the factories of Vasil'evskij Island, "that very same endlessness of chaos from which, time immemorial, many-chimneyed distances and Vasil'evskij Island watch the Senator's house."[36] Here the Ableuxov house is in the accusative as the object of the threatening gazes of the personified factories and other dwellings on the island. The macrocosmic level—houses, buildings, geographical locales—and the microcosmic—human characters—have identified interrelations.

WATER-BOUND SPATIALIZATION OF SELF

Another frequent spatialization of the Petersburger's sense of self as well as of one's ability to create as artist/poet "on the shore of desolate waves" is maritime. Given the actual topography of St. Petersburg, a series of islands and marshlands in the Neva delta on the Finnish Gulf and the Baltic Sea, these water-bound spatial models of the individual's fate are only to be expected. They usually consist of a lone boat on the river of time/life or on the sea of eternity, or a lone figure contemplating a body of water where such a boat strains against the elements. These spatializations, as we shall see, migrate as motifs from Romantic poetry. They are not as numerous as our land-based models, but, as Brodskij emphasizes, the Petersburger's special love for water and the open sea dictates that we must consider them particularly "Petersburgian."

It was not by chance that in his novel *Petersburg* Belyj gave Peter I two hypostases: first, the Bronze Horseman-Metallic Guest, and second, the Flying Dutchman. Peter's conversion of Russia into a great European power was, from the very outset, the creation of a naval power on the model of Holland or England, and, locally, Sweden. This specific purpose makes Alcaeus' old metaphor of "the ship of state" especially applicable to this capital. Petrine Russia, the reformed State, is often symbolized in the Admiralty, originally the site of wharves and later of the pre-revolutionary naval headquarters. For Mandel'štam, as we saw, this edifice was an "airy bark," "a frigate or an acropolis," "the brother of water and of sky." All these images amalgamate into a dynamic ship-of-state-in-history cluster. Peter, in the poem and in life, is building a ship with his own hands (shipbuilding being one of the first crafts he mastered on his trip to Holland in 1698). For Mandel'štam Peter's craft thus serves as an

---

[36] Ibid.

analogon for poem-construction, a concept he made literal as a bark of words set out on the "sea of language" in his essay "On the Nature of the Word." In times of periodic flooding, the entire city, as the man-made ship of world/Russian culture, resists the assaulting waves like a ship in a storm. Shipwreck and total inundation would mean "falling out of world history."

The Bronze Horseman pits Peter I against the elements as a superhuman hero who constructs an enormous ark—the city. On the more human level, a lone canoe or boat tossed about by a wild sea or loosed from its moorings is a common Romantic image of rational man in his struggle with a more powerful, chaotic nature. Geographically non-specific in earlier Romantic elegies, this journey of the "river of time which carries away all the deeds of men," in Deržavin's words, undergoes transformations in the period under discussion that bind it more and more to Petersburg as a metaphor for the city, the modern Russian man, and their troubled trajectory in time.

We recall Baratynskij's generalized presentation of modern man in his 1821 "Elegy":

Не бывать тому, что было прежде.
Что счастье мне? Мертва душа моя.[37]

That which has been can never be again.
What is happiness to me? My soul is dead.

The very pointed final stanza compares the disappointed lyric speaker's reflections on the beach with his past life as a beloved, departing boat, traversing a river of spatialized biographical time:

Гляжу я в даль моих минувших дней.
Так нежный друг, в бесчувственном забвенье,
Еще глядит на зыби синих волн,
На влажный путь, где в темном отдаленье
Давно исчез отбывший дружный челн.

I gaze into the distance of my past days.
The way a tender friend in insensate forgetfulness,
Persists in gazing upon the swells of the blue waves,
Upon the watery path where in the dark distance
His friend's departed bark vanished long ago.

A concise masterpiece elegy for the genre of lost selves, Baratynskij's poem may have helped to motivate Tjutčev's affinity for Heine's poems in which

---

[37] Evgenij Baratynskij, *Stixotvorenija i poèmy, proza, pis'ma* (Moscow: Xudožestvennaja literatura, 1951), 81.

boats and maritime imagery, the sea of eternity and the river of time, are central. The young Tjutčev translated no less than four such poems. Most striking is his rendition of "Privetstvie duxa" ("The Greeting of the Spirit"), where a deceased Teutonic knight greets the living as boats tossed on the river of time (the Rhine).[38] The image of a swimmer or sailor likewise is seen in "Korablekrušenie" ("Shipwreck"),[39] and his presentation of the poet on a ship's deck on the Rhine is seen in "Kak poroju svetlyj mesjac" ("Oh, how bright the moon sometimes").[40]

We should not be surprised to see these generalized and German Romantic images transplanted to Petersburg in Puškin's *The Bronze Horseman*. In the introduction to the poem, Peter the Great as a lone human and superhuman figure meditates on the shore, not unlike Baratynskij's lyric hero in "Elegy," although here Peter meditates on the fate of his "child" Russia, not on his own personal fate. The line "he gazed into the distance" (*vdal' gljadel*) echoes Baratynskij's poem. Puškin considered Baratynskij the greatest living elegist, and certainly knew he was echoing his poem. In a daring and optimistic swerve away from the elegiac, Puškin has his Peter craft a ship literally, as Petersburg, and figuratively, as the modern Empire which sweeps away the individual "little man" (the Finnish fisherman and his spaces) who is still present there:

… Пред ним широко
Река неслася; бедный челн
По ней стремился одиноко
По мшистым, топким берегам
Чернели избы здесь и там,
Приют убогого чухонца[41]

… Before him widely
Flowed the river. A poor canoe
Strained up the river, alone.
Among the mossy, marshy banks
Black huts appeared hither and yon,
The abode of the wretched Finn

This version of the human individual is swept away by Peter's redirection of the river (his control of historical forces) only to re-emerge in the form of the

---

[38] Tjutčev, "Privetstvie duxa," 41.
[39] Tjutčev, "Korablekrušenie," 43–44.
[40] Tjutčev, "Kak poroju svetlyj mesjac," 49.
[41] Puškin, "Mednyj vsadnik," 5: 123.

post-Petrine little man, Evgenij. The latter, in his turn, takes the only canoe-ferry left during the raging flood to find that the house that symbolized his happiness and life's project (Paraša's house) has been washed away no less than the Finn's abode and canoe. The theme of the lone boat on the dangerous Neva becomes a Petersburg theme, and recurs some years later in Tjutčev's poems to his greatest love, Denis′eva, as well as in his elegies on the loss of that love.

Some eleven years later, in 1844, Tjutčev, who was powerfully drawn to the Neva and its embankments despite their affront to his sense of self (in a way quite similar to his attraction for untamed Bavarian nature), spoke of his inexplicable bond to Petersburg and the severe climate of the North, notwithstanding his diplomatic posts in Italy:

Глядел я, стоя над Невой,	Standing above the Neva, I gazed at the
Как Исаака-великана	Golden cupola of St. Isaac the Giant
Во мгле морозного тумана	Shining in the haze
Светился купол золотой.	Of the frozen fog.
Всходили робко облака	Clouds timidly rose
На небо зимнее, ночное,	Into the nocturnal wintertime sky,
Белела в мертвенном покое	The ice-covered river
Оледенелая река.[42]	Whitened in the deadly calm.

He then expresses an elegiac desire to return to the sunny South (like Batjuškov in "Tauris"), but seems, like Annenskij later in his famous poem "Petersburg," inexplicably bound to and identified with the Northern capital, here as part of its granite embankment:

О, Север, Север-чародей,	O, North, o North, you sorcerer!
Иль я тобою околдован?	Is it that you have bewitched me?
Иль в самом деле я прикован	Or am I actually chained
К гранитной полосе твоей?[43]	To your granite strip?

Like Blok after him in *Retribution*, Tjutčev's lyric persona feels physically and mentally conjoined with Petersburg through its stone. The choice of the verb приковать to express the nature of Tjutčev's attachment to Petersburg is especially expressive, as it combines the architectural-building sense of connecting by forging or chains with two opposite meanings of emotional attachment which were common parlance in Tjutčev's day, as now. The first is negative—fear: Страх приковал меня к месту (I was rooted to the spot by fear). The

---

[42] Tjutčev, "Gljadel ja, stoja nad Nevoj," 143.
[43] Annenskij, "Petersburg," 199.

second is very positive—irresistible attraction: Петербург приковал к себе внимание (The city riveted the poet's attention). Given how unreasonable Tjutčev found his attachment to Petersburg, one could argue that a third common usage of приковать is also at play here: прикован к постели (to be bedridden). To be Petersburg-ridden is the poet's special sickness. This association of Petersburg with illness, with its accompanying delirium and hallucinations, would become a familiar motif employed by Petersburg writers to express the city's unique power both to oppress and to inspire simultaneously.

The Neva embankment assumes special importance later in Tjutčev's life because he associates it with his last great love, Denis′eva. In the year he met her (1850), he presents us in "On the Neva" with a couple in a boat floating down the river. Here we see a reprise of the motif of lovers in a boat, as in his 1835 poem "The East Grew White," transported to a Petersburg setting:

И опять звезда ныряет
В легкой зыби невских волн,
И опять любовь вверяет
Ей таинственный свой челн.[44]

And once more a star dives
In the light swell of the Neva's waves
And once more love entrusts
Its mysterious boat to it [the swell].

The lovers in the boat, called two "phantoms," have an ethereal quality, and he implores the river which "carries their boat off into the distance" to "keep on your wide expanses / the secret of the modest boat" («Приюти в твоем просторе / Тайну скромного челна»). The third poem in what can be viewed as a Tjutčevan Petersburg series begins with the all-important word *opjat′*—"once again" that was prominent in the first poem. This time, however, the poet returns not only to Petersburg, the place that is calling him, but he returns to the scene where the mysterious boat of his love had floated. Yet the boat is missing; only moonlight streams in its place, because Denis′eva has died:

Опять стою я над Невой,
И снова, как в былые годы,
Смотрю и я, как бы живой,
На эти дремлющие воды.
Нет искр в небесной синеве,
Все стихло в бледном обаянье,

---

[44] Tjutčev, "Vostok belel," 106.

Лишь по задумчивой Неве
Струится лунное сиянье.

Во сне ль все это снится мне,
Или гляжу я в самом деле,
На что при этой же луне
С тобой живые мы глядели?[45]

Once more I stand above the Neva,
And again as in past years
I too look, as if I were alive,
At these sleepy waters.

There are no sparks in the heavenly blue,
All has grown quiet in its pale fascination.
Only moonlight streams
Along the pensive Neva.

Is this all a dream that I see?
Or am I really looking at
What you and I gazed at together
In the light of this very same moon?

These poems resonate in the Acmeist poetry of Axmatova and Mandel'štam. Sharon Leiter has shown that this later poem clearly influenced Axmatova's association of her romantic life with Petersburg locales. Moreover, changes in those locales are signs of internal changes in her life and herself.[46] In "On the Neva," Tjutčev spoke of himself "once more" falling in love in the image of a star diving into the waves of the Neva. In the later poem, he is there "once more," but all is changed to such a degree that he has a sense of his own unreality. In the second poem of her *Northern Elegies*, Axmatova has the same sense of unreality and disbelief at what is happening to her:

И надо было мне себя уверить,
Что это все случалось много раз   [1: 310]

And I had to assure myself that all this
Had happened many times before

In place of the bright diving star in "On the Neva," in Tjutčev's later poem there are no sparks; all is pale and quiet. In the earlier poem, at the beginning

---

[45] Tjutčev, "Opjat' stoju ja nad Nevoj," 261.
[46] Sharon Leiter, *Akhmatova's Petersburg* (Philadelphia: University of Pennsylvania Press, 1983), 130.

of his affair, he had asked an enticing question about the "two phantoms" in the boat:

Дети ль это праздной лени
Тратят здесь досуг ночной?
Иль блаженные две тени
Покидают мир земной?[47]

Are these the children of idle languor
Spending their nocturnal leisure here?
Or are they two blessed shades
Abandoning the earthly world?

The last line suggests the notion of the Neva as the Lethe, a river into the world of the dead. In the last poem, the river-self is pensive («задумчивая Нева»), with the poet observing the scene and ruminating over the turbulent and brighter past, in virtual disbelief that he has experienced it. His disorientation expands to a sense that he is dead among the living, that he has actually departed with Denis′eva and the boat, and that the long-gone boat and pale scene are his real life from which Denis′eva, their love, and to a large extent Tjutčev himself («как бы живой») are missing. The missing boat, as in Baratynskij's "Elegy," is the absent, and more important, basic self.

Mandel′štam, called the poet of the Lethe-Neva, includes the canoe/boat (челн/челнок) in a Petersburg context that is a spatialization of remembering himself and the words of his poems, the attempt to recall words from oblivion. We recall his likening of poems to boats. Thus in his "I forgot the word I wanted to say," we read the line «В сухой реке пустой челнок плывет, / Среди кузнечиков беспамятствует слово» ("In a dry riverbed an empty canoe floats, / The Word has forgotten itself amidst the grasshoppers") [2: 113]. The implications of this beautiful pre-revolutionary poem are later amplified in Mandel′štam's allusions to "dried-up riverbeds" in the 1920s. Reference to, remembrance of, and recalling not only the word but the self in the attempt to integrate one's life is found in Mandel′štam's autobiography, *The Noise of Time*. There the poet speaks of his teacher, the literary scholar Vladimir V. Gippius, and then of himself, two Jews active in the Petersburg-Russian cultural tradition, as lacking a past, a genealogy. The literary heritage, largely aristocratic and Russian, is characterized as a "fur coat of the nobility" (барственная шуба). These two men are said to be "in a fur coat above their station" («в не по чину барственной шубе»). For Mandel′štam, his heritage lies in the literary tradition because he had been ejected from truly deep

---

[47] Tjutčev, "Na Neve," 45.

involvement in the Judaic tradition by his father's choice of a secularized life. Trying to find one's identity in the great Petersburg tradition means, again, to be a boat in a dry river:

> To remember not living people but the plaster casts struck from their voices. To go blind. To feel and recognize by hearing. Sad fate! Thus does one penetrate into the present, into the modern age, as via the bed of a dried-up river [Так входишь в настоящее, в современность как в русло высохшей реки]. [2: 103]
>
> And, you know, those were not friends, not near ones, but alien, distant people! Still, it is only with the masks of other men's voices that the bare walls of my house are decorated. To remember is to make one's way alone back up the dried riverbed![48]

This autobiographical passage is closely associated with life in literature, life and one's identity as a writer. It brings us to Axmatova's important "Third Northern Elegy" (treated below in other contexts), which is influenced by the Mandel'štam passage and which links the issues of time's destructive effect on one's sense of self and one's identity as a writer. Adapting Tjutčev's *zadumčivaja reka* (pensive river) to her own situation, Axmatova treats herself as the Neva. Here we find a dried-up Neva—that is, out of its proper bed—and it stands simultaneously for the poet and for the Petersburg literary tradition:

> Меня, как реку,
> Суровая эпоха повернула.
> Мне подменили жизнь. В другое русло,
> Мимо другого потекла она,
> и я своих не знаю берегов.   [1: 311]
>
> Like a river,
> I have been diverted by a severe epoch.
> My life has been substituted. Into another riverbed,
> Passing another by, the river has flowed,
> And I do not recognize my own shores.

These shores contain Leningrad, not Petersburg, and thus have become other. An ersatz self has emptied the true one, and like Mandel'štam, in order to find the true city she must grope blindly: «А я один на свете город знаю / И ощупью во сне его найду» ("But I only know one city in this world / And I will find it, groping, in my sleep") [2: 311].

---

[48] Osip Mandel'štam, *The Noise of Time. The Prose of Osip Mandel'štam*, trans. Clarence Brown (San Francisco: North Point Press, 1986), 113. All references to *The Noise of Time* are given from this edition.

The final source of Axmatova's Leningrad elegy is an early Mandel'štam poem in which he speaks of himself being destroyed by time and being emptied of his content, his self (in a typical instance of Petersburg negative *kenosis*): «Меня как монету срезает время / И мне уж не хватает меня самого» [1: 98] ("Time cuts me like a coin / And I haven't enough of myself left"). This sensation of loss of self is repeated in the would-be writer Parnok's exclamation in *The Egyptian Stamp*: "Look what has happened to me.... In the north I have become nothing—so little is left of me—I beg your pardon!"[49] And although he uses it in a different way, we will see something similar in Brodskij's characterization of the self, that sometimes *one* (speaking of the self in the third person, as a species of Everyman) feels "less than [a whole] one" (see chapter 7). For now we limit ourselves to examples like the above from Tjutčev, Axmatova, and Mandel'štam which show a more sea-bound spatialization of the same loss of self that we saw depicted on land in Belyj's *Petersburg* and Blok's poems.

VERTICAL PRESENTATION OF ONE'S PERSONAL PAST

In this type of identification, the self in time is represented by movement downstairs or underground into the past or up into the attic of the future. Bachelard identified this type, and what he had to say about cellars applies to Petersburg's "undergrounds," which derive their psychological meaning first and foremost from Dostoevskij's *Notes from Underground*. As Bachelard writes, "[The cellar is the] *dark entity* of the house, the one that partakes of subterranean forces."[50] The irrationality of the depths of cellars and basements was taken over by Nietzsche, who borrowed the concept and used it with reference to Russia in *The Antichrist*, and it was directly associated by Freud with the unconscious. The psychologist Carl Jung also deals with cellars and attics in *Modern Man in Search of a Soul*:

> ... the conscious [reason] acts like a man who, hearing a suspicious noise in the cellar, hurries to the attic and, finding no burglars there decides, consequently, that the noise was pure imagination. In reality, this prudent man did not dare venture into the cellar.[51]

Jung deals with the special fear of mysterious creatures lurking in the "cellars" and deep nooks of the self. Bachelard points out: "In the cellar, darkness prevails both day and night, and even when we are carrying a lighted candle, we

---

[49] Mandel'štam, *The Egyptian Stamp*, 159.

[50] Bachelard, *The Poetics of Space*, 18.

[51] Carl Jung, cited in ibid., 19.

see shadows dancing on the dark walls."⁵² He goes on to speak of buried madness and walled-in tragedy in selves and the tragedies that are the content of such "cellars."

There is not an abundance of examples in twentieth-century Petersburg poetry of cellars representing the unconscious deep ancestral past, although they do exist. Poets sometimes assume very directly the role of the underground man. Some of the descent images refer to unearthing the great cultural treasure of the past that is buried in Petersburg, and have therefore a personal and suprapersonal significance at once. Others of the vertical images of descent into the self and the past, however, are truly striking and could serve as textbook illustrations of what Jung and Bachelard describe. Such a case is presented in Axmatova's well-known poem "The Cellar of Memory" (1940):

Подвал памяти

Но это вздор, что я живу грустя
И что меня воспоминанье точит.
Не часто я у памяти в гостях,
Да и она всегда меня морочит.

Когда спускаюсь с фонарем в подвал,
Мне кажется—опять глухой обвал
Уже по узкой лестнице грохочет.
Чадит фонарь, вернуться не могу,
Я знаю, что иду туда, к врагу.
И я прошу как милости... Но там
Темно и тихо. Мой окончен праздник!
Уж тридцать лет, как проводили дам,
От старости скончался тот проказник...
Я опоздала. Экая беда!
Нельзя мне показаться никуда.
Но я касаюсь живописи стен
И у камина греюсь. Что за чудо!
Сквозь эту плесень, этот чад и тлен
Сверкнули два зеленых изумруда
И кот мяукнул. Ну, уйдем домой!
Но где мой дом и где рассудок мой?⁵³

---

⁵² Bachelard, *The Poetics of Space*, 19.
⁵³ Axmatova, *Stixotvorenija* (Leningrad: Sovetskij pisatel', 1976), 196.

The Cellar of Memory

But this is nonsense, that I live sadly,
Cut by remembrance.
I am rarely a guest of memory,
And it always upsets me.

When I descend with a lantern into the cellar,
It seems to me again a hushed collapse
Is already rumbling along the narrow stairway.
The lantern smokes, I can't turn back,
I know that I am going to the enemy.
And I beg as mercy.... But there
It's dark and silent. My holiday is over!
It's thirty years since we said farewell to those ladies,
That practical joker died of old age...
I'm late. What a misfortune!
I can't show myself anywhere.
But I touch the painting on the walls
And warm myself by the fireplace. What a miracle!
Through this mold, this smoking and decomposition
Two green emeralds sparkled
And a cat meowed. Well, let's go home!
But where is my home and where is my reason?

When the past is presented in a house in "The Cellar of Memory" we see the poetic persona experiencing a warm, somewhat pleasant return. But then she catches sight of a live cat, which creates a Poe-like atmosphere and snaps her out of the trance she fell into, immersed in her own past. In the return she temporarily takes on another self and time, and is thrown into a state of confusion: Is this my basement or someone else's? How can I be sure I will find myself and not someone else? Is this my house or have I lost my reason? Thus a descent into a past self can cause considerable disjunction and disassociation from the later self.

Axmatova uses the vertical disposition of time in space, with the past below or buried under the present, in other works. When projected on a larger area it can be called an archeological stratification of time, with the preceding cultural-temporal layers under the current time, represented by the surface of the earth. *Poem without a Hero*, of which we spoke in chapter 3 as having an upper (1940–45) and lower (1913–14) temporal plane, depicts the poet in a tower surveying her complex past and then descending into it:

Из года сорокового,
Как с башни, на все гляжу.
Как будто прощаюсь снова
С тем, с чем давно простилась,
Как будто перекрестилась
И под темные своды схожу.   [2: 103]

From the year 1940,
As from a tower, I look down on everything.
As if I am taking leave again
Of something I bade farewell to long ago,
As if I had crossed myself
And am going down under dark vaults.

Not only is this the descriptive geographical disposition of past time in the poem, as an underworld one can visit, but the entire text is verbally and musically treated as having a surface and deeper layers. Under the surface words of the text are buried other words of dead poets, multiple levels of allusion: «У шкатулки тройное дно» ("The chest has a triple bottom") [2: 128]. The possibility that the buried words of a past, dead poet-brother may emerge from her own words musically—as an overtone—or "dug up" in the work is clear: «Если чужое слово проступает» ("If someone's word bursts through"). She makes it clear that she is visited by voices *de profundis* and has a desire to dig up and around in the past: «Бес попутал в укладке рыться» ("A devil made me rummage around in the trunk") [2: 125].

The notion of Petersburg's past buried beneath a building in the city was well established in Jakov Polonskij's famous poem "Miasma,"[54] in which a ghost from the time of the construction of the Northern capital haunts the later inhabitants of a Petersburg house. The Fontanka House, for Axmatova, is inhabited by similar ghosts who will not leave her alone. The notion that the past is buried below us, or that it lies in the foundation of a building is, as we pointed out, at once architectural and archeological. It is the immanence of a past history which will not allow us to forget it or trample it with impunity. It is often associated with guilt, and demands its due. Thus the events of 1913–14 obsess the poet, and the complicity of many in the death of Knjazev—and, more importantly, in what that death is made to stand for—is not allowed to be forgotten.

Axmatova's personal-biographical treatment of this guilt and past notions is paralleled in the *oeuvres* of the other Petersburg poets by treatments of the cultural treasure of the city as buried under it. Guilt is not missing in these

---

[54] Jakov Polonskij, "Miazma," *Stixotvorenija* (Moscow: Sovetskij pisatel', 1939).

depictions either, and there is an ethical imperative to unearth the buried treasure, as in the following by Mandel'štam :

> В Петербурге мы сойдемся снова,
> Словно солнце мы похоронили в нем,
> И блаженное, бессмысленное слово
> В первый раз произнесем. [1: 85]
>
> We will gather again in St. Petersburg,
> As if we had buried the sun there,
> And we shall utter for the first time
> The blessed, senseless word.

Beauty, true poetry, has been submerged or relegated into a past or national unconsciousness. Since the buried sun is associated with Puškin and his legacy, it implies the sun of Russian poetry and the whole complex of the persecution of Puškin under Alexander I and Nicholas I, including the mishandling of his death. A collective notion of guilt on the matter of the eclipse of the sun of Puškin is prominent in the poem's second line: «словно солнце мы похоронили в нем» ("as if we buried the sun there"). It contains the implication that Puškin, who should have been buried in St. Petersburg, was not.

The ignominious handling of Puškin's burial is treated in detail in A. V. Nikitenko's *Diary* as another source of the writer's guilt:

> At Puškin's death they deceived the people; they said the funeral would be held at St. Isaac's Cathedral, but at night they transferred his body to Konjušennaja Church. Benckendorff convinced the tsar that a demonstration was in the works; they sent military pickets out all over the city and filled the crowds with detectives. In the very same manner they carried Puškin's body away into the country.[55]

At one of the way stations not far from Petersburg, Nikitenko's wife saw a simple cart covered with straw and a coffin beneath it wrapped in coarse bast-matting. Three gendarmes in the courtyard were seeing to it that post horses were quickly harnessed and the coffin rushed on its way:

> "What's this?" she asked a peasant standing nearby.
> "The Lord only knows, ma'am! Some Puškin or other has been killed and they're rushing his body away with post horses in bast-matting and straw, the Lord forgive me for saying it, like a dog."[56]

---

[55] A. V. Nikitenko, *Dnevnik v trex tomax* (Moscow: GIXL, 1955), 1: 197.
[56] Ibid., 198

In his 1915 essay "Puškin and Skrjabin," Mandel'štam also wrote about Puškin's burial: «Ночью положили солнце в гроб. Исаакий так и не дождался солнечного тела поэта…» [2: 313] ("They laid the sun in his grave at night. Isaac did not receive the poet's sun-filled body"). These lines allude, as does his poem, to the ignominious way in which Petersburg was emptied of Puškin, its greatest cultural treasure, Puškin, the buried-elsewhere and now invisible sun. The eclipse of Puškin's sun of which Mandel'štam speaks is the main subject of Xodasevič in his important 1921 essay "The Shaken Tripod," mentioned above: "Pisarevism was the first eclipse of Puškin's sun. And it seems to me the second is not far off."[57]

Mandel'štam's poem "We will gather again in Petersburg" alludes to Orpheus; the task facing the "we" in the poem is that of unearthing and raising what is buried and making it active in the present, as in another poem where Mandel'štam presents himself as a buried "head" that is, like Orpheus' severed head, still speaking poetry:

Да, я лежу в земле, губами шевеля,
Но то, что я скажу, заучит каждый школьник   [1: 214]

Yes, I lie in the earth, moving my lips,
But every schoolchild will memorize what I say

Axmatova has a kind of Antigone complex, expressed very clearly in her article «Невское взморье» ["The Nevsky Shore"]. Perhaps it is Antigone she has in mind when she writes:

Скоро мне нужна будет лира,
Но Софокла уже, не Шекспира   [2: 25]

Soon I will need the lyre of Sophocles,
Not of Shakespeare

or, in 1962:

Непогребенных всех, я хоронила их
Я всех оплакала, а кто меня оплачет?[58]

The unburied ones, I buried them all
I mourned each one, but who will mourn for me?

Being buried alive, the fate of Antigone, was something Axmatova complained about often enough, especially in the sense of being buried as a relegation to

---

[57] Xodasevič, "Koleblemyj trenožnik," 204.
[58] Axmatova, "Nepogrebennyx vsex ja xoronila ix," *Stixotvorenija*, 300.

an earlier time as though she were already dead: "They have walled me up in the 1910s," as she remarked to Viktor Žirmunskij. The Antigone responsibility of proper burial of her poet-brothers was one of the major aims of *Poem without a Hero*, and she also alludes to it in her article on Puškin, who she felt had, like herself, a burial fixation. The kind of burial Axmatova often gave these forgotten poets, weaving their words into her own in palimpsests like *PWH*, often meant unearthing them from oblivion and making them live again in accordance with Mandel'štam's imperative.

Mandel'štam is particularly fond of the Persephone myth of descent to the underworld and rebirth and re-ascent to the upper world, and he employs it in numerous poems about Petersburg. It is like an anticipation of Christ's death and resurrection, or the apparent death of a buried seed which is necessary to its reflowering, one of Vjačeslav Ivanov's favorite images. The buried Persephone, like Axmatova, goes to the lower world, but does not die: she is resurrected, returning to the upper world. Mandel'štam cherishes the hope that high culture, which he sees eclipsed and submerged or buried from the late teens of the twentieth century through the Soviet period, will return to the upper world after a dark winter of cultural discontent. In fact, he treats Petersburg as a moribund underground location as early as 1916, as the underworld domain of Proserpina:

> В Петрополе прозрачном мы умрем,
> Где властвует над нами Персефона.
> Мы в каждом вздохе смертный воздух пьем,
> И каждый час нам смертная година.
>
> Богиня моря, грозная Афина,
> Сними могучий каменный шелом.
> В Петрополе прозрачном мы умрем,—
> Здесь царствуешь не ты, а Прозерпина.   [1: 61]
>
> We will die in transparent Petropolis,
> Where Persephone rules o'er us.
> In each sigh we drink lethal air,
> And every hour is the hour of our death.
>
> Goddess of the Sea, fearful Athena,
> Take off your mighty stone helmet.
> We will die in transparent Petropolis
> Where not you, but Proserpina rules.

Proserpina's cyclical death-rebirth is associated with descent to the underworld, return, rising, and renewal. We recall Axmatova's descent in *PWH* to the underworld, whence she returns alive:

А как же может случиться,
Что одна я из них жива?   [2: 106]

And can it really happen
That I'm the only one here who is alive?

In his Petropolis poem cited here, Mandel'štam places Petersburg entirely in the underworld, as he does with the buried but preserved culture of Herculaneum. Though the Petersburgers are temporarily "buried" there (as Dante's inferno is an underworld), they can return and, he hopes, will experience spring and the renewal which are cyclically promised.

Poems in the same Mandel'štam collection, *Tristia*, present the vertical-horizontal axes more dramatically, with a Greek mythological coloring, but refer to cultural history, an overarching cultural time flow of which the individual poet's life can be viewed as a part and a contribution. These same texts, however, can be viewed as the topography of the poet's consciousness and unconscious. One such poem is his masterpiece, "I forgot the word I wanted to say":

Я слово позабыл, что я хотел сказать.
Слепая ласточка в чертог теней вернется,
На крыльях срезанных, с прозрачными играть.
В безпамятстве ночная песнь поется.

Не слышно птиц. Бессмертник не цветет.
Прозрачны гривы табуна ночного.
В сухой реке пустой челнок плывет.
Среди кузнечиков беспамятствует слово.

И медленно растет, как бы шатер иль храм,
То вдруг прикинется безумной Антигоной,
То мертвой ласточкой бросается к ногам,
С стигийской нежностью и веткою зеленой.

О, если бы вернуть и зрячих пальцев стыд,
И выпуклую радость узнаванья.
Я так боюсь рыданья Аонид,
Тумана, звона и зиянья!

А смертным власть дана любить и узнавать,
Для них и звук в персты прольется,
Но я забыл, что я хочу сказать,—
И мысль бесплотная в чертог теней вернется.

Все не о том прозрачная твердит,
Все ласточка, подружка, Антигона…
И на губах, как черный лед, горит
Стигийского воспоминанье звона.　　　　November 1920 [1: 82]

I forgot the word I wanted to say.
A blind swallow returns to the chamber of shades,
On clipped wings, to play with the transparent ones.
In memorylessness the nocturnal song is sung.

No birds are heard. Immortals do not bloom.
Transparent are the manes of the night herd.
In a dry river an empty canoe floats.
Among grasshoppers the word forgets itself.

And it grows slowly, like a tent or temple,
Now it suddenly throws itself, like a mad Antigone,
Now it falls at our feet like a dead swallow
With Stygian tenderness and a green branch.

If only we could return the shame of seeing fingers,
And the convex timidity of recognition.
I so fear the weeping of the Aonids [the Muses],
The fog, the ringing and the yawning emptiness!

But mortals are given power to love and recognize,
For them sound, too, flows through into fingers,
But I've forgotten what I wanted to say,
And a bodiless thought will return to the chamber of shades.

The transparent one keeps repeating the wrong thing,
A swallow, a friend, Antigone…
And on my lips burns like black ice
The remembrance of Stygian ringing.

We remember in *The Egyptian Stamp* that the narrator thinks of trying to phone Persephone and Proserpina in the Petersburg underworld, but "phones have not been installed." This poem is intimately connected with the one which precedes it (#112), where Persephone is present:

Когда Психея-жизнь спускается к теням
В полупрозрачный лес вослед за Персефоной,
Слепая ласточка бросается к ногам
С стигийской нежностью и веткою зеленой.　　　　[1: 80–81]

> When Psyche-life descends to the shades
> To the quasi-transparent forest following Persephone,
> A blind swallow throws itself at her feet
> With Stygian tenderness and a green branch.

The province of Persephone, her underworld from which she will rise in the above poems, is not that of the poet and his ilk, but is rather the place whence the Word and Psyche-life have gone. That mythical underworld in "I forgot the word I wanted to say" is likewise the landscape of the poet's unconscious.

In one interpretation, then, the descent is a myth portraying the temporary burial of Petersburg culture, the sun, which descends during the "night of culture," à la Vjačeslav Ivanov, only to rise again. In another interpretation, on the level of individual psychology, the Word, the poet's contribution to culture, has left consciousness and descended to the underworld, while he has tried to follow it thither to bring it back up from the Styx, the Lethe, i.e., to wrest it from the death of oblivion. The whole can be interpreted as a spatial representation of bringing a forgotten word out of the preconscious or unconscious.

Most of our poets show the Word (крылатое слово) as handicapped, on clipped wings, hampered and blind, yet willfully departing from the poet. The images used for its lostness recall Petersburg scenes in *The Bronze Horseman* such as «Бедный челн по ней [Неве] стремился одиноко» ("A poor canoe strained up the river, alone"), which here becomes an image of greater dryness and barrenness: «В сухой реке пустой челнок плывет» ("In a dry river an empty canoe floats"). Silence and a scene even emptier and drier than the desolate one on the barren shores before Petersburg's creation have here ensued.

Stanza 3 of "I forgot the word," concerning the attempt of the word to rise to the level of consciousness and become audible, is presented in an architectural metaphor as a temple or a tent. Stanzas 3 and 4 present the image of an ancient blind bard, reminiscent of Homer or of a *guslar* like Bojan mentioned in the *Lay of Igor's Host*, Russia's great extant epic, which is called a *slovo* (in modern Russian, "word"), an Old Russian genre. The nimbleness of Bojan's fingers alluded to in the opening lines of the work seems to be recalled in the poet's "desire to return shame to seeing fingers"; Antigone, as the guide of her blind father, is the agent of the modification of his sense of sight to that of touch ("seeing fingers"). The Word-Thought, down in the underworld, is disembodied, having returned to the unconscious whence it arose. The poet is left with the reverberating reminders of the escaped word: fog, ringing, and a gaping emptiness imply vagueness, lack of clarity in space and in sound, and loss of sound altogether. The poem is merely the *shade* or shadow of the real lost word. Its relation to the real "word he wanted to utter" is like that of the shadows in the cave allegory in relation to the ideal forms. The poem is the result of the poet's struggle to wrest the word from the unconscious, to pull it back, keeping it from total death. The descent to the world's innards on the cosmic level, often seen in Greek mythology, is on the microcosmic, individual level the poet's conscious incursion into his own unconscious.

The lost word of Mandel'štam's poem in the broadest sense is the lost cultural-aesthetic consciousness of the Petersburger.[59] A more readily comprehensible and very graphic presentation of the same cultural consciousness in the process of being lost is found in *The Splitting of the Atom*, Georgij Ivanov's modernist autobiographical *cri de coeur*, written in Paris on the eve of the Second World War. Mandel'štam's "atomization" of individual biography is literally expressed in this work, which bears the strong influence of Vasilij Rozanov's way of "writing the self" in *Solitaria, Fallen Leaves,* and *The Apocalypse of Our Time*. The atom being split is the erstwhile human individuality, the whole or integral man, whom Blok and others posited as still existing in the nineteenth century. Mandel'štam had commented in "The End of the Novel" that Tolstoj's *Anna Karenina* "succeeds in interesting the reader in the fate of an individual biography or a cluster of biographies" [2: 266]. In *The Egyptian Stamp*, the crisis of the "man of the past" is represented as Anna Karenina before the railroad-associated events that led to her downfall and eventual suicide. If Mandel'štam was predicting the end of such integral biographies which make the novel possible, *The Splitting of the Atom* is in resounding agreement with that postulate. Ivanov's prose work is post-novelistic and focuses on the split-off parts of consciousness and of the poet's erstwhile, more integral self—his atomic individuality. Whereas Mandel'štam's character Parnok in *The Egyptian Stamp* is said to be "held together by Petersburg alone," Ivanov blames his splitting apart on a "betrayal of Puškinian Russia."[60] What he means by this is explained in the excerpted passages below:

| Красуйся, град Петров, и стой | Be beautiful, city of Peter, and stand |
| Неколебимо, как Россия | Unshakeable, like Russia |

So Puškin exclaims with fervor, against his own premonitions ... "Nothing, nothing, silence," Gogol' mutters.[61]

---

[59] Georgij Ivanov calls this cultural complex "*Puškinskaja Rossija.*" Here again we might contrast Montaigne's positive "I don't know what I had wanted to say" (quoted in Poulet, *Studies in Human Time*, 44) with Mandel'štam's more devastating "I forgot the word I wanted to say."
[60] Georgij Ivanov, *Raspad atoma* (Paris: n.p., 1938), 75.
[61] Ibid.

... But the sunset darkens quickly and night's haze overpowers man ... it leads him into such darkness that even when he returns to the surface he doesn't recognize the fact. And he won't return ... his soul is screwed tight, by a corkscrew, what use has his soul for an unshakeability that was shaken long ago and for a beauty that has long since been rendered ugly? Dig Peter the Great up out of his grave and stick him with a cigarette butt in his mouth against the wall of the Peter and Paul Cathedral [where the tsar is in fact buried] while Red Army soldiers look on and laugh—Do that and nothing will happen. Dantès will still murder Puškin and Ivan Sergeevič Turgenev will still shake Dantès' hand, and nothing will happen, Turgenev's hand won't wither. And what do we really care about all of this in the depths of our souls?[62]

Shot through with sadness, the Russian soul-self that Puškin's Bronze Horseman and Puškin's *oeuvre* in general presuppose as human no longer exists, just as that Puškinian Russia has ceased to be. "Why has Puškinian Russia betrayed us?" Ivanov calls out plaintively.

The living world of Puškin's art is a Petersburg of different, whole human types, a human type now hardly left. The spatial representation of this crisis and the death of the whole human individuality is striking, and the tragic atomization of the fate of Anna Karenina is invoked by Ivanov, as it was by Mandel'štam. As in the case of Sof'ja Petrovna Lixutina, which we observed above, the ongoing loss of self is occurring to a self largely unawares. This is one of the most striking vertical renderings of the inner self as Petersburg space:

> What succeeded aesthetically yesterday has become impossible today, unrealized. One cannot believe in the appearance of a new Werther— one cannot imagine a notebook of verses which contemporary man will leaf through, wiping away his tears, and gaze up at the heavens with a searing hope. It is impossible. So impossible, in fact, that one can barely believe that it ever was possible. New ironclad rules envelop the world like so much raw skin, and they know no consolation from art. Moreover, these vague unrescindable, soullessly "fair" laws born of the new world or which gave birth to that world, have a retroactive force: not only is it impossible for the genius artist to create consolation, it has become virtually impossible to be consoled by past works of genius.

---

[62] Ibid., 76–77.

There are still people who can weep over the fate of Anna Karenina. There they stand on that patch of earth that is sinking with them. On that patch of soil stand the foundations of the theater where Anna, her elbows on the velvet of the loge, resplendent in torment and in beauty, experienced her shame.

It is as if the barely dimmed slanted rays—the last, as it were, refraction of what has been lost, or the confirmation that what is lost is irreparable. Soon everything will fade…

What Tolstoj foresaw before others has come to pass: the inevitable boundary line beyond which there is no consolation from imagined beauty, no tears shed over a fictional fate.[63]

This sinking of Petersburg soil, of Anna, the theater, and those Russian souls who still understand her fate is foreseen in Tolstoj's *What is Art?* (1897), in which he rejects his greatest works of art, according to Ivanov, in favor of a universally comprehensible non-art. The erstwhile depth of Russian sensibilities and aesthetic sense has been lost by the now-atomized individual, the modern human automaton. The few poetic souls who have not forgotten, who retain the lost values, are sinking with the theater and the art, its contents. The greatest spiritual achievements of Russia are being buried alive, described in individual terms by Gogol'ʹs "silence" (espoused by his character Popriščin in "Diary of a Madman"); here this sinking is a mirror of what is happening to Ivanov's hero, the poet-speaker who is helpless to halt it, in a space which is himself. This vision of Petersburg space is the contemporary fate of the dismembered autobiographical self, soon to sink entirely from view, as if it were founded on quicksand.

In his attempt to bring the word back up to the surface of consciousness, the poet is like Orpheus, who tries to bring Eurydice back up from below. In Glück's opera, a favorite of Mandel'ʹštam, Orpheus, in contrast to the Greek myths, actually succeeds in retrieving her despite her backward glance. Here, as for Mandel'ʹštam in "We will gather again in Petersburg," the feeling is that ultimately contact with the lost word will be made, and it will be retrieved.

The disjunctions between the upper and lower worlds; the loss of a past part of the self or past connections in Axmatova's "The Cellar of Memory"; the loss of one's own words, be it for reasons of fear and discouragement («Петь, вы же видите, я не могу» ["You see, I can't sing"]) or loss of cultural continuity represented by "forgetting the word one wanted to say": all these are caused by a discontinuity in time, by blows of history. Petersburg itself is dying or dead: «Твой брат Петрополь умирает» ("Your brother Petropolis is

---

[63] Ibid., 31–32.

dying") is a refrain repeated before the revolution, and with the city's submersion comes that of the culture it represented. The death of Petropolis causes and implies the death of its brother-creature, the poet who is virtually inseparable from it.

The reduction, burial, or death of Axmatova's city, the subject of her *Poem without a Hero*, is her own destruction and grinding-down—her self-forgetting. Mandel'štam depicts the same phenomenon in *The Egyptian Stamp*, where his hero's identity is shown to be Petersburg's, and he specifically alludes to the "yellow steam of the Petersburg winter, yellow snow clinging to stone slabs" of Annenskij's poem. Parnok and the narrator say: «… держусь я одним Петербургом—концертным, желтым, зловещим,… зимним» [2: 25] ("… I am sustained [held together] by Petersburg alone, the Petersburg of concerts, yellow, ominous … and wintry…"). History is the culprit in all these men's struggles to hold together (*deržat'sja*), to stabilize the self and the city and to hold on.

In the next section of the chapter we will see, in even more fragmented versions of identification, how violently unstable the city-self can be in its death.

FRAGMENTED SELVES, DISPERSAL OF THE CITY

А веселое слово—дома—
Никому теперь не знакомо,
Все в чужое глядят окно.
Кто в Ташкенте, кто в Нью-Йорке,
И изгнания воздух горький—
Как отравленное вино.

And now no one knows
The happy words "at home,"
We all gaze into an alien window.
Some are in Tashkent, some in New York,
And the air of exile is bitter—
Like poisoned wine.

Anna Axmatova [2: 131]

Oh my beloved city, dragged to uttermost death.
    Cassandra, of Troy, in Aeschylus, *Agamemnon*[64]

---

[64] *Greek Tragedies*, trans. David Greene and Richard Lattimore (Chicago: University of Chicago Press, 1960), 1: 1–60.

The fragmentation of the self in its simple form, *dédoublement* of the ego, has in Russian letters always been associated with eerie St. Petersburg, with its fog, light phenomena, and atmospheric conditions. In Gogol'''s "The Nose" it is inchoate, and it comes to complete fullness in Dostoevskij's *The Double* (*Dvojnik*), as well as in *Crime and Punishment*. In the post-revolutionary period these fragmentations come additionally to be associated with an apocalyptic catastrophe that has dealt a crippling blow to the city, and with historical adversities which result as the city writhes in its death agony, like an earthquake and its less significant but still perceptible aftershocks.

"Doubles" in the Dostoevskian sense of *The Double* are two "selves" ostensibly inhabiting the same body, a schizophrenic phenomenon. One of the "selves" is always felt to be the prior, original and more genuine one, and this "self" often feels humiliated, enslaved, insulted, or that its prerogatives have been usurped by the other self or selves. As the number of contending "I's" becomes greater, the sense of dispersal of self, loss of identity, and confusion multiplies, as does the sense of tragedy.

Let us begin with a case of two selves representing two distinct periods of a biography that are depicted poetically as confronting each other on a single Petersburg plane. The classic example of *dédoublement* "caused" in a sense by Petersburg, as we indicated, is Dostoevskij's 1846 novel *The Double*. It is clear there that the weather, not time or history, seems to bring on Goljadkin's schizophrenia:

> "This terrible weather!" thought our hero; "Listen! isn't that a flood warning? –Evidently the water is rising very fast." No sooner had Mr. Golyadkin said, or thought, this, than he caught sight of a figure coming towards him.... Mr. Golyadkin's nocturnal acquaintance was none other than himself, Mr. Golyadkin himself, another Mr. Golyadkin, but exactly the same as himself—in short, in every respect what is called his double....[65]

The second Goljadkin, called the "younger" in the novel, appears later in time, and thus the two represent somewhat different time periods coexisting on a single level.

In twentieth-century works the selves which appear are often from different periods of a biography, as in Blok's 1909 poem "The Double," where the dream of a past self materializes in the foggy Petersburg streets to address the lyric hero. Often history is clearly said or understood to have caused the fragmentation of the self. Evgenij Zamjatin's 1920 short story "The Cave"

---

[65] Fyodor Dostoyevsky, *The Double*, in *Notes from Underground/The Double*, trans. Jessie Coulson (New York: Penguin Books, 1972), 168, 173.

("Peščera"), for instance, presents the image of an icy, post-apocalyptic, and re-primitivized Petrograd—a world where both city and self are on the verge of becoming, if not already altogether transformed into, entirely different versions of themselves. Former Petersburg buildings are now rocky crags containing a receding succession of cave-like dwellings into which a new race of "cave-dwellers" retreat further and further. It is not the city that resembles a frozen wasteland; rather, we understand the triumph of the city's new "double" in the reversal of the simile—it is the rock cliffs which "resemble houses":

> ... Low, dark, thick clouds, like a vaulted ceiling, and the world one enormous silent cave. Narrow, endless passages between walls; and dark ice-coated cliffs resembling houses; in the cliffs—deep purple hollows; in the hollows, around the fire, humans, crouching. A light icy draught blows the powdery snow from under your feet, and over the white powder, the massive cliffs, the caves, the crouching humans, moves with inaudible, measured steps, some supermammoth.[66]

Likewise, the people who inhabit the caves are becoming newly ensavaged. The main character, Martin Martinyč, is racked by the struggle between two identities: his old self, still represented by his books, his Skrjabin sheet music, and his memories of Petersburg; and a new self who steals wood from his neighbor in a narrow focus on physical survival. Martin's old self is gradually losing ground in the face of a new age occasioned less by the ongoing march of time than by the frozen expanses of time's end:

> And upon the dotted line made by Martin Martinych breathing two Martin Martinyches engaged in a duel to the death: the old one, the Scriabin one, who knew "I may not," and the new one, the caveman, who knew "I must." The caveman, gnashing his teeth, knocked the other Martin Martinych down and throttled him, and Martin Martinych, breaking his nails, opened the door, plunged his hand into the stack of wood....[67]

Like the forms of Petersburg architecture which have been iced over and made unrecognizable, Martin feels that he is being literally reshaped. Zamjatin sustains the image of a Martin Martinyč made of clay, a highly impressionable and ultimately passive material that suffers the blows of time/history on his

---

[66] Evgenij Zamjatin, "The Cave," trans. Avrahim Yarmolinsky, *The Portable Twentieth-Century Russian Reader*, ed. Clarence Brown (New York: Penguin, 1985), 102.
[67] Ibid., 95.

very body. His old self is being buffeted and dented in ways that cannot be smoothed over afterwards; the marks remain and change him:

> Clayey Martin Martinych knocked against the logs, and this made a deep dent in the clay. And there was even a deeper dent when he knocked against the corner of the chest of drawers in the dark passage.... He did not hear: there were only the dully aching dents in the clay made by words and by the corners of the chiffonier, the chairs, the desk.[68]

Random flotsam and jetsam from his former life remain to knock about inside Martin's fading sense of self in the same way that the random detritus of culture remains to litter the rooms of the house:

> In the troglodytic Petersburg bedroom all was as it had been in Noah's ark not long ago—the clean and the unclean in diluvial promiscuity: Martin Martinych's desk, books, stone-age cakes of ceramic appearance, Scriabin opus 74, a flatiron, five potatoes lovingly scrubbed white, nickel-plated bedsprings, an ax, a chiffonier, firewood. And in the center of this universe was its god, a short-legged, rusty-red, squat, greedy cave god: the iron stove.[69]

This multi-leveled image of apocalyptic flood is informed not only by the myth of Noah and the Biblical flood (and corresponding associations of house/city as a "mad" and sinking ship, a common metaphor for Petersburg and its individual houses at this time) but also by the myth of Petersburg itself, especially as codified in Puškin's *The Bronze Horseman*. In this reading the scattered relics in the room become so much debris and driftwood left behind by the receding flood, the "loot" dropped by the greedy but hurrying bandits of history (to adapt Puškin's image). The iron stove has become a new version of the Bronze Horseman as metallic "idol," consuming and destroying the proofs of the "real" Petersburg, the "real" Martin Martinyč, even as it provides some measure of control against the fast-encroaching frosts. Evgenij's Paraša becomes Martin's Maša.

The very dimensionality of Martin, Maša, and the city and its buildings is slowly being ground down, flattened out. The life of the "old self," of culture, thought, and the word (Mandel'štam's "fifth element") is here subject to a tragic reduction: "Staring, dim, old woman's eyes, and everything shrinking, hunching under that fixed stare. The ceiling is caving in, the armchair, the desks, the beds, Martin Martinych himself—are all flattening out, and on the

---

[68] Ibid., 94, 100.
[69] Ibid., 92.

bed—Masha, perfectly flat, like paper."[70] It is, of course, wood and paper that are fed into the fire. Here we recall that Mandel'štam, in "Preserve My Speech," later identifies himself as poet with a living tree. The roundedness and convexity occasioned by three (or more) dimensions, that which could in some measure still be felt by the "seeing fingers" in Mandel'štam's "I forgot the word" or by Axmatova when she "gropes" for her city in her "Third Northern Elegy," is here being reduced and emptied out to two-dimensionality by the icy finger of time/history. At the end of the story, the sense of being three-dimensional flickers again, if only briefly: Martin is given the chance to "save" his Paraša. His last act as the "old" Martin Martinyč, in the cruel and paradoxical logic of the ice age, is to make the sacrifice of giving Maša a carefully-saved vial of poison instead of taking it himself. It is this brief resurgence of nobility that remains as the last link to a former Martin, a former Maša, and a former city: "She threw off the blanket, sat up in bed, pink, swift, immortal—like the water at sunset, then seized the little bottle...."[71] This episode is immediately followed by the story's conclusion, a reprise of the very first paragraph, in which it becomes clear that the city's transformation into a barren, icy landscape of rocks is complete. "Immortality" in this sense is a function of time's complete stoppage, its frozen immobility.

In *PWH* and the *Northern Elegies*, the Axmatova of the early 1940s is also estranged from her former selves by a "cruel age": «Меня, как реку, суровая эпоха повернула» ("Like a river, I have been diverted by a severe epoch") [1: 311]. In *PWH* she is not happy with the youthful self she is forced to confront in the ballroom. In *Requiem* she disclaims certain past selves at times even more emphatically, and disclaims the locales where these selves are embedded:

> Последняя с Морем разорвана связь,
> My last tie with the sea is broken,
>
> Ни в царском саду у заветного пня,
> Где тень безутешная ищет меня   [1: 310]
>
> Not in the tsar's garden by the cherished stump,
> Where an inconsolable shade is seeking me

These past selves are not fully integrable into her present life; her self evinces a tragic discontinuity presented in spatial or geographical terms.

In these works we see not only the co-presence of two selves from two temporal periods in the same space, but the association of these different past

---

[70] Ibid., 97.
[71] Ibid., 101.

selves with certain parts of Petersburg, exterior as well as interior. Thus certain parts of the city are perceived as holding "the contents" of a different parcel of dispersed biography, or "selves." In Russian literature of the Soviet period this phenomenon is associated with Petersburg most frequently because of the numerous time-levels of the city, reflected even in the different names St. Petersburg—Petrograd—Leningrad. Axmatova, gazing upon Leningrad buildings in 1945, "sees through" to the buildings of the 1870s, to the Petersburg of Dostoevskij, which is always immanent there:

> Торгуют кабаки, летят пролетки,
> Пятиэтажные растут громады
> В Гороховой, у Знаменья, под Смольным.
> Везде танцклассы, вывески менял,
> А рядом: "Henriette," "Basile," "Andre"
> И пышные гроба: «Шумилов-старший».
> Но, впрочем, город мало изменился.
> Не я одна, но и другие тоже
> Заметили, что он подчас умеет
> Казаться литографией старинной,
> Не первоклассной, но вполне пристойной,
> Семидесятых, кажется, годов.

> Pubs are open, cabs rush by,
> Five-story hulks grow up
> On Goroxovaja, by Znamen'e, near Smolnyj.
> Ballet classes everywhere, moneylenders' signs,
> And next door "Henriette," "Basile," "Andre"
> And pompous graves: "Shumilov the Elder."
> But in all the city has changed little.
> Not I alone, but others also
> Have noted that it at times
> Can seem be an old lithograph,
> Not first-class, but quite acceptable,
> Of the 1870s or so.

The lighting, the river's reflections, Petersburg's white nights, and the northern climate affect one's ability to "see through" (*prozrevat'*):

> Особенно зимой, перед рассветом
> Иль в сумерки—тогда за воротами
> Темнеет жесткий и прямой Литейный,
> Еще не опозоренный модерном,

> И визави меня живут—Некрасов
> И Салтыков… [1: 308]

> Particularly in winter, before dawn
> Or at twilight—it's then that behind the gates
> Harsh and straight Litejnyj Prospect darkens,
> Not yet shamed by *art nouveau* architecture,
> And across from me live Nekrasov
> And Saltykov…

At the end of this elegy about the place-time of the birth of her generation, Axmatova stresses that her birthplace as poet/writer, "that Petersburg," is still there, though it was destined subsequently to die, to witness and experience catastrophic "unprecedented spectacles":

> Так вот когда мы вздумали родиться
> И безошибочно отмерив время,
> Чтоб ничего не пропустить из зрелищ
> Невиданных, простились с небытьем. [1: 310]

> That's when we decided to be born
> And, measuring out the time without error,
> So as not to miss any unprecedented
> Spectacles, we bade farewell to non-being.

The co-presence of her artistic birthplace and another city, Leningrad, which she called Petersburg's opposite, is felt; access to both is possible. It was this "two-time/place quality" that Evgenij Evtušenko emphasized in his necrological poem dedicated to Axmatova in 1966.

> Ахматова двувременной была.
> О ней и плакать как-то не пристало.
> Не верилось, когда она жила,
> не верилось, когда ее не стало.[72]

> Axmatova was of two times.
> It hardly seems fitting to mourn her.
> It was unbelievable when she lived,
> it was unbelievable when she was alive no longer.

The amazement among contemporary Soviet (even Leningrad) poets that someone like Axmatova was alive witnesses the sense that part of their rever-

---

[72] Evtušenko, "Pamjati A. A. Axmatovoj," 246–48.

ence towards her was as a bridge between two ages; she had a firm foot in old Petersburg as well as in the tragedies of Soviet Leningrad. Evtušenko speaks of her death, spatializing the time periods of Axmatova's biography separately:

> Она ушла, как будто бы напев
> уходит в глубь темнеющего сада.
> Она ушла, как будто бы навек
> вернулась в Петербург из Ленинграда.

> She departed as if a refrain were departing
> Into the depth of a darkening garden.
> She went away as if she had
> Returned from Leningrad to Petersburg forever.

As if she had returned one final time to Petersburg from Leningrad: this formulation defines, and brilliantly at that, Axmatova's entire late *oeuvre* as a trip back and forth between Petersburg and Leningrad, a journey between her own and her country's present life and that of pre-revolutionary Petersburg. It characterizes her *oeuvre* as an attempt to forge a linkage, a bridge. Evtušenko appeals in religious Church Slavic to his nation and fellow poets to keep and cherish Axmatova («О, не убий»), as if, without her, there would irrevocably be "two Russias," as Belyj had warned: "The fates of our fatherland are torn in twain." Evtušenko deals with a synchronically divided Russia in the second part of his poem:

> … не убий
> ту связь времен—она еще поможет.
> Ведь просто быть не может двух Россий,
> Как быть и двух Ахматовых не может.

> … do not kill
> that linkage of times—she/it [a person / the link] will help yet.
> There simply cannot be two Russias
> Any more than there can be two Axmatovas.

As pointed out earlier, the sense of too many Axmatovas, of a self too divided, is what torments Belyj and later, what often disturbs Mandel'štam, Brodskij, and others. It leads to a desire to effect a reintegration of self, to overcome the damage wrought by time, always against great odds.

Perhaps Evtušenko used the metaphor of a bridge for Axmatova because she had viewed herself as a river turned by the Soviet period from its original bed, a feat of technology actually carried out, mostly in Siberia. In the "Third Northern Elegy" she is clearly the Neva, a Neva off-course and confused. She refers to her city and its river in similar confusion in *PWH*. There we find the context of chaos, presented clearly in Belyj's *Petersburg*, which may have suggested it to her. In Mandel'štam's *The Egyptian Stamp*, the city is presented as a huge book: the river is its spine or its contents, while the opposing sides of a drawbridge are the two sides of its cover. Critics in carriages try to drive up the sides of this "cover," but keep slipping down then in the ice. She alludes directly, it seems, to Mandel'štam's image, which is a metapoetic metaphor evoking chaos and falling:

И валились с мостов кареты,
И весь траурный город плыл
По неведомому назначенью,
По Неве иль против теченья,—
Только прочь от своих могил. [2: 117]

And carriages fell from the bridges,
And the whole mournful city floated
In an uncharted direction,
Down the Neva or against the current—
Only away from its graves.

This scene, as pointed out in chapter 3, would seem to be an image of Petersburg-Leningrad trying to flee its past. Denial of one's dead, one's sacred graves, is anathema for Antigone-Axmatova. To fail to render proper burial to the dead means denial of the personal and historical-cultural past, which is, in her view, destructive for the nation as well as for the individual. As we have seen, it is what she most struggles against when she takes up the "lyre of Sophocles."

The future is fast approaching in the third chapter of *Poem without a Hero*, but the past should not totally retreat in its wake. In the "Third Northern Elegy," as we have observed, the sadness consists of the very fact that the poet, like the city, has lost her "truer self." She is living an ersatz, a substitute life. There is an allusion here to the destructive effects of time as a river and to Deržavin's deathbed poem, the "Slate Ode":

Река времен в своем теченьи
Уносит все дела людей.[73]

The river of times in its flow
Carries away all the deeds of men.

---

[73] Gavrila Deržavin, "Reka vremen v svoem tečen'i," *Stixotvorenija* (Moscow: Sovetskij pisatel', 1963), 374.

Axmatova's elegy restates poetically Čaadaev's observation that Russia and the Russians do not have a normal history, but one falsified and tampered with, turned into a series of unrelated "improvisations" that do not organically grow out of each other:

> О, как я много зрелищ пропустила,
> ....
> ... Сколько я друзей
> Своих ни разу в жизни не встречала
>
> Oh, how many spectacles I have missed,
> ....
> How many of my friends
> I never met even once

Yet she vows that she can and will find her true shores and true self:

> А я один на свете город знаю
> И ощупью его во сне найду.   [2: 311]
>
> But I only know one city in this world
> And I will find it, groping, in my sleep.

In this image the speaker uses her "seeing fingers" and entrusts herself to a "convex timidity of recognition" (familiar to us from Mandel'štam's "I forgot the word") that is here specifically identified with her city. Likewise, the evil double who has usurped her identity is like the Leningrad that has usurped Petersburg's:

> И женщина какая-то мое
> Единственное место заняла,
> Мое законнейшее имя носит,
> Оставивши мне кличку, из которой
> Я сделала, пожалуй, все, что можно.   [1: 312]
>
> Some woman has taken
> My unique place,
> And bears my most legal name,
> Having left me a nickname out of which
> I've made as much as I could.

This statement is corroborated when the speaker, feeling estranged from the self—the successful self, perhaps, that is in Goljadkin-like or Parnok-like competition with it—complains, "I won't lie down in my own grave" («Я не в свою, увы, могилу лягу»). This is a striking statement from one so involved in the question of proper burial and commemoration, but it is present as a constant anxiety ("and who will mourn for me?"), as we see in *Poem without a Hero*:

> Я ль растаю в казенном гимне?
> Не дари, не дари, не дари мне
> Диадему с мертвого лба…   [2: 125]

> Is it I who will melt in a governmental hymn?
> Do not give me, do not give me, do not give me
> A diadem from a dead man's brow…

Here she expresses her desire not to be made into a Soviet saint with whom she cannot identify, not to become a false self in life or in death.

A false self, a misdirected Neva with a non-natural, unrecognizable city on its banks, is opposed to the genuine river and the city that are in absence. There is division in the "Third Northern Elegy" as well as the co-presence/co-incidence of selves, cities, and rivers. There is, as pointed out, a sense that time's flow has been disturbed and that the true self, river, and city have been betrayed. They are associated, as such disjunction was in Mandel'štam, with the unwritten verses, the unuttered words of the poet:

> И сколько я стихов не написала,
> И тайный хор их бродит вкруг меня
> И, может быть, еще когда-нибудь
> Меня задушит…
>   [1: 311]

> And how many of my verses I have not written down,
> And their secret chorus wanders around me
> And, perhaps, will still one day
> Strangle me…

The external space and self must be overcome and put aright by a reassertion of the more genuine inner one. When the poet says that perhaps those verses will strangle her, she implies that writing back the true Petersburg is her genuine duty, but that it may to a considerable degree cost her her life. Mandel'štam indicated something similar in his essay "Puškin and Skrjabin" when he wrote: "Memory above all, even at the price of death."[74] Paradoxically, to be true to oneself one may have to die (lose one's life) to gain it.

---

[74] This quote is only to be found in the complete version of the essay, translated by Jane G. Harris and Constance Link in *The Critical Prose of Osip Mandel'štam* (Ann Arbor: Ardis Publishers, 1979), 93–94.

Of course, this image of a divided self and divided, betrayed space probably derives from Mandel'štam's likening of the self to a coin chipped away at by time (see above, page 114; we saw a similar image in Zamjatin's Martin Martinych as a "clayey figure" battered by the scratches and dents of his age). Axmatova may be acknowledging this source when she presents the two sides of the "coin" of her life in the section entitled "Tails" ("Reška") in *PWH*. A similar sense of losing too much of the self is felt by Parnok, the Russian-Jewish would-be poet in *The Egyptian Stamp*. As his original personality crumbles, Parnok says, reminding us of Brodskij's poem "A Halt in the Desert" (see chapter 6):

> I am the last Egyptian ... I am a little bowlegged prince. I am a low Ramses-bloodsucker ... I am the prince of ill fortune.... I have become nothing—*so little is left of me.*[75]

This is the same loss of self occurring because of the advancing victory of history-time, the outer events that are emptying the inner content of the personality. If these outer forces or events upset the internal equilibrium—the memory of who one is—to a significant degree, the self can be lost, "plucked out of its biography" (in Mandel'štam's words), as happens to Axmatova in her "Third Northern Elegy."

Parnok, the original self of the narrator of *The Egyptian Stamp*, has suffered the ravages of time, and his sense of self has become compartmentalized into at least three identities: Parnok, the Russian-Jewish would-be writer; Kržižanovskij, the inimical, Goljadkin-like double (see Axmatova's double in her "Third Northern Elegy" above); and a third self that reflects upon, is aware of, and narrates the story of the other two struggling inside him. What is significant for the poetics of space-time here is that the integrality of the original would-be Jewish writer is associated with the integrity of his native house-apartment and its "Egypt"-derived things and, in a larger sense, with his extended house—Petersburg. Nabokov shows the same kind of identification with his childhood house on Bol'šaja Morskaja Street and his family estate at Vyra. Nabokov's native places are "lost" in a different way, but his sense of their and his own dispersion in space and time may very well have been directly influenced by Mandel'štam's treatment of them in *The Egyptian Stamp* and *The Noise of Time*.

While there is a certain feeling of disassociation in the images with which *The Egyptian Stamp* begins, they are hardly surreal, as some have suggested. The random and destructive effects of the tumultuous apocalyptic time in which Parnok lives are immediately obvious. For example, the cuckoo clock

---

[75] Mandel'štam,' *The Egyptian Stamp*, 159.

from which a soldier emerges and shoots the hour is associated with the American cuckoo-duel game, a rough equivalent to Russian roulette, in which soldiers shoot at each other in a totally dark room: "an American cuckoo-duel in which the opponents fired their pistols at cabinets of chinaware, at inkpots, and at family portraits."[76] Alluding distantly to Puškin's "The Shot," what Mandel'štam presents here is the clock/time destroying and dispersing the objects and heirlooms of Parnok's family seat. Left intact, these rooms would be a firm foundation for his inner world, but instead they are violently exploded and whisked away: "The centrifugal force of time has scattered our Viennese chairs and Dutch plates with little blue flowers. Nothing is left."[77] The dispersion of his "dear Egypt of objects" leads to an exodus from the original self, or a diaspora of selves.

In the third paragraph the narrator asks, "How can I rid myself of my past, separating myself from the objects which have been a part of my life?", an ambiguous question of "how can I do it, how can it happen?" Yet a feeling of guilt attends this contemplated betrayal of the past: "How can I smooth over my guilt?" This is not surprising in a poet who believed it was the writer's duty to assert the connections between past, present, and future. But the irony lies in the fact that this moral dilemma is somewhat illusory since the objects of his past are literally running out the door on their own steam, abandoning him. The piano and a large mirror are rushing headlong down the stairs. This is but the beginning of a loss of objects which commences on the first pages and symbolizes the hero's progressive sense of loss of self. Mandel'štam, like Proust (whom we have discussed heretofore), is very mindful of the importance of objects as symbolic receptacles of time past, of periods or moments in the individual's biography. He writes, "One cannot embrace the termini of a life: from the moment when one has comprehended the gothic German alphabet [as a child] all the way to the golden fat of the university's *piroshki*."[78] By association with Angiolina Bosio's biography, the Il'in map in his room represents spatialized time in *The Egyptian Stamp* in a way later adapted by Nabokov in *Speak, Memory* (see chapter 5). For Mandel'štam, as for Proust, objects, tastes, smells—experiential data—are the best means for registering one's passage through time. Yet he begins his work about a major collapse of a personality with *the disintegration or destruction of a place*; time attacks a Petersburg Jewish family home, which is at once Parnok's and to a lesser degree the narrator's.

---

[76] Mandel'štam, The *Egyptian Stamp*, 133.
[77] Ibid.
[78] Ibid., 134.

But it is not just the interior space of the house that is exploding. The larger Petersburg outside, his larger "house," the city, is subject to the same forces of disintegration. This apocalypse is in full swing in *The Noise of Time*:

> All the elegant mirage of Petersburg was merely a dream, a brilliant covering thrown over the abyss [a reference to Tjutčev] ... a chaos, the unknown womb world whence I had issued, which I feared, about which I made vague conjectures and fled, always fled.⁷⁹

The organized, outdoor Petersburg world "covers" the interior chaos of Parnok's Jewish apartment, described so well in the chapter "Judaic Chaos" of the autobiographical *Noise of Time*. The struggle between outer order and inner disorder is a reinstated, personalized version of the Apollonian-Dionysian model of *stroj* containing and holding together a swarming *roj* within that was the hallmark of the European-Mongol in Belyj's *Petersburg*. As a Jew, Mandel'štam must contend with both the Mongol and the Jewish chaos underlying Petersburg. He is doubly vulnerable. This is why the removal of the film, the surface, from the orderly Petersburg to reveal its lower level is so dangerous; the self is held together by Petersburg alone. The death and destruction of that orderly, beautiful surface are suspected and feared as imminent or as ongoing results in the destruction of the self. In *The Egyptian Stamp* Mandel'štam points out the locales in Petersburg where it would be madness to have a rendez-vous in apocalyptic days, as if they and the self were particularly vulnerable in those spots.

The narrator of *The Egyptian Stamp* speaks of how his family tries to protect itself from the deleterious effects of the seething chaos under Petersburg: "He thought of Petersburg as his infantile disease—one had only to regain consciousness, to come to, and the hallucination would vanish...."⁸⁰ His family uses all manner of antidotes against the illness of Petersburg—boiling water to prevent the bacilli from entering his organism, for example. This notion that the illness of Petersburg can be imbibed through its infested water is derived from Belyj's *Petersburg*.

Let us focus once more on the two main selves present in the novella: Parnok (the original self) and Kržižanovskij (an assimilated military officer with a Polish surname, presented as crude and insensitive compared to Parnok, and as a successful ladies' man, exactly as the second Goljadkin is seen by the first). Moreover, it cannot be overlooked that the figure of Kržižanovskij has compromising political overtones, as he has the same name of the head of Gosplan in the mid-twenties. Here, as in Dostoevskij's *The*

---

⁷⁹ Mandel'štam, *The Noise of Time*, 76–77.
⁸⁰ Mandel'štam, *The Egyptian Stamp*, 158.

Double, the two figures are unaware that they are the same person. Although he expresses the desire to, never does Parnok come out directly and confront his double as Kovalev does in Gogol''s "The Nose": "You should know your place, sir. After all, you are my very own nose!"[81] The narrator alludes to and is intellectually aware of the internal drama occurring within him enough to write a long narrative about it. All along Parnok, the original self, is associated with particular spaces in very expressive passages: "Parnok was a man of Kamennoostrovsky Prospekt—one of the lightest and most irresponsible streets of Petersburg. In 1917 … this street became still lighter with its steam laundries, its Georgian shops, where even cocoa was still to be bought, and its maniacal automobiles, the property of the Provisional Government."[82] Parnok was such a "light," somewhat irresponsible intellectual, thinly attached to reality and place, and thus fairly easy to "lose":

> There are indeed people in the world who have never been ill with anything more dangerous than influenza and are somehow hooked on to the present age at the side.… Such people never feel themselves to be grown up and, at thirty, are still finding someone to be offended by, someone whose apologies they require. They were never particularly spoiled by anyone, and yet they are as corrupt as if they had received the academic ration of sardines and chocolate all their lives. They are muddle-headed people.…[83]

Things in general are not very "pinned down" on Kamennoostrovskij: "But on Kamennoostrovsky the streetcars develop an unheard-of speed."[84] This is the speed of modern history, associated over and over again with trains and trams. The description of the street that follows is a model of the calmer ladies' man, of Kržižanovskij, Parnok's successful, more confident double, who appears and goes to the laundry on that street several pages later:

[Parnok:]
Parnok was a man of Kamennoostrovsky Prospekt…

[Kržižanovskij]:
Kamennoostrovsky: a feather-brained young man with starch in his only two stone shirts and a sea breeze in his streetcar-filled head. It is

---

[81] Gogol', "Nos," 3: 44.
[82] Mandel'štam, *The Egyptian Stamp*, 140.
[83] Ibid.
[84] Ibid.

a young dandy out of work, carrying its houses under its arm like an idle fop returning with his airy bundle from the laundress.[85]

The space is the man—the man, the space. Both selves, Parnok and Kržižanovskij, are pinned down to the same street, just as both Goljadkins occupy the same apartment. The street exhibits the characteristics of both sides of the self, the well-groomed Kržižanovskij and a *bednyj ščegol'* (poor fop) like Parnok. The Polish laundry is on the same street, of course, and when several pages later Parnok goes there to retrieve his laundry, he learns that it has already been given to Kržižanovskij. For the mentally healthy Polish laundress, there is only *one* person. Different aspects of the same street reflect different sides of the same person. Their joint attachment to the space is yet another textual proof that they are different parts of a single self.

There is a point in the novella at which Parnok, who has been progressively divested of Petersburg places, receives back many desired parts of it which he associates with himself: he receives these streets and squares, of which he had been deprived as of a patrimony, in the form of galleys and page proofs in art. This metapoetic treatment of the space concerns Parnok's aspirations as a writer and the need to possess and control the spaces in order to be a Petersburg writer and a reintegrated self. The narrator admits that he and Parnok have one thing very much in common—both are creatures of Petersburg.

The end of the novella includes attempts at resolution of this internal struggle between two confronted selves, but a reintegration of the self is not to be. Parnok is melted down and Kržižanovskij leaves for Moscow (a total break with his Petersburg foundations and deeper self), and he too appears to melt down in a hot bay window in the Moscow Hotel Selekt. Two selves are exorcised, but here the narrative breaks off; the other, narrating, self cannot go on as a writer.

Above we have discussed poems and prose texts in which two selves, temporally distinct, having arisen at different times in one Petersburg horizontal space, continue to coexist in it. In some of them parts of the space, such as the native house, are more associated with the self of one period of biography, although both are co-present. In *The Egyptian Stamp*, attachment to the same Petersburg avenue, among other clues, supports the contention that Parnok and Kržižanovskij are the same person, whereas the house that is destroyed initially is associated only with a younger self, a "purer" Parnok period. The association of the two with Kamennoostrovskij Prospekt later brings us back

---

[85] Ibid.

to a more complex version of the Goljadkin situation, in which two schizoid parts occupy virtually the same space.

In chapter 5 we will proceed to a slightly different presentation of the doubled or multiplied self, one in which the desired, often more "true" past self, cannot be accessed, despite the continued existence of its former places of residence.

5   Attempts to Reverse Time: Traveling in Space in Quest of the Integral Self

> Я родился в большой стране,
> в устье реки. Зимой
> она всегда замерзала. Мне
> не вернуться домой.
>
> I was born in a large country,
> at the mouth of a river. In the winter
> it always froze. I
> can't go back home.
>
> Iosif Brodskij, 1978[1]

In this chapter we treat identities split into more than one past self, in particular, those who cannot retrieve certain parts of their past although the place where they are (believed to be) housed can readily be found and visited. These "lost selves" are irretrievable pasts locked in existent Petersburg buildings and locales. Some poems deal with even more multiple selves (more than two or three components), and the attempt of a moving, often ambulatory subject to collect the "whole self." The poems we deal with here represent a variation on the fragmented and dispersed selves seen in chapter 4: the building or place is there but the self cannot be retrieved.

Irretrievable Selves as the Contents of Former Houses

In his essay "Less than One," Iosif Brodskij said of the current architectural function of some Leningrad buildings that their external form told him everything—that it mattered little what was in the buildings in the present. Thus the fact that the Kazan Cathedral for much of his life was a Museum of Atheism signified little. This clear aesthetic stance, a valuation of form over function ("content"), is not always felt in the works of Petersburg poets in this century. On the contrary, there are numerous contexts in which the lyric ego goes "home" to a specific Petersburg building, not necessarily a famous or

---

[1] Iosif Brodskij, "Polden' v komnate," *سočinenija Iosifa Brodskogo* (St. Peterburg, Puškinskij fond, 1992), 2: 447–48. Hereafter, all references to Brodskij's poems will be given by volume and page number in the text, with English translations by A. L. Crone and J. Day.

beautiful architectural monument, and cannot commune any longer with the spirit of the "past self" that he/she is still convinced resides in the place. Impossible or failed returns to the premises of the past, the failure of memory to accommodate us in those situations, are known in other literatures; Thomas Wolfe's famous title *You Can't Go Home Again* at once evokes them and warns us against such projects. Nevertheless, no treatment of the poet's identification with Petersburg spaces can overlook this all-important type of spatialization of self.

These spatial treatments are, as it were, psychological inversions of Puškin's very positive "I visited again" («Вновь я посетил»), which ends in the poet's experiencing a sense of his life as a whole and of the future of his line, his progeny. In a famous passage, he greets the trees as members of his household and family, and his own fears of mortality are assuaged by the fact that the trees will witness the growth and continuation of the Puškins, his grandchildren and their children.

Close to an opposite tone to Puškin's return to Mixailovskoe occurs in Fedor Tjutčev's very negative return to his birthplace, Ovstug, in 1849, in which the irretrievability of what he finds there turns quickly into rejection:

Итак, опять увиделся я с вами,
Места немилые, хоть и родные,
Где мыслил я и чувствовал впервые—
И где теперь, туманными очами,
....
Мой детский возраст смотрит на меня.

О бедный призрак, немощный и смутный,
Забытого, загадочного счастья!
О, как теперь без веры и участья
Смотрю я на тебя, мой гость минутный,
Куда как чужд ты стал в моих глазах—
Как брат меньшой, умерший в пеленах...

Ах, нет, не здесь, не этот край безлюдный
Был для души моей родным краем—
Не здесь расцвел, не здесь был величаем
Великий праздник молодости чудной.
Ах, не в эту землю я сложил
Все, чем я жил и чем я дорожил![2]

---

[2] Tjutčev, "Itak, opjat′ uvidelsja ja s vami," 151.

And so I have met you again,
Places not dear, although native,
Where I first thought and felt
And where now with foggy eyes
....
My childish age gazes upon me.

Oh, poor ghost, feeble and confused,
Of a forgotten, enigmatic happiness!
Oh, how now without faith or involvement
I look upon you, my momentary guest,
How terribly alien you have grown in my eyes—
Like a younger brother who died while still in diapers.

Oh, no, not here, not this unpeopled place
Was the birthplace of my soul–
Not here did I blossom, not here
Was celebrated the great feast of marvelous youth.
Ah, not in this earth did I bury
All I lived by and cherished!

This poem as a psychological document combines the irretrievability of the self buried in Ostvug with a rejection of the place (self) and its contents because of the poet's failure on this occasion to connect that past with the present. We know that Tjutčev wrote some more sympathetic poems as he gazed on his native country. Yet the Romantic Slavophile found on his occasional journeys home that his love for Russia often faltered when he faced its concrete realities.[3]

Innokentij Annenskij, usually far less sentimental than Tjutčev, was one of the Carskoe Selo–Petersburg poets who metaphorized a self in a building or native country estate. In the first of two such poems cited below ("Before Sunset" and "Nox Vitae"), the past is enclosed in a house which has deteriorated over time, "a memory covered by cobwebs," and which is about to be destroyed by someone's design—excised:

Перед закатом

Гаснет небо голубое,
На губах застыло слово;
Каждым нервом жду отбоя
Тихой музыки былого.

---

[3] "Lettres de Tjutscheff à sa seconde épouse, née Baronne de Pfeffel," *Starina i novizna* 18 (1914), 19 (1915), 20 (1916), 21 (1917).

Before Sunset

The blue sky goes out,
A word has frozen on my lips;
With every nerve I await the passing away
Of the quiet music of the past.

As in the case of the very disappointed Tjutčev, Annenskij returns to this place "before the sunset" of his life, full of expectations of sweet memories.[4]

Но помедли, день, врачуя
Это сердце от разлада!
Все глазами взять хочу я
Из темнеющего сада…

But slow down, o day, curing
This heart of mine from breaking!
I want to grasp everything from
The darkening garden with my eyes…

Because this place is about to be removed or is actually being removed (torn down) from space, the poetic persona rushes here for the last time to take in the memories that he knows remain there. He wants to take what is no longer left. The elements of the setting are enumerated:

Щетку желтую газона,
На гряде цветок забытый,
Разоренного балкона
Остов, зеленью увитый.

Топора обиды злые,
Все, чего уже не стало…
Чтобы сердце, сны былые
Узнавая, трепетало…[5]

The yellow brush of the lawn,
A forgotten bloom in the flowerbed,
The skeleton of the destroyed balcony
Entwined in greenery.

---

[4] "Quiet Songs" («Тихие песни»), the title of Annenskij's first collection of poetry, is borrowed from Lermontov's poem "The Angel."
[5] Annenskij, "Pered zakatom," 75.

> The evil offenses of the axe,
> All that no longer exists...
> So that the heart, recognizing its former dreams,
> Would quicken again.

The axe has not finished its work and, as an antidote to personal lack of wholeness in the future (called in the poem a "breaking of the heart" [разлад сердца]), he wants to take in his "former dreams," which have already ceased to be, but are associated with that house, and keep them for himself. How different from and more positive this image is than Tjutčev's "forgotten, [now] enigmatic happiness," upon which he looks with a patronizing denial: "Oh, how now without faith or involvement I look upon you." Tjutčev's rejection of the family manor house at Ovstug and what he experienced living in it is ultimately a failure of faith on the part of the poet who said, "One can only believe in Russia."[6] On this occasion he failed to see the importance of emotional openness towards one's past that Proust exemplifies in the attitudes of his hero. In his study of Proust, Poulet has formulated this attitude thus:

> But in order for this past to be indeed the continuer of the self and the founder of an authentic present, in order for it to be the source of our restored faith ... any moment could be regained, or better, brought to significance.... One might call it an act of faith indefinitely retarded, then tardily accomplished; as if the reality regained in memory appeared richer in import, worthier of faith than it was lately in sensation.[7]

Such an act of faith is out of the question in the Tjutčev poem above. In Annenskij, on the other hand, it seems the poet hopes it will occur, because he is convinced that that house and setting contain some part of his necessary psychological sustenance which would be the basis of a continued authentic life, albeit regained, understood, and fit into the whole belatedly. This would seem to be the case were the poem's message not powerfully qualified by the next stage in his project, the very next poem in the collection, "The Night of Life" ("Nox Vitae") in which Annenskij speaks of a garden where "the wind, the maples, the sound of the heights / With the reproach of a long-ago prayer for the dead" is heard. This may well be the same "darkening garden" of the old family house mentioned in stanza 2 of "Before Sunset." Clearly the poet has returned to what is probably the same place for the identical reasons. But there is no light here:

---

[6] Tjutčev, "Umom Rossiju ne ponjat'," 259.
[7] Proust, quoted in Poulet, *Studies in Human Time*, 305–06.

> Но… в блекло-призрачной луне
> Воздушно-черный стан растений,
> И вы, на мрачной белизне
> Ветвей тоскующие тени!

> But in the pale-ghostly moon
> The airy black outline of the plants
> And you, melancholy shades of branches,
> On the gloomy whiteness [background]!

The old Puškinian personification of plants and trees is here mixed with the double meaning of *ten'*—both shadows of plants and shades of past friends and family:

> Как странно слиты твердь и сад
> ....
> Как ночь напоминает смерть
> Всем, даже выцветшим покровом.

> How strange the firmament and garden have flowed together
> ....
> How much this night in every detail reminds us of death,
> even with its faded shroud.

He is overwhelmed by the feeling that the past buried in his family garden is not that remote.

> А все ведь только что сейчас
> Лазурно было здесь, что нужды?
> О, тени, я не знаю вас,
> Вы так глубоко сердцу чужды.

> Or still only just now
> Was it azure here, as blue as one could wish?
> Oh, shades, I don't recognize you,
> You are so deeply alien to my heart.

Despite this feeling of physical proximity, his sense of alienation from the figures he encounters is profound, and his elegiac attempt to reestablish contact with his past and past self ends in fiasco:

> Неужто ж точно, Боже мой,
> Я здесь любил, я здесь был молод,

И дальше некуда?.. Домой
Пришел я в этот лунный холод?⁸

Can it possibly be true, good Lord,
that it was here that I loved and here I was young,
And there's nowhere else?
Can it be that I have come home to this moonlit coldness?

Poulet is very eloquent on the experience of former self as former place we see in Tjutčev and Annenskij: "it is a place ... disconnected from its [erstwhile] occupant, because nothing in it responds to the demand of his thought.... Then, in the consciousness of the hostile refusal of things to put themselves in touch with the mind, [he] takes account of the depth of his solitude.... thought ... ceaselessly imposes upon us metamorphoses, which perpetually changes us into another 'self,' and ... every instant makes of us, and for us, a stranger."⁹

In Axmatova's "Fourth Northern Elegy," a work probably directly intertextually connected to these two poems of her mentor, Annenskij, the poet dramatizes the same experience of the irretrievability of a past. She admits, however, that the reason for this is that she is "dead to it," implying a failure of the faith of memory, an inability to reintegrate that particular past into the self. Lidija Čukovskaja considers this well-known work the most pessimistic in Axmatova's *oeuvre*.¹⁰ In view of the value the Acmeists placed on memory, Čukovskaja appears to be right at first perusal. Let us examine this elegy closely, however, section by section. Its subject is the slow retreat of memories and dying friends from the self, and in particular of a most important memory, which Bachelard would call an "original" memory, associated with a particular house. The situation described is identical to what we observed in the Annenskij poem above.

Четвертая

Есть три эпохи у воспоминаний.
И первая—как бы вчерашний день.
Душа под сводом их благословенным,
И тело в их блаженствует тени.
Еще не замер смех, струятся слезы,
Пятно чернил не стерто со стола,—
И как печать на сердце, поцелуй,

---

⁸ Annenskij, "Nox Vitae," 77.

⁹ Poulet, *Studies in Human Time*, 294.

¹⁰ Lidija Čukovskaja, *Zapiski ob Anne Axmatovoj, 1952–62* (St. Petersburg: Neva, 1996), 2: 130 ff.

Единственный, прощальный, незабвенный…
Но это продолжается недолго…

Reminiscence has three epochs.
And the first is like yesterday.
The soul is under their [the reminiscences'] vault,
And the body blissful in their shadow.
Laughter has not yet died down, tears pour forth,
The inkspot is not erased from the table,
And a kiss is like a seal upon the heart,
The only, farewell, unforgettable kiss…
But this does not last long…

Here we see a deceased friend (or one from whom the speaker has been otherwise separated) under the "vaulted ceilings" of reminiscence, suggestive of a church and funeral service:

Уже не свод над головой, а где-то
В глухом предместье дом уединенный,
Где холодно зимой, и летом жарко,
Где есть паук и пыль на всем лежит,
Где истлевают пламенные письма,
Исподтишка меняются портреты,
Куда как на могилу ходят люди,
А возвратившись, моют руки мылом,
И стряхивают беглую слезинку
С усталых век—и тяжело вздыхают…
Но тикают часы, весна сменяет
Одна другую, розовеет небо,
Меняются названья городов

There's no more vault overhead, but somewhere
In a dull suburb there is an isolated house,
Where it's cold in winter and hot in summer,
Where there's a spider and dust on everything,
Where flaming letters smolder
And imperceptibly portraits change,
A place people go as to a grave
And, coming back, wash their hands with soap,
And wipe away a fleeting tear
From their eyelids—and sigh heavily…
But the clock ticks, one spring

> Replaces another, the sky grows rosy,
> The names of cities are changed

This last remark reminds us of "Soviet" time and the fate of St. Petersburg. The poet continues alluding to that public aspect of loss of memory and the official taboo placed on the past, particularly on the Silver Age, which was the formative period of Axmatova's life and the period of her poetic debut. People are unwilling to reminisce partly because they are afraid, while others cannot because they have been arrested or killed:

> И нет уже свидетелей событий,
> И не с кем плакать, не с кем вспоминать.
> И медленно от нас уходят тени,
> Которых мы уже не призываем,
> Возврат которых был бы страшен нам.

> Eyewitnesses of events are no longer here,
> There's no one to cry with or reminisce with,
> And our shades slowly leave us,
> And we don't summon them any more,
> Their return would be frightening to us.

The question arises here as to whether Axmatova, so dedicated to remembering her dead poet-brothers (in her Antigone stance) is speaking in the elegy of herself personally or of the common situation of people in Russia and elsewhere or both.

> И, раз проснувшись, видим, что забыли
> Мы даже путь в тот дом уединенный.

> And once awakened, we see we have even forgotten
> The way to that isolated house.

Both internal and external political factors (totally absent in Annenskij's poems) conspire to produce a virtual loss of a part of people's biographies. This is what Mandel'štam meant when he said, "Today Europeans are plucked out of their biographies" [2: 269]. Yet the memory of what has been lost remains, and we rush frantically to regain it:

> И, задыхаясь от стыда и гнева,
> Бежим туда, но (как во сне бывает)
> Там все другое: люди, вещи, стены,
> И нас никто не знает—мы чужие.

And, choking from shame and anger,
We rush there, but (as in a dream)
Everything is changed: people, things, the walls,
And no one knows us—*we* are the outsiders.

This devastating statement is followed by the repetition of the message in a colloquial form that reads as harsh and ironic: «Мы не туда попали» ("We've come to the wrong place"). It is common for Axmatova to use simple colloquialisms in very tragic situations, thereby elevating the colloquialism and ironizing or making light of the situation in which it is uttered. Here the poet seems to parrot the comment of the current residents of the house. It is, of course, an only too correct statement, but uttered without an inkling of the «туда» (thither/there) the poet sought to reach.

Axmatova's «Мы не туда попали, Боже мой!» ("We've come to the wrong place, Good Lord!") reads like an echo of Annenskij's slightly shorter «Неужто ж точно, Боже мой!» («Can it possibly be true, good Lord"). Axmatova's continuation is somewhat longer but clearly inspired by his two poems, constituting not an imitation of Annenskij but a variation on a theme of Annenskij:

И вот когда горчайшее приходит:
Мы сознаем, что не могли б вместить
То прошлое в границы нашей жизни,
И нам оно почти что так же чуждо,
Как нашему соседу по квартире,
Что тех, кто умер, мы бы не узнали,
А те, с кем нам разлуку бог послал,
Прекрасно обошлись без нас—и даже
Все к лучшему… [1: 313]

And this is when the most bitter thing occurs:
We realize that we could not accommodate
That past into the bounds of our life
And that it is almost as alien to us
As to our neighbor,
That those who died we'd no longer recognize
And those we parted from
Got along famously without us and that it's even
All for the best…

The very many poems of Axmatova which constitute conversations with dead poets, conversations often far livelier than her dialogues with the living, belie the final statement of the "Fourth Northern Elegy." The weight of the evidence dissuades us from taking Axmatova literally when she speaks of such rank alienation from her own past and says that it is "all for the best." Few were the people of Axmatova's generation who were as able as she to recall, re-evoke, and recreate in poetry the vivid world of the Silver Age. Nevertheless, she too had the experience of meeting stone walls, and perhaps she wished to give it vivid expression here in poetry, as Annenskij had done.

Most problematic is the line "it's even all for the best," which represents a radical departure from Annenskij's despair that he cannot cure his heart from breaking in any final and effective way. Where Axmatova is concerned, we are familiar throughout her *oeuvre* with the sense that some pasts should be left dead and not rummaged in, as, for example, in her "Third Northern Elegy":

> Мне ведомы начала и концы,
> И жизнь после конца, и что-то,
> О чем теперь не надо вспоминать. [1: 311]
>
> I know ends and beginnings,
> And life after the end, and something
> It's better not to reminisce about.

This is not, it seems to us, the case of the "Fourth Elegy." Because of the fact that a particularly "severe epoch" can speed and encourage the process of forgetting, Axmatova has interjected twentieth-century historical-political realities into Annenskij's (not temporally specific) thematics. Yet the simple fallibility of memory also comes into play. At the opening of her memoir of Mandel'štam entitled "Pages from a Diary," her first comment is about Lozinskij's death depriving her of someone with whom she could have reminisced and checked the veracity of her memory's version of things: "And Lozinskij's death somehow broke the thread of my reminiscences...." [2: 166]. The degree of Axmatova's isolation in the forties in talking about Mandel'-štam's death and other such matters is quite clear from Isaiah Berlin's conversations with her in 1946, as recorded in *Personal Impressions*:

> Then she spoke her own poems from *Anno Domini*, *The White Flock*, *From Six Books*— "Poems like these, but far better than mine [her known assessment of Mandel'štam as a superior poet to herself, *not* Gumilev] were the cause of the death of the best poet of our time, whom I loved and who loved me..."[11]

---

[11] Isaiah Berlin, *Personal Impressions* (New York: Viking Press, 1980), 193.

In 1953, the year of Stalin's death, she dares to complain and be ironic about enforced or legislated amnesia. This can also be seen as a reproach to herself inasmuch as the other *Northern Elegies*, and especially the third, show some self-recrimination for allowing herself, to whatever degree, to participate in the general trend of forgetting. The passive "My life has been substituted. Into another riverbed, / Passing something alien, the river has flowed, / And I do not recognize my own shores" is transmuted in the "Fourth" (1945) into the active "We realize that we could not accommodate / That past into the bounds of our life."

Sometimes it is impossible; sometimes the small changes in the interior of a house, as well as the new people that the Soviet state has now assigned to live in that house, who have never heard of "us," nor know that *we* once inhabited these rooms—all this can sometimes conspire to kill all connection *we* should be able to feel with the place. Sometimes it effectively robs us of our own past and we superficially shrug off the loss of that self: "it's even all for the best." Yet this comment is part of an entire section following a colon which is preceded by this framing sentence: "And this is when the most bitter thing occurs." At first reading, it may seem that "the bitterest thing" is that we are outsiders in the very much changed and now alien place to which we returned. Yet after several perusals we see that "the bitterest thing" may be the fact that we passively shrug this new status of alienation off and lie to ourselves about it, that we try to suppress and devalue the past associated with the place and underestimate its importance for our present life. If this is so, the whole poem takes on a completely different complexion. It does not then preach the cavalier forgetting that so upsets Čukovskaja, but rather the message that losing one's past *and then acting as if it is unimportant or even better for "life"* is the real tragedy, a message Čukovskaja would find more palatable. Perhaps the very fact that the last lines are ambiguous enough to admit of these two interpretations guarantees that the actual thought will reach the reader one way or another. Even if he understands it as Čukovskaja does, he will think he is disagreeing with Axmatova, when actually he has been pushed to the conclusion she wants him to reach by a more contrary path.

The whole striving of Axmatova's poetic and prose work corroborates our conclusions concerning her elegy on the "epochs of remembrance." The avowed aims of her prose memoirs, published with commentary by L. I. Mandrykina and by Axmatova's close friend, the scholar Vitalij Vilenkin, contradict any notion of Axmatova's succumbing gracefully to the loss of memory and saying "so what?" She wanted in the "unwritten book" which is her memoirs to put together certain important parts of her past life and herself, "that this might remain." She did not believe in the consecutivity of memory or in "respectable" biographies which falsify by subjecting things to a strict chronological order: "Any attempt at coherent [chronological] memoirs is a falsification; no human memory is constructed to remember things in order.... It doesn't matter where one begins: in the middle, the end, or the beginning" [2: 178].

"Pro domo mea," which can be rendered in Russian as «за свой дом», is the opening section of this biographical book. Vilenkin is most likely correct in his assumption that "The subtitle of the first section, 'Pro domo mea,' refers essentially to the conception of the book as a whole" [2: 178]. The part on Mandelʹštam is but a chapter of a whole which links him intimately to her creative life and that of her generation. Her long-term struggle in prose and poetry to relate to and to immortalize her relation to the great cultural figures of her past in the face of natural and unnatural forgetting and amnesia show her constantly trying to wrest from *mea domus* whatever she can. The pain and the repeated attempt to "come home" are the truth of the story, one fraught with failures and disappointments, which inspire the poet to keep up her struggle against oblivion.

A clear case of a former self still inhabiting a former house is found in Axmatova's "There my shade has remained and is melancholy," written in 1917:

Там тень моя осталась и тоскует,
Все в той же синей комнате живет,
Гостей из города за полночь ждет
И образок эмалевый целует.
И в доме не совсем благополучно:
Огонь зажгут, а все-таки темно...
Не оттого ль хозяйке новой скучно,
Не оттого ль хозяин пьет вино
И слышит, как за тонкою стеною
Пришедший гость беседует со мной?   [1: 167]

There my shade has remained and is melancholy,
It is still living in the same dark blue room,
Awaiting guests from the city after midnight
And kissing the enamel icon.
And it's not completely comfortable in the house:
They left a fire, but it's still dark...
Isn't that why the new mistress is bored?
Isn't that why the master drinks wine
And listens how behind the thin walls
The guest who came is talking to me?

This poem shows part of the self left behind in a former house in which the lyric persona lived with a lover or husband. The shade of herself is there, still doing what she used to do (receiving guests), and as a kind of immanent spirit in the house she keeps the new wife/mistress of the house on edge and the master upset.

Another interesting image of the relationship between the self and its former haunts can be found in Brodskij's 1962 poem "Everything is strange for a house's new tenant." Here, however, the emphasis is on a former self who has *not* remained behind. Like Axmatova, Brodskij presents his poem partly from the point of a view of a new tenant/self who, because of a lingering sense of someone else's having inhabited the space, does not feel "at home" in his new lodgings. In fact, this residue of a former self is sensed not so much through its actual presence, as through the loyalty of the *space*—the rooms and furniture—to its previous tenant. Brodskij is typically very specific about the details of rooms, and he is as preoccupied with interiors and furniture as he is with the details of façades:

> Все чуждо в доме новому жильцу.
> Поспешный взгляд скользит по всем предметам,
> чьи тени так пришельцу не к лицу,
> что сами слишком мучаются этим.
> Но дом не хочет больше пустовать.
> И, как бы за нехваткой той отваги,
> замок, не в состояньи узнавать,
> один сопротивляется во мраке.
> Да. Сходства нет меж нынешним и тем,
> кто внес сюда шкафы и стол и думал,
> что больше не покинет этих стен;
> но должен был уйти, ушел и умер.
> Ничем уж их нельзя соединить:
> чертой лица, характером, надломом.
> Но между ними существует нить,
> обычно именуемая домом.   [1: 200]

Everything is strange for a house's new tenant.
[His] quick glance slides across all the objects,
whose shadows so don't suit the newcomer,
that they themselves are anxious about it.
But the house doesn't want to stand empty anymore.
And as if because of the lack of that courage,
the lock, in no condition to recognize anyone,

> alone protests in the gloom.
> Yes. There is no similarity between this one and the one
> who brought the shelves and table in here and thought
> that he would never leave these walls;
> but he had to go away, he went away and he died.
> There's nothing now to unite them:
> a facial feature, character, a crack [a nervous breakdown].
> But a thread does exist between them,
> one that is usually termed a house.

The possibility that the former tenant (the one who "went away and died") and the new tenant are parts of the same self is made clear by the word "now" (*už*) in line 13, as well as in line 14 by a hint at some traumatic "splitting" occasioned by a *nadlom* (a crack or nervous breakdown, in the best tradition of Petersburg doubles). Thus we have a new self who in no way resembles the old one, and in fact is utterly unrecognizable to the very space where he had previously lived.[12] Similarly, the space itself seems "foreign" to the newcomer. The self that "went away and died" is in fact a powerful presence in his *absence*, felt by both the rooms and the new tenant. The walls, furniture, and even the lock on the door *remember* "the one who brought the shelves," and do not want to adjust to another resident, despite their equally strong desire not to remain empty. The house does not recognize "this one," nor can it retrieve "that one," and yet, as a spatial image of memory, it provides the one connection they share. The space in this poem is, indeed, the only thing "holding together" the fragmented parts of the personality described herein.

Both here and in the Axmatova poem "There my shade has remained," the former self has physically moved (or even "died"), but psychologically for all concerned that former self is still *there*, whether as a full-blown presence that "lives in the same dark blue room" or as a painfully-felt absence. In another of Brodskij's poems from 1962, "I embraced those shoulders," we find a variant of the fragmented self: the speaker has physically returned, expecting his shade to have remained, but finds it not there to greet him. Here again we find the same specificity of detail in descriptions of interior space that we saw in the previous poem:

> Я обнял эти плечи и взглянул
> на то, что оказалось за спиною,

---

[12] Here we might recall Poulet's comment on Montaigne's philosophy of self: "The feelings of the past self become as enigmatic to the present self as those of a sranger" (Poulet, *Studies in Human Time*, 44). For Brodskij, however, this is not a joyful diversity but a rather painful sense of alienation and foreignness.

и увидал, что выдвинутый стул
сливался с освещенною стеною.
Был в лампочке повышенный накал,
невыгодный для мебели истертой,
и потому диван в углу сверкал
коричневою кожей, словно желтой.
Стол пустовал. Поблескивал паркет.
Темнела печка. В раме запыленной
застыл пейзаж. И лишь один буфет
казался мне тогда одушевленным.

Но мотылек по комнате кружил,
и он мой взгляд с недвижимости сдвинул.
И если призрак здесь когда-то жил,
то он покинул этот дом. Покинул.   [1: 163]

I embraced those shoulders and looked
at what happened to be behind [her] back,
and I saw that the pushed-out chair
was flowing into the lit-up wall.
The light bulb was of a high voltage
not advantageous for the worn furniture,
and that's why the couch in the corner was gleaming,
Its brown skin virtually yellow.
The table was empty. The parquet shone.
The stove was dark. In a dust-covered frame
a landscape froze. And only
the sideboard seemed to me then to be animate.

But a moth circled around the room
and he moved my gaze from immobility.
And if a ghost once lived here,
well, it has left this house. Left it.

Here the "shoulders" appear to be those of a beloved (or, rather, formerly beloved) woman. No sooner does the poet embrace them on the threshold than he searches the premises for the shade of his former self that should be in the house. He hopes to recognize himself in the configurations of the furniture, to be able to fit himself into the place and into the love relationship once more. The furniture looks dead, faded, and yellow. Everything is less animated than he had hoped. As we read the cold, objectivized treatment of the items of furniture scrutinized, we feel the coldness and alienation from the place and person that the man is experiencing, an alienation made more intense by the fact that he is still locked in the embrace. This room is the landscape of his inner self at that moment. The self is as dead as the room. A moth and the buffet are the only signs of animacy left there. The final two sentences convince us, by emphatic use of reiteration, that the self he came there to find has long since departed this place. Here there is no question of a space that protests this departure: this is a de-animated space, not the highly sensitive lock and walls that we saw in "Everything is strange for a house's new tenant."

Our treatment of these failed attempts to retrieve a self embedded in a place would be incomplete without one more poem of Brodskij, again a much more ironic one on the surface than Axmatova's "Fourth Northern Elegy" but one involved just as profoundly in the return and just as full of disappointment at the irretrievability of a past self (and thus perhaps even closer to Tjutčev). Brodskij's bitter irony in some poems borders on that of another Petersburg poet, the émigré Georgij Ivanov, whose negativity grates on some readers. Here is an example of Ivanov's negations:

Хорошо, что нет Царя.
Хорошо, что нет России,
Хорошо, что Бога нет.
....
Хорошо—что ничего.[13]

It's good there is no tsar.
It's good there is no Russia,
It's good there is no God.
....
It's good that there is nothing.

Let us consider how Brodskij treats his return in his 1961 poem "You go back to your hometown" (part of the cycle *July Intermezzo*) in which the "hometown" is Petersburg. The influence of Axmatova's ironic "and it's even all for the best" is quite clear, as is Mandel'štam's "Leningrad":

Воротишься на родину. Ну что ж.
Гляди вокруг, кому еще ты нужен,
кому теперь в друзья ты попадешь.
Воротишься, купи себе на ужин

какого-нибудь сладкого вина,
смотри в окно и думай понемногу:

---

[13] Georgij Ivanov, "Xorošo, čto net carja," 52.

> во всем твоя, одна твоя вина.
> И хорошо. Спасибо. Слава Богу.   [1: 87]

> You go back to your hometown, so what?
> Look around, who else needs you,
> whose company will you fall into.
> You go back, buy yourself for supper
>
> some sort of sweet wine,
> look out the window and think a little:
> it's all your fault, yours alone.
> And that's good. Thank you. Thank God.

The Blokovian image of the poet drinking alone—*in vino veritas*—in "Neznakomka" is compounded by the very alienated homecoming here. Brodskij then continues with a series of anaphorae:

> Как хорошо, что некого винить,
> как хорошо, что ты никем не связан,
> как хорошо, что до смерти любить
> тебя никто на свете не обязан.
>
> Как хорошо, что никогда во тьму
> ничья рука тебя не провожала,
> как хорошо на свете одному
> идти пешком с шумящего вокзала.

> How good it is that there's no one to blame,
> how good it is that you have no ties,
> how good it is that you're not obliged
> to love anyone until death.
>
> How good it is that no one's hand
> ever led you into darkness,
> how good it is to walk alone in this world
> from a noisy train station.

Here follows the ending of the poem, which exceeds Axmatova's "Fourth Northern Elegy" in ambivalence and retains Tjutčev's rejection of the native place. It is similar to Tjutčev's in the poet's disappointment at the lack of a sense of home and rejection of it as the abode of his original self, mixed with the sense that that self is in him and that he is just rejecting and denying it. The Romantic disappointment, disillusionment, and harsh treatment of the native place indeed approach Tjutčev's:

Как хорошо, на родину спеша,
поймать себя в словах неоткровенных
и вдруг понять, как медленно душа
заботится о новых переменах.

How good it is, rushing home,
to catch yourself in insincere words
and suddenly understand how
slowly the soul concerns itself with new changes.

This ending is a masterpiece of ambiguity. In one interpretation, the more adult self that is returning realizes that all his denial of his feelings about returning to Petersburg is nonsense, that all the phrases beginning "how good it is" have been insincere, except the last. The soul at first seems to be happy and not worried or willing to face the fact that the returning self is a somewhat different person from the one who he thinks remains in that place. This interpretation, if it is what Brodskij has in mind, calls forth structural and strategic echoes in the poem «Тоска по родине» ("Missing Home"), a work by one of his most admired poets, Marina Cvetaeva.[14] There the émigré who says that she lives in a "house, and one that doesn't know it's mine / Like a hospital or barracks," denies any importance to a native city, country, or house. This haunting image is combined with a description of herself as an extreme loner with no house, a "Kamčatka bear without an ice floe." Taming bears and the personification of the bear, even providing them with the name and patronymic Mixail Semenovič, is a very *Russian* custom, and it can be argued that this metaphor already goes a long way to Russify this "soul born somewhere or other." She states in quite extreme terms that past connections have no meaning for her in the art of "word weaving":

Мне все равны, мне все равно
И может быть всего равнее
Роднее бывшее всего.

All people are the same to me, everything is the same to me
And perhaps I am most indifferent
To that which I once loved most.

This contrary position reminds us of Lermontov's in his poem "Gratitude." After saying that no place matters, neither city nor country, Cvetaeva undoes it all in the final sentence.

---

[14] See especially Brodskij's *Razgovory o Cvetaevoj* (Moscow: Nezavisimaja gazeta, 1988).

Но если по дороге куст встает
Особенно рябина…[15]

But if a bush appears on the road
Especially a snowberry bush…

Then all the above is cancelled out, and in Brodskij's poem "insincere words" are a species of lies to the self, to numb the self (perhaps like Axmatova's "all is for the best").

Yet the other, equally feasible interpretation of the concluding lines of the last stanza of Brodskij's "You go back to your hometown" is quite different. It implies that as he was leaving the busy train station, having been met by no one, he caught himself full of sentimental "nonsense" and replaced it with a commonsensical, and true, ending: his present self has no real connection with the place to which he is returning. Sentimental ideas about homecoming are a Romantic nostalgic myth that deserves to be exploded, and are exploded in the poem. This is tantamount to a rejection of a Romantic younger self who espoused such ideas and would have been dismayed by such a return.

Yet the ambiguity of the ending, the fact that it admits of two diametrically opposed interpretations, signifies rather that both these attitudes are alive in Brodskij, representing a synchronic split, as similarly opposed attitudes do in Cvetaeva's poem. He both affirms and rejects the hold of the place and the past upon him. Tjutčev does the same, rejecting the youthful self at Ostvug more cruelly, but no more convincingly, and perhaps even protesting too much.

AMBULATORY ATTEMPTS TO RETURN TO THE SELF AND TO REACH PETERSBURG'S CENTER

In this type of poem, multiple past selves are dispersed over a large territory of greater Petersburg which functions as a "great house" whose center the lyric ego is walking through and wishes to regain. The plurality of selves hidden in the wider space makes this model, as well as the goal of reaching the center city/center self, more complex. Brodskij, like Mandel'štam, is a very ambulatory poet.

W. H. Auden, a favorite of Brodskij's, treats the body as a city (probably Dublin) in his poem on the death of Yeats, a poem Brodskij certainly knew:

---

[15] Cvetaeva, "Toska po rodine," *Stixotvorenija* (Moscow: Sovetskij pisatel', 1964), 304–05. Nabokov makes the same point, but specifically about Petersburg: "the mental image of matted grass on the Yayla, of a canyon in the Urals or of salt flats in the Aral Region, affects me nostalgically and patriotically as little, or as much, as, say, Utah; but give me anything on any continent resembling the St. Petersburg countryside and my heart melts" (*Speak, Memory*, 250).

> ... it was his last afternoon as himself,
> The provinces of his body revolted,
> The squares of his mind were empty,
> Silence invaded the suburbs[16]

This image of the poet's dying body as a city presents his arms and extremities as the suburbs, while his torso, heart, and mind, etc., are its central squares. Perhaps Brodskij had Auden in mind when he wrote the following in 1967:

> ... город
> обычно начинается для тех,
> кто в нем живет, с центральных площадей
> и башен.
> А для странников—с окраин.   [2: 48–49]

> ... for those who live in it the city
> usually begins
> from its central squares
> and towers.
> But for wanderers, it begins from the outskirts.

Brodskij has called Petersburg a part of the heart of Russia—the mediastinum. As a many-time heart patient, he has a heightened awareness of the anatomical cavity which encases the heart, and such a metaphor betrays identification and involvement.

In his 1962 poem "From the Outskirts to the Center," Brodskij presents a series of locations, all of which lie on a horizontal plane within the city through which he moves. He gives us an example of the walking poet-wanderer attempting to return to the city center, which symbolizes a return to the center of the self. The placement of this poem in the collection *A Halt in the Desert* immediately after "You go back to your hometown" influences our reading of the latter in that it points up once again the obvious ambiguities on which that work ends. "From the Outskirts to the Center" emphasizes the poet's centripetal movement, towards the center of a unified self, mind, and heart that are the object of his quest. Brodskij borrowed his first line, "I visited again," from Puškin, emphasizing that this is a reintegrative journey, although the place visited, unlike Puškin's Mixailovskoe and Tjutčev's Ovstug, is not a family's country estate, which Brodskij, of course, did not possess. He spent his childhood in old, central Petersburg, and tries to go back there.

---

[16] W. H. Auden, "On the Death of W.B. Yeats," *Selected Poetry* (New York: Random House, 1958), 52.

He begins with Puškin's famous line, but then, like Tjutčev («Итак опять я увиделся с вами, / Места немилые, хоть и родные» ["Again I saw you / Places not dear, although native"]), casts aspersions on the idyllic quality of the locale. Brodskij writes with greater irony vis-à-vis its ugliness, and is ironic about the fact that his "loves" occurred in these unromantic locales:

> Вот я вновь посетил
> эту местность любви, полуостров заводов,
> парадиз мастерских и аркадию фабрик,
> рай речных пароходов   [1: 217]
>
> Here I have visited again
> this locale of love, isthmus of industrial plants,
> paradise of workshops and Arcadia of factories,
> paradise of river ferries

This is possibly the most complete de-idyllization of Petersburg in the entire tradition: an adult realism recontextualizes what was experienced by youth as a beautiful "paradise," an idyllic "Arcadia." The lyric hero is situated in the industrial area directly east of the city center across the Neva, in one part of what Belyj's narrator in *Petersburg* had imagined as the "many-chimneyed distances" separated from the historic heart of the city:

> я опять прошептал:
> вот я снова в младенческих ларах.
> Вот я вновь пробежал Малой Охтой сквозь тысячу арок.
>
> I whispered again:
> Here I am again in my childhood haunts [Lares].
> Here I have again run through Malaja Oxta through a thousand
>   archways.

Here the almost incantatory power of Puškin's phrase is made clear as the poet draws attention to his own repeated utterance of it. Now he is following a familiar route, perhaps in the hope that he will encounter his own past selves along the way (as the saying goes, "Our Lares are always with us"). The next stanza alludes to Gumilev's vision of simultaneous access to multiple points in space and time in "The Tram that Lost Its Way," here suggesting the possibility that the speaker will have a similarly transcendental experience of a multi-dimensional Leningrad. Then, just as Tjutčev confronted his double for a moment, the noise of the tram accompanies the moment when Brodskij's hero faces one of his doubles:

за спиною трамвай
прогремел на мосту невредимом,
и кирпичных оград
просветлела внезапно угрюмость.
Добрый день, вот мы встретились, бедная юность.

behind my back a tram
rumbled on an unharmed bridge,
and the gloominess of the brick fences
suddenly shone through.
Good day, here we've met again, poor youth.

This greeting with a younger self in an atmosphere of gloom seems directly drawn from Tjutčev's 1849 poem:

И где теперь туманными очами,
При свете вечереющего дня,
Мой детский возраст смотрит на меня.

And where now with foggy eyes,
In the light of fading day,
My childish age gazes upon me.

Yet whereas Tjutčev's return has no allusion to music, sounds of the past—the aural accompaniment to Brodskij's ambulatory journey—are important. In "Before Sunset," Annenskij had wanted to hear the music of his own Russian past. Axmatova, when she hears the music in *PWH*, cannot silence it. Brodskij's music is the sound of trams, of Dixieland jazz, train whistles, factory whistles, and steamboats on the river Neva. For example, in another vision prompted by a sound association, Brodskij's speaker hears the "jazz of the suburbs" and suddenly sees himself indoors, leaning over his "native record player" and listening to Dixieland jazz:

не душа и не плоть—
чья-то тень над родным патефоном,
словно платье твое вдруг подброшено вверх саксофоном.

neither spirit nor flesh—
someone's shade over the native record player,
as if your dress were suddenly thrown up like a saxophone.

The appearance of this youthful self, like others he meets on his journey towards the center, is associated with the places the speaker is re-encountering and the sounds he hears; he sees these versions of past selves as "shades." They have a real spatio-temporal presence for him, but they are not animated; they are "neither spirit nor flesh." As he continues on his way, the pluralization of meeting places in Brodskij's poem (unlike Tjutčev's) serves to multiply the number of former selves met. They are numerous youthful selves at different junctures:

> … в подворотнях, в парадных
> ты стоишь на виду
> на мосту возле лет безвозвратных

> … in the entryways and front doors
> you stand in plain view
> on the bridge next to unreturnable years

The latter image is a remarkable example of spatialized time, of its presentation in physical "chunks" (which Belyj had been the first to do with Petersburg spaces). Brodskij's lyric hero stands on a bridge next to a "pile of years," which seem themselves to be architectural features as much as the bridge.

As the speaker continues to walk, he keeps encountering youthful selves, and addresses them in what seems to be an ongoing echo of Tjutčev's earlier poem:

Tjutčev	Brodskij
Мой детский возраст смотрит на меня.	Добрый день. Ну и встреча у нас. До чего ты бесплотна:
……………………	……………………………
Смотрю я на тебя, мой гость минутный,	До чего ты бедна. Столько лет, а промчались напрасно.
Куда как чужд ты стал в моих глазах—	Добрый день, моя юность. Боже мой, до чего ты прекрасна.
Как брат меньшой, умерший в пеленах…	
My childish age gazes upon me. … I look upon you, my momentary guest, How terribly alien you have grown in my eyes— Like a younger brother who died while still in diapers.	Good day. What a meeting this is. How fleshless you are: … How poor you are. How many years, and they fled by in vain. Good day, my youth. My God, how beautiful you are.

In his much longer poem, Brodskij sees the meagerness of the places of his youth, but does not reject the pieces of the youthful selves as Tjutčev had rejected his "childish age," whom he treated as a "younger brother who died while still in diapers." Brodskij acknowledges that he is meeting dead selves, but he wants to find them again and revivify them. This is a main purpose of his return.

He then appears to recall a particular winter from his youth and the events thereof, and as he moves towards the center of the city he searches for the self he had been during that time:

> Это наша зима.
> Современный фонарь смотрит мертвенным оком,
> предо мною горят
> ослепительно тысячи окон.
> Возвышаю свой крик,
> чтоб с домами ему не столкнуться:
> это наша зима все не может обратно вернуться.

> This is our winter.
> A contemporary streetlight looks on with a dead eye,
> before me burn blindingly
> thousands of windows.
> I raise my cry
> so that it won't bump into the houses:
> this is our winter that just can't come back to us.

He recognizes that winter, the experiences of that time, and his own past self embodied in the familiar spaces of the city, but despite his impassioned attempts to call to that self ("I raise my cry"), he cannot actually retrieve it (it "can't come back"). Only in death, according to Brodskij, will all the selves and life as a whole—including the self of that important past winter—be recollected and reintegrated:

> Не до смерти ли, нет,
> Мы ее не найдем, не находим.
> От рожденья на свет
> ежедневно куда-то уходим

> Not until death, no,
> We won't find our winter, we don't find it.
> From our moment of birth
> we are daily departing for somewhere

Brodskij spatializes this centrifugal movement with the specific topography of Petersburg/Leningrad, with which the lyric hero deeply identifies; the city itself, after all, becomes more like "Petersburg" and encounters more of its "past selves" in its central regions.

The speaker goes on to describe in more detail the fragmentation of the self: one's whole life is a dispersion of various selves, as if one were called from the innermost center of oneself into the suburbs, enticed by someone. We are constantly running in different directions, summoned by a self out there on the periphery:

> ежедневно куда-то уходим,
> словно кто-то вдали
> в новостройках прекрасно играет.
> Разбегаемся все. Только смерть нас одна собирает.

> we are daily departing for somewhere,
> as if someone in the distance
> in the new sections of town is playing marvelously.
> We are constantly running in different directions. Only death alone
>   collects us.

The last line admits of two readings: 1) we all (all our "selves") keep running in different directions, and 2) we keep constantly (adverbial use) running in different directions. The image of multiple selves collected by death has a clearly existentialist ring, and reminds us of the dynamism of the personality of Montaigne once more. Brodskij's image of a self overwhelmed by centrifugal forces derives from the dynamics of the personality advanced by Vjačeslav Ivanov and elaborated by Osip Mandel'štam in "The End of the Novel." For Mandel'štam, the ego is a dynamic tension caused by centrifugal (decomposing) forces and centripetal forces of cohesion. Centripetal forces for Mandel'štam are those connected with biography, memory, and a structure of personality. Centrifugal forces are those which tend to de-centralize, de-individualize, break a unified personality down into multiple, disconnected selves, destroying the sense of identity. In this chapter we have dealt with writers who feel that they have lost their self-center and that other, often inimical, doubles have come to dominate them. Time, as we have seen earlier, effects this change for many twentieth-century Petersburg writers, weakening the self's ability to remain intact. Such centrifugal forces affected Blok as winds in a window opened to the future; in Mandel'štam, we have the image of a coin at which time is chipping away; and in Zamjatin's "The Cave," we saw a self made of clay affected permanently by the dents and marks of time. In "The End of the Novel," Mandel'štam speaks aesopically about the dynamics of the individual personality and the great assault against individualism in the early 1920s:

> The measure of the novel is human biography or a system [of them...] moreover, the novel [parallel to the ego] holds together compositionally only so long as the centripetal forces of our solar system remain alive within [the self-sun] and as long as the centrifugal forces, those from the center to the periphery, do not prevail over the centripetal ones. [2: 268]

In Mandel'štam's metaphor, the self is a solar system whose sun must hold its planets within its orbit to exist as a self. He then goes on to make the analogy between the functioning of the novel as a system and the human personality as a system of memories explicit and even apocalyptic:

> The future of the novel will be no less than the history of the reduction to dust of biography as a form of personal existence. What is more, we will witness the catastrophic collapse of biography. [2: 269]

For Brodskij in "From the Outskirts to the Center," death may be the true gatherer of man's many selves, but he is determined to find a certain "winter" along the way. He characterizes death as a great meeting, which is reminiscent of the rising of all souls on Judgment Day. Axmatova alludes to such a gathering when she meets so many deceased friends in *PWH* (some of whom she says are her doubles, hence other "selves"); and, speaking to Ol'ga Glebova-Sudejkina, the main heroine of the Petersburg in *PWH*, the poet-persona says: "You are one of my doubles." Brodskij similarly describes the finding of his multiple doubles or selves:

> Значит, кто-то нас вдруг
> в темноте обнимает за плечи,
> и полны темноты,
> и полны темноты и покоя,
> мы все вместе стоим над холодной блестящей рекою.

> So someone suddenly
> embraces us by the shoulders in the dark,
> and full of darkness,
> and full of darkness and tranquillity,
> we all stand together over the cold shining river.

In this image, the doubles suddenly act upon the speaker: their vague shapes embrace him. Unlike Goljadkin, whose evil double emerges from the moment in space and time when the older self is standing over a Petersburg bridge railing and peering into the water below, the "darkness" that enters Brodskij's speaker at a comparable moment is associated with *peace*—he had been in search of his double/past self all along. As he collects his dispersed selves, he asks *who*, which self, is indeed doing the collecting:

> Неужели не я,
> освещенный тремя фонарями,
> столько лет в темноте
> по осколкам бежал пустырями,
> ....
> Неужели не я? Что-то здесь навсегда изменилось.

> Can it be that it's not I,
> illuminated by three lanterns,
> who has run for many years in darkness
> along bits of glass through desert places,
> ....
> Can it be that it's not I? Something here has changed forever.

After asking who the collecting self is (and indeed doubting that it is the present self), he speaks of a mystical lone figure who moves along, much as the "sad, tall one" in Belyj's *Petersburg*, and like the ethereal Christ figure at the end of Blok's *The Twelve*:

> Кто-то новый царит,
> ....
> кто-то вечно идет возле новых домов в одиночку.

> Someone new is reigning,
> ....
> someone eternally walks alone near the new buildings.

In the ongoing march of time/history, new versions of the self (those who, at least temporarily, "reign") are always in search of their past counterparts in the spaces of the city. Brodskij's "From the Outskirts to the Center" is more like Axmatova's *PWH* than her "Fourth Northern Elegy" in the sense that there is no separation of the dead from the living. They meet on the same plane, and they are both immanent in Petersburg-Leningrad spaces:

> Значит, нету разлук.
> Значит, зря мы просили прощенья
> у своих мертвецов.

> So there are no separations.
> So we asked forgiveness
> from our dead in vain.

Thus, as the poet discovers, there seems to be a cyclical pattern of death-life-death implied in the patterns of centrifugal and centripetal movement here. And the Petersburg spaces through which he walks have the ability to retain features of lost—even dead—selves (including those of the poet). We remember, after all, that Brodskij's Petersburg is a "paradise of river ferries," where the Neva is the Lethe, and he is going to the *other, the ideal Petersburg*:

То, куда мы спешим,
....
дорогая страна,
постоянный предмет воспеванья,
не любовь ли она? Нет, она не имеет названья.
Это—вечная жизнь:
поразительный мост, неумолчное слово,
проплыванье баржи,
оживленье любви, убиванье былого,
пароходов огни
и сиянье витрин, звон трамваев далеких,
плеск холодной воды возле брюк твоих вечношироких.

The place to which we scurry
....
is a dear land,
the constant object of praise,
isn't it love? No, it doesn't have a name.
It is eternal life:
a striking bridge, a word that can't be silenced,
the floating by of a barge,
the renewal of love, the murder of the past,
the light of ferries
and the shine of store windows, the ringing of distant trams,
the splash of cold water near your eternally wide trousers [bell bottoms].

Nothing is forgotten by this ideal Petersburg's spaces: even the men's bell-bottom fashion of Brodskij's youth, immortalized in Aksenov's novel *The Burn* (*Ožog*) in a character symbolizing the 1950s in Russia, is here made into more than a passing fad. In Petersburg/Leningrad's "eternalizing" spaces, versions of past selves, along with their particular characteristics, become incorporated into the city. Brodskij then congratulates himself on the recovery of parts of himself from the past. It is a congratulation quickly tempered, however, by an ironic affirmation of loss—what he has "found" no longer belongs to him, but to the city and its "cold shining river":

Поздравляю себя
с этой ранней находкой, с тобою,
поздравляю себя
с удивительно горькой судьбою,
с этой вечной рекой,
с этим небом в прекрасных осинах,
с описаньем утрат за безмолвной толпой магазинов.

I congratulate myself
on this early find, on you,
I congratulate myself
on my amazingly bitter fate [life],
on this eternal river,
on this sky with its marvelous aspens,
on the description of things lost beyond the silent crowd of stores.

Although Petersburg's spaces allow the speaker to recognize his former selves and even interact with them, he will remain "less than one" until he dies, when death will prove to be the one thing all his selves have in common.

Mandel'štam had described such an otherworldly Petersburg in his 1930 poem "Leningrad":

Петербург! Я еще не хочу умирать:
У тебя телефонов моих номера.

Петербург! У меня еще есть адреса,
По которым найду мертвецов голоса.   [1: 158]

Petersburg! I don't want to die yet:
You have my telephone numbers.

Petersburg! I still have the addresses
By which I'll find the voices of the dead.

It was this same moribund quality that made Xodasevič call his Petrograd memoirs *Necropolis*, and prompted Axmatova to describe her reunion with the dead in *PWH*. "Leningrad," in which Mandel'štam repeatedly addresses the city as Petersburg, also has to do with a poet in search of former selves and a former city. We have mentioned how it, like Brodskij's poem, casts Petersburg as the place in which the poet desires to contact the dead (and his own dead selves). It also reminds us of the childhood illness imagery which we discussed in *The Egyptian Stamp*:

> Я вернулся в мой город, знакомый до слёз,
> До прожилок, до детских припухлых желёз. [1: 158]

> I returned to my city, familiar to the point of tears,
> To its veins, to its children's swollen glands.

This sick Petersburg refers to the sickly child Mandel′štam once was when he lived there, and Petersburg is by contiguity that sick child, his "child's age." We are further reminded of Dostoevskij's personification of the city in spring as a lovely young girl who is dying of consumption in "White Nights." In *The Egyptian Stamp* that mortally ill girl becomes Jewish and represents Memory, of which there is little left. The poet in "Leningrad" receives his guests up the back stairs of the Petersburg apartment:

> …в висок
> Ударяет мне вырванный с мясом звонок,
>
> И всю ночь напролёт жду гостей дорогих,
> Шевеля кандалами цепочек дверных. [1: 158]

> …Into my temple
> A bell pulled out with its flesh strikes,
>
> And all night long I await dear guests,
> Shaking the door chains like leg irons.

This co-presence of living and dead selves appears to have influenced *PWH*, where Axmatova is visited by a series of just such past selves, associates, and friends, although she does not summon them by phone or otherwise. Frantic phone calls to Persephone, to the underworld, we recall, were also made by Parnok in *The Egyptian Stamp*. The difference in Mandel′štam's contact with the dead and Brodskij's in "From the Outskirts to the Center" (or even Axmatova's) is that Mandel′štam's 1930s poem depicts something violent and sinister in the Leningrad to which the poet returns. In it the speaker's violent death seems to be a possibility at any moment. This feeling is increased by the repeated exclamation "Petersburg, I do not want to die yet!" uttered as a spell to keep him alive. The heavy chains on the door and the ripped-out doorbell convey a sense of murderous violence. It was about this "Leningrad" that Mandel′štam wrote three poems in December and January of 1930–31. In the second one, he admits how much he is still drawn to Petersburg, and in the last he prays to make it safely through the night without something nightmarish happening:

> Помоги, Господь, эту ночь прожить,
> Я за жизнь боюсь, за твою рабу…
> В Петербурге жить—словно спать в гробу.　　　　　　[1: 160]
>
> Help me, Lord, to live through this night,
> I fear for life, for your servant…
> Living in Petersburg is like sleeping in a coffin.

Though the Petersburg he returns to is already largely dead, he believes there is still present in it an underlying spirit that enables him to call it "my city." Mandel′štam was drawn back "though he foresaw the coming executions and fled the mutinous activities" [1: 159]. Brodskij's "From the Outskirts to the Center" was written in the Xruščhev era, and is much more positive than any of these three by Mandel′štam. Mandel′štam's "Leningrad" is devoid of Tjutčcv's hostility towards the "child's age" he meets in Ovstug. Another of Mandel′štam's poems, "With the imperial world," evokes the same images of childhood Petersburg seen in *The Noise of Time*, though with much greater compression. This poem first denies the "reality" or meaning for an adult of the childhood experiences recounted so vividly in such chapters of the autobiography as "French Ladies and Mutineers." Yet after two stanzas of denying that anything in his life was very centrally connected with the old Russian imperial world («с державным миром»), he admits that that world still holds him in its grip. As we shall see in much detail in chapter 9 below, this logically unresolvable problem is raised very poignantly in *The Noise of Time*, in a passage concerning the formative effects of Petersburg on the author as a small Jewish boy. It clearly influenced Brodskij's similar confessions in "Less than One," with the obvious exception that Brodskij described in much greater specificity and detail the influence of architecture on his intellectual and aesthetic formation, whereas Mandel′štam demonstrated the architectural influence in his poems. Mandel′štam wrote:

> The Petersburg street awakened in me a craving for spectacle, and the very architecture of the city inspired me with a kind of childish imperialism: I was delirious over the cuirasses of the Royal Horse Guard and the Roman helmets of the Cavalry Guard, the silver trumpets of the Preobrazhensky band.…
>
> All this mass of militarism and even a kind of police aesthetics may very well have been proper to some son of a corps commander.… but it was completely out of keeping with the kitchen fumes of a middle-

class apartment, with father's study, heavy with the odor of leathers ... with Jewish conversations about business.[17]

But what had I [as a Jewish child] to do with the Guards' festivals, the monotonous prettiness of the host of the infantry and its steeds, the stone-faced battalions flowing with hollow tread down the Millionnaya, gray with marble and granite?[18]

His answer is a kind of confession of love for the city as a large human creature, inspired mainly by its architecture:

And I say now, without a moment's hesitation, that at the age of seven or eight all of this—the whole massif of Petersburg, the granite and wood-paved quarters, all the gentle heart of the city [Brodskij's "mediastinum"] with its overflow of squares, its shaggy parks, its islands of monuments, the caryatids of the Hermitage, the mysterious Millionnaya Street, where there were no passers-by and where only one small grocery store had wormed itself in among the marble, but especially the General Staff Arch, the Senate Square, and all Dutch Petersburg I regarded as something sacred and festive.[19]

In "From the Outskirts to the Center," Brodskij speaks of his returning self as he moves inward; this self is aware of and reflects upon other "selves" he meets. He is a mediator, an alienated self that is free from too heavy a burden of memory (and in any case, why should *he* remember, if the city does it for him?):

Поздравляю себя!
Сколько лет проживу, ничего мне не надо.
Сколько лет проживу....

I congratulate myself!
How many years will I live, needing nothing.
How many years will I live....

But the rejection and conclusion is partly an excuse, because his return is ultimately a failure. The further in he goes, the less he feels that he is "a resident of the places"; he is rather a go-between, an interloper, not one lodged anywhere. The voice on the outskirts keeps calling him thither, preventing his concentrating on himself: he keeps being dispersed. Each return is a failure:

---

[17] Mandel'štam, *The Noise of Time*, 74.
[18] Ibid., 76.
[19] Ibid., 72–73.

Сколько раз я вернусь—
...словно дом запираю,
сколько дам я за грусть от кирпичной трубы и собачьего лая.

How many times will I return—
...it's as if I'm locking a house,
how much will I give for the sadness I feel from the brick chimney and
 a dog's bark.

His return to the center is more the locking up of a house, which punctuates his inability to open it, penetrate, and retrieve its inner depths, than the regaining of its contents, although his attempts to do so are repeated and painful. The whole narrative here is a painful play in which the words of a typical greeting in Russian after a long separation are repeated: «Сколько лет, сколько зим» "How many summers, how many winters [has it been since we last saw each other]?" In this poem Brodskij has taken Mandel'štam's dynamics of the personality, specifically the type in which the centrifugal forces are very compelling, and he has spread that dynamic self onto the entire topography of the Northern capital. He particularly narrates his walk back inward in which he attempts to cure himself, to make himself whole by reassembling the pieces. It is a complex reworking of "You go back to your hometown," carried out in the reverse order.

Underlying ambulatory returns of this type is Mandel'štam's famous passage about the exiled Dante trying to re-attain the center of his beloved Florence, not only by walking, but by writing:

> Love of the city, passion for the city, hatred for the city—that is the material of *The Inferno*. The rings of hell are nothing but the Saturnine rings of emigration. For an exile, his only, forbidden and irretrievably lost city is scattered everywhere. He is surrounded.... [2: 402]

Here Mandel'štam speaks of the exiled writer's attempt to "write his way back" to the heart of his city/self. For Brodskij, exiled in "From the Outskirts" from his former selves if not yet from Russia and Petersburg, this center remains elusive. The elegiac cast we have observed in this poem would take on an entirely new meaning, of course, in the Petersburg poems written after Brodskij's enforced emigration, when his walks through the city become an exclusively mental and creative exercise.

ABOLISHED TOWERS: THE FAILURE OF ARCHITECTURE TO CONTINUE SHAPING CONSCIOUSNESS

> Je suis … le veuf, l'inconsolé,
> Le prince d'Aquitaine à la tour abolie
> Gérard de Nerval, "El Desdichado"[20]

The motif of the "abolished tower" is prominent in Petersburg poetry from the destruction of Paraša's house in *The Bronze Horseman*, which drives Evgenij mad, to the removal of beautiful buildings in the twentieth century. Each loss is a blow to the city and its poets. Removal and disappearance are a constant threat and a painful reality. The 1989 book *Lost Architectural Monuments of Leningrad*[21] attests eloquently to this problem. The traditional curse that the city will be emptied out is emphasized by Brodskij with his usual irony: "the geometry of this city's architectural perspectives is perfect for losing things forever."[22] Brodskij, however, refuses to believe in the possibility of the total deletion of Petersburg's buildings. He takes his cue not only from Nerval, but from Axmatova, who asked in reference to Nerval's poem, «Кто знает как пусто небо / На месте упавшей башни?» ("Who knows how empty the sky is / In the place where a tower has fallen?") [1: 258]. The real question here is not the commonplace "how empty is it?" but "*how, in what way, is it empty?*" The implication is clearly that an "abolished tower" is a non-neutral emptiness, a more pregnant emptiness than one where there had been no tower in the first place. The abolished tower has what Brodskij calls "negative tangibility," and what Nabokov refers to as "unreal estate."[23] Such abolition is similar to Freud's description of conscious negation:

> The simple negative insertion transformation is a way to unsay what one is saying. Negation is addition because it has to include the positive statement it seeks to deny in its assertion. 'It is not my mother' [or 'he has an abolished tower'] is … a negative added to a positive. In this sense, negation is always tantalizing, provocative and ambiguous, a positive descriptive force which implies and promotes the very idea or thing it seeks to deny. It is an absence yoked to a presence, or a presence-evoking absence.[24]

---

[20] Gérard de Nerval, "El Desdichado," *Les Chimères* (Lille: Girard, 1949), 5.
[21] *Utračennye pamjatniki Leningrada* (Leningrad: Fond kul'tury, 1989).
[22] Brodsky, "A Guide to a Renamed City," *Less than One*, 74.
[23] Brodsky, "Footnote to a Poem," *Less than One*, 260; Nabokov, *Speak, Memory*, 40.
[24] Maire Jaanus, *Literature and Negation* (New York: Columbia University Press, 1979), 206–07.

In a similar way, Mandel'štam was very aware of the positive role of abolitions in art. He spoke of the hole that remains after a doughnut is eaten, a hole which still retains its shape. Writing about now-absent buildings of Petersburg and now-absent Petersburgers, Brodskij says that negative tangibility "impart[s] to non-existence the quality of an active process. The absence of usual … signs of being is not equated with non-being but *surpasses being in its tangibility* [italics ours]."[25]

Clinging to Petersburg buildings is a strategy for retaining one's best or original self. Failure to receive sustenance, a "source of support," from solid buildings because they are crumbling, or actively being razed to the ground, causes a predicament for the Petersburg poet: what is being abolished is a part of himself, that which formed and sustained him. Brodskij provides an excellent example of the ongoing abolition of a building and the ongoing loss of a sense of self and national tradition from the loss of architecture in his 1966 poem «Остановка в пустыне» ("A Halt in the Desert"). This Petersburg poem depicts a stop in a cultural wasteland, implying ironically that the city's negative *kenosis* has gone very far, and that the "shore of desolate waves" has been rendered a desert (*pustynja*) once again by the mid-twentieth century. This desert is in effect the undoing of Peter's complex project and a kind of fulfillment (and not only morphologically) of Tsarina Evdokija's curse, "May this place be empty!" The process of negation is dramatic in this poem, which tells how Petersburg is being emptied of its buildings. We cite it in large sections:

> Теперь так мало греков в Ленинграде,
> что мы сломали греческую церковь,
> дабы построить на свободном месте
> концертный зал. В такой архитектуре
> есть что-то безнадежное. А впрочем,
> концертный зал на тыщу с лишним мест
> не так уж безнадежен: это—храм,
> и храм исскуства.
> ……………………………………
> Жаль только, что теперь издалека
> мы будем видеть не нормальный купол,
> а безобразно плоскую черту.
> Но что до безобразия пропорций,
> то человек зависит не от них,
> а чаще от пропорций безобразья.

---

[25] Brodsky, "Footnote to a Poem," 260. Being is often equated by the Symbolists and others with writing—to name a thing is to call it into being.

Прекрасно помню, как ее ломали.
Была весна, и я как раз тогда
ходил в одно татарское семейство,
неподалеку живщее. Смотрел
в окно и видел Греческую церковь.
Все началось с татарских разговоров;
а после в разговор вмешались звуки,
сливавшиеся с речью поначалу,
но вскоре—загулшившие ее.
В церковный садик въехал экскаватор
с подвешенной к стреле чугунной гирей.
И стены стали тихо поддаваться.
Смешно не поддаваться, если ты
стена, а пред тобою—разрушитель.

....
Потом туда согнали самосвалы,
бульдозеры…И как-то в поздний час
сидел я на развалинах абсиды.
В провалах алтаря зияла ночь.
И я—сквозь эти дыры в алтаре—
смотрел на убегавшие трамваи,
на вереницу тусклых фонарей.
И то, чего вообще не встретишь в церкви,
теперь я видел через призму церкви.

Когда-нибудь, когда не станет нас,
точнее—после нас, на нашем месте
возникнет тоже что-нибудь такое,
чему любой, кто знал нас, ужаснется.
Но знавших нас не будет слишком много.
Вот так, по старой памяти, собаки
на прежнем месте задирают лапу.
Ограда снесена давным-давно,
но им, должно быть, грезится ограда.
Их грезы перечеркивают явь.
А может быть, земля хранит тот запах:
асфальту не осилить запах псины.
И что им этот безобразный дом!
Для них тут садик, говорят вам—садик.
А то, что очевидно для людей,

собакам совершенно безразлично.
Вот это и зовут: «собачья верность».
И если довелось мне говорить
всерьез об эстафете поколений,
то верю только в эту эстафету.
Вернее, в тех, кто ощущает запах.

Так мало нынче в Ленинграде греков,
да и вообще—вне Греции—их мало.
По крайней мере мало для того,
чтоб сохранить сооруженья веры.
А верить в то, что мы сооружаем,
от них никто не требует. Одно,
должно быть, дело нацию крестить,
а крест нести—уже совсем другое. [2: 11]

....

Сегодня ночью я смотрю в окно
и думаю о том, куда зашли мы?
И от чего мы больше далеки:
от православья или эллинизма?
К чему близки мы? Что там, впереди?
Не ждет ли нас теперь другая эра?
И если так, то в чем наш общий долг?
И что должны мы принести ей в жертву?

There are so few Greeks in Leningrad now
that we tore down the Greek Church
in order to build in the empty space
a concert hall. In such architecture
there's a certain hopelessness. And yet
a concert hall with over a thousand seats
is not so hopeless: it's a temple,
and a temple of art.

....

Only it's a pity that now from the distance
we'll no longer see a normal cupola,
but an ugly flat line.
But where the ugliness of proportions is concerned,
man depends less on them
and more often on the proportions of ugliness.

I remember perfectly how they tore it down.
It was spring, and I often visited a certain Tatar family
which lived nearby. I would look out
the window and see the Greek Church.
It all began with the Tatar conversations;
and later sounds mixed into the conversation
which at first blended with it
but soon drowned it out.
An excavator drove into the church garden
with a wrecking ball on it.
And the walls began to give in.
It's silly not to give in if you're
a wall, and there's a destroyer in front of you.

....

Then they brought in dump trucks,
bulldozers… And once, of a late evening,
I was sitting in the ruins of the apse.
Night was shining in the ruins of the altar.
And I—through these holes in the altar—
gazed at the rushing trams
and the string of dim streetlights.
And things that you never find in a church
I then saw through the prism of the church.

Someday, after we're gone,
that is to say, after our deaths, there will
arise in our places something
which will horrify anyone who knew us.
But there won't be many who did.
That's how, by ancient memory, dogs
raise their leg in the same old place.
The fence was torn down long, long ago,
but they see the fence in a daydream.
Their daydreams cross out reality.
And maybe the earth retains that smell:
asphalt can't overpower the smell of a dog.
And what is this ugly building to them!
For them there is a garden here, a garden, I tell you.
And things that are obvious to people
are totally irrelevant to dogs.

That's what they call "canine loyalty."
And if I had to speak
seriously about the relay race of the generations,
this is the only relay race I believe in.
Specifically, in those who have a sense a smell.

There are so few Greeks in Leningrad now,
and there aren't many in general outside of Greece.
At least, there are too few
to save the buildings of faith.
And to have faith in that which we build,
well, no one demands that.
It's apparently one thing to convert a nation,
but to bear the cross is something else again.

....

Tonight I look out the window
and think about where we have gotten to.
And what we are further removed from:
Orthodoxy or Hellenism?
And what have we come nearer to? And what is ahead?
Is another era awaiting us?
And, if so, what is our common duty?
And what must we sacrifice to it?

"A Halt in the Desert" is a *poèma* in unrhymed iambic pentameter, a meter used often for meditative moods by Puškin. Brodskij presents the problem of Petersburg's loss of beautiful architectural monuments, which is tantamount to Brodskij's loss of self. His diction is, as Puškin's often is, the colloquial Russian of the period. Like Puškin, Brodskij waxes more eloquent, using archaisms and more elegant turns of phrase when his attitude towards the event justifies it. At other times he is bitterly ironic, and the many short sentences and enjambments add an occasional choppiness to the language, which jars and supports the ironic stance.

We remember from his prose that Brodskij especially stressed the beauty and importance of churches among those buildings that comprise his "Peter." In his essay on Mandel'štam, "The Child of Civilization," Brodskij names what he considers the "strands" of Petersburg culture: it was "the capital of Imperial Russia, whose dominant religion was Orthodoxy, whose political structure was inherently Byzantine"; it was "the mediastinum of ... Russian Hellenicism"; Petersburg was "the spiritual center of [the empire], and in the beginning of the century the strands of that current were merging there the way they do in Mandelstam's poems."[26]

At first perusal, "A Halt in the Desert" may seem to be a straightforward meditative monologue, but it complains about more than the razing of a specific church, or buildings in general. The event the poet witnesses from the household of his Tatar acquaintances is raised in the course of the poem to the level of a symbol of the loss of Petersburg, and to a large degree of the loss of self. If we take literally the opening line, "There are so few Greeks in Leningrad now" («Теперь так мало греков в Ленинграде») then when we hear its chiastic refrain («Так мало нынче в Ленинграде греков») many lines later, we can only take it symbolically after the intervening material. "Greek" here means both Orthodox Christian and Hellene, someone who understands both these traditions and appreciates the beauty of form and proportion like Hellenic Greeks did. Brodskij vacillates between an emphasis on pagan Greek culture and aestheticism and Greek Orthodox religion. This is an old Petersburg habit: these are the two poles Merežkovskij moves back and forth between in pendulum fashion. Both of these elements that went into Petersburg converge in this church. The Greeks in the poem are Brodskij himself and the "old dogs" who remember the Church and still "see" its beauty. The contours of that beauty seem to be Brodskij's greatest preoccupation as he repeatedly contemplates the ugliness and lack of proportion of its replacement. Earlier we read in Brodskij that a true Petersburger was bound to associate virtue with proportion. Here he rephrases this sentiment in a chiasmus, saying that men do not depend on the ugliness of proportions, but on the proportions of the ugliness (*bezobrazie*), a word that could even convey atrocity. Greek Petersburg for Brodskij was a place of beauty; Leningrad is a place with a preponderance of vulgarity and ugliness/atrocity.

Russia's destructiveness, often directed against herself and her own achievements, is strongly experienced by the poet, and he feels some guilt for it as he ponders Russia's historical problems. It is not by chance that the Church is destroyed to the music of the Tatar language. We recall the adage: "Scratch a Russian and you'll find a Tatar." The Tatars were traditional destroyers of ancient Rus', and in this poem modern technology has been added to their arsenal of weapons. Petersburg poets such as Mandel'štam associate Tatar cruelty with Muscovy, and this image may contain some of the same anti-Soviet/anti-Moscow connotations.

Brodskij personifies the collapsing walls of the church, thus identifying with those walls as he apostrophizes them with the familiar *ty*, in a comment which is concomitantly directed to the reader/listener: «Смешно не под-

---

[26] Brodsky, "The Child of Civilization," *Less than One*, 130–31.

даваться, если ты / стена, и перед тобою—разрушитель» ("It's silly not to give in if you're / a wall, and there's a destroyer in front of you"). This reminds the reader familiar with Mandel′štam of his interesting personification of trees as heroes who resist felling, even when it is inevitable. Brodskij excludes such heroics as a possible option here: the church is felled easily and puts up no resistance. It, and his generation of poets perhaps, lack Mandel′štam's mettle.

Brodskij then places himself inside the partially ruined church, and looks at nocturnal Leningrad through the prism formed by that dismantled building. What he sees is a modernized cultural wasteland, a place being rapidly returned to its primeval state. He is repelled by what he knows will be its future ugliness: «мы будем видеть не нормальный купол, / а безобразно плоскую черту» ("we'll no longer see a normal cupola, / but an ugly flat line"). His attachment to the partially dismantled building entails a sense of disenfranchisement from what he possessed by right in his childhood—the right to be molded and formed by the beauty of buildings such as this one. Now, without leaving "Peter," he is being dismantled along with it.

After making this point, he turns from meditation upon himself, the church, and his generation to the breaking of tradition that such barbarous acts imply. Something frightening will replace us, in the same way the concert hall has now replaced the church and we, like it, will be forgotten. As an antidote to this forgetting he introduces his "Greek dogs"—old dogs, who, as the English adage (which Brodskij, as a translator from the English, certainly knew) has it, "can't learn new tricks." These dogs are a modern hypostasis of the Hellene/Greek, although outsiders may treat this person as a "cur." Perhaps he alludes to the mangy dog at the crossroads of history in Blok's *The Twelve*. These dogs return to urinate as of old on the church's fence, despite the fact that it is gone, because they still see it. They remain faithful to what has been "torn down." Their inner vision (daydreams) crosses out the new, ugly reality. This ability to smell the past and see through to it even when its physical objects have been removed is Brodskij's religion of culture: «верю … в тех, кто ощущает запах» ("I believe in those who have a sense of smell.") It is here that he closes the frame which consists of the first line and its chiastic reworking:

> Now there are so few Greeks in Leningrad
> So few now in Leningrad Greeks there are

He continues treating the Greeks as bearers of Orthodox religion, using variants on the root *ver* (*fidel, faith*):

- собачья *вер*ность (canine loyalty, i.e., the needed quality, faithfulness to the self and to Petersburg-Russian culture)
- *вер*ю в тех (I believe in those, i.e., his ideal)
- *вер*нее (more correct or probable)
- сооруженья *вер*ы (buildings of faith)
- *вер*ить в то, что мы сооружаем (to have faith in that which we build)

Still, in the modern day no religious-cultural building or construction of any kind is possible. Thus the poem which begins with the following chiasmus:

безобразие пропорций	ugliness of proportions
пропорции безобразья	proportions of ugliness

ends with a chiasmus on buildings of faith, which are churches on the one hand and on the other, the mental edifice of belief, of building up faith. It is clear that his generation is building things that no one, neither Greeks nor anyone else, believes in. He then comments in another two lines that are a chiasmus with an internal sonic chiasmus:

```
            A    B
Одно, должно быть, дело нацию крестить,
а крест нести—уже совсем другое [дело]
     b                          a
```

Here the chiasmic structure is very interesting in that the elements A (*delo*) and B (a sonic element, *nac*, which turns to *nes*) are crisscrossed inside. Inasmuch as chiasmus gives a pithy, aphoristic sound to two-line statements, because of its frequent use in the Bible, these chiasmata may be perceived as particularly highlighted parts of the poem's message. In this poem they are numerous:

A	греки		Ленинград	B
C	безобразие		пропорций	C
D	пропорции		безобразья	C
B	Ленинград		греки	A

E	сооруженья		веры	F
F	верить		мы сооружаем	E

G	одно дело	H	нацию крестить	I
I	крест нести	H	другое дело	G

Not only is this a work about the destruction of architecture, but the insistent presence of chiasmus expresses formally the canceling effect that is occurring. A-B—B-A expresses a sequence in which there is a change followed by a reversion to the original state. Just as Peter the Great began in an empty place and filled it with beautiful buildings, so the place of beautiful buildings is now experiencing their cancellation and being rendered empty once more. Chiasmus, in its witty, tongue-twisting repetition of the same roots in quick succession, can also cause momentary confusion or delayed comprehension; these effects of wit, confusion, and the irony of the very structured form these statements are in makes the poem's message a kind of sad architectural joke. Thus even in an unrhymed *poèma* in a kind of meditative elegy (close in form to a monumental elegy), the structural outlines of the work are given in sharp relief. There is a strong sense of balance and proportion in this long work, which is about the *destruction* of things beautifully balanced and proportioned. Thus there is a kind of tension between the work's message and its very graceful form, a form that neither the enjambments nor the occasional very colloquial diction manage to destroy. They are like vernacular adornments (gingerbread) on a classical edifice.

The very coda of the poem poses historiographical questions about Russia's future path which at the same time concern what Brodskij himself, as a Russian poet, should be or become. There is a clear case made in the work that Petersburg has been unable to remain faithful to itself through the blows of history—what Blok calls historical vengeance. Petersburg has largely lost its path, and the poet is having great difficulty holding on to his faith and his own path. Gazing out of his window onto the "window on Europe," he feels as if he is in a desert. Yet the desert is an ambiguous symbol because it is negative on the one hand (as in Eliot's *Wasteland*), but it is there that Puškin and Isaiah have the experience of renewal that makes them prophets and that puts them on an even truer path. Brodskij asks:

И от чего мы больше далеки:
от православья или эллинизма?

And what are we further removed from:
Orthodoxy or Hellenism?

Leningrad is far away from both strains of Petersburg (Petropolis) that he holds dear. He senses that he is on the brink of a new age and that he must change himself to be ready for it. He is a "Greek," and there is nothing in the environment in which he can have faith—neither architectural beauty nor spiritual beauty (religion)—and he tries to cope in his poem with the inner emptiness which that fact produces in him. If these buildings, including churches, shaped his character/content when he was a schoolboy, their removal is causing him to be emptied out; like the walls of the church, his faith and personality are "caving in." Such poems represent his protest against the bulldozer. What Brodskij expresses in this poem is the progressive loss of Russia's former cultural content which causes his "loss of himself." Like Puškin's prophet in the desert, he bears witness to that which only "blind ones" (poets), like himself, and "old dogs" can see: "daydreams cross out reality."

The emptying process of Petersburg, and the emptying and devastation of Brodskij's sense of self that it causes and symbolizes, is what we have called a negative *kenosis* (see p. 8). It implies a greater tragedy and greater suffering than traditional Orthodox *kenosis*. According to Father Fedotov, in the Russian notion of sainthood and Christology, Christ (or a saint in imitation of him) sacrifices himself, pouring his divinity completely out into the world, thus divinizing the world and rendering himself empty of divinity—i.e., fully human. His divinity is a positive element spread throughout the world.

The emptying-out of Petersburg and the devastation of the lives of Petersburgers we see as the subject of the poems in this and the preceding chapter is a perverse variation on *kenosis*, virtually a negative *kenosis*. The process of emptying out is projected on an enormous, supra-individual being—the city. Its architectural monuments as well as its churches are destroyed, "devoured by a hungry state" (in Mandel'štam's words), and a parallel process of psychological divestment, the negative *kenosis* of the individual Petersburger, occurs. In the poetic identification between self and space that we have been presenting, however, both Petersburg and the self who lives there are united in their common suffering; the process of divestment undergone is one that domesticates the formerly antagonistic city and, as we shall see in part 3, sometimes idyllizes those ominous forces which had seemed to come from within the city itself. Thus it is that the threat of emptiness comes from the outer storms of Time and History, while within the city space, poets like Brodskij can declare that both Petersburg's buildings and Petersburg poets "feel most at home in the foul weather of late fall or of premature spring and its showers mixed with snow and its impetuous disoriented squalls."[27]

DEHISTORICIZED ELEGIAC RETURNS TO PETERSBURG: THE CASE OF NABOKOV

One may wonder why Nabokov's numerous written returns to Petersburg and his native places in *Speak, Memory* and in his poetry were not included in our section on "ambulatory attempts to return" above. His returns *are* often ambulatory, and their aim seems to be self-reintegration. Indeed, the subtitle of *Speak, Memory*, "An Autobiography Revisited," makes it sound as though his project should fit squarely in the Puškin-inspired "I visited again" category of self-space identification. Yet such is not the case. Though Nabokov's returns have the external earmarks of the (positive) Puškinian and (negative) Tjutčevan return, in which a self changed by time confronts an irretrievable past self, they are in fact a Nabokovian subversion of the tragic significance of multiple selves. His returns minimize the effects of time's passage on selfhood in a unique way. We include this interesting case in the "historical" category because Nabokov, rather than denying history's effects on the self (a strategy typical in the "ahistorical" type of identification to be seen in chapters 6–8), writes these effects into a pattern subject to his own control, thereby in a sense "dehistoricizing" them.

The subversion here consists in the totally imaginary aspect of the place returned to—so-called "Petersburg"—and the amount of control to which the quest is subjected. We are told early on in his autobiography that Nabokov's Petersburg no longer exists—it is entirely inaccessible in empirical space and has dropped out of time/history, replaced by a paltry parody of itself, Soviet Leningrad. Nabokov's return, then, is the most cerebral and imaginary of the ones discussed in this chapter, a return and a destination totally enclosed and controlled in his rather solipsistic selfhood.

An important caveat must be voiced here: Nabokov's autobiographical and lyric persona is not to be confused with those characters in his fictional art who are under history's sway, diminished and psychically devastated by the revolution and other historical events. These fictional characters do sometimes undertake physical returns to Petersburg/Russia in search of a sense of personal wholeness. Not so their creator: he resists any admission that history,

---

[27] Brodsky, "Less than One," *Less than One*, 90.

despite its very real and painful upheavals, had caused him personally the loss of self that the hero of his novel *Podvig* (*Glory*), for example, feels and undertakes to rectify. Nabokov executes an imaginary, mental return, but never could or would equate Soviet Russia with *his* destination. In *Speak, Memory* (or, in Russian, «Другие берега», *Other Shores*), he is at great pains to emphasize "other," but not in the sense of Herzen's title,[28] where the "other" means non-Russian, European shores. It may seem that Nabokov's shores differ in that they are not geographical, but temporal. Yet they are in fact more intangible even than time-boundedness would suggest. His shores exist outside of the usual temporal flow; they are "unreal estate" that Nabokov nevertheless owns, delimits, and controls as one would a piece of property. He begins his autobiographical project by looking across to this *other*, intangible and yet still creatively accessible shore: "…from my present ridge of remote, isolated, almost uninhabited time, I see my diminutive self celebrating on that August day 1903, the birth of sentient life."[29] The shore image occurs again with allusion to the river Oredež near his family estate, this time from the opposite direction:

> The house, I am told, still stood there in 1940, nationalized but aloof, a museum piece for any sightseeing traveler…. the fair Oredezh had a festive air at that spot. Farther down … it was deeply suffused with the reflections of great, romantic firs (the fringe of our Vyra); and still further downstream, the endless tumultuous flow of a water mill gave the spectator … the sensation of receding endlessly, as if this were the stern of time itself.[30]

Nabokov's "other shores," then, are not those of the Mediterranean resorts where he penned the memoir, but are rather "another kind of shore," the shores of his childhood Petersburg which cannot be returned to physically because the place itself has been rendered totally "other."

Nabokov's "unreal estate," for which he quests and which he revisits in his autobiographical and lyrical pieces, is the creation of an excessively controlling elegist. He says his autobiographical impulse is to "follow … thematic designs [in his] life,"[31] designs which were, are, and will be for him part of a highly individual pattern that is preconceived and of which he is preeminently aware aforetimes. He is not genuinely "writing his way back" to recapture lost time or lost selves. He does not really admit that history has dealt him divisive or

---

[28] *From the Other Shore*, a collection of autobiographical and historical essays, written 1847–50.
[29] Nabokov, *Speak, Memory*, 22.
[30] Ibid., 72–73.
[31] Ibid., 27.

killing blows; that is to say, it is not that the blows dealt had no effect on him, but that they were *anticipated and part of the pattern*.

In chapter 10 of *Speak, Memory* Nabokov documents his birth as a poet ("the summer of 1914, when the numb fury of verse-making first came over me").[32] In particular, these pages show the teenage Vladimir as an elegist. Beautiful descriptions of the composition of his first elegy are followed by passages which show that the plan of his life dictated the generic choice. His elegiac stance produces controlled elegies that anticipate and mitigate their own sadness, and this stance is the model of Nabokov, the autobiographer.

The elegy protects Nabokov from the blows of time/history not retrospectively, but anticipatorily. His attitude toward Petersburg-Russia and his self-identification with them is best exemplified in his first love for Tamara, who is elevated virtually into a symbol of Nabokov's Russia. Tamara, his first mature love, and his coming-of-age as a man and as a poet-elegist are anticipated; he is waiting to meet, fall in love, possess, *and lose* her: "It seems hardly worthwhile to add that, as themes go, my elegy dealt with the loss of a beloved mistress—Delia, Tamara or Lenore—whom I had never lost, never loved, never met but was all set to meet, love, lose."[33] He writes elegies of prospective sadness and future nostalgia. Thus he expects and parries the blows of time and fate like a chessmaster who sees the game many moves ahead. This personal ability to outwit history is the hallmark of Nabokov as elegist and autobiographer. In *Poem without a Hero* (see chapter 11), Axmatova seems to know in the early 1940s that she will have a "guest from the future" in 1946 (as the final work stands), but she does not anticipate the outcome of the journey to her past and confrontations with past selves that the *poèma* narrates. Axmatova is perplexed, and has even been "turned from the riverbed" of her early life by the "real twentieth century." She is broken, divided, and alienated from her youthful self by the revolution and other events of her biography: «Все расхищено, предано, продано» ("Everything is plundered, betrayed, and sold off"). Nabokov treats the historical cataclysms of his young life as *expected* events time had in store—the Bolševik revolution fulfills his life pattern. He knew it would come, as he knew he would suffer over the loss and separation from Tamara. Time, in imitation of a pre-controlled elegy, obliges him with a concrete Tamara whom he loves, loses, and leaves. The role of the revolution in this chain of events is its expected role, and he strolls across the Tsarist/Soviet time boundary unbroken. Rather than fragmenting Nabokov's

---

[32] Ibid., 215.

[33] Ibid., 225. What seem to be references to Tibullus (Delia, his beloved) and Poe (Lenore) are in fact probably references to Mandel'štam's collection *Tristia*, where Delia is mentioned in the poem "Ja izučil nauku rasstavan'ja" and Lenore is mentioned in the poem "Solominka."

selfhood, history is treated as cementing or fulfilling it. At the end of chapter 11 of *Speak, Memory*, just after the young Nabokov has recited his first elegy to an appreciative mother, he looks into a mirror, and we catch him in the act of anticipating a divisive future and immediately reorganizing the "pattern" of his self to encompass this catastrophe, long before it actually happens:

> Looking into my own eyes, I had the shocking sensation of finding the mere dregs of my usual self, odds and ends of an evaporated identity which it took my reason quite an effort to gather again in the glass.[34]

The deliberate juxtaposition of this prescient moment with his first attempts at writing poetry show clearly that the controlled elegy is his autobiographical approach to the integration of self and (Petersburg) space.

Interestingly, Nabokov projects his own controlling elegiac stance onto many members of his own generation of Russians, dubbing them "geniuses" of memory.[35] In *Speak, Memory* Nabokov points out at least thrice the excessive propensity of his generation to store up details from the soon-to-be-eclipsed world where they spend their childhood. He also claims that it was a hereditary trait in his family: "The act of vividly recalling a patch of past is something that I seem to have been performing with the utmost zest all my life…"[36] His mother, in particular, is portrayed as similarly clairvoyant about Petersburg's future. She was a major force in the development of his exceptional retrospective faculty:

> "*Vot zapomni* (now remember)," she would say in conspiratorial tones as she drew my attention to this or that beloved thing in Vyra.… As if feeling that in a few years the tangible part of her world would perish, she cultivated an extraordinary consciousness of the various time marks [marks viewed in space] distributed throughout our country places. She cherished her own past with the same retrospective fervor that I now do her image and my past. Thus, in a way, I inherited an exquisite simulacrum—*the beauty of intangible property, unreal estate.*… [italics ours] Her special tags and imprints [spread in space] became as dear and as sacred to me as they were to her.[37]

Nabokov claims the death and therefore physical absence of the Petersburg world in which he grew up, the abolition of "the kind of Russian family to

---

[34] Ibid., 227.
[35] Ibid., 25.
[36] Ibid., 75.
[37] Ibid., 40.

which I belonged—a kind now extinct...."[38] Thus, as we see, Nabokov admits that history has had (will have) an effect on him and those people and places he loves; otherwise his and others' special talent for memory would not hold such significance.

In such an admission, Nabokov seems nostalgic, but he also then largely denies that the harsh time he lived in has forced him to lose his childhood; after all, he has seen it coming. He reserves the right to yearn for that childhood even before it has been lost, although he is sure he will reintegrate it into his life "to help him endure further losses," ensure his wholeness, and complete the "thematic design" that encompasses even such disruptive historical events:

> Beneath the sky
> Of my America to sigh
> For *one* locality in Russia[39]

This "locality" is fairly large, including the old capital with the lovely mansion Nabokov grew up in, and the family estates in the St. Petersburg district such as Vyra, Batovo, and Rožestveno. Different memories and childhood-to-adolescent "selves" with experiences including first love are dispersed throughout those places. He claims to want to render these experiences truthfully, to recall them fully, for he himself has falsified them and forced their forgetfulness by "loaning" them to characters in his fictional works. While not denying the craftsmanship aspect of all writing, including autobiography and memoir, Nabokov insists that in this particular work he is fashioning and rendering *himself* more than he is anything else. The dispersal of self which his autobiographical exercise addresses is as much a literary as it is a temporal phenomenon:

> I have often noticed that after I had bestowed on the characters of my novels some treasured item of my past, it would pine away in the artificial world where I had so abruptly placed it.... its retrospective appeal had gone and, presently, it became more closely identified with my novel than with my former self, where it had seemed to be so safe from the intrusion of the artist.[40]

Not only time, but even the writer's craft had served to disperse Nabokov's once unified self. Once again, however, this is a disruptive force under the ever-watchful control of the elegist who counts such disruption as a necessary part of the overall, (re)-integrated pattern: "The break in my own destiny af-

---

[38] Ibid., 79.
[39] Ibid., 73.
[40] Ibid., 95.

fords me in retrospect a syncopal kick that I would not have missed for worlds."[41]

The retrieval of items of Nabokov's past from his novels is essential because time/history is destructive to them when they are lent to his novelistic characters. Time/history grinds down and empties his novelistic heroes the same way it does a lyric poet who acknowledges time. But it must be recalled that Nabokov the writer of fiction *controls, even creates, that time and history* and lets his characters writhe under its blows. As we shall see in chapter 10, his character Lužin, with whom he has a great deal in common, lacks control over biographical time, which he perceives as his enemy in a life-and-death chess game. Lužin's outcome is tragic. Nabokov the autobiographer, by contrast, ends his book in 1940 with the diligent and successful solution of a *chess problem*, and as his son Dmitri stands between his parents the way he did at age three, we see an end which is a beginning, the symmetrical, controlled, and *solved* puzzle of Nabokov's successful defense against history/time.

While Brodskij is ambivalent about trips imagined in space, Nabokov believes that they are possible and salubrious:

> I confess I do not believe in time. I like to fold my magic carpet, after use, in such a way as to superimpose one part of the pattern on another. Let visitors trip. And the highest enjoyment of timelessness—in a landscape selected at random—is when I stand among rare butterflies and their food plants. This is ecstasy.... It is like a momentary vacuum into which rushes all that I love.[42]

These Proustian epiphanies visit Nabokov with a certain frequency. Places recalled *are* himself:

> I see again my school room in Vyra, the blue roses of the wallpaper, the open window. Its reflection fills the oval mirror above the leathern couch where my uncle sits.... A sense of security, of well-being, of summer warmth pervades my memory. That robust reality makes a ghost of the present. The mirror brims with brightness; a bumblebee has entered the room.... Everything is as it should be, nothing will ever change, nobody will ever die."[43]

---

[41] Ibid., 250.

[42] Ibid., 139. This thought bears an uncanny resemblance to certain comments about Henri Bergson in Mandel'štam's "Puškin and Skrjabin." For further discussion, see chap. 9, below, p. 305.

[43] Ibid., 76–77.

This full receipt of the past he is seeking, as well as the sense of stoppage of time, the eternity of the moment, renews Nabokov. He does not write himself back, but writes himself "whole." He imagines himself, like Brodskij, as a wanderer on foot. He would not be admitted to the USSR, but he wants to be a ghost there, an invisible observer. In Brodskij the ghosts were the past selves ("neither spirit nor flesh"). Just as Brodskij wished to attain a particular winter, so does Nabokov. In Nabokov the émigré the invisible ghost is the *present* self, and the past characters and selves he is creating are more "solid."[44] They, like the rushing butterflies, will confer on him more substance, and his programmed return is bound to be successful.

In the story of Mademoiselle O., Nabokov's most memorable governess, he returns as a ghost to the winter of 1905–06:

> I was not there to greet her; but I do so now as I try to imagine what she saw and felt at that last stage of her fabulous and ill-timed journey....
>
> I can visualize her, by proxy ... and vainly my ghostly envoy offers her an arm that she cannot see. ("There I was, abandoned by all, *comme la Comtesse Karenine*"....) Zahar takes over—a burly man in sheepskin.... I hear the snow crunching under his felt boots....
>
> Very lovely, very lonesome. But what am I doing in this stereoscopic dreamland? How did I get here? Somehow, the two sleighs have slipped away, leaving behind a passportless spy standing on the blue-white road in his New England snowboots and stormcoat.... The snow is real, though, and as I bend to it and scoop up a handful, sixty years crumble to glittering frost-dust between my fingers.[45]

This crumbling of snow is the binding of past and future. Time is concretized in a melting evanescent substance, chosen also by Axmatova as the temporal substance in *PWH*, where the past melts into the future («как тогда снежинка на руке / доверчиво и без упрека тает» ["like then a snowflake on the hand / melts trustingly and with no reproach"]). Nabokov goes back and walks forward; he "continue[s] for another stretch along my private foot-

---

[44] This "ghostliness" of the present self revisiting Petersburg (here the country estate) is also expressed by his fictional character Fedor Godunov-Čerdyncev in *The Gift*: "Perhaps one day, on foreign-made soles with heels long since worn down, feeling myself a ghost despite the idiotic substantiality of the insulators, I shall again come out of that station and ... walk along the footpath that accompanies the higway...." Vladimir Nabokov, *The Gift*, trans. Michael Scammell and Vladimir Nabokov (New York: Vintage International), 25.

[45] Nabokov, *Speak, Memory*, 98–99.

path which runs parallel to the road of that troubled decade."[46] In a similar way, in the autobiographical present (1951) he accompanies his mother out to buy the huge Faber pencil for her sick son at Treumann's store. In these revisits to past moments he more fully experiences Mademoiselle's arrival than he had in life at the time, and the same may be said of his mother's efforts on his behalf. This is what Poulet calls achieving the moment that had been unachieved in [its] time,"[47] that is, giving it greater meaning belatedly. It is fuller because it is embellished in art.

In chapter 9, part 3 of *Speak, Memory*, Nabokov deals with memories directly connected with the city and his rides to school. And later, in his romance with his first love, Tamara, they are forced to continue their summer love affair in a wintertime Petersburg with nowhere to hide or meet privately. That winter in Petersburg is depicted as particularly hard. This passage is a classic in the Petersburg tradition: "… we were reduced to exploring the wilderness of the world's most … enigmatic city. Solitary street lamps were metamorphosed into sea creatures … by the icy moisture on our eyelashes." Their experience transforms space:

> As we crossed the vast squares, various architectural phantoms arose with silent suddenness right before us. We felt a cold thrill, generally associated not with height but with depth—with an abyss opening at one's feet—when great, monolithic pillars of politic granite … zoomed above us to support the mysterious rotundities of St. Isaac's Cathedral. We stopped on the brink, as it were, of these perilous massifs of stone and metal, and with linked hands, in Lilliputian awe, craned our heads to watch new colossal visions rise in our way—the ten glossy-gray atlantes of a palace portico … or that enormous column with a black angel on its summit that obsessed, rather than adorned, the moon-flooded Palace Square.…[48]

Here we have a totally metapoetic comment on the superior status of verbal creations like Puškin's poetry to architectural monuments, here the Alexander Column: the angel on the column strives upward "to reach the subbase of Puškin's 'Exegi monumentum.'"[49] All these walks and rides with Tamara around Petersburg became poems. Nabokov's elegiac quest for his past, which constitutes the whole of *Speak, Memory* and the happy finding of some beloved people and former selves, is very Proustian (although it actually goes be-

---

[46] Ibid., 29.

[47] Poulet, *Studies in Human Time*, 306.

[48] Nabokov, *Speak, Memory*, 237.

[49] Ibid.

yond the Proustian project). It is a prose version of the return to Petersburg already seen in some of the poetry above.

Yet, as we have seen, Nabokov's anticipatory control of coming sadness is a different stance from that of the post-revolutionary writers treated here, who are seeking in physical and imagined Petersburg space abolished selves that history deprived them of, in many cases embedded in destroyed or drastically altered buildings. Mandel'štam had written of the last Egyptian, the would-be Jewish poet Parnok, «Я князь невезенья» ("I am the prince of ill-luck"), a line referring clearly to Gérard de Nerval's first *chimère* "El Desdichado."[50] Nerval's protagonist, an Orphic figure who descends to help a Eurydice rise to the upper world, is described as "le Prince d'Aquitaine à la tour abolie" ("the prince of the abolished tower"), just as a nobleman such as Nabokov, who inherited a large estate shortly before the revolution, is a prince of "unreal estate," i.e., of an abolished country, but one that still exists as a Nervalian pregnant emptiness.

The figure described by Nabokov as controlling elegist is both circular and spiralate (he envisions his own life as "a colored spiral in a small ball of glass");[51] in describing the pattern of his life, present and future feed into the past, while the past feeds into the lyric or autobiographical present (here we are reminded again of his understanding of time as a "folded magic carpet"). This is a strategy Nabokov employs and elaborates in his novel *The Gift* as well as in his own autobiography. The extra dimension of art and the possibilities of a life conceived of as a controlled elegy are what allow the circle, in turn, to gain three-dimensionality as a spiraling "design" and an exit from mere repetition (the unfortunate case of Nabokov's fictional hero Lužin, as we shall see in chapter 9). The blows of history are real and acknowledged; they are responsible for his reliance on "unreal estate" and his physical separation from "other shores." Yet these divisive historical events do not prevent a realization of self-integrity, but, in fact, ensure that Nabokov the anticipatory elegist/biographer will not be "diverted" from his path/pattern like Axmatova claims she has been. The forward-looking young elegist who anticipates needing memory to sustain him and his generation is mirrored by the backward-looking biographer who *is* sustained by that very memory, and in whose hands time crumbles away like snow. A model of this perfectly-balanced recession of time inscribed in space, where self is identified with the key images of "shore," "Petersburg," and "Petersburg house," can be found in a poem written by Nabokov in 1929, cited in full below:

---

[50] *Dicha* in Spanish means "luck" or "good fortune."
[51] Ibid., 275.

Для странствия ночного мне не надо
    ни кораблей, ни поездов.
Стоит луна над шашечницей сада.
    Окно открыто. Я готов.

И прыгает с беззвучностью привычной,
    как ночью кот через плетень,
на русский берег речки пограничной
    моя беспаспортная тень.

Таинственно, легко, неуязвимо
    ложусь на стены чередой,
и в лунный свет, и в сон, бегущий мимо,
    напрасно метит часовой.

Лечу лугами, по лесу танцую—
    к кто поймет, что есть один,
один живой на всю страну большую,
    один счастливый гражданин.

Вот блеск Невы вдоль набережной длинной.
    Все тихо. Поздний пешеход,
встречая тень средь площади пустынной,
    воображение клянет.

Я подхожу к неведомому дому,
    я только место узнаю…
Там, в темных комнатах, все по-другому
    и все волнует тень мою.

Там дети спят. Над уголком подушки
    я наклоняюсь, и тогда
им снятся прежние мои игрушки,
    и корабли, и поезда.[52]

For nighttime wandering I need
    neither ships nor trains.
The moon stands above the chessboard garden.
    The window is open. I am ready.

And with customary soundlessness,
    like a cat across the gate at night,

---

[52] Vladimir Nabokov, *Vsemirnaja biblioteka poèzii* (Rostov-na-Donu: Feniks, 1998), 268–69.

> my passportless shadow jumps
> > onto the Russian shore of a frontier stream.
>
> With secrecy, lightly, invulnerably
> > I cover the walls one after another,
> and the sentry aims in vain at the moonlight,
> > at the dream running past.
>
> I fly through fields, I dance in the forest—
> > and who would understand that there is one,
> one live soul in this whole big country,
> > one happy citizen.
>
> Here is the shine of the Neva along the long embankment.
> > Everything is quiet. A late stroller,
> meeting a shadow amid the deserted square,
> > curses his imagination.
>
> I walk up to a mysterious house,
> > I recognize only the place...
> There, in dark rooms, everything is different
> > and everything agitates my shade.
>
> Children are asleep there. I bend over
> > a corner of the pillow, and then
> they dream of my former toys,
> > and ships, and trains.

In this fantastic quest for a lost self (selves), Nabokov effects a return to Petersburg, one that is clearly not dictated by physical laws of distance ("I need neither ships nor trains"). In this nighttime journey, the poet's intent to tie together strands of his self/life-design is made clear in the first stanza by the image of the "chessboard" in the garden. Unlike his fictional character Lužin, who envisions his life as a vicious circle of malevolently-repeating chess moves, Nabokov as controlling elegist takes comfort and creative joy in the chessboard, which allows him not only to discern a design in his life, but to take part in creating it. Whereas Lužin's grand defense is his leap into nothingness (his suicide), the lyric persona here jumps out of his window "onto the Russian shore" in a literalization of the autobiographical project he would undertake more than twenty years later. He creeps, dances, flies across Russia until he reaches Petersburg, where he proceeds to stroll through the city in the manner of other Petersburg writers in search of lost selves.

Once in Petersburg, the lyric persona encounters a "late stroller" frightened by Nabokov's ghostly presence on the empty city square (much like Akakij Akakievich in Gogol''s "The Overcoat") and sleeping children in the house that used to be his. Yet despite the triumph of the "shadow" who has managed to steal back onto the "other shore," our hero finds that this is not, after all, "the right" Russia/Petersburg. As in his story, "A Museum Visit," the dreamlike world he has wandered into is made doubly so by the fact that this is Soviet Russia/Leningrad. His "passportless shadow" is shot at by a border guard; his house is "mysterious," "everything looks different," and the only way he knows it *is* his house is by its spatial coordinates. All of these changes "agitate [his] shade." History *has* affected his life.

How, then, does Nabokov as controlling elegist employ the "chessboard" in the first stanza as proof of an integrative rather than an entrapping design in his life? By means of a typical sleight-of-hand move, Nabokov actually effects a return *within a return* in this poem. Although at first glance the house is no longer his and contains no trace of his former, childhood self, we soon find that not only is his old self actually still there, but this previous self depends upon the appearance of the present (future) poet who has returned to his native city. The lyric hero finds his sleeping childhood self in the children over whom he leans; through this recognition he manages to "crumble time" as well as space. He returns to his younger self, who in turn *dreams* of the future self who will be displaced in space and time: the children/young Nabokov dream of the same "ships and trains" mentioned in the first stanza. Thus the dreaming child anticipates the "wandering" life of a future self, and presumably the elegiac nature of such wandering in the world, away from the "one locality." We can see another version of this reciprocal dreaming in the "late stroller," who can be identified as another possible self met with in the hero's "nighttime wandering." This lone walker senses Nabokov's ghostly presence on the square, and "curses his imagination," that is, some sort of extrasensory dread which parallels the same feeling experienced by the young Nabokov in *Speak, Memory* (albeit with Tamara) on the moonlit Palace Square. In this way, the return in space effected in the poem does not actually become authentic for Nabokov until a concomitant return in time, conceived of as the binding of two temporal planes *equally aware of each other*, is intimated. This is more than a Proustian return in art; it is a return-memory which depends upon the reciprocal action of a prescient self in the past who anticipates this moment long before it actually happens.

Nabokov's strategy as controlling elegist is the last, transitional step in our progression through historical presentations of identification between self and space. In the next three chapters we will examine ahistorical types of identification, in which the self denies that time/history has wrought any sort of change on Petersburg or the self intimately bound up with it.

Part III

Petersburg and the Idyllic Chronotope: "Ahistorical" Treatments of Space

> What Euterpe and Urania have in common is that both are Clio's seniors.
>
> Iosif Brodskij[1]

In the three preceding chapters on "historical" treatments of Petersburg space in poetry and prose, the city space and the Petersburg poet-self were for the most part adversely assaulted by events unfolding in time, and were battling and resisting those forces. The self so assaulted was never whole and never ideally integral; it never experienced the peace which comes with the feeling of being co-extensive with what one considers one's true self. Concomitantly, architectural monuments, in Brodsky's inimitable words about the Admiralty, are "embattled spirits" in the same way as the human individual. Although this sense of solidarity between self and space itself represents a significant new development in the Petersburg tradition, the battle rages as a creative/biographical process, and victory is never complete; it is partial and tentative, if it can be spoken of at all.

The "ahistorical" mythologization or metaphorization of Petersburg space is quite different. It represents the poet-self as victorious over the destructive forces that we saw assaulting the personality in chapters 3, 4, and 5. The fact that Petersburg is such a constantly conflicted space, always viewed as subject to a tragic emptying process over time, makes this claim of victory even bolder and the strategies of the embattled self—all artistic—even more heroic and miraculous.

In chapter 2, a dismissive attitude towards historical time and time's passage in general was observed as a characteristic of the "feeling," emotional type of elegiac hero (see discussion p. 42). His selfhood remains intact no matter

---

[1] Joseph Brodsky, "Letter to Horace," *On Grief and Reason* (New York: Farrar, Straus and Giroux 1995), 441.

how great the assaults upon it. The lyric hero in the ahistorical Petersburg tradition that we will present in the coming chapters has much in common with him. Moreover, many of the poetic statements in this part of the tradition take place out of time, in a dream time alternative to actual history, and are comparatively impervious to its flux and change. Such a dismissive attitude towards time can include the notion that time for Petersburg and the Petersburg poet has stopped, and does not flow as it would in a biographical or autobiographical novel. In these poems, time becomes a profound eternal moment.

It should therefore come as no surprise that time-space relations in the ahistorical treatments in part 3 are the opposite of modern novelistic time, in which constant changes—that which constitutes the "new" in the very concept of the "novel"—wreak losses and disruptions in the life of the hero. The time-space relations in the texts below are the least likely to occur in actual Petersburg space—they appertain to the wish-fulfillment type of elegy, such as Batjuškov's "Tauris," and to Baxtin's idyllic chronotope. Urban idyll or urban pastoral are, except in the very modern period with which we deal, a contradiction in terms. The rural tranquillity of the idyll here occurs within the ubiquitous anti-idyll of conflicted Petersburg space. In these treatments, the anti-idyllic "place" assaulted and changed by time is called Leningrad, and Leningrad does not impinge on the poet's being or creative power in any meaningful way.

The Petersburg idyll in the Silver Age and its aftermath is not that of the shepherd or agricultural laborer, though Brodskij often takes his inspiration from Latin bucolic poetry (for example, Virgil's *Georgics*). It is a writer's idyll, in which Petersburg becomes the sacred locus of active, continued creativity, a veritable "Petersburg of the spirit." This idyll is the unity of all the great past and present contributors to the tradition, as a family by choice—the work of generations of writers renewed and carried forth in the modern writer's *oeuvre*. In this description, we recognize the oft-formulated Acmeist view of creation as at once retrospective and future-oriented. Brodskij expressed this sense of continuity in his essay on Axmatova, "The Keening Muse": "If Akhmatova was reticent, it was at least partly because she was carrying the heritage of her predecessors into the art of this century."[2]

The creative Petersburg writer's idyll of which we speak claims that as long as Petersburg buildings stand as sustenance to the self—a self which derives, as Axmatova most demonstratively does, its content and substance from them—then that writer-self will perpetuate Petersburg in art in a cyclical fashion. Baxtin describes time-space relations in the idyll as "an organic fastening-

---

[2] Brodsky, "The Keening Muse," *Less than One*, 39.

down, a grafting of life and its events to a place, to a familiar territory with all its nooks and crannies...."[3] He goes on to enumerate a list of aspects of rural nature such as mountains and valleys, which in our identification with the cityscape have been substituted by recognizable architectural attributes of St. Petersburg. The only thing in Baxtin's rural list that is common to country and city is "one's own home."[4] He continues:

> Idyllic life and its events [here, works] are inseparable from this concrete, spatial corner of the world where the fathers and grandfathers lived.... This little spatial world is limited and sufficient unto itself, not linked in any intrinsic way with other places, with the rest of the world.[5]

We note this sense of a linkage of generations, of a family connected with the preceding Petersburg tradition, in Mandel'štam's speaking of his true ancestors in his autobiography as earlier Petersburg writers, the "masks of other men's voices" (*maski čužix golosov*, [2: 103–04]), rather than his actual relatives.[6]

The perennial presence of the great Petersburg voices of the past to the modern writer makes them all contemporary in an idyllic present which their new art participates in and perpetuates. Baxtin emphasizes that history is totally weakened by the unity and tenacious changelessness of idyllic space: "this unity of place ... weakens and renders less distinct all the temporal boundaries between individual lives and between various phases of one and the same life."[7] Speaking of the "blurring of all the temporal boundaries made possible by a unity of place," he emphasizes the proper idyll's anti-urban essence. The basic processes of life are connected with the cyclical processes of nature. The rhythmical (natural) organic time of the idyll is directly opposed to the frivolous, fragmented time of city life or even historical time. Such a connection to nature emphasizes the ahistorical aspect of the writer's idyll, which in Petersburg is attached to a civilization-and-history-rich urban space, a space quite diametrically opposed to "nature."

---

[3] Baxtin, "Forms of Time and Chronotope in the Novel," 225.

[4] Ibid.

[5] Ibid.

[6] Mandel'štam could well have been referring here to the voices of Russian authors recorded by Sergej Ignat'evič Bernštejn, head of the phonetics laboratory at the Petrograd Institute of the Living Word (*Institut živogo slova*) starting in 1918. (We are grateful to Nina Perlina for this suggestion.)

[7] Ibid.

The very grounded-to-Petersburg presentation of the Petersburg poet as a stable, whole, productive, and unperturbed powerful self, who creates beauty and recreates his personal Petersburg—the Petersburg he knows, sees and experiences (chapter 6); the Petersburg he has made his own and carries within him in emigration or exile; the buried, inner Petersburg (chapter 7)—all are particularly prominent in Nabokov and Axmatova. The ability to exteriorize one's inner Petersburg onto Leningrad or any other space, dominating that space, is the subject of chapter 8. This exteriorization of an inner Petersburg can occur as a bursting-out and filling of space with one's mental, psychic Petersburg—one that is unabashedly personal and emblematic of powerful creativity. It answers in the affirmative the haunting question of Mandel'štam's "Admiralty": "Doesn't this chastely-constructed ark deny the dominance of space?" On the other hand, retreat into an enclosed, very private space—a room, a nook—may be necessary to retrieve the creative Petersburg buried within the psyche before its bursting out and then being foisted on any actual landscape, dominating it.

The idyllic, quietly or boldly triumphant mood—triumph claimed over temporal assaults—is praised in Brodskij's assessment of Axmatova's strength: "The comprehension of the metaphysics of personal drama betters one's chances of weathering the drama of history."[8] The Petersburg writer's idyll is striking in a tradition fraught with tragedy, anxiety about change, and actual monumental changes. To proclaim an idyll in the dark Petersburg environment, where the self has been buffeted about and found wanting, a "has-been" (*byvšij čelovek*) from another devalued epoch, is an especially forceful gesture, in which spatial reality overcomes temporal reality. To find idyllic a native place usually associated with the non-idyll; to find safety, permanence, and stillness in the midst of a storm; to choose the perenially inhospitable and unsettled as home in beautiful evocations of idealized, felicitous space, is an assertion of the greater metaphysical (ontological) reality of what Brodskij calls the "second [indestructible] Petersburg, the one made of verses and of Russian prose."[9] In these chapters we examine varying degrees to which temporality is erased or ignored, and positive space dominates a foreign and/or hostile "other" space.

Some of the most interesting texts of spatialization of self consist of the history-ridden, non-idyllic Petersburg cradling the idyllic Petersburg within. The latter is a wish fulfillment realized in art as a kind of eternal reality and as a potential to overcome the anti-idyll, to render the most conflicted space serene and felicitous. This idyll within the anti-idyll is the obverse of Tjutčev's

---

[8] Brodsky, "The Keening Muse," *Less than One*, 41.

[9] Brodsky, "Guide to a Renamed City," *Less than One*, 93.

"resplendent cloak" (*blistatel'nyj pokrov*) thrown over an abyss, where an island of order (*stroj*) floats on a sea of chaos (*roj*). For Tjutčev, the *roj*, associated later with Dionysian creativity, is the greater, basic reality. For the modern tradition, the tranquil, beautiful, eternal flowers of Petersburg art within are more powerful and can become all-encompassing, capable of impressing themselves on the space and on the wider world, irrespective of what occurs in history. This is the unabashed claim of Mandel'štam's "We will gather again in Petersburg, / As if we had buried the sun there.... The immortal flowers are still blooming." The Dionysian power of art is no longer presented as a destructive chaos, but as a time-stopping, all-powerful peace and beauty, like the "*pokoj i volja*" (peace and will) that Blok, after Puškin, claimed the poet most needs. Tragedy is stemmed and supplanted by the eternal tranquillity of deathless art, where "nothing will ever change, nobody will ever die."[10]

The urban idyll or pastoral, particularly where Petersburg is concerned, represents the city's very considerable assimilation in the mind of the modern artist and the Russian national consciousness. The civilized city has become the homey, safe, comforting cradle for the modern artist's creativity, just as nature had been for the shepherds of pastoral tradition as well as for Tjutčev and the Romantics.

---

[10] Nabokov, *Speak Memory*, 77.

6

THE VISIBLE PETERSBURG AND THE DOMINANCE OF SPACE

In chapters 3, 4, and 5 below we treated identifications with space which constantly increased in the complexity with which they acknowledge the determinative effects of forward-moving history. In texts dealing with the pre-revolutionary period such as Belyj's *Petersburg* and Blok's *Retribution*, we observed attempts to stave off the terrible apocalyptic events that were generally felt to be imminent. Blok, as we saw in chapter 3, presents the figure of a poet wandering on the Neva embankment who sees the impending future, with the Russian debacle at Tsushima and the tragedy of Bloody Sunday moving towards him and Petersburg on a horizontal plane. Suddenly Peter the Great, like the martyrs Boris and Gleb in "The Life and Courage of Aleksandr Nevskij,"[1] appears with his navy in a gesture of protecting his city and its inhabitants in the new, hostile age.

We cite this scene as a striking example of the historical treatment of Petersburg space, one in which the lyric persona is obsessed with history and its frightful events, and in which he attempts to slow, stave off, or at best avert events which imply the end of Petersburg. In symmetrical contrast, our first examples of the *ahistorical* treatment of space and self in the city involve the denial that any apocalyptic disaster could affect the continued existence of a particularly Petersburg identity. It asserts the fulfillment of the wish implicit in the texts treated in chapter 3: the horizontal movement of time has not impinged upon the integrity of Petersburg or of the self/writer who dwells there. According to this strategy of denial, history (Soviet history) is said to have stopped where Petersburg is concerned, to have detoured around Petersburg, or at any rate to have had no significant effect upon it. Nothing has been irretrievably lost or irreparably damaged, and thus the elegiac cast of the Petersburg poems and prose in this part of our book is challenged by resilient selves and spaces; they correspond to the type of elegiac hero who does not admit that he has been truly affected by the passing of time and its losses (see chapter 2 above). In an even more striking proof of this resilience, Petersburg continues to exist and shape the consciousness of writers and

---

[1] "Tale of the Life and Courage of the Pious and Great Prince Alexander Nevsky," *Medieval Russia's Epics, Chronicles, and Tales*, ed. Serge A. Zenkovsky (New York: Dutton, 1989), 235–54.

thinkers who were born after the nominal transformation of Petersburg into Leningrad.

Almost all of our poets resort occasionally to such an ahistorical strategy of denial, treating the Sovietization of Petersburg/Russia as a temporary and superficial phenomenon. This denial, importantly, involves a mutual clinging for support between architectural monuments of the capital and the self. No matter what happens, as long as these monuments stand, Petersburg and its past remain intact, as do the selves identified with them. Correspondingly, as long as the self (in particular, the writer-self) continues to project his inner vision of integrality upon his surroundings, Petersburg spaces will never be Leningrad spaces. Whereas in its historical manifestations, such an identification between self and space signifies an impending or already-accomplished doom that will have drastic effects on both, in the ahistorical case it is a solidarity of strength which unites the two partners in a stubborn resistance to forward-moving history and the ravages of time. It is typical of the always-paradoxical Petersburg idea that the beauty and strength of the "true city" and its steadfast writers in these instances of denial are in fact heightened by the very forces which presume to disturb them.

In framing the special relationship between self and Petersburg space in this and succeeding chapters, we can say that two opposed qualities of the city's architecture stand in defiance of the forward press of Soviet history. First, the sheer weight and mass of the buildings resist being swept away, so that although the city sustained serious physical damage during the Civil War, World War II, and the Blockade, most of its defining grandiose forms and their configuration of a special type of space remain intact. Second, in spite of this solidity, these masses represent *par excellence* Bachelard's notion of space as compressed time.[2] As we saw in part 1, Petersburg buildings, monuments, and streets retain the memory not only of the past they have witnessed, but also act as "receptacles" of the people who have lived there, their thoughts and experience, and even of literary characters and situations created by them.[3] Stone is thus composed of palimpsestic layers of abstraction. If in previous incarnations of the Petersburg myth it is precisely this paradoxically immaterial quality of the city's structures which leads to the disturbing notion that it

---

[2] "At times we think we know ourselves in time, when all we know is a sequence of fixations in the spaces of the being's stability—a being who does not want to melt away, and who, even in the past, when he sets out in search of things past, wants time to 'suspend' its flight. In its countless alveoli space contains compressed time. That is what space is for" (8). We adapt this notion of the suspension of time in space for the ahistorical strategy under discussion in this chapter.

[3] See also Roman Jakobson, *Puškin and his Sculptural Myth*, trans. John Burbank (The Hague: Mouton, 1975).

could be ready to fly up, to disappear at any moment, this very same quality here constitutes its secret strength, its readiness to be *internalized*, to itself be sustained, by those authors who continue to write it. The Underground Man, in identifying himself with "the most abstract and premeditated city in the world," asks "Where are the primary causes I can rely upon, where's the foundation?"[4] As if in a fittingly paradoxical answer to his question, in the ahistorical context under discussion here, Petersburg and the creative self who draws upon it for support are *rooted* in its spaces both physically and psychologically, and they cannot be swept forward with history.

In this chapter we will see how the "real" Petersburg (a spatial, not temporal entity) exists underneath its visible surface, and how access to it can result in a communion with the past, a present moment infused with the past in a kind of Proustian eternal moment. In this sense we can interpret literally the seminal role of memory in effecting a mutually sustaining dynamics between the physical city and the represented city, as Lachmann has so well described it.[5] In keeping with the two-way interaction we have been continually stressing, the "memory" mentioned here is not only the Petersburg author's, but also the city's. In later chapters, we will describe how such communion can lead to the creation of an idyllic writer's world, or to a sense of traveling up and out of time instead of horizontally forward to a preordained destiny of tragic emptiness. In removing time's layers, Petersburg writers access their own and the city's past, which for some writers aids them in breaking "out" beyond the inexorable movement of history.

It is important to note that many of our writers exhibit more than one type of identification with space, even within a single work, so that the act of "clinging for support" to Petersburg structures or locales may not be interpreted entirely consistently from one work to the next, or even from one line to the next. For example, in *Petersburg*, as we have seen in many of our discussions of the "historical" treatment of identification, both Apollon Ableuxov and his son Nikolaj cling to buildings in moments of duress, specifically to those of Petrine Petersburg, thereby identifying with them. Thus when Nikolaj envisions the antechamber of his house being swallowed by the abyss, he also feels that he himself is being emptied out. However, in some instances Apollon and Nikolaj, along with the revolutionary Aleksandr Dudkin, would also qualify as fictional prototypes exhibiting denial of history's effects on the Petersburg tradition and on the self. The staunch position of Apollon's yellow stone mansion implies his own self. Thus, although he is surrounded in his

---

[4] Fyodor Dostoevsky, *Notes from Underground*, 2nd ed., trans. Michael Katz (New York: Norton, 2001), 13.

[5] See Lachmann, *Memory and Literature*, 19.

own home by ominous evidence of a plot to assassinate him, he manages for the better part of the novel to deny the facts that stare him in the face. He lives in a solipsistic world that he has created for his own purposes, and resents real-world intrusions. According to the narrator, when Senator Ableuxov is confronted with the double agent Morkovin-Voronkov, he "does not accept on principle the existence of such people." With the same farsightedness as Blok's lone wanderer in *Retribution,* his vision reaches as if across the water to the threatening elements contained in the more socially marginalized area of "the islands." Apollon is made very anxious by this apparition, yet in his identification with the buildings themselves, he stalwartly refuses to really believe that any force could compromise his security. His solipsistic denial mechanisms are prodigious. Such statue-like impenetrability, which, in Apollon's case, recalls the city's intimidating grandeur rather than the more human features of identification mentioned in other examples, is felt by Dudkin from his vantage point on Vasil'evskij Island: "From over there rose Petersburg: there buildings blazed out of a wave of clouds. There, it seemed, hovered someone spiteful, cold. From over there, out of the howling chaos someone stared with stony gaze, skull and ears protruding into the fog."[6] The force of Apollon's stern resistance and the complicity he feels with his city in it seem to be validated in the response of the anthropomorphized islands: "From far, far away, as though farther off than they should have been, the islands sank and cowered in fright; and the buildings cowered; it seemed that the waters would sink and that at that instant the depths, the greenish murk would surge over them."[7] Although Apollon himself is not a writer of Petersburg, such bald denial of reality and the effects of current events "on principle" is characteristic of the denial which is the subject of this chapter. It represents a rejection of the fulfillment of Evdokija's prophecy "Petersburg will be emptied out."

In *Petersburg,* as we have seen, the capital's past and its historical continuity are said to be retained in the lines and parallelipipeds of its original urban design. In the section of the fourth chapter entitled "The Summer Garden," the former grandeur of the garden as Peter had designed it, helping Leblond, has faded: "Time sharpens its teeth for everything—it devours body and soul and stone.... The garden had shrunk and now cowered behind the bars."[8] Despite this statement of degenerative historical progression, the garden is still a pervasive locus of spatialized, tangible time. Here sights and sounds of old Petersburg are visible and audible to modern strollers in the park, who sense

---

[6] Bely, *Petersburg,* 13.

[7] Ibid., 9.

[8] Ibid., 97.

the Petrine past so vividly that it invades the present, and even for a brief moment halts and supplants it:

> The evening atmosphere thickened. The heart felt as if there were no present, as if out of those very trees the somberness would be illuminated by a quivering bright green light. The bright red huntsmen with horns upraised would elicit melodic organ swells from the zephyrs.[9]

The continued existence of buildings, gardens, architectural ensembles, and sculpted figures as a pretext for denying history's effects on Petersburg and the self is also clearly present in the lyric poems and autobiographical passages of the Acmeists and their successors. It is perhaps in the Acmeist program, in its concern with the continuity of memory and monuments of culture, that such a poetic resistance of history is most strongly asserted and felt. In his 1921–22 poem "Under arches of ancient quiet" Mandel′shtam, in a three-way association, links the creative self, the solid and memory-laden physical structure of St. Isaac's Cathedral in Petersburg, and the preservative function of world cathedrals and the Christian cultural tradition in general. The "grain of deep and absolute faith" which is both the poet's creative gift and the internalized, carefully preserved Petersburg is kept, stored intact in "the deep bins" of the church, characterized, along with other world churches, as "granaries of air and light":

> Люблю под сводами седыя тишины
> Молебнов, панихид блужданье
> И трогательный чин—ему же все должны;—
> У Исаака отпеванье.
> ....
>
> Соборы вечные Софии и Петра,
> Амбары воздуха и света,
> Зернохранилища вселенского добра
> И риги Нового Завета.
>
> Не к вам влечется дух в годины тяжких бед,
> Сюда влачится по ступеням
> Широкопасмурный несчастья волчий след,
> Ему ж вовеки не изменим.

---

[9] Ibid., 99.

Зане свободен раб, преодолевший страх,
И сохранилось свыше меры
В прохладных житницах, в глубоких закромах
Зерно глубокой, полной веры.   [1: 91]

Under arches of ancient quiet, I love
The wandering services and requiems
And the touching ritual—all yield to it—
At a St. Isaac's funeral.

The eternal cathedrals of Sophia and Peter,
Granaries of air and light,
Storehouses of universal [ecumenical] good[s]
And threshing floors of the New Testament.

It is not to you that the courageous spirit
Will be drawn in hours of trouble;
Drawn hither, up the steps are the wide,
Sullen wolf-tracks of misfortune, which we will never betray.

For the slave is free who has overcome fear,
And the grain of deep and absolute faith
Has been preserved beyond measure
In these cool granaries and deep bins.

The poet's self is kept safe and whole in the space and structure of St. Isaac's, which is linked to other famous buildings (the St. Sophia Cathedral in old Constantinople and St. Peter's in Rome) safeguarding faith and culture; here we have the literalization of Mandel'štam's pronouncement in "The Word and Culture" that "culture has become a church" [2: 265]. The troubled spirit is refreshed, restored, by its contact with this repository—an affirmation of self within a concrete structure, a Bachelardian "protective" space. In fact, St. Isaac's in Petersburg is given pride of place among cathedrals in its strength and preservative function because of its constant association with tragedy (*nesčast'e*, misfortune), more than the other churches mentioned—it is precisely to *this* shelter within the tragedy-ridden Petersburg space that the self is drawn. And it is in "overcoming" this misfortune and fear that one is allowed access to the ultimately unassailable structure of the church/self. It is as if assaults on the self and Petersburg space only serve to prove their integrity. The deep identification between the creative self and the Petersburg structure first explored metapoetically by Mandel'štam in his 1913 "Admiralty" has here become a defiant stance, a faith-filled conviction in the eternal creative moment contained in and by the cathedral—memory which will triumph over this new time of troubles, activated in the promise of the "grain" to eventually take root and bear fruit (much like his "buried sun" elsewhere). The cathedral represents a resilient and stable space, a suspended eternal moment which is the source of strength for those who enter.

Mandel′štam's denial of history is perhaps most clear in his poem "We will gather again in Petersburg," which evokes the city as a charged, theatrical *space* (here, both the interior of the Marinskij Theater and its exterior, Theater Square) with its own particular laws governing dark and light, day and night, and thus time and history in general. The period of "the blackness and universal emptiness of Soviet night" is shown to be temporary, and there is confidence that the "buried sun," which only the poetic elect in the poem can see anyway, will rise again. The hated bridge patrol, the alien, bureaucratic "low hypocrite" who is attacked in the work, will never see the buried sun or understand its significance. Moreover, poets may be killed («Гаси, пожалуй, наши свечи» ["Extinguish, if you will, our lights"]), but the sun of the Puškinian poetic tradition, of Petersburg art and beauty (equated with the very spaces of the city), is inextinguishable and will prevail through the Soviet night until the coming of a great future: «Все поют блаженных жен родные очи, / Все цветут бессмертные цветы» ("The native eyes of blessed women are still singing, / The immortal flowers are still blooming"). The "low hypocrite" in the poem is dismissed with the same opprobrium as are those indirectly responsible for Puškin's death in Lermontov's "On the Death of the Poet" (1837), and Dantès in Tjutčev's poem on the same theme ("… before our human justice [he] will eternally be branded … as a regicide").[10] Shortly before Mandel′štam's poem was written, Rozanov had emphasized the eternal power of the sun in *The Apocalypse of Our Time*: "Try to crucify the sun and you will see what a god is."[11] Indeed, in Mandel′štam's *Tristia* there is the hope that the sun of Russian culture cannot be in eclipse for long. Mandel′štam does not share the pessimistic forebodings on the question of Puškin's survival in Russian culture expressed by Blok and Xodasevič at the Puškin Celebration in 1921.[12] In chapter 8 we will further explore this notion of burial and sun as another type of spatial expression of the denial of history in Petersburg letters.

The optimistic view expressed in "We will gather again in Petersburg," the view that great art and the city that preserves this art in its spaces exist eternally and cannot be threatened, is even found in the *oeuvre* of Georgij Ivanov,

---

[10] Tjutčev, "29-oe janvarja" (1837), 127.

[11] Rozanov, *Apokalipsis našego vremeni*, 444.

[12] See chap. 4 above.

generally regarded as a more pessimistic figure. He uses Mandel'štam's first line as an epigraph for his poem "A quarter century has passed abroad" (quoted in chapter 4, p. 93), written later in France. The "prophecy" he mentions («... пророчество мертвого друга / Обязательно сбыться должно» ["... our dead friend's prophecy / Will have to come true"]) is the one in Mandel'štam's great poem. Ivanov's answer is not only an affirmation of Mandel'štam's faith, but also an answer to Blok's fatalistic "Night, the street, the streetlight, the druggist's shop," with its line «Живи еще хоть четверть века— / Все будет так. Исхода нет» ("Live another quarter century— / Everything will be the same. There is no exit").[13] "We *will* gather in Petersburg" is Ivanov's echoing affirmation across the decades—and across the intervening miles between France and Russia—that there is an exit from this vicious circle.

Powerful denial of the ravages of history is rarer in Axmatova's presentations of self and space, and when it is present, it is expressed more subtly. Her *oeuvre*, as we have seen, is filled with poems demonstrating the difficulty of retaining memories and former selves. Axmatova's denial consists in her almost Symbolist assertion that there are "two cities" at the delta of the Neva—Leningrad the impostor-double and Petersburg, the true one. As we indicated earlier, Evtušenko, in a wonderful poem on Axmatova's death, defined her entire *oeuvre* as a trip back and forth between these two cities. Axmatova is characterized as the living spirit of Petersburg wandering through Leningrad.[14] Of course, there is a pessimistic and ominous undertone in Evtušenko's poem in that the "incredible" presence of Petersburg in Leningrad, made possible by Axmatova's "bridging life," may well have been taken away with her final return to the necropolis. The poets who remain must vow to keep that "Petersburg spirit" alive lest access to it be denied. He calls on the present generation to keep Petersburg art and Russian art, equated here in a Brodskian fashion, alive as a reinvigorating force for Russia. This poem, surprising from a Muscovite, addresses the same issues of self-division, doubling, Axmatova/pseudo-Axmatova, and Petersburg/Leningrad that the poet herself had treated in her *Northern Elegies*.

In her very tortured "Second Northern Elegy" (1942), Axmatova asserts the existence of the true city through a denial of the present Leningrad, which is the objective correlative of the horrors of her present and recent past life. It is the horrible product of a history that is the opposite of progress, a return to savagery and barbarism (*odičanie Peterburga*). She can barely hear the sounds of the true city. Like Axmatova herself in Evtušenko's poem, it is as if the

---

[13] Blok, "Noč', ulica, fonar', apteka," 172.
[14] Evtušenko, 247 (see chap. 4, pp. 133–34).

sounds have retreated to the world of the dead: «... звуки города—как с того света / Услышанные, чуждые навеки» ("... the sounds of the city— heard as if from the other world, / Alien forever").

Yet in the "First Northern Elegy" ("Prehistory"), Axmatova is sometimes able to peer through the present buildings and see the facades of another epoch:

[... город] подчас умеет
Казаться литографией старинной,
Не первоклассной, но вполне пристойной,
Семидесятых, кажется, годов.
....
Темнеет жесткий и прямой Литейный,
Еще не опозоренный модерном

[1: 308]

[... the city] at times
Can seem to be an old lithograph,
Not first-class, but quite acceptable,
Of the 1870s or so.
....
Harsh and straight Litejnyj Prospect darkens,
Not yet shamed by *art nouveau* architecture

In this elegy, Axmatova is aided by architecture in her breakthrough to the past, to the Petersburg of Dostoevskij, by buildings that have survived from that period. In fact, as she states, "the city has changed little" («Но, впрочем, город мало изменился»). As for Mandel'štam and, later, Brodskij, for Axmatova the physical and visual aspect of the city retains the spirit of Petersburg, and she feels her personal past and present to be permanently and indelibly marked on the places where she lived: "Our shades are under the arch on Galernaja Street forever"; "Our footsteps are forever in the Hermitage halls."

We see the same idea reflected negatively when Axmatova laments the destruction of these places. The tendency to hope that they retain and in certain circumstances will yield forth the past in a flood of Proustian recollections is seen in the "Fourth Northern Elegy" ("There are three epochs to remembrance"), where the lyric persona's hope is dramatically frustrated. In her poem on the German destruction of Carskoe Selo ("O, woe is me! They have burned you down"), Axmatova presents the corollary of the notion that buildings hold and yield forth memories and the content of the past, that is, that the destruction of buildings will destroy the memories. Her poem is addressed to the fire-ravaged town:

> О, горе мне! Они тебя сожгли!
> О, память что разлуки тяжелее
> ....
> И в прошлое теперь уж нет лазейки
>   [1: 315]

O, woe is me! They have burned you down!
Oh, memory that is worse than separation!

And now there is no longer a loophole to the past.

Although the late Axmatova constantly does "break through" to the past in the form of lively conversations and even meetings with dead poet-friends, she is less sanguine about man's hold on the past. This is ironic because it is largely to her that we are indebted for our vivid sense of the life of the bohemian world of Silver Age Petersburg. In her late poetry, in works such as *Poem without a Hero*, we feel that dead, but so lively, Petersburg past to be immanent in the city. In a similar way, in Mandel'štam's poem "Leningrad," the poet brags of his ability to commune with the immanent, if invisible, Petersburg: «Петербург! У меня есть еще адреса, / По которым найду мертвецов голоса» ("Petersburg! I still have the addresses / By which I'll find the voices of the dead") [1: 158]. The course of Soviet time has not succeeded in "emptying out" Petersburg or the selves who are anchored there.

BRODSKIJ'S DENIAL: STONES AND WORDS AS ANTIDOTES TO HISTORY

In chapter 5 we cited several examples of Brodskij's "historical" presentation of Petersburg space and self, which involve above all a dispersal of identity, the whittling-down of the self and of Petersburg structures which signifies a loss of meaning, a chaotic "emptying-out" of order and significance. Like many of the poets discussed here, however, Brodskij's identification of the creative self with the spaces and structures of his native city is often conflicted, represented in the process of its formation rather than as a crystallized, formulaic correspondence. In Brodskij we see a specially-constructed vision of Petersburg and self: it is an Escher-like conflation of eternal and temporally/historically-bound categories, the continuous protected space within the equally real, constantly assaulted non-idyll of which we spoke in the introduction to this section. As we will show in this chapter, he identifies his formation as a writer and his creative self with a staunchly standing Petersburg which can be discerned through its post-war ruins and in the words of its poets. Yet, as the one figure in our study who was not formed as a writer during the great Silver Age of Petersburg art, Brodskij's identification with Petersburg takes on a slightly different cast. It is a positive assertion built out of ruins, or negatives. Perhaps more than any of the poets we quote, Brodskij's approach is paradoxical: his method of positive solidarity rests upon the almost *a priori* assumption of the ravages the city and his "self" have undergone. Petersburg's existence is all the more amazing in Brodskij's experience because it is precisely through the prism of its ruins and its almost Dostoevskian industrial districts as much as the grandeur of past epochs that the city's structures and spaces assert their force as a shaper and inspirer of minds for his generation. Brodskij and his artistic life are a strange proof of Petersburg's resilience; he is a kind of Petersburg artifact. For this reason the denial of ravaging history that we speak of for Brodskij involves a slightly different psychology of self and space than is implied in other Petersburg writers who deny history.

When Brodskij chooses to take an ahistorical stance (which is often), no one expresses this position more eloquently. The intellectual soundness of the position of denial outlined here is not at issue. The beauty and inspirational force and the cogency of its bravado are. In fact, it is one of the interesting paradoxes of the Petersburg poetic tradition that Brodskij, as disciple of Mandel'štam and Axmatova in his love for the architecture of the past, is the greatest and most powerful proponent of the denial of history of which we speak. Born in 1940, Brodskij had not personally experienced that past; and yet he is able not only to access it, but also to assimilate it as his own in his communion with Petersburg architecture and poetry. Such an affirmation is all the more forceful and effective precisely because he never lived *during* Axmatova's Petersburg (although he "lived it" in her and others' words). His experience of it strengthens the notion discussed in these chapters that the city's true identity is based in its architecture and its interaction with its writers rather than an assumed conformation to historical movement. If the buildings and the historical center of the city are still there, the Petrine spirit and all that it implies is extant and communicated to the inhabitants. They "read the book" of the edifices and pavement. Not accidentally, Brodskij depicts this interaction between self and Petersburg space in textual terms: the city's structures preserve the text of its identity and past, just as writers preserve and support its stones in their texts. If the Petersburg of the word, Russian poetry and prose about Petersburg, is still known and read, the city is alive and well, and Soviet history and culture are powerless weapons against it.

In his book of English essays about himself, world culture, and his relation to it, *Less than One*, Brodskij includes two frankly autobiographical pieces, the title essay and "In a Room and a Half." The latter refers to the space which he and his family occupied in Dom Muruzi on Litejnyj Prospekt, where two other Petersburg writers, Dmitrij Merežkovskij and Zinaida Gippius, lived before and during the revolution. A third essay, "A Guide to a Renamed City," may also be qualified as autobiographical because of the author's powerful identification with the city therein. Brodskij's orientation towards the spatial environment and the visual aspects of things in both his essays and his Petersburg poetry is the most marked of all our poets, extreme even in a group with a heightened architectural and visual orientation. He is manifestly aware of this fact: "Visual aspects of life, I am afraid, always mattered more to me than its content."[15] Indeed, his poetic eye regularly focuses not only on particular Petersburg houses, streets, canals, etc., but also on the city's spatial arrangement. He pays meticulous attention to the horizon, perspectives, and the trajectory of vision in this carefully designed urban space and the flat landscapes which surround it. "Content" is discovered *through* and shaped by these forms; internal, intangible realities are accessed through solid weight, imposing structure, and the logic of urban planning.

Petersburg space, as we know, also shapes the selfhood of its writers and thinkers. In the essays mentioned, Brodskij's visual and spatial presentation of the city is juxtaposed with the poet's explorations of self and identity, the psychological implications of which in turn parallel, both implicitly and explicitly, Petersburg and its structures. Of particular relevance for our topic are Brodskij's remarks on his conception of the self enduring within time and space. In the essay "Less than One," for example, Brodskij denies the importance for him of the passage of time (linear history) on his personality, "Soviet time" being the only kind he had ever lived through himself. This is in large part a denial of the destructive effects of time on the individual (contradicted, of course, elsewhere in his work). He writes:

> Either because of some basic flaw in my mind or because of the fluid, amorphous nature of life itself, I have never been able to distinguish any landmark, let alone a buoy. If there is anything like a landmark, it is that which I won't be able to acknowledge myself, i.e., death. There was never such a thing as childhood. These categories—childhood, adulthood, maturity—seem to me very odd, and if I use them in conversation occasionally, I always regard them mutely, for myself, as borrowed [and not really applicable].[16]

Evident in this view is Brodskij's aversion to categorization and the limitations on self which any kind of definition, and especially the most conventional

---

[15] Brodsky, "Less than One," 22.
[16] Ibid., 16.

definition ("childhood, adulthood, maturity," Soviet citizen), implies. Indeed, the less sharply defined the self, the less it can be threatened by mere temporal/historical circumstance. This assertion is followed by a clear denial of the effect of time's passage on his life:

> I guess there was always some "me" inside that small and later, somewhat bigger shell around which "everything" was happening. Inside that shell the entity which one calls "I" never changed and never stopped watching what was going on outside. I am not trying to hint at pearls inside. What I am saying is that the passage of time does not much affect that entity ... to get a low grade, to operate a milling machine, to be beaten up at an interrogation, or to lecture on Callimachus in a classroom is essentially the same.... The dissatisfaction of a child with one's parents' control over him and the panic of an adult confronting a responsibility are of the same nature. One is neither of these figures; one is perhaps less than "one."[17]

When "one" speaks in the third person, impersonally, as in the expression, "one would hope...," it is never the *whole of oneself* who is the subject; rather, it is the part that would stand in for Everyman—a diluted, generalized self. Subjectively, one senses the incompleteness of that "one," an incompleteness that for Brodskij paradoxically becomes a way of asserting his independence. This inner being can never be fully defined or categorized according to life stage, personality, or situation—in Baxtinian terms, it is "unfinalizable." Outer circumstance cannot affect the "me" within precisely because that "me" is "less than one" to begin with. What may look like a lack of integrality, of wholeness ("less," not "more than one"), is thus actually a strategy of preserved selfhood.

The complicity between stones and words in Soviet-era Leningrad/Petersburg works in a similar way: the layers of "compressed time" in its spaces ensure that Axmatova, like other Petersburg writers, sees an "1870s Petersburg" through Leningrad, that Dudkin, like Evgenij, sees the Bronze Horseman clattering through its streets. Petersburg, too, in this sense is less than the prescribed "one" of "Leningrad"; it finds a secret strength in not being finalized as the Soviet "impostor city." The "fluid, amorphous" boundaries that in the age of Gogol' and Dostoevskij had often seemed to foreshadow its lack of solidity and eventual ruin are now seen as a liberating alienation from Leningrad reality into the "Petersburg" of spaces and texts. Brodskij, especially in his early poetry, asserts this essential inviolability of Petersburg. He can see the Petrine, Puškinian, and Dostoevskian cities clearly, and, moreover,

---

[17] Ibid., 16–17.

strongly identifies with the fictional inhabitants of that time—all through a spatial/architectural medium, as in the following excerpt from chapter 29 of his "Petersburg Novel" (*Peterburgskij roman*, 1961):

> Канал туманный Грибоедов,
> сквозь двести лет шуршит вода,
> немного в мире переехав,
> приходишь сызнова сюда.
>
> ....
>
> Канал ботинок твой окатит
> и где-то около Невы
> плеснет водой зеленоватой,
> —мой Бог, неужто это вы.
>
> А это ты. В канале старом
> ты столько лет плывешь уже,
> канатов треск и плеск каналов
> и улиц свет в твоей душе.
>
> И боль в душе. Вот два столетья.
> И улиц свет. И боль в груди.
> И ты живешь один на свете
> и только город впереди. [1: 82]

Foggy Griboedov Canal,
the water plashes across 200 years,
you've moved around in the world a little,
you come here once again.

The canal drenches your shoe
and somewhere near the Neva
the greenish water will splash,
—my God, could this really be you [pl.].

But it's you [sg.] How many years in the
old canal have you been floating already,
the ropes' crack and the canals' splashing
and the light of the streets in your soul.

Pain, too, in your soul. For two centuries.
And the light of the streets. And the pain in your breast.
And you live all alone in the world with only the city ahead.

In a play involving water reflection and Russian varieties of the pronoun "you" (singular vs. plural and/or formal) Brodskij employs the common Petersburg literary device of the lone wanderer observing his face in the canal below. In the context of the entire poem, we can recognize here not only Puškin's tormented Evgenij, but a range of youthful Dostoevskian heroes. Brodskij's lyric persona reads himself into the memory (the plural "you") of the canal, a space which contains the accumulated effects of two hundred years' worth of memories (including the reflections of literary characters). Also evoked here is Blok, whose Petersburg spaces can sometimes overwhelm the speaker, aware as he is of his fleeting role in a part that has been played cyclically, over and over again, in the very same spaces. We see such an entrapping repetition in his "Night, the street, the streetlight, the druggist's shop" as well as in his 1909 poem "On the Islands" ("Na ostrovax"):

> Чем ночь прошедшая сияла,
> Чем настоящая зовет,
> Все только—продолженье бала,
> Из света в сумрак переход.[18]

> With whatever light the evening of yesterday shone,
> With whatever voice that of today calls,
> It's all just a continuation of the ball,
> The crossing from light into darkness.

A similar repetition of passage from light into darkness and back was described by Belyj in chapter 8 of *Petersburg*, as Nikolaj and Apollon pace back and forth in the hall of their Petersburg house—their last conversation before the explosion of the bomb, one in which steps toward a rapprochement of sorts are taken. Blok's use of the image in the context of Petersburg spaces reaffirms in a rather negative way the "sameness" of Petersburg space, its inviolable inner "self." In his "Petersburg Novel," Brodskij asserts his own stance above the water as evidence of Petersburg's unchanged inner essence (as one in a line of repeating characters); yet he also breaks himself off from that Everyman sense of "one" by articulating his reflection as the *singular* "you" rather than the plural. "You live all alone in the world," despite the "pain in your breast" is thus made into a paradoxically positive assessment of the poet's position. "The city"—its spaces, structures, and sounds—is the poet's anchor, his only constant companion; Petersburg and the self both resist the passage of time.

---

[18] Blok, "Na ostrovax," 168.

Brodskij observes in himself little or no development; he sees his "self" as a solid, uncrackable nut for which space is a lot more real than time. This fact of his own psychic orientation he applies to his characterization of Peter the Great:

> In general he [Peter] was in love with space, and with the sea in particular.... A man of sober mind, though of frightful drinking habits, he regarded every country where he set foot—his own included—as but a continuation of space. In a way, geography was far more real to him than history, and his most beloved directions were north and west.[19]

Space thus contains time rather than being controlled by it. In other essays and poems Brodskij asserts that time is the superior category because it is an abstraction of matter, and in his later poetry makes a conscious effort to explore this superiority. Nevertheless, it is his basic identification with space that is essential to Brodskij as a poet: "When it comes to collapsing time, our trade, I am afraid, beats history, and smells, rather sharply, of geography."[20] Peter's city is Brodskij's original model for such a space:

> Когда-нибудь, со временем, пойму,
> что тоньше, поучительнее даже,
> что проще и значительней пейзажа
> не скажет время сердцу моему.   [1: 56]

> In time, someday, I'll understand
> that time will say nothing to my heart
> that is subtler, more instructive, even,
> simpler and more important than the landscape [will].

Brodskij's visual orientation associates him intimately with the spaces of his own city, amidst which he is often ambling in his poems, as many Petersburg writers and literary characters have done. This is a peculiarly meditative kind of activity, one that is more liable than any other to effect a psychic bond between stones and self. He claims that St. Petersburg naturally inclines one to such ambling:

> It's the northern light, pale and diffused, one in which both memory and eye operate with unusual sharpness. In this light, and thanks to the directness and length of the streets, a walker's thoughts travel far-

---

[19] Brodsky, "A Guide to a Renamed City," *Less than One*, 72.
[20] Brodsky, "Letter to Horace," *On Grief and Reason*, 441.

ther than his destination.... In his youth, at least, a man born in this city spends as much time on foot as any good Bedouin.... It's because to walk under this sky, along the brown granite embankments of this immense gray river, is in itself an extension of life and a school of farsightedness.[21]

Space and walking through it in this idiosyncratic approach to life is substituted for elongation in time, and the streets themselves are credited with the channeling of thought and its aspirations to the abstract, represented here by a heightened capacity for cultural memory. For Brodskij, one sense of the "extension of life" and "farsightedness" to be gained by walking the streets of Petersburg is that of a cultural past he can see clearly and become part of through his spatial meanderings. This street vision is also closely bound to his own personal past: "a man with normal eyesight can make out at a distance of a mile ... the age of the tail following him." Here we are reminded of Belyj's characterization of Dudkin's close relationship to the Petersburg streets: "You bring home with you what you have experienced on the streets, in squalid restaurants, in tearooms. Then what was he returning home with? His experiences dragged after him, like a tail invisible to the eye. Aleksandr Ivanovič experienced the experiences in reverse order, as they retreated behind his own back."[22] For both Dudkin and Brodskij, the psychological and emotional space of selfhood is intimately related to the life and space of the physical Petersburg—a memory-laden space which, in the ahistorical presentation under discussion here, follows one doggedly rather than falling off in chunks as for Sof'ja Petrovna.[23]

Brodskij continues, "There is something in the granular texture of the granite pavement next to the constantly flowing, departing water that instills in one's soles an almost sensual desire for walking."[24] Walking is associated in Blok, Mandel'štam, and Brodskij with the creation of metrical feet, poetry as human temporal movement through the world. In this emphasis on walking in Petersburg, Brodskij has his clearest antecedent in the *flâneur* hero of Dostoevskij's "White Nights." That character, like Brodskij, and to some extent like Belyj's ambulatory Nikolaj Apollonovič and Aleksandr Dudkin, evinces a most intimate attitude towards Petersburg buildings, as if they were

---

[21] "A Guide to a Renamed City," 89.

[22] Bely, *Petersburg*, 64.

[23] And for both, it might be mentioned, the "tail" (*xvost*) in question has the additional meaning of police surveillance (for Dudkin, the double agent Morkovin/Voronkov, and for Brodskij, the KGB).

[24] Brodsky, "A Guide to a Renamed City," 89.

people or friends. In the following passages we see the warm relationship between Dostoevskij's hero and both the people and houses he encounters on his daily walks through the city:

> ... there is an old gentleman I see every day on the Fontanka Embankment with whom I have practically struck up a friendship. He looks so thoughtful and dignified, and he always mutters under his breath, waving his left hand and holding a big knotty walking-stick with a gold top in his right. I have, I believe, attracted his attention, and I should not be surprised if he took a most friendly interest in me. In fact, I am sure that if he did not meet me at a certain hour on the Fontanka Embankment he would be terribly upset. That is why we sometimes almost bow to one another, especially when we are both in a good humour. Recently we had not seen each other for two days, and on the third day, when we met, we were just about to raise our hats in salute, but fortunately we recollected ourselves in time and, dropping our hands, passed one another in complete understanding and amity. The houses, too, are familiar to me. When I walk along the street, each of them seems to run before me, gazing at me out of all its windows, and practically saying to me, "Good morning, sir! How are you? I'm very well, thank you. They're going to add another storey to me in May"; or, "How do you do, sir? I'm going to be repaired tomorrow"; or "Dear me, I nearly got burnt down, and, goodness, how I was scared!" and so on and so on. Some of them are great favourites of mine, while others are my good friends. One of them is thinking of undergoing a cure with an architect this summer. I shall certainly make a point of coming to see it every day to make sure that its cure does not prove fatal (which God forbid!). And I shall never forget the incident with a pretty little house of a pale pink hue. It was such a dear little house; it always welcomed me with such a friendly smile, and it looked on its clumsy neighbours with such an air of condescension, that my heart leapt with joy every time I passed it. But when I happened to walk along the street only a week ago and looked up at my friend, I was welcomed with a most plaintive cry, "They are going to paint me yellow!" Fiends! Savages! They spared nothing, neither cornices, nor columns, and my poor friend turned as yellow as a canary.[25]

---

[25] Fyodor Dostoevsky, "White Nights," *Great Short Works of Fyodor Dostoevsky*, trans. David Magarshack (New York: Perennial, 1968), 148.

This famous passage and the friendly human relations and dialogue with the houses and buildings of Petersburg is repeated in the work of Brodskij, who sees himself as if educated and formed by those façades and friendly buildings, which he loves in almost the same way. In Brodskij's poetic and prose passages we can make out not only a similar affection for, but also a distinct identification with the city:

> … I remember this city at a time when it didn't look like "Leningrad" [his early childhood]—right after the war. Gray, pale-green façades with bullet and shrapnel cavities; endless, empty streets, with few passersby and light traffic; almost a starved look with, as a result, more definite and, if you wish, nobler features. A lean, hard face with the abstract glitter of its river reflected in the eyes of its hollow windows. A survivor cannot be named after Lenin.
>
> Those pockmarked façades behind which—among old pianos, worn-out rugs, dusty paintings in heavy bronze frames, leftovers of furniture … a faint life [Brodskij's, among others] was beginning to glimmer. And I remember, as I passed those façades on my way to school, being completely absorbed in imagining what was going on in those rooms with the old, billowy wallpaper.[26]

Like Brodskij's own personal "uncrackable nut" of selfhood, Leningrad has an unchangeable, Petersburgian center whose identity has remained intact. In its ruins, Petersburg is "less than one"—as we have seen, a paradoxically positive evaluation in Brodskij's philosophy. In the same kind of inward motion familiar to us from the poem "From the Outskirts to the Center," Brodskij describes his need to affirm for himself the reality of the "center," the besieged yet intact kernel of being and meaning ("what was going on in those rooms"). He discovers this inner essence by reading the buildings as books; they are his mentors and models:

> I must say that from these façades and porticoes—classical, modern, eclectic, with their columns, pilasters, and plastered heads of mythic animals or people—from their ornaments and caryatids holding up the balconies, from the torsos in the niches of their entrances, I have learned more about the history of the world than I subsequently have from any book. Greece, Rome, Egypt—all of them were there.… And from the gray, reflecting river flowing down to the Baltic, with an occasional tugboat in the midst of it struggling against the current, I

---

[26] Brodsky, "Less than One," 4–5.

have learned more about infinity and stoicism than from mathematics and Zeno.[27]

In a relatively new city without archeological layers dating back to Greece and Rome, history is represented spatially; all periods coexist, mixed on a horizontal plane, and consecutivity loses importance. This creates an unusual unity ("compression," in Bachelardian terms) of space and time, one in which identity is not significantly threatened by circumstance.

Roman Timenčik has pointed out that the form of Petersburg streets has influenced the classical lines and even the enjambments in Petersburg poetry.[28] Brodskij is the poet who most emphasizes the derivation of his aesthetic and poetic principles from Petersburg's architecture and visual aspects. The city's spaces taught him not only the history of the world, but also gave him his ideas of beauty and of how poetry should be formed:

> Such was the history of Russian aesthetics that the architectural ensembles of St. Petersburg, churches included, were—and still are—perceived as the closest possible incarnation of such an [a better] order. In any case, a man who has lived long enough in this city is bound to associate virtue with proportion. This is an old Greek idea; but set under the northern sky, it acquires the peculiar authority of an embattled spirit and, to say the least, makes an artist very aware of form. This kind of influence is especially clear in the case of Russian or, to name it by its birthplace, Petersburgian poetry.[29]

This is the aesthetic tradition and credo of the poets Brodskij admires, and of Brodskij himself. The complicity from stones to words to stones is very clear in it. We saw in chapter 5 that the old, embattled "Greeks" in Leningrad were not only churches, but also poets, and Brodskij himself in his poem "A Halt in the Desert." This association between spatial and poetic form is especially poignant in Brodskij's post-1972 career, when the spaces of Petersburg continue to haunt and shape his verse. The poet and the city continue to support each other even in a state of extreme dislocation, thus testing to its farthest limits the abstract nature of solid stone in Petersburg:

> Я родился и вырос в балтийских болотах, подле
> серых цинковых волн, всегда набегавших по две,

---

[27] Ibid., 5.

[28] Roman Timenčik, "Poètika Sankt-Peterburga èpoxi simvolizma/postsimvolizma," *Trudy po znakovym sistemam* 18 (Tartu: 1984), 117–24.

[29] Brodskij, "A Guide to a Renamed City," 83.

> и отсюда—все рифмы, отсюда тот блеклый голос,
> вьющийся между ними.... [2: 403]
>
> I was born and grew up in the Baltic bogs, next to
> the grey zinc waves, always running in twos, and this is
> the origin of all my rhymes, and that faded voice
> winding among them....
>
> И дрова, грохотавшие в гулких дворах сырого
> города, мерзнущего у моря,
> меня согревают еще сегодня. [3: 17]
>
> And the wood crackling in the resounding courtyards of the
> damp city freezing by the sea
> Still warms me today.

But not only is Brodskij, the man and the artist, formed by the quality and look of the buildings of Petersburg: he claims his entire generation is. There is, as we might expect, an uncanny resemblance for him between those starving, pockmarked postwar façades and his own post-war generation. The substitution of a building for a person and vice versa that is characteristic of identification with Petersburg spaces is endemic in Brodskij. Here is an example in which the crowd vaguely recalls Belyj's human myriapod (*ljudskaja mnogonožka*):

> ... every time a natural or premeditated disaster takes place, you can spot in a crowd a pale, somewhat starved, ageless face with its deep-set, white, fixed eyes, and hear the whisper: "I tell you, this place is cursed!" You'll shudder, but a moment later, when you try to take another look at the speaker, the face is gone. In vain, your eyes will search the slowly milling crowds, the traffic creeping along: you will see nothing except the indifferent passersby and, through the slanted veil of rain, the magnificent features of the great imperial buildings.[30]

The faceless person substituted by an equally faceless building has the majesty of the elderly Petersburg woman in *Requiem*, of whom Axmatova wrote: «Что-то вроде улыбки проскользнуло по тому, что некогда было ее лицом» ("Something like a smile flashed across what had once been her face") [1: 361].

Petersburg is still alive in these shabby but tenacious survivors, kept carefully within the "structure" of the self: "Poorly dressed but somehow still ele-

---

[30] Brodsky, "A Guide to a Renamed City," 74.

gant ... broken, growing old, they still retained their love for the non-existent ... thing called 'civilization.' Hopelessly cut off from the rest of the world, they thought that at least that world was like themselves.... As I write this, I ... almost see them standing in their dilapidated kitchens...."[31] It is the city's, as its inhabitants', special strength that they remain "cut off" from the course of history which has engendered Leningrad. This sustaining memory effected by metonymic representation works both ways, for the very material of Petersburg also remembers its human inhabitants, no matter what means to efface them are taken: "... however repainted and stuccoed, the ceilings and façades of this unconquered city still seem to preserve the stain-like imprints of its inhabitants' last gasps and last gazes."[32] For Brodskij, Petersburg's harrowing experiences in the twentieth century have only served to prove in the extreme that the relationship between space and self here is an enduring and (re-) generative safeguard of the city's true identity.

The lean, mean buildings among which Brodskij walked in the post-war city of his childhood had the same traits as the people of his generation of Petersburgers. The special metonymic association between self and city we have been describing here has, as always, a visual basis: the form of Petersburg's stone, the lines and twists of its streets and squares. It is by this means that a relationship of proximity becomes one of affinity with the city, a process Brodskij describes in a 1987 poem set in Rome, *"Na via Džulija"* ("On Via Giulia"):

> ... Городам, Теодора, тоже
> свойственны лишние мысли, желанье счастья,
> плюс готовность придраться к оттенку кожи,
> к щиколоткам, к прическе, к длине запястья.
> Потому что становишься тем, на то смотришь,
>   что близко видишь.   [3: 143]

> ... Cities, too, Theodora,
> have unnecessary thoughts, the desire for happiness,
> plus the readiness to claim one's shade of skin,
> ankles, hairdo, wrist's length.
> Because you become what you look at, what you see up close.

Thus for Brodskij and his own immediate post-war generation, the character as well as the aspect of Petersburg was assimilated. Despite all the odds and the "drab hell, with a shabby materialist dogma and pathetic consumerist grop-

---

[31] Brodsky, "Less than One," 29.
[32] Ibid., 91.

ings" that Leningrad and Soviet Russia became, he remained aloof from and did not participate in Soviet life, which he calls dismissively "immediate reality":

> My generation, however, was somewhat spared. We emerged from under the postwar rubble.... We entered schools, and whatever elevated rubbish we were taught there, the suffering and poverty were visible all around. You cannot cover a ruin with a page of *Pravda*. The empty windows gaped at us like skulls' orbits, and as little as we were, we sensed tragedy. True, we couldn't connect ourselves to the ruins, but ... they emanated enough to interrupt laughter.... In those postwar years we sensed a strange intensity in the air; something immaterial, almost ghostly.[33]

In this case it is the ruins, the negative forms described precisely by their omission from Soviet "elevated rubbish" that inspire a sense of living continuity with Petersburg. Buildings as receptacles of the past, of memory play an especially important role in Brodskij's work and for Brodskij's generation; they literally contain the Petersburg idea, here in the form of "negative tangibility," an absence that translates into a more real presence than Soviet rhetoric. Damaged Petersburg structures powerfully transmit this idea, this inner essence, to Leningraders. The ravages of war and history have not effaced this transmitting capacity.

Part and parcel of the enduring nature of Petersburg space is its existence in the words of Petersburg writers; thus Brodskij asserts the dependence of his generation of Petersburgers on books. In addition to their cultural reliance on architecture and stones, they were dependent on the word:

> If we made ethical choices, they were based not so much on immediate reality as on moral standards derived from fiction. We were avid readers and we fell into dependence on what we read.... More than anything else, novels would affect our modes of behavior and conversations, and 90 percent of our conversations were about novels. It tended to become a vicious circle, but we didn't want to break it. In its ethics, this generation was among the most bookish in the history of Russia, and thank God for that.[34]

Such a dependence on literature had always been a trait of life in Petersburg. In Toporov's description of the classic Petersburg text, for example, "... it is just as hard to conclusively decide what in the text is from the city and ...

---

[33] Brodsky, "Less than One, " 26–27.
[34] Ibid., 28.

more often—what in the city is from its text."³⁵ Thus a reliance on the word is in itself a form of endurance of the Petersburg aesthetic. Books and architecture became the main realities whereas (Soviet) reality itself was regarded as nonsense or nuisance. This generation, like Brodskij, was made up of people who dropped out of the forward movement of Soviet life, treating it as a lesser, superficial phenomenon:

> The instinctive preference was to read rather than to act. No wonder our actual lives were more or less a shambles. Even those of us who managed to make it through the very thick woods of "higher education," with all its unavoidable lip service to the system, finally fell victim to literature-imposed scruples and couldn't manage any longer. We ended up doing odd jobs ....³⁶

They dropped out in order to remain true to the civilization which Petersburg holds and symbolizes. The march of history has not obliterated Petersburg or the selves/words therein contained; it and they remain "cut off," uncrackable, voluntarily less than the monolithic "one" of Soviet cultural time, and intent on forging for themselves a dynamic relationship with the city through new artistic efforts.

It was not, characteristically, only the Petersburgers of Brodskij's generation who became dependent on the word; so did the city itself, with its buildings:

> ... such was [the] mastery of [Petersburg writers'] material ... that in no time something strange began to happen to the city. The process of recognizing these incurably semantic reflections, loaded with moral judgments, became a process of identification with them. As often happens to a man in front of a mirror, the city began to fall into dependence on the three-dimensional image supplied by literature.... the city started to peer more and more intently at that looking glass which the Russian writers were carrying ... through the streets, courtyards, and shabby apartments of its population.... Russian literature caught up with reality to the extent that today when you think of St. Petersburg you can't distinguish the fictional from the real.³⁷

As much as Brodskij receives real sustenance from Petersburg's words and stones during the post-war period, he in turn sustains the "inner me" of the

---

³⁵ Toporov, "Peterburg i peterburgskij tekst russkoj literatury," 282.
³⁶ Brodsky, "Less than One," 28–29.
³⁷ Brodsky, "A Guide to a Renamed City," 80.

city and buttresses its spatial presence by his own writings—his own part in the dynamic exchange denying the effects of time. Once again, proximity leads to mutual affinity and identity in this enchanted space.

It is important to remember that the denial of external Soviet reality and the ravages of Soviet history is not the only position Brodskij takes in his Petersburg poetry. It is, however, very striking in his *oeuvre*, and when present it is based on a tripartite system of mirror images and identifications that works something like this:

Creative Petersburg man creates buildings and ensembles
➤ A creates B

Creative Petersburg writers create Petersburg literature
➤ C creates D

A complicity of architecture/space and words creates the Petersburg creative man
➤ B and D create A and C

Writers and architects are dependent on and identified with Petersburg architectural spaces
➤ A and C are dependent on B

Writers and architects are dependent on Petersburg literature
➤ A and C are dependent on D

Petersburg spaces are dependent on Petersburg literature
➤ B is dependent on D

This closed system of internal identifications is self-sufficient, and has no need of extra-Petersburg influx or influence. Man and place are identified with the verbal art. Verbal art and man are dependent on place. The only meaningful dynamism derives from these inner connections.

Like the young Brodskij himself, who dropped out of Soviet school and the path expected of a Soviet youth, Brodskij portrays his city suddenly "dropping out of Soviet life/history":

> ... the city of the Bronze Horseman galloped into its future ... treading on the heels of its little men and pushing them forward. And one day a train arrived at the Finland Station, and a little man emerged from the carriage and climbed onto the top of an armored car.
>
> This arrival was a disaster for the nation but a salvation for the city. For its development came to a full stop.... This city froze as if in total

mute bewilderment before the impending era, unwilling to attend it....[38]

It's perhaps in reference to the modesty of that October 25 night enterprise that the city has been termed in official propaganda "the cradle of the Revolution." And a cradle it remained, an empty cradle, and quite enjoyed this status. To a degree, the city escaped the revolutionary carnage. "God forbid us to see," said Pushkin, "the Russian debacle, meaningless and merciless," and Petersburg didn't see it. Civil war raged all around ... and a horrible crack went through the nation ... but here, on the shores of the Neva, for the first time in two centuries, quiet reigned and the grass started to shoot up through the cobblestones of the emptied squares.... the city was left to itself and its reflections....

... Petersburg, having nowhere to withdraw to, came to a standstill—as though photographed in its nineteenth-century posture.[39]

Indeed, many of his Petersburg poems convey this sense of motionlessness, a feature of Brodskij's closed Petersburg system, the eternally-repeating and self-sufficient chronotope that we saw earlier in "Petersburg Novel." And although for Brodskij such suspension in time is not always as unambiguously positive as for other Petersburg writers (Nabokov, for example), it effectively combats the supposedly inevitable line of history represented by Soviet reality. He continues emphasizing that the buildings have dropped out and are as out of place in Soviet life as people like himself: "A strange consolation comes from the notion that these stones have nothing to do with the present and still less with the future. The farther the façades go into the twentieth century [space as time], the more fastidious they look, ignoring these new times and their concerns."[40] Failing to recognize or denying Soviet history and life, "Petersburg" and its culture is punished and debunked by Soviet reality, just as Brodskij, for his non-conformism and extreme denial of Soviet reality, was rejected by it. What he says about Petersburg's reaction to this situation is actually a direct statement of his own attitude. In answer to Gumilev's "*zabludivšijsja tramvaj*" which has careened out of control in time and space, taking its poet captive, Brodskij chooses to jump down, "drop off" the unstoppable tram—a gesture which refuses the superiority of the temporal dimension, and emphasizes the poet's communion with space instead:

Ты плыви. Ты раскачивай

---

[38] Ibid., 85.

[39] Ibid., 88.

[40] Ibid., 90.

фонарики угнетенья
в бесконечное утро
и короткие жизни,
к озаренной патрицианскими светильниками
метрополитена
реальной улыбке
человеческого автоматизма.

Увози их маленьких,
их неправедных, их справедливых.
Пусть останутся краски
лишь коричневая да голубая.
Соскочить с трамвая
и бежать к заливу,
бежать к заливу,
в горизонтальном пейзаже
падая, утопая.

[1: 43 (1960)]

Float along. Swing
the lights of oppression
into the endless morning
and into short lives,
toward the real smile
of human automatonism,
lit up by the patrician
lamps of the metro [subway].

Carry them away, the small ones,
the righteous and unrighteous ones.
Let only the colors of brown
and blue remain.
Jump down off the tram
and run to the gulf,
run to the gulf,
falling, drowning
in the horizontal landscape.

In his address to the tram, the poet reveals the extent to which the passengers are held captive by the means of transportation (tram, subway) which carry them along, making them helpless automatons of history. He asserts his individuality, and, more, his living force, by jumping down. Such psychological and moral rebellion has been a characteristic trait of many Petersburg literary heroes, from Evgenij to Dudkin. In Brodskij's time, this tendency toward self-determination manifests itself perhaps even more strongly. Among the characteristic features of Leningraders he lists "a degree of haughtiness toward the rest of the country. Mentally, this city is still the capital."[41] He projects his attitude onto Petersburg/Leningrad, with which he is almost totally identified:

> Like some of Dostoevsky's characters, Leningrad derives pride and almost a sensual pleasure from being "unrecognized," rejected; and yet it's perfectly aware that, for everyone whose mother tongue is Russian, the city is more real than anywhere else in the world where this language is heard.[42]

This passage is followed by Brodskij's moving assertion that it is Petersburg prose and poetry in the Russian language which ensure the reality of the city. The thoughtful reader does not miss the point that it is Brodskij's prose and poetry, despite any politically motivated attempts to discredit him, which ensure his status as the *real* leading poet of the postwar period.

Brodskij's virtual identification of Petersburg's reaction to the Bolševik Revolution and his own reaction, as a Petersburger and Petersburg poet, to Soviet life and reality, is unusual in a poet of his generation. It has a clear antecedent, however, in Axmatova's depiction of Petersburg and poets like herself in "Petrograd in 1919" («Петроград в 1919-ом году»), a poem treating, long before Brodskij's birth, the conscious, deliberate internalization of the pre-revolutionary city and its architecture against the "cold winds of the new time." We cite this brief poem in its entirety to show the community of reaction and images—in both Brodskij's view and Axmatova's denial during the actual revolutionary period in Petrograd—claiming that "Petersburg," which Brodskij said had nowhere to retreat to, actually retreated within:

> И мы забыли навсегда,
> Заключены в столице дикой,
> Озера, степи, города
> ....
> Никто нам не хотел помочь
> За то, что мы остались дома,
> За то, что, город свой любя,
> ....
> Мы сохранили для себя

---

[41] Ibid., 93.
[42] Ibid.

Его дворцы, огонь и воду.

Иная близится пора,
Уж ветер смерти сердце студит,
Но нам священный град Петра
Невольным памятником будет.

[1: 326]

We forgot forever,
Locked in the wild capital,
Lakes, steppes, cities [the rest of Russia]

No one wanted to help us
Because we remained at home,
Because, loving our city,

We preserved for ourselves
Its palaces, its fire and water.

A different age is nearing,
The winds of death already chill to the heart,
But the holy city of Peter for us
Will be a captive monument.

Here Axmatova speaks, as Brodskij was to do some forty years later, of the internalization of Petersburg by the Petersburg poet. The process begins with the citizens of Petrograd being imprisoned (*zaključeny*) in the revolutionary and civil war-torn city, a clear notion of detention and enclosure. In this state they forget the Russia outside of Petersburg, represented by the lakes, steppes, and other Russian cities, which in their turn have forgotten Petersburg. Petersburgers were abandoned, not aided in that terrible 1919 "because we stayed home and, loving our city, preserved its buildings for ourselves," as Axmatova writes. Suddenly, mid-poem, the Petersburgers' remaining home ceases to be the result of external necessity and becomes an act of will. It becomes their duty to preserve the city's "palaces, fire and water." Axmatova's Petersburgers "commit the city to memory" as Nabokov's generation is said to have done, and thus save it from death, internalizing it in memory. The city becomes an unwitting and not fully willing prisoner inside its citizens. From being enclosed in the city, the citizens enclose it inside themselves.

The Petersburg within, the one that is invisible for the non-initiate, is the standard of beauty and culture, the "buried sun" of the modern Petersburg tradition. In light of this inner Petersburg, the poets wreak their harsh judgment on contemporary Leningrad, the ersatz, impostor city—what Axmatova called in 1924 "Petersburg's opposite." In his autobiographical essays, Brodskij avers that Petersburg went in the same way into the hearts of his own generation, infecting them with its civilization, its sense of proportion and aesthetic form, and even channeling their aspiring ideas. It became the inner content of its poets and writers—they saved it and it saved them in a mutual imprisonment-salvation that Axmatova described and foresaw in the tragic year 1919. And Petersburg withdrew from external reality and objective Soviet history. The name of the city that remained part of it was Leningrad, a name that grates on Brodskij's ears.

In our next chapter we move from the self's communion with a visible Petersburg still accessible through its buildings and spaces to the sometimes idyllic Petersburg that is buried within the poet. This "burial of St. Petersburg" is the next step in our investigation of the denial of the importance of history.

7

The Buried Sun and the Invisible Petersburg: A Reconstructed Writer's Idyll

> А ночного солнца не заметишь ты
> But you will not notice the night sun
> Osip Mandel′štam [1: 85]

> Я много узнал мне неведомых лиц,
> Зрел тварей волшебных, таинственных птиц,
> По высям творенья, как бог, я шагал
>
> I recognized many people I had not known,
> I saw magical beasts and mysterious birds,
> I walked along the heights of creation like a god
> Fedor Tjutčev[1]

In many instances of the Petersburg poet's higher vision of his city and denial of history, he identifies himself with a space that reminds us of the Symbolist's idealized and transcendent worlds and visions. Axmatova alluded to such a space, echoing Blok: «Как вы были в пространстве новом, / Как вне времени были вы» ("How in a new space you were, / How out of time you were").[2] In this form of identification with space, "Petersburg" comes to mean the idealized creative space-time of the artistic community—specifically, those conditions that allow for optimal creativity, be it past, present, future, or potential. The ability to create beautiful works of art that affect and transform the outer world as well as their creator himself comes to be called "Petersburg."[3] This ability/creative space is clearly the antonym of the Soviet, negative Leningrad, which is treated as a kind of hell. Nevertheless, as Sharon Leiter has pointed out very emphatically in her study *Axmatova's Petersburg*, when there is a hidden Petersburg world, access to it is usually place-bound. One must reach "the 'world behind the mirror' of unrealized events or the

---

[1] Tjutčev, "Son na more," 94.
[2] Blok, "Milyj brat! Zavečerelo," 111: "Словно мы—в пространстве новом, / Словно—в новых временах."
[3] For example, the poet Xodasevič becomes Orpheus in his "Ballada," treated in detail in chap. 8 below. It is also discussed in detail in Bethea, *Khodasevich*, 237–50.

shadow world of the past through the visual, palpable Leningrad world," and "for Axmatova ... the bridge to that invisible world is always the visual...."[4] Thus, as we saw above in chapter 6, Axmatova spoke of buildings and architectural ensembles as "loopholes to the past," implying that their removal would bring about total rupture with that past.

This "Petersburg" is the opposite of Leningrad. It is an idyllic place-state. It represents no particular epoch or time, but a recurrent, ever-potential state—a Petersburg which is possible as long as Petersburg poets can envision it and carry its image and spirit within them. The notion of Petersburg as an idyll and the poet as a piping shepherd of sorts represents a more intense strategy of defiant ahistoricism than that which we saw in chapter 6. It draws upon the understanding codified by Brodskij as "less than one,"[5] but is more dynamic than the "frozen" or suspended-time approach to "the real Petersburg/self" that we typically find in Brodskij, and more adamant about the strictly positive nature of this timeless state of being, its potentialities equal to its actualities. In the vision of the city discussed in this chapter, Petersburg is a sustained belief supported and embodied by its writers and its spaces, which jointly contain its ever-presence. This idyll is all the more forceful and defiant for its existing in an urban space, and, moreover, in an urban space with all the earmarks of a chaotic and soulless hell. If in the nineteenth-century Petersburg tradition, the city's "abstract and premeditated" qualities were a source of constant anxiety and even terror, the identification between space and self occasioned by a solidarity against twentieth-century history counts "Petersburg's" insistent abstraction, here associated with the ideal and creative, as salvific. The realm of the ideal is the true Petersburg, the true self. The city of the mind is a place-condition of repose, joy, and perpetual creative possibility. The elegiac mode of loss and mourning is overpowered here because all Petersburg's potentialities are coexistent; the idyllic mode of identification between self and space proves to be a potent variant on identification based in the elegiac mode.

We see this positive city in Xodasevič's 1925 poem "Petersburg," written about his enormously productive "Petersburg period":

Петербург

Напастям жалким и однообразным
Там предавались до потери сил.
Один лишь я полуживым соблазном
Средь озабоченных ходил.

---

[4] Leiter, *Akhmatova's Petersburg*, 130 ff.
[5] See chap. 6, pp. 220–21.

Смотрели на меня—и забывали
Клокочущие чайники свои;
На печкак валенки сгорали;
Все слушали стихи мои.

А мне тогда в тьме гробовой, российской,
Являлась вестница в цветах,
И лад открылся музикийский
Мне в сногсшибательных ветрах.

И я безумел от видений,
Когда чрез ледяной канал,
Скользя с обломанных ступеней,
Треску зловонную таскал,

И, каждый стих гоня сквозь прозу,
Вывихивая каждую строку,
Привил-таки классическую розу
К советскому дичку.[6]

Petersburg

To pitiable, monstrous misfortunes
People there gave themselves over 'til sapped of strength.
I alone like a half-alive seduction
Wandered among the worried ones.

They would look at me and forget
Their bubbling teapots;
They burned their felt boots on their stoves;
They were all listening to my verses.

And then in the Russian-imperial, gravelike darkness,
A female messenger in flowers appeared to me,
And a musical mode was opened to me
In winds that knocked you off your feet.

And I went mad from visions,
When across the icy canal,
Sliding from broken steps
I dragged a stinking cod,

---

[6] Vladislav Xodasevič, *Sobranie sočinenij*, ed. Nina Berberova (Munich, 1961), 1: 23.

And chasing each line of verse through prose,
Dislocating each line,
I grafted a classical rose
Onto the Soviet wilding.

In this poem, Xodasevič looks back on his period of Orphic poetic power, best exemplified in his most famous poem of the period, "Ballad" (treated in chapter 8). The poet here speaks in a state not unlike Puškin's in "The Prophet" or Tjutčev's in "A Dream at Sea"—that is, in a state of higher vision which allows him access to the true city, an enchanted world completely opposed to the communal kitchens and "gravelike darkness" of Leningrad. The content of his "Petersburg" is idyllic, despite the fact that the city around him is literally dying and falling apart. His skill and craft as a poet, described in detail in the last stanza, enables him not only to tap into Petersburg, but also to sustain it through his own powers of creation. In contrast to Blok's "wind, wind!" that diverts modern man and Petersburg from their path and ensures that "man cannot stand on his feet" in *The Twelve*, the "winds that knocked you off your feet" here are associated with a transforming creativity and access to the idyllic spaces of the "true" city. As we saw above, Xodasevič spoke in his memoirs about the dying of Petersburg/Petrograd perhaps more eloquently than anyone else, and he virtually equated Puškin in the grave with Petersburg in *its* grave.[7] In his poem "Petersburg," however, his statement of poetic power despite the terrible winters and hunger of the period (1918–22) reminds us of Mandel'štam's vision of the buried or night sun in "We will gather again in Petersburg," which of course preceded and influenced Xodasevič's poem.

Poems casting Petersburg as the writer's idyllic place-time represent a fairly rare, but very important strategy of denial of history in post-revolutionary Russian literature. Its greatest and most influential poem is, in fact, this very same masterpiece of Mandel'štam's, the 1918 "We will gather again in Petersburg," referred to repeatedly in these pages. As we saw in chapter 4, an atmosphere of death and dying pervades this poem, compounded by the notion of a major governmental threat to poetry and poets via allusion to the ignominious circumstances of Puškin's death and funeral. In Mandel'štam's poem there are fewer topical references than in Xodasevič's later poem to the physical hardships of life that consumed Petrograders at that time. His Russian darkness is more mythical and more apparently apocalyptic:

---

[7] See discussion in chap. 4, p. 119.

> В черном бархате советской ночи,
> В черном бархате всемирной пустоты [1: 85]
>
> In the black velvet of Soviet night,
> In the black velvet of universal emptiness

In both poems the hellish reality of contemporary Petrograd is opposed to the highly idealized Petersburg, which is not the prosperous city of the *ancien régime*, but a marvelous haven for the writer and creative person, the place where Puškin should have been buried: «Словно солнце похоронили в нем» ("As if they had buried the sun there"). It is particularly after the 1917 revolution that the word "Petersburg" loses its connection with the visible world and connotes more and more an idyllic time-place, the refuge of the family of poet-friends, a longed-for state ever sought-after and only occasionally triumphantly achieved. In the context of the Petersburg idyll, the process of "ensavagement" (*odičanie*) to which the city was subjected in the immediate post-revolution years, and which we described in very negative terms in chapter 3, becomes a paradoxical kind of pastoralization. In the ahistorical idyll, primitivization becomes a positive value, such that "in the face of devastation, the 'city of culture' regains its lost natural paradise."[8] Thus the frequent mention during this period of grass growing in the Petersburg streets can acquire very positive tones. Viktor Šklovskij, for example, writes, "In Petersburg it smells of spaciousness and the sea. Green grass is everywhere.... The city has gone pastoral.... A paradise lost and regained."[9] In "The Word and Culture," Mandel'štam speaks in a similar way of the newly idyllic Petersburg:

> The grass on the Petersburg streets are the first forerunners of the virginal forest that will cover the place where modern cities are. This bright, tender greenness, amazing in its freshness, belongs to a new, spiritualized nature. Verily Petersburg is the foremost city in the world. The race of modernity, its speed, is measured not by subways and not by skyscrapers, but by the merry grass that is penetrating through from under the city stones. [2: 264]

Mandel'štam does not limit his pastoral Petersburg to a reprise of a primitive ("virginal") time, but casts its rampant grass in the role of a kind of avant-garde herald of world culture. The creative idyll, as in "We will gather again," is thus not limited by constraints of temporality. And nature and culture, perhaps for the first time in Petersburg history, are no longer battling each other. If the idyllization of the city stands in direct opposition to the process of en-

---

[8] Boym, *The Future of Nostalgia*, 137.
[9] Viktor Šklovskij, *Xod konja*, quoted in Boym, *The Future of Nostalgia*, 136–37.

savagement that we observed in our discussion of "historical" treatments of self and space, then negative *kenosis* here starts to turn into its opposite. Rather than emptying out its own void or chaos onto its poet-selves, here Petersburg, having been "emptied" to the point where grass is growing in its streets, becomes the source of the self's retreat into the idyllic creative spaces of the "second Petersburg: the one made of prose and Russian verse," as Brodskij put it.

This writer's idyll sometimes takes on the quality of the shadow world as represented in Belyj's *Petersburg*. In *Myth and History*, Mircea Eliade elaborated the notion of the sacred and profane dimensions of any life, one participating in linear history and the other eternal and out of mundane time. That mythical and sacred world exists parallel to the empirical world. We see it, for example, in the life of Puškin's "Poet" (1826). In his profane life, that poet is the most mundane of persons: "Among the insignificant children of the world, perhaps he is the most insignificant." But this is so only "until Apollo needs his service," at which point he takes on his holy prophetic mission, becoming Apollo's emissary and acquiring all the special visions and hearing associated with that superhuman role. Sometimes he has a vision of the world of the dead; at other times he merely hears a chorus of voices to which only the poet has access, a *"tajnyj xor"* ("secret choir") of inspiration. The Petersburg poet can move easily from the everyday profane world into the sacred Petersburg world, or have it invade his empirical space and everyday life to take him over (as Xodasevič goes "mad from visions"). Jakov Gordin remarks on the surprising frequency of terms designating "enlightenment," higher vision, and access to the "sacred" in the immediate post-revolutionary years, and mostly among Petersburgers, drawing attention to the "sensation of 'the nearness of the miraculous,' 'the blessed,' and an unheard-of higher life, all in the midst of unprecedented trials and humiliations...."[10] In Mandel'štam's "We will gather again in Petersburg," that higher world can be seen and participated in only by the community of poets, the "we" who will gather. "Somewhere," according to the poem's variant lines, "the sweet choruses of Orpheus," the indestructible poet who continues singing after he has been beheaded, "are still heard." Yet the philistine, the official, the governmental detractors and regimenters of poetry and art, whom he brusquely addresses with the familiar *ty* form, are unable to see this "second Petersburg," which is more important and ultimately more real: «А ночного солнца не заметишь ты» ("But you will not notice the night sun").

---

[10] Jakov Gordin, *Perekličkа vo mrake: Iosif Brodskij i ego sobesedniki* (St. Petersburg: Puškinskij fond, 2000), 92.

This higher world becomes visible and audible to Axmatova in *Poem without a Hero* when the crowd comes in and she reacts: «Венеция дожей … / Это рядом» ("The Venice of the Doges … / Is nearby"). This "Venice of the Doges" or "the land of satin half-masks" is what Axmatova calls the real Petersburg, the creative one. The everyday Leningrad is compared to a provincial city, Luga, which is even less distinguished in the Soviet period than it was before the revolution, and thus an extremely debunking metaphor. The distance from the present empirical Leningrad of the 1940s to the sought-for idyllic writer's haven called Petersburg is associated with the evocative powers of the poet's mind, with nothing material. Distance here becomes mental, internal:

Между помнить и вспомнить, други,
Расстояние—как от Луги
До страны атласных баут.   [2: 98]

Between not forgetting and strong remembrance, friends,
There is a distance as great as that from Luga
To the land of satin half-masks.

Of course, Axmatova's Petersburg as represented here has qualities of a pastoral paradise, a curious urban Arcadia peopled not by peaceful peasants, but by colorful, creative bohemian artists, actors, dancers, and impresarios. In Konstantin Vaginov's 1928 novel *Kozlinaja pesn'* (*Goat Song*), the Petersburg writer's idyll, the so-called last bastion of Petersburg and world culture in Soviet Leningrad, has similar qualities of pastoral antiquity: "the philosopher played an ancient melody … women rose to their feet and began dancing in pairs among flowers on the meadow."[11] Nabokov's version of Arcadia in his 1969 novel *Ada* (here the estate called Ardis) is a multiply-sublimated and metapoetic treatment of an idyllic space ultimately evoking his own family estate and the creative Petersburg powers with which it was connected. The group of émigré authors performing in Paris and Berlin, depicted elsewhere in Nabokov and others, are the ghostly remainders of that world.

We pointed out in the introduction to this section of the book that Petersburg is an unlikely candidate for idyllic status. The fact that it is a large urban environment would disqualify it, and its very tragic and complex negative mythology from the time of its founding would seem to render a Petersburg idyll impossible. Yet Mandel'štam, Nabokov, the artist Benois, and

---

[11] Konstantin Vaginov, *The Tower*, trans. Benjamin Sher (New Orleans: Sher Publishers, 1997), 74, 76. Vaginov uses the Russian title *Kozlinaja pesn'* (*Goat Song*) as a literal translation of the Greek "tragedy" (*tragoidia*), so named because of the costumes of actors and singers representing satyrs.

even Brodskij fly in the face of such restrictions, fashioning for themselves an idyllic Petersburg formative period, specifically envisioned as the poet's childhood in an urban idyll. Brodskij, realizing the oxymoronic humor of his idyll, makes fun of his own attitudes towards the city: «Вот я вновь посетил … парадиз мастерских и аркадию фабрик» ("Here I have visited again this … paradise of workshops and Arcadia of factories").[12] Such incongruous statements reflect the coexistence of the *klassičeskaja roza* (classical rose) and the *sovetskij dičok* (Soviet wilding) of Xodasevič's poem cited earlier. In his essay "Flight from Byzantium," Brodskij wrote that he had subjected himself to inoculations of Xodasevič's "classical rose" for the greater part of his life.[13] Indeed, the mixture of the "prose of everyday Soviet life" in language and imagery with the "classical roses" of the "second Petersburg" is ever present in Brodskij's Petersburg poetry.

Petersburg poets, then, attempt to make Petersburg stand for heightened creativity and a community of creators, enthusiasts of art, and poet-friends («Все слушали стихи мои», "They were all listening to my verses"). As all idylls, according to Baxtin, severely limit themselves to a set of basic activities in the lives of the idyllic personages, so here the subjects are limited: creativity, communion with poet-artist-friends, pure poetic imagination, and an elevated state of special hearing and vision experienced in those pursuits (Puškin's «и звуков, и смятенья полн», "full of sounds and commotion" from "The Prophet"; Xodasevič's « лад … музикийский … в сногшибательных ветрах / И я безумел от видений…», "a musical mode … in winds that knocked you off your feet / And I went insane from visions" from "Petersburg"; and Axmatova's «музыка дикого мэтра, / ленинградского дикого ветра», "music of a wild maestro, / of the wild Leningrad wind" from *Poem without a Hero*). Perhaps this "Petersburg" has qualities of the family idyll, but represents a family of poets instead of blood relations, one in which, as Baxtin emphasizes, "the deep *humanity* of idyllic man himself [read: poet] and the humanity of his human relationships are foregrounded, as is the *wholeness* of idyllic life.…"[14]

Baxtin further speaks of the destruction of the idyll as a significant part of modern literary history, and points out that there are survivals of it that appear in modern novels, when a personage of idyllic provenance appears in the corrupting atmosphere of the modern city, bringing along his idyllic baggage: "a fragmentary penetration of isolated elements of the idyllic complex," "'a

---

[12] Brodskij, 2: 217.

[13] Brodsky, "Flight from Byzantium," *Less than One*, 395–96.

[14] Baxtin, "Forms of Time and Chronotope in the Novel," 233.

man of the people'" is often of idyllic descent.[15] Our poet appearing in Petrograd or Leningrad, as Xodasevič describes himself doing in his poem "Petersburg," is just such an idyllic messenger. Coming from this idyll or carrying his Petersburg within him, he injects himself as an isolated element of that idyllic complex into Leningrad/Petrograd, and tries to graft elements of this Petersburg onto the non-Petersburg in which he physically finds himself.

This desire to project the ideal, the idyll onto the patently non-idyllic can be seen in a very ironic Petersburg poem written by Brodskij in the United States in 1976, «Развивая Платона» ("Embroidering on Plato"). This poem represents an inversion of the strategy used in Brodskij's earlier poem "From the Outskirts to the Center" (see chapter 5), where Petersburg-Arcadia is mercilessly de-idyllized. Although the city is not named as such in "Embroidering on Plato," it is the world of "Petersburg" within Soviet Leningrad that is being idyllized here in a complex and ironic way. It is a city in which the poet attempts to re-graft the "classical rose" of Petersburg onto the mundane, prosaic, and even vulgar character of the Leningrad which surrounds (surrounded) him:

> Я хотел бы жить, Фортунатус, в городе где река
> высовывалась бы из-под моста, как из рукава—рука,
>   и чтоб она впадала в залив, растопырив пальцы,
> как Шопен, никому не показывавший кулака.
>
> Чтобы там была Опера, и чтоб в ней ветеран-
> тенор исправно пел арию Марио по вечерам;
>   чтоб тиран ему аплодировал в ложе, а я в партере
> бормотал бы, сжав зубы от ненависти: «баран».
> ....
> Там была бы Библиотека, и в залах ее пустых
> я листал бы тома с таким же количеством запятых,
>   как количество скверных слов в ежедневной речи,
> не прорвавшихся в прозу. Ни, тем более, в стих.
> ....
> И там были бы памятники. Я бы знал имена
> не только бронзовых всадников.…   [2: 394]

I would like to live, Fortunatus, in a city where a river
would stick out from under a bridge like a hand from a sleeve,
    and it would empty into a gulf, spreading its fingers
like Chopin, who didn't show anyone his fist.

---

[15] Ibid., 235.

There would be an Opera there, and in it a veteran-
tenor would diligently sing the Mario aria in the evenings;
    and a tyrant would applaud him in the box seat, while I, in the pit,
would mumble, grinding my teeth in hatred, "old goat."
....
There would be a Library there, and in its empty halls
I would leaf through tomes with as large a number of commas
    as there are dirty words in everyday speech,
words that don't make it into prose, much less into verse.
....
And there would be monuments there. I would know the names
of more than just the bronze horsemen....

In each stanza, institutions of Petersburg's classical creative community, represented both abstractly (as ideal Platonic forms with capital letters) and architecturally, coexist with degrading conditions of Soviet *byt*.[16] At the end of the poem, the poet is driven out of his city, and apparently is happy about it:

И когда бы меня схватили в итоге за шпионаж,
подрывную активность, бродяжничество, менаж-
    а-труа, и толпа бы, беснуясь вокруг, кричала,
тыча в меня натруженными указательными: «Не наш!»,—

я бы втайне был счастлив, шепча про себя: «Смотри,
это твой шанс узнать, как выглядит изнутри
    то, на что ты так долго глядел снаружи;
запоминай же подробности, восклицая "Vive la Patrie!"

And when, in the end, they would grab me for espionage,
subversive activity, vagrancy, menage-
    à-trois, and the crowd, raving around me, would yell,
poking me with their work-hardened fingers, "He's not one of us!"

I would secretly be happy, whispering to myself, "Look,
this is your chance to find out what something you've seen so long
    from the outside looks like from the inside;
so remember the details, exclaiming, "Vive la Patrie!"

---

[16] For interesting commentary on the "Mario aria" (from the opera *Tosca*) and on Fortunatus as addressee (an Auden subtext), see Maija Könönen, *"Four Ways of Writing the City": St. Petersburg-Leningrad as a Metaphor in the Poetry of Joseph Brodsky*, Slavica Helsingiensia 23 (Helsinki: University of Helsinki, 2003), 196–98 and 219–24.

From the foregoing it would seem that Brodskij's ideal city has not managed to transcend its real trappings, and that the very fact of his ultimate expulsion from the place represents the inaccessibility to him of the "Petersburg" creative circle. However, Brodskij's desire to idyllize the non-idyllic works more effectively in the poem's structure.

Each of the 16 stanzas in the poem is framed by the subjunctive mood (*by*). In this way, Brodskij writes *as if* wishing, *as if* what he states is in opposition to fact, not a real possibility, but an ideal world. For Brodskij in 1976, his native city has actually become more ideal than real; in one sense, the subjunctive mood represents an elegiac wish of something he cannot access (at least physically) now. However, the second line of the poem (quoted above) begins a chain of "wishes" that reveal quite a differently-directed technique. Petersburg *is*, in fact, a city where the "river [sticks] out from under a bridge, like a hand from a sleeve." As we read further, we realize that Brodskij is describing not something that *might be* for him (a wish fulfillment), but something that already *was* part of his own experience:

По отсутствию дыма из кирпичных фабричных труб
    я узнавал бы о наступлении воскресенья
и долго бы трясся в автобусе, мучая в жмене руб.

By the absence of factory smokestacks
    I would know that Sunday was on its way
and I would be shaken around in a bus for a long time, tormenting a
    ruble in my grasp.

Here, as in the final two stanzas describing the poet's arrest, we recognize concrete and biographically accurate details of the poet's life in 1960s/70s Leningrad. The subjunctive context of such details represents more than the familiar elegiac device of "if I only could, I would go back and live it again." The elegy typically acknowledges an indicative past or present (one that did actually happen/is happening, whether ideal or not) as a background against which a sense of loss or wishing occurs. Here, in contrast, Brodskij turns what we know to be his real experience in Leningrad into something that did not happen, but he wishes had. Moreover, he further distorts the poetics of the elegy in "wishing for" and looking back with apparent nostalgia on the clearly non-idyllic (his own exile, for example). In one sense, "Embroidering on Plato" could be seen as a deeply ironic explosion of the Romantic myth of the exiled poet, addressed to those (himself included) who see the very circumstance of exile, of a Puškinian disjunction between the poet and the *tolpa* ("crowd") as desirable, something to be wished for. However, the juxtaposition of Leningrad and Petersburg in the poem is too charged for us not to consider that in another sense, Brodskij is seriously examining his own creative self and a formative space. The subjunctivization of a clearly indicative set of circumstances recasts Brodskij's physical association with his native city as a timeless idyll, "re-inoculating," to some extent, the rather compromised manifestations of "Petersburg" in Leningrad shown in the poem. This re-aestheticization—a Platonizing or idealizing—of Petersburg in the form of the poem (with its classical mood, diction, and line length) actually works to confirm Brodskij's continuing contact with "Petersburg," even outside of Russia. This Petersburg is internalized within him, and it is the exercise of memory («запоминай же подробности», "so remember the details") which allows him access to the writer's idyll, the true *Patrie*. There is an endless, repeating loop between the *fact* of his actually having been exiled and the *wish* that he could be. "Looking from the inside" (*iznutri*), that is, from his idyllic "Petersburg" (even if he himself happens to be abroad), enables the poet to engage in an endless, quasi-idyllic, creative potential, reaffirming the "classical" Petersburg sullied by its contact with non-idyllic Leningrad. It is a version of the state of "higher vision" we have seen in Xodasevič and others who employ this strategy. Participation in the Petersburg writer's idyll is enacted in the repeating desire to *go back*.

We say "quasi-idyllic" because Brodskij's ironic tone remains throughout the poem; what is important here is the clear desire, the exercise in casting the non-idyllic as idyllic. A fondness for Petersburg (rather than Leningrad) is unmistakable here, as is an undying love of certain places—the Hermitage, a coffee house—which is very reminiscent of the beloved, somewhat idyllic Petersburg Mandel'štam associates with his youth in *The Noise of Time* and with Parnok's youth in *The Egyptian Stamp*. And just as in the latter work, the poet in "Embroidering on Plato" finds himself being singled out as an alien element and captured, arrested, although not lynched as in *The Egyptian Stamp*. It is as if the mood of the city has not changed much since the days described in Mandel'štam's prose. Brodskij's will to idyllize the non-idyllic is similar to Mandel'štam's in "We will gather again in Petersburg":

Дикой кошкой горбится столица,
На мосту патруль стоит,
Только злой мотор во мгле промчится
И кукушкой прокричит.
Мне не надо пропуска ночного,
Часовых я не боюсь:
За блаженное, бессмысленное слово
Я в ночи советской помолюсь.   [1: 85]

The capital hunches like a wild cat,
A patrol stands on the bridge,
Only an evil motorcar speeds through the haze
And calls out like a cuckoo.
I don't need a night pass,
I am not afraid of sentries:
For the blessed, senseless word
I will pray in the Soviet night.

Here the speaker blatantly denies that the rules of Soviet law and reality have any application to him; instead, he invokes the "blessed, senseless word" of the Petersburg creative idyll over the noise of the speeding car.

The speaker in Nabokov's 1929 poem "For nighttime wandering I need…" (discussed in detail in chapter 5), in language very similar to Mandel'štam's, likewise calls upon and himself participates in the Petersburg idyll. Mandel'štam's hero "[does not] need a night pass" (не надо пропуска ночного), while Nabokov's "need[s] neither ships nor trains" for his "nighttime wandering" (для странствия ночного мне не надо ни кораблей, ни поездов); Petersburg is a self-sufficient idyllic system that requires no external means or permission for our poets to access it. It is an idyll that can be felt even in darkness. Petersburg poets of this age must of necessity become nocturnal animals who can see at night: while Mandel'štam's Petersburg "hunches like a wild cat" (дикой кошкой горбится) in the shape of its bridge, as if its very structures were frightened of and hostile toward the Soviet sentries keeping watch there, Nabokov's speaker "jumps … like a cat across the gate at night" (прыгает … как ночью кот через плетень) across miles to eventually reach Petersburg. Even measures taken to interfere with the poet's praying for or jumping into the Petersburg creative idyll do not impinge upon the idyll's integrity. Mandel'štam clearly states that he is "not afraid of sentries" (часовых я не боюсь), and Nabokov uses the same word in describing his own invincibility: "the sentry aims in vain" (напрасно метит часовой). Brodskij shows the same ability to see and determination to find the ideal Petersburg, the same lack of fear of threats in the empirical city:

В сумерках я следил бы в окне стада
мычащих автомобилей, снующих туда-сюда
   мимо стройных нагих колонн с дорическою прической,
безмятежно белеющих на фронтоне Суда.

At twilight I would follow through the window the herds
of mooing cars rushing hither and thither
   past columns with Doric coiffures,

calmly white on the Court Building façade.

Like Mandel′štam, he turns his arrest into something not to be feared, but a learning experience, an opportunity to understand his city "from the inside." The people who will reject him are Mandel′štam's «черные души», «низменные святоши» ("black souls," "low hypocrites"). We have seen in Brodskij, too, this paradoxical sense that the current city is in no way a candidate for the idyllic status that our poets confer upon it. It was also clear in Axmatova's 1922 denial that the place in which she was living had nothing at all to do with "Petersburg," that it was, in fact, non-Petersburg: «Петербург превратился в свою противоположность» [2: 199] ("Petersburg has turned into its opposite"). In her memoirs of Osip Mandel′štam, she said virtually the same of Carskoe Selo, which had been renamed "Detskoe."

CREATIVE CONTINUITY IN PETERSBURG AND CARSKOE SELO

For all the unlikelihood that Petersburg would be treated as an idyllic time-place, it in fact emerges in certain very influential poems of the twentieth century as a place of serenity and calm, a true cradle of creativity made all the more cozy and comfortable by the contrast of the chaos and storms without. In the pre-revolutionary period largely marked by historical examples of self-space identification, Axmatova encapsulates this paradoxical sense of Petersburg as nurturing space: «Был блаженной моей колыбелью / Темный город у грозной реки» ("The dark city by an ominous river / Was my blissful cradle") [1914].[17] With such a formulation, Axmatova follows Puškin in *The Bronze Horseman*, asserting a Petersburg writer's idyll against the narrative backdrop of flood and destruction:

> Люблю тебя, Петра творенье,
> ....
> Твоих задумчивых ночей
> Прозрачный сумрак, блеск безлунный,
> Когда я в комнате моей
> Пишу, читаю без лампады[18]
>
> I love you, Peter's creation,
>
> The transparent twilight, the moonless
> Shine of your pensive nights,
> When in my room

---

[17] See also Day, chap. 4 ("The Unsettled Home").
[18] Puškin, Mednyj vsadnik," 5: 131.

> I write and read without a lamp

Indeed, even after the revolution Axmatova would continue asserting the idyllic basis of the writer's Petersburg, again drawing upon Puškinian models of tranquil well-being, transferring to the city all the qualities we are used to associating with Carskoe Selo!

No one would dispute that Carskoe Selo is an idyllic time-place in Deržavin, in Puškin, in the Puškin Pleiad, especially Del′vig and Kjuxel′beker, occasionally in Žukovskij and Tjutčev, and in Annenskij and two Acmeists, Axmatova and Gumilev. This aspect of Carskoe Selo has been treated by Roberta Reeder, in the context of the difficulty of a return there, as well as by Anna Lisa Crone.[19] It has also been treated by Renate Lachmann as a "memory place" linked to Petersburg in its complex palimpsestic poetics, especially in the Acmeist tradition.[20] Significantly, while there are poets almost exclusively associated with Carskoe Selo, such as Komarovskij, most of the great writers who can be called "Carskoe Selo poets" are either simultaneously "Petersburg poets," or, as in the case of Innokentij Annenskij, made extremely important contributions to the Petersburg tradition. Nabokov mediates between urban and country idyll in an analogous way, with the substitution of his family's estates Batovo and Vyra as his Carskoe Selo. The great exception to this double-centeredness is Osip Mandel′štam, and Axmatova emphasizes in her memoirs of Mandel′štam that there are no idyllic associations with the town in his *oeuvre*: "There is not nor can there be a topic such as 'Mandel′štam and Carskoe Selo.'"[21] This impossibility, as we will see here, is not insignificant.

The idyllic vision of Carskoe Selo was created in art over some 140 years, from Deržavin to Axmatova. Baxtin, in his discussion of chronotopes in prose, lists some of the hallmarks of the idyll as a literary type, such as unity of place in the "life of generations," which "renders less distinct all the temporal boundaries between individual lives and between various phases of one and the same life." In emphasizing this unity of place, he asserts that "idyllic life and its events are inseparable from this concrete, spatial corner of the world where the fathers and grandfathers lived and where one's children and their children will live."[22] In transferring this characteristic from Carskoe Selo to the city, the Petersburg idyll our writers try collectively to create contrasts sharply

---

[19] Anna Lisa Crone, "Axmatova and the Passing of the Swans: Horatian Tradition and Carskoe Selo," *Tsarskoe Selo: A Sense of Place*, ed. Barry Scherr and Lev Loseff (Columbus, OH: Slavica Publishers, 1994), 88–112. See note 34 below for Roberta Reeder.

[20] Lachmann, *Memory and Literature*, 252 and 243–55.

[21] Axmatova, "Listki iz dnevnika," 2: 192.

[22] Baxtin, "Forms of Time and Chronotope in the Novel," 225.

with the many treatments of Petersburg space presented here in earlier chapters. Petersburg spaces and selves do not only cling to each other for support, do not only defiantly resist the very notion of time through a shared and mutually-reflecting memory, but actually catch themselves in the act of *creating* each other in a constant and always-accessible (because always place-bound) intercommunion. This treatment of Petersburg, in fact, represents a great attempt to reinterpret its space—to make it stand for something radically different in the national memory. The "content" of Peterburg—its inner being/meaning—becomes sustaining, life-giving, rather than chaotic and voidlike.

Let us recall the idyllic characteristics of Carskoe Selo which were conferred upon the town in the poetry of Deržavin, Puškin, Del'vig, Kjuxel'beker, and lesser poets of the 19th century. It is these idyllic traits that our poets in turn confer upon Petersburg in their strategy of denial of history and identification between self and space. Carskoe Selo is the place of sacred higher life; first, it is the place where monuments to the nation's past were erected by Catherine II, but secondly, and more importantly, it is the place of the inner heroism of the anointed poet, the cradle of his creativity. Thus it was the place of a higher principle of self, and, although the first Carskoe Selo poets elegiacally lament the loss of a former time, a former self—a loss not acknowledged in the kind of Petersburg denial discussed in this chapter—it is their kind of idyllic identification of self with a specifically creative space that finds resonance in the twentieth-century Petersburg aesthetic. The truest self existed in Carskoe, in communion with poet-friends; it is the true homeland associated with youthful inspiration and purity. These correlations are very powerfully expressed in Kjuxel'beker's poem "Carskoe Selo." In Puškin's 1829 "Reminiscences in Carskoe Selo," he returns there as a prodigal son.[23] In Kjuxel'beker's poem, his return is a failure, because Carskoe has changed and because Puškin and Del'vig are not with him. Carskoe in this poetry is a place of attempted returns, even on a yearly basis, to mark the anniversary of the graduation of the first Lycée class. These returns can be both real, as in Kjuxel'beker's poem, and imaginary, as in Puškin's Lycée poem written during his exile in Mixailovskoe to be read at the gathering. The imaginary returns are often more positive than the actual ones, and sometimes give the poet the Proustian sense of achieving a state belatedly, perhaps more than it was ever achieved at the time. Thus Carskoe Selo as "homeland" is envisioned as an inspired state of creativity based on a shared sense of community with poet-friends.

---

[23] Puškin, "Vospominanija v Carskom sele," 3: 189.

The actual physical returns, by contrast, are usually accompanied by a deep sense of exile *in situ*, that the place has changed, that lyric heroes are not able to retrieve from it what is there, and that it does not yield itself to them fully.[24] Disappointment causes the Carskoe Selo poems to become meditations on what has been lost or cannot be fully retrieved, in the elegiac mode. However, the speaker in many of these poems dwells for so long on happy memories and a continuing, indissoluble bond between poet-friends that these components of the poem tend to challenge the elegiac cast. The Carskoe Selo elegy often asserts an idyllic creative state in the present of the poem, the conjuring-up of those elements in art, in poetry. The poet puts back the missing elements of that Carskoe Selo which is within him. In Kjuxel′beker's poem, for example, the poet's elegiac lament is mitigated somewhat by the affirmation of his creative homeland:

> Ничто души моей от вас не удалит!
> И в песнях сладостных и в славе состязанье
> Друзей-соперников тесней соединит![25]
>
> Nothing will distance my soul from you!
> Competition will unite friends-rivals even closer
> In sweet songs and glory!

The disappointed Kjuxel′beker evokes what is missing so lovingly that he seems to bring it back:

> Здесь мирные места, где возвышенных муз
> ....
> Порыв к великому, любовь к добру впервые
> Узнали мы, где наш тройственный союз
> Союз младых певцов, и чистый и священный
> Был дружбой утвержден!
>
> Here are peaceful places where we first
>
> Knew the exalted Muses' impulse
> Towards greatness and love of goodness,
> Where our triple alliance, the alliance of
> Young poets, pure and sacred, was affirmed in friendship!

---

[24] We observed this problem in chap. 5, p. 145 ff.
[25] Vilgel′m Kjuxel′beker, "Carskoe Selo," *Izbrannye proizvedenija* (Leningrad: Sovetskij pisatel′ 1967), 1: 95–96.

He closes on a note that Carskoe would be its idyllic self and that he would be at peace there only with them, with the missing Puškin and Del′vig. It is not, thus, merely a homeland of space/place, but of the mind and creative spirit as well:

> При вас, товарищи, моя утихнет кровь.
> И я в родной стране забуду на мгновенье
> Заботы, и тоску, и скуку, и волненье,
> Забуду, может быть, и самую любовь!

> With you, comrades, my blood will grow calm.
> And in my native land, I will forget for a moment
> Concerns and melancholy, boredom and excitement,
> I might even forget love itself!

It was this poem, perhaps, that provoked Puškin's most famous lines on the same subject in his 1825 poem "October 19":

> Друзья мои, прекрасен наш союз!
> Он, как душа, неразделим и вечен—
> ....
> Все те же мы: нам целый мир чужбина;
> Отечество нам Царское Село.[26]

> My friends, our alliance is wonderful!
> It is indivisible and eternal like the soul—

> We are always the same: all the world is a foreign land to us;
> Our fatherland is Carskoe Selo.

For Puškin, the creative space represented and inspired by Carskoe Selo is linked to the unsundered self, the "indivisible and eternal" soul. It is Puškin, too, in his 1823 "Carskoe Selo," who best expresses the longed-for idyll of Carskoe, an imaginary return so alive and explicit that it is a successful return through art:

> Воспоминанье, рисуй предо мной
> Волшебные места, где я живу душой,
> Леса, где я любил, где чувство развивалось,
> Где с первой юностью младенчество сливалось
> И где, взлелеянный природой и мечтой,
> Я знал поэзию, веселость и покой…

---

[26] Puškin, "19 oktjabrja," 1: 475–76.

> Веди, веди меня под липовые сени,
> Всегда любезные моей свободной лени,
> На берег озера, на тихий скат холмов!…
> Да вновь увижу я ковры густых лугов,
> И дряхлый пук дерев, и светлую долину,
> И злачных берегов знакомую картину,
> И в тихом озере, средь блещущих зыбей,
> Станицу гордую спокойных лебедей.[27]

> Reminiscence, conjure up for me
> The magic places where I live in my soul,
> The forests where I loved, where feeling developed,
> Where infancy melded with first youth,
> And where, coddled by nature and reverie,
> I knew poetry, gaiety, and serenity…

> Lead me, oh, lead me under the linden trees,
> Ever favorable to my free laziness,
> To the shore of the lake, the quiet slope of hills!…
> That I may see again the thick carpets of meadows
> And a withered clump of trees and a bright valley,
> And the familiar picture of grain field shores
> And in the quiet lake, amidst shining swells,
> A proud flock of tranquil swans.

This is truly the most idyllic evocation of Carskoe Selo in the poetic tradition, especially considering that most of the descriptions of it in Puškin emphasize what is missing at the moment of speech. In this tradition, Carskoe is often a place of absences, as in his 1825 Lycée anniversary poem:

> Кого еще недосчитались Вы?
> Кто изменил пленительной привычке?
> Кого от вас увлек холодный свет?
> Кто не пришел, кого меж вами нет?

> Who else is missing?
> Who has betrayed our captivating habit?
> Whom has the cold world attracted away from us?
> Who failed to come? Who is not amongst you?

At the end of the poem, Puškin internalizes the absence motif. He foresees a time when all but one of his classmates will be dead, and places the essential

---

[27] Puškin, "Carskoe Selo," 1: 371.

Carskoe Selo inside the figure of the last surviving Lycée student (Gorčakov ended up outliving them all): «Кому из нас под старость день Лицея / Торжествовать придется одному?» ("Who of us in old age will have to celebrate Lycée Day alone?") Such a poetics of absence or "negative tangibility," however, only serves to render poetic assertions of continuity among the creative community more effective, and to justify the internalization of the "homeland" in one of the Lyceé-selves.

In his poem "The Swan of Carskoe Selo,"[28] Žukovskij internalizes the great poetic haven of Puškinian Carskoe Selo in the figure of the great Catherinian swan-poet, who imagines himself alone, without his poet-friends, in Carskoe in 1851. That swan does not fit into the society of the younger swans:

> Ты на молодое смотришь поколенье
> Грустными очами; прежнего единый
> Брошенный обломок, в новый лебединый
> Свет на пир веселый гость неприглашенный,
> Ты вступить дичишься в круг неблагосклонный
> Резвой молодежи....

> You gaze upon the younger generation
> With sad eyes; a lonely, abandoned
> Ruin from the past, into the new cheerful swan society
> You are an uninvited guest,
> You are skittish about entering the circle
> Of frolicsome youth ill-disposed toward you....

The time-honored metaphor of poet-swans, taken from Plato's *Republic* and popularized in Russia by Deržavin's rendering of Horace's beautiful "Non usitata" (the poem «Лебедь», "The Swan"), was used by Del'vig to refer to Puškin (in his poem «Пушкину», "To Puškin": «Кто, как лебедь цветущей Авзонии» ["Who, like a swan of flowering Ausonia (Italy)"]) and became a traditional epithet for poets associated with Carskoe Selo. Žukovskij's poem is a vital link in this tradition. Žukovskij's swan is in a changed Carskoe; the true, great Deržavinian-Puškinian Carskoe Selo is buried in him, inside him, and he is encouraged to rejoice in this fact. He still sees what is invisible to others: «Но не сетуй, старец, пращур лебединый: / Ты родился в славный век Екатерины» ("But do not complain, old man, great-grandfather swan / You were born in the great age of Catherine").

---

[28] Žukovskij, "Carskosel'skij lebed'," 247 ff.

In the same way, our poets feel that the true Petersburg lies buried within them, among them, as a shared mental and spiritual space accessible through their own participation in the ongoing creation of this "Petersburg." Sometime Petersburg poet Roman Gul′ expressed this notion in the title of his memoirs, «Я унес Россию» (*I carried Russia away*), as did Nabokov in his 1923 poem "Petersburg": «Ты растаял, / ты отлетел, а я влачу виденья / в иных краях…» ("You have melted away, / you have flown away, while I carry around visions in other countries").[29] At the end of the Žukovskij poem the beautiful song of the great swan, the music of the true Carskoe Selo, is heard for the last time. In the twentieth century, this tradition prompted Gumilev to write on the occasion of Annenskij's death: «Был Иннокентий Анненский последний / Из царскосельских лебедей» ("Innokentij Annenskij was the last / Swan of Carskoe Selo").[30] Annenskij had written of Carskoe Selo a few years before, emphasizing the fragile presence in the town of those idyllic values and qualities that were now non-existent everywhere else: «Там все, что навсегда ушло» ("Everything is there that has disappeared forever").[31]

Axmatova, who grew up in Carskoe Selo and whose early poetry is as much associated with the town as with Petersburg, wrote in 1916 «Так вот одна осталася / Считать пустые дни» ("And here I remain alone / To count the empty days") [1: 175], alluding to her separation from two of the other swans of Carskoe Selo, Annenskij (because of his death) and Gumilev (due to the circumstances of their personal lives). In the poem, Axmatova casts herself as the very last swan of Carskoe Selo, rushing there to commune with the absent swans, just as Kjukel′beker had hoped to feel the presence of Del′vig and Puškin on his return in 1819. It is clear from a perusal of her Carskoe Selo poems that Axmatova envisions her Carskoe Selo period as an innocent, idyllic one, as Puškin had, before she knew the mixed values and harsh facts of a more grown-up Petersburg world. In her later poetry she disassociates herself from that innocent personage, who was not able to face the difficulties of the twentieth century:

Показать бы тебе, насмешнице
И любимице всех друзей,
Царскосельской веселой грешнице,
Что случится с жизнью твоей— [1: 364]

---

[29] Nabokov, "Peterburg," *Vsemirnaja biblioteka*, 202.
[30] Nikolaj Gumilev, "Pamjati Annenskogo," *Stikhotvorenija i poemy* (Tbilisi: Merani, 1988), 210.
[31] Annenskij, "L. I. Mikulič," 211.

> If I could have shown you, prankster,
> And favorite of all your friends,
> Cheerful sinner of Carskoe,
> What would become of your life—

It is as if that playful and spoiled young poetess has no connection with the woman in the prison lines of hellish Leningrad that she became during the purges. She underlines this in the last poem of *Requiem*, insisting that a monument to her could not be erected in Carskoe («Не в царском саду у заветного пня, / Где тень безутешная ищет меня» ["Not in the tsar's garden by the cherished stump, / Where an inconsolable shade is seeking me," 1: 310]). She says that the only fitting monument to her (besides her poetry, which is her monument, as it was Puškin's) must be placed in the prison yard where she waited, suffering with other wives and mothers of arrested and imprisoned men.

Yet the tradition of Carskoe Selo as the setting of the poet's idyll, the idyllic place where the family of poet-friends could create and flourish, was still alive in Axmatova's 1916 poem, where her return to Carskoe is successful, and communion with the missing poets does take place. Although she does not expect it, in an icy Mallarméan scene she encounters in Carskoe on that return,[32] the missing poet-swans are set free from their graves under the ice, as Deržavin had portrayed himself being set free in "The Swan." Axmatova's swans fly upwards, immortal:

> Но так бывает раз в году,
> Когда растает лед,
> В екатеринином саду
> Стою у чистых вод.
> И слышу плеск широких крыл
> Над гладью голубой.
> Не знаю кто окно открыл
> В темнице гробовой.

> But thus it happens once a year,
> When the ice melts,
> In the Catherinian garden
> I stand by the clear waters.
> And I hear the splashing of wide wings
> Over the smooth blue waters.

---

[32] A reference to Mallarmé's famous swan poem "Le vierge, le vivace et le bel aujourd'hui."

I don't know who opened a window
In the dungeon of the grave.

After the revolution, Carskoe is less and less a topic of Axmatova's poetry, and Petersburg, the more adult world of the "real twentieth century," is the scene of a far-from-idyllic biography and creative life. In *Poem without a Hero*, she flees fast with the oncoming, frightening age, running to the garden in Carskoe Selo, where youthful love and the Muses will console her («Где все девять мне будут рады», "Where all nine will be glad to see me"). As she retreats, the real, non-idyllic twentieth century invades Petersburg along the embankments. As Roberta Reeder has pointed out, the contrast of the idyll and the non-idyll in *Poem without a Hero* is clear enough.[33]

Yet abandonment of Carskoe Selo as the place-time of idyllic, serene creativity does not mean that a writer's idyll leaves Axmatova's poetry altogether. In Mandel′štam, all the idyllic motifs of Puškin's Carskoe Selo were summed up in the word "Petersburg." No matter what the harsh and frightening realities of "Leningrad" in his poem of the same name ("I returned to my city, familiar to the point of tears"), "Petersburg" is there and he can still find it. In the same way, Kjuxel′beker seems disappointed at first in the real Carskoe, but then finds his way back to the longed-for idyllic one in art. Mandel′štam, in an even more dramatic challenge to the elegy, puts idyllic motifs into Petersburg in his longing attitude to return to the place of eternal poetic beauty: «И блаженное, бессмысленное слово / Мы в первый раз произнесем» ("And we will utter for the first time / The blessed, senseless word") [2: 85]. Axmatova, for whom, in direct contrast to Mandel′štam, Carskoe Selo had been an extremely important place biographically and poetically, directly grafts the Carskoe Selo idyllic complex of motifs onto Petersburg. Only thus can we understand the full implication of the Petersburg space we encounter in her 1959 «Летний сад» ("The Summer Garden"):

Я к розам хочу, в тот единственный сад,
Где лучшая в мире стоит из оград,
Где статуи помнят меня молодой,
И я их под невскою помню водой
В душистой тиши между царственных лип
Мне мачт корабельных мерещится скрип.
И лебедь как прежде плывет сквозь века
Любуясь красой своего двойника.

---

[33] Roberta Reeder, "Tsarskoe Selo in the Poetry of Anna Axmatova: The Eternal Return," *The Speech of Unknown Eyes: Akhmatova's Readers on Her Poetry*, ed. Wendy Rosslyn (Cotgrave: Astra, 1990), 2: 293.

И замертво спят сотни тысяч шагов
Врагов и друзей, друзей и врагов.
И шествию теней не видно конца
От вазы гранитной до двери дворца.
Там шепчутся белые ночи мои
О чьей-то высокой и тайной любви.
И все перламутром и яшмой горит,
Но света источник таинственно скрыт. [1: 319]

I want to return to the roses, to that unique garden,
Where the world's best fence is,
Where the statues remember me in my youth,
And I remember them covered by Neva's waters,
In the redolent silence among the regal lindens
I sense the creaking of ships' masts.
And the swan as of old floats through the ages
Admiring the beauty of its own double
And one hundred thousand footsteps sleep the sleep of the dead,
Footsteps of friends and enemies, enemies and friends.
And there's no end in sight to the procession of shades
From the granite vase to the door of the palace.
That's where my white nights whisper
About someone's exalted and secret love,
And everything burns with mother-of-pearl and jasper
But the source of the light is mysteriously hidden.

The wish expressed in the first line of the poem is actually fulfilled by the poet in and through the ensuing verses. Place (the Summer Garden) is affirmed as a continuum of space-time; it is the "non-present" (read: non-temporal) condition found in the very same Summer Garden in Belyj's *Petersburg*.[34] Self and space remember each other. Each has internalized the other, establishing a double strength against historical threats. Axmatova, however, increases the intensity of such identification by specifically relating it to a Carskoe Selo-like "homeland" of creative pursuits and mingled voices ("redolent silence"; "the swan"; "footsteps"; "whisper").

Sharon Leiter has analyzed Axmatova's poem in terms of a garden of memory, showing how an actual, visible architectural place serves in Axmatova's poetry as an access to hidden, buried worlds. Leiter relates the poem to Axmatova's 1914 poem «Тот голос, с тишиной великой споря» ("That voice which argued with a great silence") [1: 136] as well as to the 1913

---

[34] See chap. 6, pp. 212–13.

poem from *Verses about Petersburg* «Сердце бьется ровно, мерно» ("My heart beats evenly, measuredly") [1: 116], a poem about the meetings of lovers under the arch on Galernaja Street and in the Summer Garden.[35]

While Leiter is correct in seeing this poem as a "return [to the themes of those poems] developing the imagery to a full-scale evocation of one of Petersburg's sacred places,"[36] it is more than that: it is a return to the idyll of Carskoe Selo. There is not another poem in the language closer to Puškin's "Carskoe Selo," with its invocation to memory: «Веди, веди меня под липовые сени» ("Lead me, oh, lead me under the linden trees"). While the place evoked is clearly the Summer Garden, with its beautiful wrought-iron fence, the attitude of desire to return recalls Puškin's toward Carskoe Selo. And the mood of the place reminds us of Puškinian passages such as this one in «Городок» ("The Town"), written in 1815, while Puškin was at the Lycée:

> ....
> Любимые творцы!
> ....
> Мой друг! весь день я с ними,
> То в думу углублен,
> То мыслями своими
> В Элизий пренесен.
> Когда же на закате
> Последний луч зари
> Потонет в ярком злате,
> И светлые цари
> Смеркающейся ночи
> Плывут по небесам,
> И тихо дремлют рощи,
> И шорох по лесам,
> ....
> И я в тиши ночной
> Сливаю голос свой
> С пастушьею волынкой.[37]

Dear creative ones!

My friend! I spend all day with them,
Either I am immersed in meditation

---

[35] Leiter, *Akhmatova's Petersburg*, 130 ff.
[36] Ibid., 130.
[37] Puškin, "Gorodok," 1: 95.

Or I am transported in thought
To Elysium.
When at sunset
The last ray of light
Drowns in the bright gold,
And the bright tsars
Of darkening night
Float through the heavens,
And the groves slumber quietly,
And there's rustling in the forest,

And I in the silence of night
Join my voice
To the shepherd's reed.

For Axmatova, the presence of a Carskoe Selo idyllic mood causes a kind of superimposition of Carskoe Selo onto Petersburg in that there are many specific details that correspond with evocations of Carskoe in Puškin's Lycée poetry:

Carskoe Selo (Puškin) [38]	Letnij sad (Axmatova)
Не се ль Элизиум полнощный Прекрасный Царскосельский сад?	И шествию теней не видно конца
Здесь каждый шаг в душе рождает Воспоминанья прежних лет	И замертво спит сотни тысяч шагов Врагов и друзей, друзей и врагов.
И быстрым понеслись потоком Враги на русские поля.	
В безмолвной тишине почили дол и рощи	В душистой тиши между царственных лип
Веди, веди меня под липовые сени	
И тихая луна как лебедь величавый Плывет в сребристых облаках	И лебедь как прежде плывет сквозь века Любуясь красой своего двойника.
Isn't the beautiful Carskoe Selo park A northern Elysium?	And there's no end in sight to the procession of shades

---

[38] From Puškin, "Vospominanija v Carskom Sele," 2: 276 and "Carskoe Selo," 1: 371.

Every step here gives rise in my soul
To memories of years past
	And one hundred thousand footsteps
	   sleep the sleep of the dead,
	Footsteps of friends and enemies,
	   enemies and friends.

And enemies rushed in a swift stream Onto the Russian fields.	

In the wordless silence the vale and
   groves reposed
	In the redolent silence among the
	   regal lindens

Lead me, oh lead me under the linden trees	

And the silent moon like a grand swan
Floats in the silvery clouds
	And the swan as of old floats through
	   the ages
	Admiring the beauty of its own
	   double

Friendship with statues in Axmatova's verse was first a motif associated with Carskoe Selo in such poems as «А там мой мраморный двойник» ("And there my marble double"). Her famous poem "Carskoe Selo Statue," which begins with the words «Уже кленовые листы / На пруд слетают лебединый» ("And maple leaves are already falling down upon the swan pond"), treats the same statue Puškin evoked in his poem of the same name. Later in the war period, the same familiarity with the statues of the Summer Garden appear, as in "Nox." The atmosphere of subdued and mysterious lighting is often associated with Carskoe Selo in Puškin, and here with the Summer Garden; white nights are also associated with Petersburg *and* with Carskoe, as in Axmatova's «Белые ночи» ("White Nights"). Though there have often been a few token swans in the Summer Garden, the great lone swan floating through the ages has clear associations with Carskoe, and unifies and completes the Carskoe Selo mood and atmosphere of Axmatova's "The Summer Garden." It represents a union of many of the Carskoe Selo motifs, not least of which is the importance of those who are no longer here. The longing mood of Annenskij's poem "L. I. Mikulič" and the presence/absence of roses therein rounds out the duality of evocation in Axmatova's poem:

Там воды зыблются светло
И гордо царствуют березы
Там были розы, были розы,
Пускай в поток их унесло.
Там все, что навсегда ушло…
Скажите «Царское Село»—

И улыбнемся мы сквозь слезы.[39]

There the waters swell brightly
And the birches rule proudly
There were roses there, there were roses
Even if they were carried off in the current.
Everything is there that has disappeared forever…
Say the words "Carskoe Selo"
And we will smile through our tears.

In her Petersburg poem, Axmatova has thus transported many of the Carskoe motifs to a Petersburg space, which has gained all the idyllic associations of Carskoe Selo. It has also at the same time acquired a sense of timelessness based in, but more defiant than the elegies about Carskoe. The poem is an attempt to invoke the beautiful and idealized Petersburg in one of its most beautiful gardens by giving it the idyllic associations of Carskoe Selo, which Annenskij had called the repository of all the positive values "that had disappeared elsewhere." These idyllic qualities are hinted at, not clearly delineated, in accordance with Brodskij's very Symbolist (and specifically, Mallarméan) idea of "negative tangibility," such that "the absence of usual signs of being … is not equated with non-being." When evoked in beautiful poetry, this absence "surpasses being in its tangibility."[40] In art the absent, abolished object, place, or "tower" is put back, and put back in a form potentially more beautiful and idealized than it ever was in real, psychological experience.

☙ ❧

The notion of longing for and creation through art of an idyllic existence is related both to the place and the poet who is so powerfully identified with it—his/her creative spirit and life. In *Speak, Memory*, Nabokov deals with writing as the externalization of what is inside the poet's being. The buried sun is not only the great poetry of Puškin, it is the greatest potential and creativity buried in each Petersburg poet; it is *his Petersburg*. The Petersburg poet must make the "blessed, senseless word" of Mandel'štam's poem worthy of Puškin; it must rise from his unconscious and shine for all who can see and appreciate it. The buried sun, the hidden Petersburg, in accordance with Mandel'štam's future perfective gerundive,[41] is the imperative to openly reveal the great

---

[39] Annenskij, "L. I. Mikulic," 211.
[40] Jaanus 204–06 (see chap. 5, n. 24).
[41] This category of ethical obligation of the artist or the incumbency upon him to write certain things is connected by him with the Latin gerundive, a category of obligation which he terms *dolženstvovanie* in "The Word and Culture" [1: 85].

"inner Petersburg," the Petersburg of the spirit. And this must be done with full knowledge that the Russian world is not ready to receive it: "I bring the Revolution gifts which it is not yet prepared to receive," Mandel'štam wrote in the 1920s in answer to a Soviet questionnaire [2: 259]. The inner Petersburg, the buried sun, must be revealed for those who can and will see. The externalizations of these inner Petersburgs is the subject of chapter 8.

8

CHANGING, MASTERING, AND AMAZING SPACES

Не отрицает ли пространства превосходство
Сей целомудренно построенный ковчег? [1: 29]

Doesn't this chastely-constructed ark
Deny the dominance of space?

                        Osip Mandel′štam

Собиратель пространства… [1: 203]

Он дирижировал кавказскими горами
И машучи ступал на тесных Альп тропы,
И, озираючись, пустынными брегами
Шел, чуя разговор бесчисленной толпы.

Толпы умов, влияний, впечатлений
Он перенес, как лишь могучий мог…. [1: 207]

Collector of space…

As a conductor he orchestrated the Caucasian mountains,
And entered the tight paths of the Alps waving,
And hearing the speech of a numberless crowd,
H strode [*like Peter—ALC*] through deserted shores..

A crowd of intellects, events and impressions
He bore as only a mighty one could….

In the above excerpts from Mandel′štam's poetic homages to Andrej Belyj, written on the occasion of the latter's funeral in 1934,[1] Belyj is shown to be a collector, master, and conqueror of linguistic and actual space. In his novel *Petersburg*, Belyj changed and altered the spaces of the northern capital in the

---

[1] Mandel′štam's poems to Belyj are #288 ("Golubye glaza i gorjaščaja lobnaja kost′"); #289 ("10-ogo janvarja 1934") [1: 204–05], its variant version, #290 [1: 205–06], and its second variant #291 [1: 206]; #292 ("Emu kavkazkie kričali gory") [1: 206–07] and its variant, #293 ("On dirižiroval kavkazkimi gorami) [1: 207], and #294 ("Otkuda privezli? Kogo? Kotoryj umer?") [1: 207].

minds of the city's writers in a way that influenced most subsequent descriptions of and identifications with Petersburg in the twentieth-century tradition. Mandel'štam depicts Belyj and his dazzling use of language as a figure skater chased by time/history through spaces which he fills and modifies with words (including new grammatical and case forms) and images: «Сочинитель… / Конькобежец и первенец, веком гонимой взашей / Под морозную пыль образуемых вновь падежей» [1: 203] ("Composer … / Ice skater and first-place winner, with the age chasing you out / To the [music of] frozen dust of cases ever newly formed"). This image of Belyj, whose *Petersburg* Mandel'štam admired but also criticized in his early polemics with Symbolism, combines all the aspects of the creative prose poet in his mastering of space: he is a figure skater, and the frozen dust his skates throw up is the music of his creative activity. The figures he produces are ever new verbal forms, which also create new visual forms in space. Such an active *changing* of physical space by the word is a striking example of the relationship between self and space that we focus on here as the most powerful of our ahistorical models in Petersburg.

COLLAGE AND SUPERIMPOSITION

For Mandel' štam, here and elsewhere, a poem or artistic prose passage is a vessel set out by its creator to voyage on a sea of language.[2] Unlike other vessels, it leaves eternal marks on that language and on that expanse, overcoming the supremacy of the space that pre-existed its appearance.

In the twentieth-century post-revolutionary idyllic treatment of Petersburg, changes are wrought on Petersburg spaces by the artist/poet. In her 1959 poem "The Summer Garden," Axmatova, through a complex collage effect, superimposes traits of Carskoe Selo, associated with her youth, upon the Summer Garden. The Petersburg locale thereby receives the idyllic associations of the poet's creative haven that had been formerly associated with Carskoe Selo in Russian poetry in general and in Axmatova's *oeuvre* in particular.

The superimposition of an inner vision, an inner Petersburg upon a foreign external locale changes and dominates that space. In *The Bronze Horseman* it was the filling of a space with a realized dream, the placing of a city where there had been nothing. In some works, such as Axmatova's "First Northern Elegy," the poet's role is more than that of a passive observer or seer. In this poem Petersburg is treated like a layered photograph or lithograph whose hidden levels can sometimes be seen. Looking at Leningrad in the 1940s, one can occasionally see through to the Petersburg of the 1870s (the

---

[2] Mandel'štam, "O prirode slova," 2: 258–59. See chap. 4 below for a discussion of maritime images of Petersburg space.

"Russia of Dostoevskij"). Bringing the gardens of Carskoe Selo and all their semantic baggage into the Summer Garden is admittedly a more complex phenomenon because the imagery is not limited to a series of archaeological/temporal layers from the same geographical place. Here another locale is actively transported and transposed into Petersburg. By uniting two gardens which represent two periods of her life and work, Axmatova powerfully underscores the identity of her life with the collaged place.

This type of superimposition or collage is certainly not the only example of alteration of Petersburg space, but it is more frequent for émigré poets to superimpose Petersburg upon a foreign locale than vice versa. A more usual version of this type of superimposition is prominent in Andrej Tarkovskij's Italian-made film *Nostalgia*, concerning a homesick Russian writer in Italy.[3] There the hero, who alludes repeatedly to a nineteenth-century Russian writer in his same situation, has a recurrent vision of his native Russian village as he gazes upon the Italian countryside and various Roman locales. Suddenly dreamy Russian rural scenes are superimposed upon the clearly Italian environment, which is Russified and marked by Tarkovskij's (and his hero's) psyche in this manner. Argentine writer Jorge Luis Borges often claimed that although he thought he had lived in various European cities while he was abroad, these cities were illusionary and he had been, was, and always would be only in Buenos Aires. This reminds us unfailingly of the constant presence of "only Petersburg" in Axmatova's verse, the one that she could find, "groping, in [her] sleep" [1: 311]. Pasternak emphasized this perennial Petersburg in Axmatova: «Какой-то город явный с первых строк / Встает и отдается в каждом слоге» ("A certain city, obvious from the first lines, / Arises and resounds in every syllable").[4] This "certain city," was, of course, also "obvious" in Brodskij's poetry and essays, even when he was clearly speaking of other cities: "For somebody with my birthplace, the city [Venice] emerging from these pages was easily recognizable and felt like Petersburg's extension into a better history, not to mention latitude."[5] In these cases the created unity of space implies a unification of the biography despite exile or other spatial movement.

A very clear superimposition of Petersburg onto a foreign space in the émigré canon is seen in Xodasevič's "Sorrento Photographs," where Petersburg displaces Naples. The poem is framed by these lines:

---

[3] *Nostalgia*, dir. Andrej Tarkovskij, Opera Film Produzione, 1983.

[4] Pasternak, "Anne Axmatovoj," 199–200.

[5] Joseph Brodsky, *Watermark* (New York: Farrar, Straus & Giroux,1992), 38.

Воспоминанье прихотливо.
Как сновиденье—оно
Как будто вещей правдой живо,
....
И так же, вероятно, лживо…[6]

Reminiscence is capricious.
Like a dream,
Reminiscence seems alive with prophetic truth

And yet seems, just as likely, deceptive…

Petersburg, as real or as a mirage, is seen by Xodasevič on his Amalfi sojourn, and is evoked through the intersection of two arts, poetry and photography:

Встает Неаполь из паров,
И заиграл огонь стеклянный
Береговых его домов.
Я вижу светлые просторы,
Плывут сады, поляны, горы,
А в них, сквозь них и между них—
Опять, как на неверном снимке,
Весь в очертаниях сквозных,
Как был тогда, в студеной дымке,
....
На восьмигранном острие
Золотокрылый ангел розов
И неподвижен—а над ним
Вороньи стаи, дым морозов,
Давно рассеявшийся дым.
И, отражен кастелламарской
Зеленоватою волной,
Огромный страж России царской

Вниз опрокинут головой.
Так отражался он Невой,
Зловещий, огненный и мрачный,
....
Ошибка пленки неудачной.[7]

---

[6] Vladislav Xodasevič, printed in Bethea, *Khodasevich*, 156–60.
[7] Ibid.

Naples rises from the steam
And there begins to play the glazed fire
Of the houses on its shoreline.
I see bright expanses,
Gardens, glades, and mountains float,
And in them, through them and betwixt them,
Again as in a bad photograph,
All in its perforated outlines,
Just as it was then in the cold smoke,

In its eight-faceted sharpness
The golden-winged angel is pink
And motionless; and over it
Flocks of sparrows, the steam of frosts,
Dispersed long, long ago.
And reflected in the
Greenish waves of Castellamare
The great guardian of tsarist Russia [the Bronze Horseman]

Is standing on his head.
Thus he was reflected in the Neva,
Ominous, fiery and gloomy,

An error of defective film.

The very diction of the opening iambic tetrameters about Naples' birth from steam calls forth to the reader Petersburg's appearance from the fog, while lines such as «береговые его дома» ("houses on its shoreline") elicit in the reader the «береговой его гранит» ("granite of its shoreline") of Puškin's Petersburg. David Bethea has shown in detail how Petersburg and other Russian locales are superimposed upon Sorrento and intertwine with the Italian cityscape that the poet is surveying and that his companion (Gor'kij's son, Maksim) is photographing. The "Petersburgization" of Naples is like Tarkovskij's Russification of Italy. It is in some sense reminiscent of Kandinskij's repeated painting of Moscow and Chagall's constant depiction of Vitebsk. Its aim is the assertion of one space-bound identity, of the unity of one's biography, that one always and everywhere is Russian and carries his Russian space within him, exteriorizing it onto any horizons. Such an identity of self and Petersburg space is especially strong in Nabokov, whose sense of superimposed worlds is a consistent feature of his and his heroes' creative work. In *The Gift*, Nabokov's characterization of the presence of Petersburg on a Berlin street also draws upon cinematographic art:

> Crossing Wittenberg Square where, as in a color film, roses were quivering in the breeze around an antique flight of stairs ... he walked toward the Russian bookshop ... it seemed as if on this German street there had encroached the vagabond phantom of a Russian boulevard, or as if on the contrary a street in Russia, with several natives taking the air, swarmed with the pale ghosts of innumerable foreigners flickering among those natives like a familiar and barely noticeable hallucination.[8]

Certainly the notion of superimposition of realities was not new in the Petersburg tradition. For better and for worse—and most of all for worse—the city's status as "window to Europe" and its European architecture had always prompted a feeling of double identity, of incongruously mixed worlds. Yet if Herzen had said, not altogether flatteringly, in 1843, "What distinguishes Petersburg from other European cities is the fact that it looks like all of them,"[9] then for post-revolutionary émigrés it is precisely such a tendency for mimicry that ensures the constant and successful evocation of Petersburg abroad.

Gazing on the Seine from his exile in France, Aleksandr Benois would often see the Neva instead. Though Georgij Ivanov is forced to admit that «Лучезарное небо над Ниццей / Навсегда стало небо родным» ("The resplendent sky above Nice / [had] become once and for all [his] native sky"), he ends his poem on a note implying that his true homeland, Petersburg, may still be reachable in art, affirming his irrational belief in a spiritual Petersburg.[10] Another famous case of multiple collages of other places upon Petersburg and vice versa is Gumilev's 1921 masterpiece, "The Tram That Lost Its Way," written shortly before his death.[11] It reflects the influence of H. G. Wells' time machine as the speed of the racing tram overtakes space, lost "in an abyss of times." Space-time is contracted, and the tram and its riders are in Petersburg, Paris, and Egypt simultaneously in a kind of technologically-induced ubiquity which Nabokov, as we shall see presently, associates with poems and the "positional" quality of poetry in general:

> Мы проскочили сквозь рощу пальм,
> Через Неву, через Нил и Сену

---

[8] Vladimir Nabokov, *The Gift*, trans. Michael Scammell and Vladimir Nabokov (New York: Vintage, 1991), 166.

[9] Aleksandr Herzen, quoted in Boym, *The Future of Nostalgia*, 121.

[10] See chap. 4, n. 9.

[11] See chap. 2, n. 21.

> Мы прогремели по трем мостам.
> We galloped through a palm grove,
> Across the Neva, the Nile and the Seine,
> We thundered across three bridges.

In certain passages the place-time appears to be revolutionary France, with clear reference to the guillotine and beheadings, yet in the final stanzas the wild ride has clearly returned to Petersburg:

> И сразу ветер знакомый и сладкий,
> И за мостом летит на меня
> Всадника длань в железной перчатке
> И два копыта его коня.
>
> Верной твердынею православья
> Врезан Исакий в вышине…
>
> And immediately the wind is familiar and sweet,
> And behind the bridge onto me rush
> The Horseman's hand in its iron glove
> And the two hooves of his horse.
>
> Like the faithful firmament of Orthodoxy
> St. Isaac's is carved on high…

The speed here is such that various place-bound layers are superimposed on Petersburg, the point of departure, and it is Petersburg that is altered by the action of the runaway tram representing the accelerated time of history "out of control," as we saw in chapter 3.

In Brodskij's ironic poem "Embroidering on Plato," as we saw in chapter 7, any city for him, even (and especially) the ideal city, will have the specific architectural traits of Petersburg.[12] The rejection of the poet by the populace at the end of that poem may have reference to Plato's negative attitude toward poets. It may also have been influenced by another example of a "visit" to Leningrad-Petersburg whose decidedly anti-idyllic results serve to warn against the dangers of a too-powerful superimposition of place: Nabokov's short story «Посещение музея» ("A Visit to A Museum"), written in the late 1930s.[13] The narrator/main character, planning a visit to a provincial French town, promises to search in its museum for a Lerois portrait of a Petersburg nobleman, the grandfather of an elderly acquaintance. He did not really in-

---

[12] See analysis in chap. 7, pp. 247 ff.
[13] Nabokov, "Poseščenie muzeja," *Vesna v Fial'te* (Ann Arbor: Ardis, 1978), 99–116.

tend to keep his promise, being wary of his acquaintance's tendency toward "flights of fantasy." However, the narrator-hero is brought by happenstance to the museum, and in the surreal atmosphere of the tale, he manages to find the painting, though the curator denies that the museum has such a work. The narrator-hero leads the amazed curator to the room where he first saw it and finds it once more, but the curator immediately disappears, and the small provincial museum mysteriously expands to Hermitage-like proportions, with an endless labyrinth of corridors. He runs, frightened and unable to exit the building, and when he finally does escape, he finds that Soviet Leningrad has supplanted the small French town of Mont Isère and that he, with his foreign clothing and demeanor, like the hero of Brodskij's poem, is an undesirable element, a potential victim or scapegoat. He experiences a moment of panic and tries to remove all traces of France from his person, but is detained and harassed by the Soviet authorities. The lesson learned here concerns the political realities of the Soviet Union and the undesirability of the speaker, who is clearly unable to creatively control the consequences of the "collage," in the once- and always-beloved place. His brush with present-day Leningrad is frightening: "this was not the Petersburg of my memory, but the one in reality, the present-day one, forbidden for me, hopelessly enslaved and hopelessly familiar. A semi-ghost [I] stood in a lightweight foreign suit in indifferent snow on an October night somewhere on the Mojka or the Fontanka." This superimposition is virtually a lesson against excessive or idyllic daydreaming about returns to Petersburg, a warning that "certain cures for nostalgia are more dangerous than the disease itself."[14] Detained by the Soviet authorities, the hero sums up the fruitlessness of such reverie-nightmares: "since then I have sworn never again to carry out the errands of another's madness."[15] He has, in effect, been subjected to changed spaces through the agency of his "fantasy"-prone acquaintance. Indeed, superimposition as higher vision can border precariously on hallucination when not subject to the ordering consciousness of the powerful creator or the tempering irony of the anti-idyllist. Unlike Brodskij's lyric hero in "Embroidering on Plato," Nabokov's character is not able (and has no desire) to control this negative reality by frequent "returns" and impositions of the wished-for Petersburg.

Thus in many of these superimpositions of Petersburg onto European locales, the poet-lyric ego is to some degree a passive recipient, pervaded by a vision, prey to a dream or nightmare, or mistakes what he sees on a photo. In some ways, being inside "someone else's dream" or appearing on "another photograph" is a metaphor for reading; the poet's power to change spaces can

---

[14] Boym, *The Future of Nostalgia*, 277.
[15] Ibid., 116.

even have unwanted effects upon the reader. If the "reader," as in "A Visit to a Museum," allows the space to master him, it will deprive him of his identity, and in the case of Soviet Leningrad, it will dominate him. In chapter 9 we will investigate in more detail the effects and implications of such "stolen identity" in Mandel'štam's *The Egyptian Stamp* and Nabokov's *The Defense*. We shall now turn to a series of changes or alterations of Petersburg spaces in which the poet takes a more powerful creative role, actively mastering the space.

Mastering and Amazing Space

Nabokov makes clear in his 1927 poem «Расстрел» ("Death by Firing Squad")[16] that a return to Russia of the type depicted in "A Visit to a Museum" threatens him with death, but a death that becomes beautiful in its association with that space. Even the thought of an ending more terrible than that in "A Visit to a Museum" cannot deter him from the creative act of superimposing native spaces onto a European "safe exile":

> Но сердце, как бы ты хотело,
> чтоб это вправду было так:
> Россия, звезды, ночь расстрела
> и весь в черемухе овраг.

> But my heart, how much you would like
> it really to have happened:
> Russia, the stars, the night of the execution
> and the ravine abloom in racemosa.

Of course, one could also read this poem to mean that physical death would be preferable to imagined returns or nostalgic longing for Russia. Actual return to Soviet Leningrad for Nabokov means enslavement of his personality and the removal of his traits of identity. To exist there he would have to lose all marks of identification and, as he puts it in "A Visit to a Museum," «остаться идеально нагим» ("remain ideally nude").[17] He foreswore such temptations to think nostalgically of *Soviet* Russia even more dramatically in a 1944 poem, at a time when some émigrés were particularly sympathetic to the Soviet Union because of its valiant fighting in World War II:

> Каким бы полотном батальным ни являлась
> советская сусальнейшая Русь,

---

[16] Nabokov, *Vsemirnaja biblioteka poèta*, "Rasstrel," 158. The poem is discussed in connection with the theme of nostalgia in Nabokov and the nightmarish turn of this theme in the late 1920s in Inna Brojde, *Ot Xodaseviča do Nabokova* (New York: Hermitage, 1990), 71–73.

[17] "Poseščenie muzeja," 105.

какой бы жалостью душа не наполнялась,
не поклонюсь, не примирюсь
со всею мерзостью, жестокостью и скукой
немого рабства—нет, о, нет,
еще я духом жив, еще не сыт разлукой,
увольте, я еще поэт.[18]

No matter what a battle canvas
that Soviet, most gaudy Rus′ might make,
no matter how much pity should fill my soul,
I will not bow down, I will not reconcile myself
to the abomination, the cruelty and boredom
of dumb slavery, no, oh, no!
I am still alive in spirit, I've not yet had my fill of separation;
It could not be otherwise, I am still a poet.

For Nabokov the return to Petersburg can only take place in art, to the eternal "Sankt-Peterburg" of his 1924 poem, where he describes the "real" city, the one with which he is identified and whose spaces have been marked and altered by Petersburg writers such as Aleksandr Puškin:

Бледно-зеленые ветрила
дворцовый распускает сад.
Орлы мерцают вдоль опушки.
Нева, лениво шелестя,
как Лета льется. След локтя
оставил на граните Пушкин.[19]

Pale green sails
Are let loose by the palace garden.
The eagles glimmer along the edge.
The Neva, lazily rustling,
Flows like the Lethe. Puškin left
the trace of his elbow on the granite.

Nabokov is here probably referring to the the Mars Field side and the Neva side of the Summer Garden. The last image probably implies that Puškin (represented by the statue of him seated, leaning on his elbow in Carskoe Selo) had also visited the Summer Garden, like Onegin, and has left his per-

---

[18] Nabokov, *Vsemirnaja biblioteka poèta*, 332.
[19] Ibid., 230–31.

manent marks on Petersburg, every bit as much as on Carskoe. This is what Axmatova effected, as we saw above, in her poem "The Summer Garden."

It is, of course, Puškin-Peter who provides the most important models of how man in moments of heightened creativity becomes *master of space*. In some representations in the Petersburg tradition, the creative man first withdraws into an enclosure, a private small room, and then is enabled to break all barriers and be victorious over space through art. In the other, most frequent, type, he is virtually propelled by the force of music or inspiration to a seashore landscape where he must battle Nature, the wild element. That nature is often a metaphor for the wild, untamed Russian tongue which he must submit to the control of the music he hears within. These dynamic depictions of creativity as mastery of space have four possible stages:

- enclosure in a small space;
- music–inspiration;
- "bursting out," breaking the bonds of three dimensions, and
- the implied encompassment of wide, limitless horizons.

The first type of creative mastery of space in Petersburg, as discussed below, emphasizes the first three stages, whereas the second type includes the second, third, and fourth stages more prominently. Our examples of the first variant will be drawn from Nabokov, Belyj, Xodasevič, and others. The second variant, more obviously Puškin-inspired, includes poems from Mandel'štam, Pasternak, and Brodskij.

Variant I: Up and Out from Enclosure

The first variant of the creator acting upon his space begins typically with enclosure in a room to work, symbolizing spatially a withdrawal deep into the self, a retreat to one's private, creative space of the type Virginia Woolf treats in *A Room of One's Own*. The room here means inner freedom. Having listened to the inner music of one's being or personal memory («тихая музыка былого»), one is armed to burst out of oneself, out of Petersburg, out of all spatial limits in an orgy of self-transcendence which is a Dionysian creative act. This bursting from the self and the room can be so powerful that it can even bring on a sense of loss of self-definition. "The creative hand lifting the filmy layers from Petersburg might become infected with diphtheria," says the narrator in *The Egyptian Stamp*.[20] One may fall into the abyss one is revealing, lose oneself and the Petersburg one is fashioning. There are some things that cannot be directly revealed and must remain enclosed in orderly forms. But the risk of some loss of self is necessary for growth and for the conquest of

---

[20] Paraphrase of *The Egyptian Stamp*, 159.

space. There must be a dramatic outpouring of the self, a creative act that changes, molds, and transforms the space—the Petersburg—onto which it erupts. Will this often terrible beauty save Petersburg, as Dostoevskij wished art to save the world? Will Petersburg's negative *kenosis* be reversed thereby?

Vladimir Nabokov wrote of internalizing space-times through obsessive memory and then of composing and creating poetry as affecting and orchestrating the outside spaces from within:

> But then, in a sense, all poetry is positional: to try to express one's position in regard to the universe embraced by consciousness is an immemorial urge. [*Nota bene*: his universe is a mental one, contained in consciousness.] The arms of consciousness reach out and grope, and the longer they are the better. Tentacles, not wings, are Apollo's natural members.... while the scientist sees everything that happens in one point of space, the poet feels [and sees] everything that happens in one point of time [in many spaces]. Lost in thought, he taps his knee with his wandlike pencil, and at the same instant a car (New York license plate) passes along the road, a child bangs the screen door of a neighboring porch, an old man yawns in a misty Turkestan orchard, a granule of cinder-gray sand is rolled by the wind on Venus, a Docteur Jacques Hirsche in Grenoble puts on his reading glasses, and trillions of other such trifles occur—all forming an instantaneous and transparent organism of events, of which the poet ... is the nucleus.[21]

This cosmic sweep reminds us of Blok's ubiquitous awareness of small things happening all over the capital as well as inside its restaurants in poems like «Незнакомка» ("The Unknown Lady"), or of Nikolaj Gumilev's "The Tram That Lost Its Way," which is a stronger case of a bursting-out into the wider world. Such are the large spatial canvases which hold a wealth of events in what Nabokov calls the "cosmic synchronization" in poetry.[22] Here the dominant lies in the artist's consciousness going out to fix, to affect the outside in art, forming Petersburg anew and leaving his trace on it. Nabokov calls his poems "stripes of paint on a roadside rock or ... a pillared heap of stones marking a mountain trail."[23] Nabokov, of course, put his mark on the "sea of language," as did our "ice-skating" Belyj and Mandel'štam. He even has a 1925 poem entitled "The Ice Skater" ("*Kon'kobežec*") in which, like Mandel'štam, he links the intricate and beautiful patterns carved out by skates on ice to the

---

[21] Nabokov, *Speak, Memory* 218.
[22] Ibid.
[23] Ibid., 217.

poet's masterful word-designs.[24] In his autobiography he describes his movement in space while composing different poems—walking out of doors, sitting, pacing in a room. It is as if all manner of events are out in the world and he must move about to capture these pieces of beauty («прекрасного разрозненные части»), to select and collect them, and to hold them together and focus them in the poem.

Clearer cases of the enclosure and bursting-out model occur in Belyj, Xodasevič, and Axmatova. Nabokov's "cosmic synchronization" is an overcoming of the limits of space and a deepening of time. Pasternak wrote of such eternal moments with reference to Puškin's creation of Petersburg poetry and to Peter's creation of Petersburg: «Минуту длился этот миг / Но он и вечность бы затмил» ("This minute lasted an instant / But it could eclipse eternity").[25] Rozanov, in a short aphorism on the creativity of the philosopher Kant, provides another apt example: «Кант никуда не ездил. Он сидел в своем немецком городке, но от такого сидения двинулись миры»[26] ("Kant never went anywhere. He sat in his little German town, but thanks to Kant's sitting still, whole worlds moved"). Such movement is literally what is depicted in our first variant of mastery of space.

In chapter 1 of Belyj's *Petersburg*, the following important passage occurs:

Сосредотачиваясь в мысли, Николай Аполлонович запирал на ключ свою рабочую комнату: тогда ему начинчало казаться, что и он, и комната, и предметы той комнаты перевоплощались мгновенно … в умопостигаемые символы чисто логических построений; комнатное пространство смешивалось с его потерявшим чувствительность телом …[27] а сознание, отделясь от тела, непосредственно соединялось с электрической лампочкой письменного стола, называемой «солнцем сознания». Запершися … он чувствовал тело свое пролитым во «вселенную», то есть в комнату; голова же этого тела смещалась в головку пузатенького стекла электрической лампы….

И сместив себя так, Николай Аполлонович становился воистину творческим человеком.[28]

---

[24] Nabokov, *Vsemirnaja biblioteka poèta*, 243.

[25] Pasternak, 161.

[26] Rozanov, *Opavšie list'ja*, 1: 45.

[27] In this displacement, Annenskij comes to mind: «Я не знаю, где *вы* и где *мы*, / Только знаю, что крепко мы слиты» ("I don't know where you are and where we are, / All I know is that we are inextricably bound" (Annenskij, "Peterburg," 199).

[28] Belyj, *Peterburg* 44–45.

> Concentrating on his thoughts, Nikolaj Apollonovič would lock himself [a habitual action] in his work room: then it would begin to seem to him that he and the room and the objects in the room were reincarnated instantly ... into rational symbols of purely logical constructions; the room's space would get mixed up with his body, which had lost sensitivity ... and consciousness, separating from the body, would unite with the electric lamp bulb on the desk, which was called "the sun of consciousness." Having locked himself up, he felt his body poured out into the universe, that is, into the room. The head of his body was displaced into the head of the paunchy glass of the bulb....
> And having displaced himself thus, Nikolaj Apollonovič would become a truly creative person.

Here, alone in his room, the young Neo-Kantian undergoes a disembodiment—his inner self, his mind, is spread out through the room. This is a Dionysian experience, not unlike the description elsewhere of Nikolaj being torn apart like the Greek god.[29] Nikolaj is in an exalted state, a creative ecstasy. Since Belyj's character is creating philosophy, the electric light of his consciousness is all-important. An animation of space, of the things in the room, occurs, and all things are transformed into philosophical or Symbolist symbols, as extensions of Nikolaj's self and his body. Sending the self out from its center into the environment is exactly parallel to the tentacled embrace emanating from Nabokov's nucleus of consciousness. This model shows on a small scale what Belyj is doing in the novel as a whole—he is encompassing and transforming the objects of Petersburg space:

> Здесь, в своей комнате, Николай Аполлонович воистину вырастал в предоставленный себе самому центр—в серию из центра истекающих логических предпосылок, предопределяющих мысль, душу и вот этот вот стол: он являлся здесь единственным центром вселенной, как мыслимой, так и не мыслимой, циклически протекающей во всех зонах времени.[30]

> Here, in his room, Nikolaj Apollonovič grew indeed into the center he had imagined to himself—into a series of logical presuppositions emanating from the center [like light streaming from a light bulb] which predetermined his thought, his soul and yes, this very chair. He ap-

---

[29] In the chapters "Strašnyj sud" (235–40) and "Dionis" (257 ff.), Nikolaj Apollonovič feels as if he is being torn apart like Dionysus.

[30] 45.

peared here as the only center of the fathomable and unfathomable universe, which flows forth cyclically in all the aeons of time.

This hyperbolic passage and reference to aeons show the extent of Nikolaj Apollonovič's overcoming temporal limits by his mental activity in the enclosed room. Dolgopolov relates the use of the term *aeon* to the Gnostic system of Valentinian, where it means «вечное бытие» ("eternal existence"), which is, according to Vladimir Solov′ev's article on Valentinianism, "the world of aeons, from which all things derive and to which returns all that which is capable of perceiving truth."[31] It is the deeper world beyond the visual, sensual world, *a realiora* (the more real realm) in Symbolist terms. Belyj himself, in "The Crisis of Thought," spoke about breaking through to the more real spheres: "… and in the philosophy of the Gnostics there went forth endless ladders of aeons, so that with their help, consciousness, which was torn apart by ecstasy, would be able to grope to reach something.…"[32] Here again we have reference to mental groping in order to encompass the world without.

These trances and transcendent experiences of Nikolaj Apollonovič were certainly familiar to Nabokov, who considered Belyj's *Petersburg*, along with Proust's *À la recherche du temps perdu* and Joyce's *Ulysses*, among the greatest novels of the twentieth century. Nikolaj Apollonovič's experience as rendered here directly inspired, in our opinion, one of the greatest Petersburg poems of all time, Xodasevič's "Ballad," also a favorite of Nabokov's.

Xodasevič knew Belyj well; as Moscow writers, they both shared very important "Petersburg periods," although Xodasevič's occurred later, after the revolution, between 1919 and 1922, when he lived at the Petrograd *Dom iskusstv* (House of Arts) where Mandel′štam and numerous other leading Petersburg writers resided in those years.[33] It was while he was there that Xodasevič wrote what are generally considered his best collections, «Путем зерна» (*The Way of the Grain*) and «Тяжелая лира» (*The Heavy Lyre*), as well as his brilliant lecture on the deaths of Blok and Gumilev and his lecture on Puškin, "The Shaken Tripod." A large part of his memoirs, entitled «Некрополь» (*Necropolis*), refers to this period of his life.

---

[31] Vladimir Solov′ev, "Valentin i Valentinianstvo," *Enciklopedija Brokgauza-Efrona*, 1891, 5: 404–06.

[32] Belyj, "Krizis mysli," quoted in *Peterburg*, 648.

[33] See, for example, Olga Forš's novel about the House of Arts *The Crazy Ship* (*Sumašedšij korabl′* [Washington, DC: Kamkin, 1964]).

Gregory Freidin is quite right when he finds intertextual echoes between Mandel'štam's 1918 "In Petersburg we shall meet again," in which Orpheus is present and figures explicitly in the variant lines, and Xodasevič's "Ballad."[34] We quote the Xodasevič poem in its entirety below. The three stages of enclosure, hearing inner music, and bursting through the enclosure are again obviously present. The creative figure is here not a philosopher but a poet-prophet. The italicized sections appear to be derived from the Belyj passage:

Баллада	Ballad
Сижу, освещаемый сверху,	I sit, illuminated from above,
Я в комнате круглой моей.	In my round room.
Смотрю в штукатурное небо	I gaze at a plaster sky,
На солнце в шестнадцать свечей.	At a sixteen-watt sun.
Кругом—освещенные тоже,	Around me illuminated also
И стулья, и стол, и кровать.	Are the chairs and the desk and the bed.
Сижу—и в смущенье не знаю	I sit in confusion and don't know
Куда бы мне руки девать.	What to do with my hands.
Морозные белые пальмы	Frozen white palms
На стеклах беззвучно цветут.	Silently grow on the windowpanes.
Часы с металлическом шумом	My watch with its metallic sound
В жилетном кармане идут.	Ticks away in my vest pocket.
О, косная, нищая скудость	Oh, sluggish, wretched meagerness
Безвыходной жизни моей!	Of my life without exit!
Кому мне поведать, как жалко	Whom can I tell how sorry I am
Себя и всех этих вещей?	For myself and all these things?
И я начинаю качаться,	*And I begin to sway,*
Колени обнявши свои,	*Having embraced my knees,*
И вдруг начинаю стихами	*And I suddenly begin in oblivion*
С собой говорить в забытьи.	*To talk to myself in verse.*
Бессвязные, страстные речи!	Incoherent, passionate speeches!
Нельзя в них понять ничего,	Nothing in them is comprehensible,
Но звуки правдивее смысла,	But sounds are truer than sense
И слово сильнее всего.	And the word is stronger than all.

---

[34] See Gregory Freidin, *A Coat of Many Colors: Osip Mandelstam and His Mythologies of Self-Presentation* (Berkeley: University of California Press, 1987), 239 ff.

И музыка, музыка, музыка Вплетается в пенье мое, И узкое, узкое, узкое Пронзает меня лезвие.	And music, music, music Weaves itself into my song, And a thin, thin, thin Blade cuts into me.
Я сам над собой вырастаю, Над мертвым встаю бытием, Стопами в подземное пламя, В текучие звезды челом.	I grow up over myself, Over my former dead being, With my feet in subterranean flames And my forehead in the flowing stars.
И вижу большими глазами— Глазами, быть может, змеи,— Как пению дикому внемлют Несчастные вещи мои.	And I see with large eyes, Perhaps the eyes of a serpent, How my poor things attend to My wild singing.
И в плавный вращательный танец Вся комната мерно идет, И кто-то тяжелую лиру Мне в руки сквозь ветер дает.	And in a flowing turning dance My whole room spins, And someone through the winds Hands me a heavy lyre
И нет штукатурного неба И солнца в шестнадцать свечей: На гладкие черные скалы Стопы опирает—Орфей.[35]	And then there is no plaster sky And no sixteen-watt sun: Onto the smooth rocks of Pieria Orpheus himself sets foot.

It is not difficult to see the influence of Belyj's passage on this poem. Xodasevič begins alone in his room, which, unlike Nikolaj's study, is both a study and bedroom. Belyj displaces the mind of Nikolaj into the lamp, calling it "the sun of consciousness" and seeing it as "the source of all thought." This is clearly what gave Xodasevič the idea for the prominence in his poem of the light bulb, which he also calls a "sun." What was a lamp becomes the special light of the poet's consciousness. Everything Xodasevič sees is transformed and basks in this special light. The first sign of transformation of the meager things in the room is the poet's pity on them. He shows a special closeness and emotional attitude to furniture that we later associate with Brodskij. He pities and empathizes with the objects in the room and thus animates them. He has an identical attitude towards himself, and puts his things together with himself in the same logical series, using a grammatical construction reserved for animate beings to refer to both: «Кому мне поведать, как жалко / Себя и всех этих вещей?» ("Whom can I tell how sorry I am / For myself and for all these things?"). In contrast, however, to the room described in Brodskij's "I em-

---

[35] Xodasevič, "Ballada," 1: 134.

braced those shoulders" (discussed in chapter 5), Xodasevič's things come alive rather than remaining eerily still. Real transformation begins when all the objects get involved in a rhythmic Dionysian dance. He and they fall into a trance in this music, in which sounds rather than meaning are most important. This priority is an echo of Mandel'štam's free, unfettered Acmeist word, not enslaved to any particular meaning, the "blessed, meaningless word." Stanza 6, with its «бессвязные, страстные речи! / нельзя в них понять ничего» ("incoherent, passionate speeches! / nothing in them is comprehensible"), describes a not fully coherent word, such as the partially lost one in Mandel'štam's "I forgot the word I wanted to say."[36] The cult of the word and its sound value as music, in addition to its other attributes, take on additional significance in the Petersburg poet's project. In Mandel'štam's "We will gather again in Petersburg," the buried Puškin is like the invisible Petersburg buried inside the contemporary poet. It is inside him, and he must unearth it from the depths of himself, like that forgotten Word. Puškin and the Orphic Dionysus, both images of the night sun,[37] are present in both poems. Xodasevič is under a kind of Orphic imperative of the Mandel'štamian kind. He must "be Orpheus" again, and the poem ends in this very positive consummation. Mandel'štam elsewhere refers to himself as the severed head of Orpheus, still speaking and prophesying (although underground, rather than in a river as Orpheus did): «Да, я лежу в земле, губами шевеля, / Но то, что я скажу, заучит каждый школьник» [1: 214] ("Yes, I lie in the earth, moving my lips, / But every schoolchild will memorize what I say").

In Mandel'štam, too, it is clearly the Orphic Word and music that must be unearthed:

Где-то хоры сладкие Орфея
И родные темные зрачки
И на грядки кресел с галереи
Падают афиши-голубки.   [Variant, 1: 454]

Somewhere are the sweet choruses of
Orpheus, and dark native eyes,
And upon the upper balconies
Poster-doves fall.

Of course, Mandel'štam's poem is set inside a theater, where he is watching Glück's *Orfeo ed Euridice*. Significantly, in this libretto Euridice, despite

---

[36] See chap. 4, p. 121.
[37] Discussed by Vjačeslav Ivanov, in *Dionis i pradionisijstvo* (Ph.D. diss., University of Baku, 1924).

Orpheus' fateful look back, is still successfully retrieved and brought to the upper world again, like a lost and wandering Word-Psyche or Word-Persephone.

Xodasevič's poem is extremely musical in sounds and metrically hypnotic. It consists of amphiabrac trimeters with a very high percentage of realized ictuses and alternating feminine and masculine rhymes. The very reliable stress pattern gives the poem its rocking, dancing sound, supporting its explicit content. Xodasevič emphasizes the gradual process of the transformation of the creative person more than Belyj, and he also emphasizes the consequent effect of that change first upon the room, then upon the outside. In both texts the creator has the first inkling of change:

Belyj: «тогда ему начинчало казаться, что и он, и комната, и предметы той комнаты перевоплощались» ("then it would begin to seem to him that he and the room and the objects in the room were reincarnated")

Xodasevič: «я начинаю качаться» ("I begin to sway")

Both are "opened up," like Puškin's prophet in the desert, and they grow out of themselves, transcending themselves:

Belyj: «Здесь ... Николай Аполлонович воистину вырастал в ... центр» ("Here ... Nikolaj Apollonovič grew indeed into ... the center")

Xodasevič: «Я сам над собой вырастаю, / Над мертвым встаю бытием» ("I grow up over myself, / Over my former dead being")

Both become masters of the universe in these hyperbolic passages representing the power and presumption of man in a true moment of creativity: both become legendary, God-like figures. In Xodasevič the trance begins in stanza 5; he is cut open by the blade of music in stanza 7; exits from himself in 8; and is Orpheus in Pieria by the end. In Belyj, Nikolaj's consciousness becomes the center and source of everything, from the nearby table to all things, fathomable and unfathomable. Thus in these two texts creative men first retreat into an enclosure, and from deep concentration burst out to affect and change the outer world.

There is one remarkable case of "a room of one's own" which is the negation of the creative mastery of space we describe. True to the local patriotism of these Petersburg writers, the poem in question involves a *Moscow* apartment, not a Petersburg one, where such mastery could indeed occur. This is Mandel'štam's «Квартира тиха, как бумага» ("The apartment is quiet, like paper"), written in response to Pasternak's comment that Mandel'štam at last had an apartment (in Naščokin pereulok) and that he should be able to write now. Gregory Freidin has astutely seen that this poem is an "anti-Ballad," a negative poem counteracting Xodasevič's most positive one analyzed here. This Moscow space is consistently treated by Mandel'štam as *not his*, just as Nabokov treated the Leningrad he fell into in "A Visit to a Museum," but here rather as the space for some compromised writer, where only terrible hack work could be written. We compare parts of Xodasevič's "Ballad" and Mandel'štam's Moscow poem below:

Xodasevič:

Сижу—и в смущенье не знаю
Куда бы мне руки девать.

I sit in confusion and don't know
What to do with my hands
[where to put my hands].

Mandel'štam:

А стены проклятые тонки,
И некуда больше бежать,
А я как дурак на гребенке
Обязан кому-то играть.   [1: 196]

But the damn walls are thin,
And there's nowhere to run to,
And like a fool I am obliged
To play for someone on a comb.

Mandel'štam then says that what he will compose there will be «наглей комсомольской ячейки / и вузовской песни наглей» ("more obnoxious than a Komsomol cell, / more obnoxious than a school song"). They will be songs fit to educate future executioners: «присевших на школьной скамейке / учить щебетать палачей» ("to teach young executioners / seated on the school bench how to chirp"). They will contain the resentment of this young Soviet generation, and will be the diametric opposite of real Petersburg poetry: «и столько мучительной злости / таит в себе каждый намек» ("oh, how much tormenting malice / there is hidden in each allusion"). In contrast, the true music of poetry and sound reigns in the verses of his contemporary, Axmatova, when she reads aloud. The last lines cited above are an inversion of his lines from "Your Beautiful Pronunciation": «и столько воздуха и шелка / и ветра в шепете твоем» ("oh, how much air and silk / and wind there are in your whisper") [1: 197]. Mandel'štam's Moscow apartment is treated as the place of destruction of real poetry and of the real poet, who is turned there into a second-rate hack. To move into some rooms is tantamount to total self-betrayal.

Our final example of Variant I takes us back to Petersburg, this time to the Šeremet'ev Palace on the Fontanka, where Axmatova and other creative types were allotted rooms in the 1930s and where the Axmatova Memorial Museum is now. The text, Axmatova's difficult *Poem without a Hero*, has been touched on here in various contexts; it, too, represents a complex example of creativity (a creative dream or transcendent experience) occurring in a room whose small confines are burst, first into the ballroom in the same palace, and then to Taškent, Siberia, and the whole Russian empire. We will discuss the *Poem* separately and in more detail in chapter 10.

Variant II: Mastering the Elements

> In general, he was in love with space, and with the sea in particular.[38]
>
> Brodskij, on Peter the Great

In our second model of mastery of space in Petersburg, a lonely creator, instead of being tightly enclosed from the world in a room, finds himself alone, confronting the immense expanses of the sea or the Neva. Bachelard has pointed out that confrontation with enormous spaces usually incites in man thoughts of eternity; boundless space becomes a psychological metaphor for unbounded time.[39] Thus what man does in the face of the unbounded is his gesture towards the whole world and eternity.

If in "Ballad," Xodasevič bursts from his room in the House of Arts and emerges climbing the rocks of Pieria as Orpheus, surveying a large space over which he is master, in our second variant the end part of this process, the rush to the new place and domination over it, is emphasized. Underlying most of the examples here in general, and particularly those that omit the first part, enclosure in a room, is Puškin's 1827 poem «Поэт» ("The Poet"). When Apollo needs the poet in the man, the latter is virtually ejected out of his regular life and propelled onto wild and immense open shores. This dash to a wide expanse of water, sea, or land is the spatial model of creativity. One's head must be filled with thought or musical sound that somehow orchestrates the mad dash:

> Бежит он, дикий и суровый,
> И звуков, и смятенья полн,
> На берега пустынных волн,
> В широкошумные дубровы…
>
> He rushes wild and severe
> And filled with sound and confusion,
> To the shores of desolate waves,
> To the wide-sounding groves…[40]

---

[38] Brodsky, "A Guide to a Renamed City," 72.
[39] Bachelard, *The Poetics of Space*, 182 ff.
[40] Puškin, "Poèt," 3: 65.

Six years later "the shore of desolate waves" gained its permanent Petersburg connection in *The Bronze Horseman*. «На берегу пустынных волн» ("On the shore of desolate waves") is perhaps Puškin's most famous line. On the shores of the very wide Neva, with the Baltic Sea in the distance and the flat emptiness of the landscape, Peter becomes a poet-creator of another kind. Merežkovskij called Peter a "poet of action" (*podvig*) while he called Puškin a "contemplative statesman" (*poèt sozercanija*).[41] In a cosmogony reminiscent of that in Genesis, Puškin's Peter the Great makes his historical gesture against the background of boundless space and eternity. Like the poet in the 1827 poem, Peter there is filled with thought:

На берегу пустынных волн
Стоял *он*, дум великих полн,
И вдаль глядел. Пред ним широко
Река неслася...

On the shore of desolate waves
He stood, filled with great thoughts,
And gazed into the distance. Before him
The river coursed widely...

And he effectively filled the wide horizon with these thoughts, as made clear in Puškin's 1828 *Poltava*: «Лишь ты воздвиг, герой Полтавы, / Огромный памятник себе» ("You alone, hero of Poltava / Erected yourself a huge monument").[42] Thus Peter's "thought" becomes incarnate.

In Mandel'štam's "Admiralty," again there is an important, though much less obvious, comparison of the poet and the architect to Peter the Great. The Admiralty in that poem is the product of the creative act, and it also stands as a symbol of Petersburg as a whole and the cultural side of the Petersburg project. The question of whether such beauty arises as "the whim of a demigod" (*prixot' poluboga*) or through the painstaking work of an artisan is resolved in favor of the latter. Both the building as «воде и небу брат» ("brother to sea and sky") and Peter in the lines «Служа линейкою преемникам Петра, / он учит: красота—не прихоть полубога» ("Which served as a yardstick to Peter's successors, / It [/He] teaches that beauty is not the whim of a demigod") are the joint antecedents of the masculine singular "*он*." Peter, the artisan-tsar, taught the first lessons of creativity embodying both inspiration—the great thoughts—and craft. The difficulty of building in the swampy place chosen, of creating anything *ex nihilo* is constantly in the background,

---

[41] Merežkovskij, *Izbrannoe*, 10.

[42] Puškin, *Poltava*, 5: 63.

and yet the nothingness challenges man to fill it. Creative man, faced with silence and emptiness, fashions an Admiralty or poem to fill the void. Mandel'štam asks: "Doesn't this chastely-constructed ark / Deny the dominance of space?"

The greatest denial of space's dominance in Mandel'štam's poem occurs when the building begins to move like a boat. It is given the same dynamic qualities that the Bronze Horseman acquires in Puškin's *poèma* when it comes down off its pedestal and courses through the city. The boat-words and images (*lad'ja, mačta, fregat, kovčeg*), as well as mention of the anchors that are actually there, help to make the edifice a boat. When it breaks loose from its foundations and moves out to the open seas, we have the same triumphant dynamic gesture, here no longer of Peter or the architects of the Admiralty, but of Petersburg-Russia as a whole, the ship of the Russian state's culture that will conquer space and "universal seas" (*vsemirnye morja*).

In chapter 2 we saw that Mandel'štam employs the Admiralty in, for the most part, a metapoetic function, with some elements of identification as an artist with Peter the Great. It is used by other poets, however, and by Brodskij specifically, as one of his "embattled spirits," in the full sense of what we call identification. Brodskij, who is under the powerful influence of Mandel'štam in much of his thinking about his native city, wrote of such images that the challenge of excessive space was the reason for Petersburg developing as it did and ultimately becoming the capital of Russian letters (see chapter 6, p. 224) He describes how the architects overcame the flat, open expanses near the Neva's delta:

> For the last half of the eighteenth and the first quarter of the nineteenth century, this city became a real safari for the best Italian and French architects, sculptors, and decorators.... And yet whatever the architects took for the standard in their work—Versailles, Fontainebleau, and so on—the outcome was always unmistakably Russian, because it was more *the overabundance of space* [emphasis ours] that dictated to the builder where to put what on another wing....[43]

The filling and appropriation of space then becomes the basic model for the free creative man and his act. The Admiralty, an exemplary building, teaches such mastery of space ("[serving] as a yardstick to Peter's successors"). The latter are all those involved in the Petersburg project after his death, especially artists, architects, and architects of the Word. Mandel'štam had concluded: «Нам четырех стихий приязненно господство, / Но создал пятую сво-

---

[43] Brodsky, "A Guide to a Renamed City," 76–77.

бодный человек» ("The dominance of four elements is agreeable to us, / But free man created a fifth element"). This fifth, purely human, creation is language, which also "takes off" from Petersburg. In Brodskij's words, the city became a departure point, a port and harbor, both literally and metaphysically: "There is no other place in Russia where thoughts depart so willingly from reality: it is with the emergence of St. Petersburg that Russian literature came into existence."[44] As the Admiralty "took off" in Mandel'štam's poem, ripping itself from its foundations, so Russian literature left its cradle, the harbor, setting sail to influence the world on a sea of language.

Our final example of comparison of the creative man (the Petersburg poet) to Peter the Great and his expansive creativity as depicted in *The Bronze Horseman* is found in Pasternak's brilliant "Variations on a Theme from Puškin" in his collection «Темы и вариации» (*Themes and Variations*).[45] In his Puškin cycle, the parallel is far clearer than in Mandel'štam's poem inasmuch as the cycle is constructed partly as a riddle, encouraging the Russian to try to understand the enigma of its greatest sphinx, Aleksandr Puškin, for both Russia and for universal culture. Pasternak here ponders this problem and presents some of his interesting thoughts on it in poetic form. The poems of this cycle again unite the elements we have seen heretofore: the lone figure rushing to the shore, the burst of creativity in which he hears inner music and has inner visions, and a definite effect wrought on the horizon, on the Petersburg outside. Pasternak places Puškin onto the same shore of the Neva where Peter had stood, thus equating their activity and their achievement as Merežkovskij had before him.

In Pasternak we see Puškin creating his "Petersburg," which is the novel in verse *Eugene Onegin*. Here the storm from *The Bronze Horseman* which nearly destroys Petersburg is internalized—it is inside Puškin's head:

На берегу пустынных волн
Стоял он, дум великих полн.
Был бешен шквал. Песком сгущенный,
Кровавился багровый вал.

On the shore of desolate waves
Stood he, filled with great thoughts.
The squall was wild. Thickened with
Sand, the purple wave was bloody.

---

[44] Brodsky, "Less than One," 76.
[45] Pasternak, "Temy i variacii," 161–66.

Throughout the cycle there are allusions to another Puškinian shore, the seashore of the opening of *Ruslan and Ljudmila* and the desert sands of that other important metapoetic work about the anointing of the great poet, "The Prophet" (1836). The sand of that desert here becomes mixed with the silt and sand of the Neva and the Baltic Sea in the waves inside the poet's head.

The "anger" or "fury" of those waves against the shore becomes the heightened internal state of the poet:

> Такой же гнев обуревал
> Его, и, чем-то возмущенный,
> Он злобу на себе срывал.

> The same kind of anger enraged him,[46]
> And, made indignant by something,
> He vented his malice upon himself.

The outer and inner here are parallels: as the sea angrily sends its waves against the shore, so the creator indignantly and furiously vents his storm on himself, spewing out words and water:

> В его устах звучало «завтра»,
> Как на устах иных «вчера».

> "Tomorrow" on his lips sounded
> Like "yesterday" on the lips of ordinary men.

The power of his words is likened to Jehovah's. So quickly did his words become deeds that he uttered them with the kind of certainty regular mortals must reserve for the past. His thoughts create the future:

> Еще не бывших дней жара
> Воображалась в мыслях кафру,
> Еще не выпавший туман
> Густые целовал ресницы.

> A heat of days that have not yet come
> Was conjured in the thoughts of the Kaffir
> A fog not yet rolled in[47]
> Kissed his thick eyelashes.

Puškin's thoughts are presented as predicting and forming future Russian life. He creates an internal storm which is destined later to "fall out," pouring from

---

[46] The root of the verb here is *bur*, or "storm."
[47] Fog, of course, is a constant Petersburg attribute.

the poet's head into reality. Petersburg will be constituted from the inside of his head outward. The highlighted element in this creative storm is "haze":

> ... Его роман
> Вставал из мглы, которой климат
> Не в силах дать, которой зной
> Прогнать не может никакой,
> Которой ветры не подымут
> И не рассеют никогда
> Ни утро мая, ни страда.

> ... His novel [*Eugene Onegin*]
> Arose from a haze which no climate
> Is able to produce, which no heat
> Of any kind can chase away,
> Which the winds cannot raise
> And which neither the May morning
> Nor suffering can ever disperse.

The "haze" of this creative storm is shown to be indestructible and "*nerukotvornaja*" (not created by mere nature), powerful in a way that natural storms cannot be. It is an absolute storm. The poet is possessed by it and its force absolutely. Here the wildness and sternness of Puškin's "Poet" is no longer inside of him but in an element which we have seen is very important for this model of creativity: those qualities are externalized upon and given to the space which is being mastered by art. Just as Nabokov said that Puškin had left the traces of his elbows on the granite, here it is not architecture which is filling the space, but a verbal construction (*Eugene Onegin*). Pasternak characterizes the space as altered by the poet. The poet, by his activity («бежит он дикий и суровый» ["he rushes wild and severe"]) pours out wildness and severity; as a result the space is transformed and the novel rises from the haze, as Petersburg had done in *The Bronze Horseman*:

> Был дик открывшийся с обрыва
> Бескрайный вид. Где огибал
> Купальню гребень белогривый,
> Где смерч на воле погибал,
> В последний миг еще качаясь,
> Трубя и в отклике отчаясь,
> Борясь, чтоб захлебнуться вмиг
> И сгинуть вовсе с глаз. Был дик

Открывшийся с обрыва сектор
Земного шара, и дика
Необоримая рука,
Пролившая соленый нектар
В пространство слепнущих снастей…

Wild was the endless view that
Opened from the precipice. Where
The white-maned crest encircled the bathhouse,
Where the free whirlpool was dying down,
Still rolling a last moment,
Trumpeting and despairing in its echo,
Struggling to fill its lungs with water in an instant
And drown, disappearing from view. Wild was
The sector of the earth that opened
From the precipice, and wild was
The boundless hand
That poured this salty nectar
Into a space of riggings that were going blind…

Puškin, like Peter on horseback with his extended hand, is dazzling the empirical Petersburg with its sleepy boats in the harbor. They are blinded by his vision, by the honey that he pours on them. Honey is an ancient Greek metaphor for poetry repopularized prior to Pasternak's writing this poem, most notably by Vjačeslav Ivanov, Gumilev, and Mandel'štam. Puškin poured out this nectar for long periods, in the many years of work on the novel in verse («на протяженье дней и дней» ["over the course of days and days"]). The rarity and admiration-inspiring quality of the book, of Puškin in general, and of creative experiences of this kind for the poet as well as its value for the reader are all encapsulated by Pasternak brilliantly in the gaze upon the space. The space is first espied and then filled, and Puškin, through whom this occurs, as well as later poets and the reader himself are all amazed, uplifted, and gratified:

На редкость дик, на восхищенье
Был вольный этот вид суров.

Wild to the point of rarity, severe
To the point of ecstasy was that free view.

We hear the echo of Mandel'štam here: "But free man created a fifth [dimension]." The fifth dimensions here are language and aesthetic feeling, a sense that nature lacks. In Pasternak's words, the Puškin phenomenon is explained in questions and answers, riddle-fashion:

Что было наследием кафров?
Что дал царскосельский лицей?
....
Два моря менялись в лице

What was the legacy of the Kaffirs?
What did the Lycée at Carskoe Selo give us?

Two seas intermingled in one man

One was the sea—the Baltic Sea and the Neva at Petersburg—and the other was the sea of the Russian language:

Стихия свободной стихии
С свободной стихией стиха.

The nature of free nature [was mixed]
With the free nature of verse.

In Puškin, the elements of free, wild nature combined with the free nature of verse and poetry. He not only burst onto the shore, but called forth creations there as Peter had, making that Petersburg shore what Mandel'štam had called an "amazed space" (*izumlennoe prostranstvo*).[48] The creative winds and storms of the poet thus stand in opposition to the wind against which "a man cannot stand up" in the historical versions of Petersburg self and space presented in part 2; changing, mastering, and amazing spaces is the most powerful ahistorical strategy engaged in by our Petersburg writers.

---

[48] Mandel'štam speaks of amazed spaces in "V xrustal'nom omute kakaja krutizna," 1: 75, in the line «И с христианских гор в изумленном пространстве». Axmatova wrote of amazed mirrors, in her "First Northern Elegy," «… зеркал, каренинской красою изумленных».

Part IV

Mixed Models of Petersburg Space and Self

In part 2 (historical identifications with Petersburg space) and part 3 (ahistorical identifications with Petersburg space [those that deny history]), we have traced and analyzed specific spatial models and strategies of identification. The first group, dominated by time, admits the tragic losses and self-division that time/history causes. Thus it focuses on the blows time has given to Petersburg and the Petersburg writer in the traditional sense of the Romantic elegy; its divergence is that the struggling self is post-Romantic in sensitivity, and the spaces are urban rather than rural or pastoral.

In part 3 we saw ahistorical (atemporal) treatments that claim imperviousness to time's assaults for both the city and the creative self. These poetic constructions represent the Petersburg artists' monuments against time, monuments that grow stronger in our discussion from chapter 6 to chapter 8. In these models of suspended time and the overcoming of emptiness, there is much of the "wish fulfillment" type of elegy that runs counter to present fact (as analyzed above in chapter 2). Such treatments of space present idyllic alternative realities which stand against and replace the so-called empirical reality. They are attempts to exit from historical time and oppose its destructive emptying force in art. They refute the emptying-out of Petersburg and of themselves in the creative act, creating new realities which, as Brodskij says, act upon the empirical space: "... the city began to fall into dependence on the three-dimensional image supplied by literature.... today when you think of St. Petersburg you can't distinguish the fictional from the real."[1]

Brodskij, our youngest poet, who did not live in pre-revolutionary Petersburg at its cultural apogee in the Silver Age, is nevertheless quite insistent on the point that great art/poetry can "take you there," can replace the damage time has wrought on the space, and enable one to experience the space "in its fullness." His important corollary to this belief is his assumption

---

[1] Brodsky, "A Guide to a Renamed City," 80.

that Petersburg space "falls into dependency on" great poetic art and cannot help being changed by its own (literary) reflections.[2] As in Axmatova's "First Nothern Elegy," we look at the present-day Litejnyj Prospekt and cannot help but see the "Russia of Dostoevskij" and Nekrasov; the mirrors still hold Anna Karenina's beauty. Life and art are mutually reflected, and reflected such that the space is essentially changed, and art and life are thus intimately melded. Rank empiricists will never be able to see the "true Petersburg," Mandel'štam's "night sun." As victims of their own philistinism (*nizmennyj svjatoša*) and rigorously non-artistic natures, such non-poets and non-artists will remain impervious to poetry's leaps and flights. These are the flat Leningraders, rooted in a tediously boring and greatly impoverished Soviet present.

As we have indicated heretofore, most of our Petersburg writers have in their *oeuvres* elegiac texts of both the historical and ahistorical types. Yet, as we have seen, Blok (after his initial, "Beautiful Lady" period), Tjutčev, Belyj, Rozanov, Georgij Ivanov, and at times Axmatova (in her *Northern Elegies*) and Mandel'štam (in his identification with Ovid in *Tristia*) tend to emphasize time/history-inflicted loss and the present resulting lack in the self. By the same token, Nabokov, Xodasevič (in his brief "Petersburg period"), and Brodskij tend to deny history's (the Soviet world's) power or victory over them or over Petersburg. Despite these general proclivities, we have emphasized both approaches all along in all authors treated, including those who display both models in specific poems.

In this fourth and final section of our study, we shall analyze a series of masterpieces in terms of a *conflict* of historical and ahistorical tendencies. In chapter 9, the conflict will be demonstrated in two genres, autobiography and novel. We will examine separate works by the same author: first, the autobiographies of Mandel'štam (*The Noise of Time*) and Nabokov (*Speak, Memory*), and second, their respective novels *The Egyptian Stamp* and *The Defense of Lužin* (*The Lužin Defense*). In our final chapter, we shall examine perhaps the most complex work in the entire tradition of self-identification with Petersburg space, Anna Axmatova's *Poem without a Hero*, where the two conflicting tendencies are powerfully co-present in a single work.

It is quite to be expected that Axmatova's work, a generically Romantic narrative poem, is not a lyric poem—not an elegy *per se*, despite its many elegiac qualities. It is a narrative work whose heroine changes and develops. In its powerful elegiac cast, Axmatova's lyric persona is rooted in history and cultural memory, in which she has borne many losses. We introduce the notion of the sanguine elegy as a tool to illustrate her refashioning of this elegiac cast: through the poem she moves towards wholeness, a new integrality with her

---

[2] Ibid.

erstwhile self and Petersburg, and finally, towards full integrality with the rest of Russia. *PWH* is the ultimate "bridging structure" in Petersburg spatial poetics.

9

PETERSBURG SPACE AS CREATIVE AND DESTRUCTIVE MEMORY: RECOVERED HEALTH AND TRAGIC SICKNESS IN MANDEL′ŠTAM AND NABOKOV

> There are indeed people in the world…, muddle-headed people who know nothing more than a few chess moves but are still eager for a game just to see how it will turn out.
>
> Mandel′štam, *The Egyptian Stamp*[1]

We have seen in chapters 6, 7, and 8 above the denial of the effects of history on the Petersburg individual, and how Mandel′štam, Nabokov, and Brodskij treat Petersburg memory as a salubrious, curative, virtually parenting presence in their early lives, one that allowed them to be strong Petersburg artists to the end. The happy Petersburg-born child is able to maintain a connection with his Petersburg youthful self for the duration of his life, and it has so imprinted itself on his identity-being that despite history and the tragedies that befall his city-space in his lifetime, his inner Petersburg remains the touchstone of a unified identity that keeps him whole enough to become a great Russian artist. We have also seen that this triumphant presence of the strong artist-self was best registered in Mandel′štam's and Nabokov's autobiographical works (respectively, *The Noise of Time* and the three versions of Nabokov's autobiography *Conclusive Evidence*, *Other Shores* [*Drugie berega*], and *Speak, Memory*).[2]

In spite of all this, both writers have to admit, even in their autobiographies, an impediment to their full entrance into and continuation in the imperial literary tradition. The impediments are different in each case, but they appear at only slightly different periods in the writers' lives. In both, earliest childhood is presented as decisively positive, tending towards the idyllic (see chapter 7), and very formative for the artist.

Mandel′štam's "impediment" is the fact that he is a Jew whose artistic tendency is to contribute to an aristocratic, imperial literature in which before his generation (including the Jewish Muscovite Pasternak) there are no leading Jewish writers that he can hark back to as his forebears. Therefore his great

---

[1] Mandel′štam, *The Egyptian Stamp*, 140.
[2] All references here are from *Speak, Memory*.

predecessors are "the masks of other men's voices," voices that he loves, and that should be alien, but in fact are "his own." Thus he declares in *The Egyptian Stamp* the attempt to throw off the protective family crest—a glass of boiled Petersburg water—and drink in freely the bacilli-infested water of his city and to open the windows and let in the diphtheria-filled air. "... the least influence of Judaism overflows all of one's life," he writes ironically, and it fills the chaotic Jewish apartments of his childhood with different smells.³ He wants to open the windows and let in the real Petersburg from outdoors, as the world of the streets is his life's breath as a writer/artist. In the last chapter of his autobiography Mandel'štam is further formed by the inspiring literature classes of his Jewish teacher of Russian literature, Vladimir Gippius. Dressed and acting like the very aristocratic Konstantin Leont'ev in his fur *mitra* (bishop's mitre)—and indeed Mandel'štam's description of Gippius would well fit the photograph of Leont'ev in the first volume of the pre-revolutionary edition of his collected works—the intrepid Vladimir Vasil'evič was on such familiar terms with the great aristocratic literature that the young man coming to his professor's apartment felt he was going to visit "Literature" in person. Like Gippius, Mandel'štam is indicating that, whatever the contradictions, he was going to warm himself from the cold of imperial state literature, in "a fur coat above his station."⁴ This reference to clothing again harks back to his childhood as described in the early chapters of the autobiography. Though he describes his apartment as bourgeois (*meščanskaja*), he plays daily in the Summer Garden, where only children in "aristocratic clothing" are admitted (no one in *meščanskoe plat'e* was allowed to enter that sacred Petersburg space). Being a Jew distances one from the great Russian tradition, but Mandel'štam, by love for the language and by an act of will, envelops himself in it, taking it on like a mantle.

Nabokov, as a Russian aristocrat of ancient Tatar lineage, like the hero of Belyj's novel *Petersburg*, has a noble pedigree of which he virtually boasts. It is not difficult for Nabokov to find people of his estate and his ilk in the history of Russian letters: he has the right genealogy. His father was significantly involved in the Duma and in the Kerenskij government; thus it is the Bol'ševik Revolution that alienates Nabokov's father from politics and his class of origin from the territory of Russia, and provides the "distancing" element that Jewish heritage had been for Mandel'štam. The great Petersburg literary tradition is being interrupted, and Russian literature is entering a second stream.

---

³ Mandel'štam, *The Egyptian Stamp*, 77.

⁴ «В не по чину барственной шубе»: this is the title of the last chapter of Mandel'štam's autobiography. Having the given name Joseph, Mandel'štam exploits this special connection with coats.

Nabokov accepts that there is no *edinyj potok* (single stream), and chooses to continue the 18th–19th century tradition though physically distant from Russia. Like Roman Gul', he "takes his Russia with him."[5]

Both these writers are fetishists of architecture, of space, and of memory. Nabokov claims to be particularly able to take his Petersburg with him and reconstitute it because he was a child of a generation with a genius-like capacity for remembering, a generation that committed everything to memory as if it had a strange premonition of what was to come. This is tantamount to an expectation of later nostalgia, of a future elegy. It is very significant that in *Speak, Memory* Nabokov's first poem is an elegy, as if for his generation it could not be otherwise. It is, moreover, an elegy of prospective loss and prospective nostalgia because he has not yet even met Tamara, the young Muse who melds later in the work with the Russia he has lost. Nabokov is *elegiac before experience*; he becomes a poet because he is about to meet, fall in love with, and lose his beloved. Life obliges him later with the actual beloved, and the revolution causes him to effectively lose Tamara (Russia). Though he chafes at the formal restraints of the elegy form (in particular, its hackneyed rhymes), his first poem fits the genre; it is an elegy, and though he laughs at his youthful self gently, it is probably true that that youthful self fervently believed in its tones of loss. He says that his first poetic composition, which he recites to his mother with such emotion, bears all the marks of his individuality, and is expressive of his intimate being: "the nearer my poem got to its completion, the more certain I became that whatever I saw before me would be seen by others."[6] The description of his emptied self that he sees in the mirror immediately after belching forth his poem ("the mere dregs of my usual self, odds and ends of an evaporated identity which it took my reason quite an effort to gather again in the glass"[7]) is in no wise a rejection of the poem as a product of his true, deepest self, but rather a confirmation of how much of that self he put into his art.

Nabokov's elegism and his attitude towards the elegy deserve more attention than they have received. As with chess problems, Nabokov likes to innovate in forms that have fixed rules. To play with and control the elegy of the backward-looking variety (his first poem is not a subjunctive wish-fulfillment elegy[8]); to control a future-to-become-past; and to parry a blow that has been struck by an imaginary opponent are all quintessentially Nabokovian strategies. They are not unrelated to Brodskij's attempts, however effective or

---

[5] «Я унес Россию». See chap. 7, p. 259.

[6] Nabokov, *Speak, Memory*, 221.

[7] Ibid., 227.

[8] See chap. 2 on varieties of elegy.

unsuccessful, to remove himself from human psychological time/experience and view them from the standpoint of Time, Language, or other superindividual positions.

Like Nabokov, Mandel'štam was the Acmeist who, along with Axmatova, considered specific, individual memory as the highest value: «Память прежде всего—даже ценою смерти» ("memory above all, even at the price of death"), he wrote in "Puškin and Skrjabin."[9] They are aware, as Nabokov is, of the vulnerability of such memory which constitutes the personality, and the uniqueness of the individual Petersburg-bound memory is for both Nabokov and Mandel'štam the memory of who they are—creatures of Petersburg.

The two excessively upbeat autobiographies under discussion present the evident denial of the negative aspects of Petersburg being and a fine disregard for the tragedy associated with the space in a long series of literary works, as catalogued in the studies of Nikolaj Anciferov. It is perhaps most poignantly a disregard for the schizophrenic doubling of personality in the madness of the characters in Gogol''s Petersburg tales and Dostoevskij's *Dvojnik* (*The Double*). As if to counter all this and consign it to oblivion, in their respective autobiographies Mandel'štam and Nabokov present idyllic, very protective, and obviously privileged Petersburg childhoods and formative years.

The Petersburg "selves" of Mandel'štam and Nabokov are highly original and idiosyncratic, as is to be expected. We shall, nevertheless, highlight some things their differently configured spaces as self have in common. In their childhoods, for example, they share many types of experience: economic affluence, powerful educated parents, education for both in the elite and progressive Tenišev School, a series of French governesses, daily strolls in the imperial parks and central places of the city, a series of tutors and lessons, dachas in the Petersburg (Pavlovsk) and Finland regions, and association with the powerful, whether in the Jewish (Ginzburg, Sinaini) or gentile (Kerenskij, Miljukov) communities. Both childhoods were pervaded by literature, music (prominent piano teachers) and the arts, museum-going, and trips abroad—all adding up for both writers to a childhood-to-early adulthood that was as supportive for future artistic achievement as Pasternak's in Moscow had been. For both these writers, the early association with "this kind of" Petersburg and the memory of it is the rich formative material of their artistic selves which enabled them to weather the slings and arrows of later cultural and material impoverishment, internal exile (Mandel'štam) and actual exile from the city and Russia (Nabokov). Which of these "exiles" was more of a change of space/place is a moot point.

---

[9] See chap. 4, n. 74.

Nabokov refused to acknowledge a changed Petersburg; in his autobiography he asserts that that world no longer exists on the physical plane. Mandel′štam, who remained in the Soviet Union, tries to minimize the importance of the loss of "imperial Petersburg," the *deržavnyj mir* of the poem "With the imperial world I was only childishly connected" [1: 159]. It becomes clear in the second half of this poem, however, that the umbilical attachment of childhood is decisive in the life of a Petersburg writer. In the poem "Leningrad" ("I returned to my city, familiar to the point of tears"), written during his visit there in 1931, it is quite clear that his connection with "his Petersburg" is as strong as ever, that he is still in every important sense the same child who took cod liver oil and had swollen glands, and that the Petersburg "sickness" in a Petersburg artist-child is a sickness for life; in fact, it *is* one's artistic life. This association between illness and inspiration—a form of the higher vision characteristic of the idyllic Petersburg—is made clear in an earlier poem, "… The courage of midnight maidens" («… Дев полуночных отвага»):

И гораздо глубже бреда	And much deeper than the ravings
Воспаленной головы	Of an inflamed head
Звезды, трезвая беседа,	Are stars, sober conversation,
Ветер западный с Невы.	And the west wind from the Neva.
	[1: 27]

By accessing this same creative sickness in Leningrad, Mandel′štam can magically contact and commune with the voices of his Petersburg dead—they are no more dead for him than are Nabokov's dear departed when he writes, "I confess I do not believe in time. I like to fold my magic carpet, after use, in such a way as to superimpose one part of the pattern upon another."[10] Mandel′štam had earlier written the following passage on time and space:

> To preserve the principle of unity in the whirlwind of changes [read: history], contemporary philosophy in the person of Bergson … offers us the theory of a system of phenomena. Bergson examines phenomena not in the order of their temporal consecutivity [historical order], but rather under the guise of their extension in space. He is interested exclusively in the internal connection of phenomena. He liberates this internal link from time and considers it in its self [*otdel′no*] … images/phenomena linked internally form as if a fan whose parts can be unfolded in time [in historical/temporal order] At the same time the fan can be mentally folded up. [2: 242]

---

[10] Nabokov, *Speak, Memory*, 139.

The fan here, as well as the "rolled-up manuscripts ... smeared with time" in the epigraph of *The Egyptian Stamp* obviously remind us of Nabokov's folded magic carpet. The similarity of these metaphors for the way events in life can be viewed in time is so great that one could think Nabokov's was influenced by Mandel'štam's.

Not surprisingly for the authors of the present study, these cases of disregarding the historical sequentiality of events find an extreme "spatial extension": "And the highest enjoyment of timelessness—in a landscape selected at random [BUT, for Nabokov, almost always a Petersburg one] ... is like a momentary vacuum into which rushes all that I love."[11] Mandel'štam's undying dead voices take on flesh in his works just as they do in the autobiography of Nabokov, who proclaims:

> I see again my schoolroom in Vyra, the blue roses of the wallpaper, the open window. Its reflection fills the oval mirror above the leathern couch where my uncle [Vasilij Rukavišnikov] sits.... A sense of security, of well-being, of summer warmth pervades my memory. That robust reality makes a ghost of the present. The mirror brims with brightness.... Everything is as it should be, nothing will ever change, nobody will ever die.[12]

This presentation of beloved childhood places, as in the autobiographical works of Mandel'štam and his "return" poems in 1931, is "felicitous space"[13] at its best. Nothing time can present—no revolution or civil war—can rend its serene, secure, and salubrious permanence. The idyllic childhood basis sustains and enables one to remain whole throughout one's whole life.

This "beautiful lie," however, is only half of the truth about Mandel'štam and Nabokov. The older writer acknowledges the deleterious effects of the revolution for himself and Petersburg culture in his 1927 fictional work *The Egyptian Stamp* and even more so in the non-fictional "Fourth Prose," where he defends the honor of the pre-Soviet bourgeois world among other things, the world of the *byvšie ljudi* (has-beens) like Parnok. In turn, Nabokov says that his childhood was idyllic by calling it such, but demonstrates that he understands that not every Petersburg artist had such a childhood in his 1929 novel *The Defense of Lužin*.[14] Lužin the artist-as-chess-grandmaster has not had the happy Petersburg childhood of Mandel'štam or Nabokov, and

---

[11] Ibid.

[12] Ibid., 76–77.

[13] See Bachelard, *The Poetics of Space*, xxxv.

[14] Vladimir Nabokov, *The Defense*, trans. Michael Scammell and Vladimir Nabokov (New York: Perigee-Putnam's, 1964). Citations used here are from this translation.

Nabokov clearly wants Lužin's collapse to be associated with his *pre*-revolutionary Petersburg experience. He refuses to grant the revolution (history) that much power over the artist. Thus he attempts to present a Russian Petersburg hero untouched by the historical cataclysms of the early twentieth century, but still a victim of "the tooth of time"—one, like himself, a Petersburg scion of nobility, Aleksandr Ivanovič Lužin.

Thus Mandel'štam and Nabokov, two of the writers most associated with Petersburg and its nearby spaces, represent themselves as being formed and rendered strong as artists by their Petersburg connection and associations (the memory of their Petersburg self) in their autobiographies.[15] At the same time, however, both of them, in fictionalized treatments of young Petersburgers extremely similar to themselves, very convincingly presented the opposite case: the tragic fates of Russian artistic genius in the early twentieth century.

These "opposite" heroes are Mandel'štam's gifted young Petersburg artist/creative man, the would-be writer Parnok, a Jew contributing to the pre-revolutionary Russian tradition, and Nabokov's Lužin, a genius chessmaster contributing universally to the chess art, like the famous Alexin and other great Russian chessmasters. The fact that Parnok, like Dreyfus, has the ambition of becoming a diplomat in the Russian foreign service (as did the aristocrat Konstantin Leont'ev, who served in Greece as gentleman-diplomat and writer) and that Lužin's art is chess does not in the least obscure the fact that these are two Petersburg creative geniuses in very complex difficulties. In both cases, unlike Mandel'štam and Nabokov themselves, who persevered and became the glory of modern Russian poetry and prose of the period, their "alter egos," even doubles—Parnok and Lužin—were not adequately sustained by their respective Petersburgs. These fictional artists were in one manner or another destroyed, losing their creativity, their lives, or both.

No writer wants to present his failure or demise while still alive, so these fictional self-presentations are filled with much material to support the fact that Parnok is *not* Mandel'štam, but one of his weaker tendencies, and that Lužin is *not* Nabokov. The strong Mandel'štam is rather like the narrator of the story about the split Goljadkin-like character Parnok-Kržižanovskij, or like the powerful Jewish tailor Mervis who created them both. Nevertheless, in many sections of the text the narrator confuses whether Parnok is "I" or "he" (which the reader can certainly perceive as the narrator's psychic instability), and seems to have had an identical childhood apartment and family and virtually the same relatives as Parnok. He also seems to know too much about the inner life of Parnok the child not to have actually been Parnok pure and

---

[15] Mandel'štam's was written in 1923–24, while Nabokov's was written only in the late 1940s–50s.

simple. Nevertheless he, the narrator, whom one could see as the adult writer/artist, betrays his Parnok-self, of which he also makes merciless fun in places, much as Dostoevskij appears to make fun of Goljadkin while telling the story of *The Double* partly in a voice virtually Goljadkin's own, as Baxtin has textually demonstrated.[16] His confusion between the first and third persons and his obvious sympathy with and understanding of Parnok do not stop him from creating a truly powerful non-assimilated Jewish artist, the tailor Mervis, who has "created" Parnok before the revolution by giving him a *vizitka* (morning coat) which is understood to be his soul. Parnok had a life while he still had this coat:

> There lived in Petersburg a little man with patent leather shoes.... His name was Parnok. In early spring he would run out onto the street and patter along the still wet sidewalks with his little sheep hooves.
>
> His desire was to get a position as a dragoman in the Ministry of Foreign Affairs, persuade Greece to undertake some risky adventure, and write a memorandum.[17]

The narrator writes this in an emphatically past tense, and later allows Mervis the tailor to kill Parnok off and create Kržižanovskij, Parnok's opposite. Mervis decides that creative-dreamer, "musical, concert-going," old-world Petersburg creatures like Parnok are no longer viable, and destroys him, stealing back Parnok's *vizitka*-soul, ripping it off his back just as the coat was ripped from Akakij's back in the same Petersburg almost one hundred years before.

A great deal has been made of Mervis as an artist in the text: it is assumed that he is up to something much more important than tailoring. He is associated with Homer because of his blind, prophetic eyes, and even because of the wrinkles in his blind physiognomy that are said to be visionary. He is, moreover, compared to Dostoevskij, "a flogged convict ... an inmate in a Russian flophouse ... an epileptic."[18] At times he is even reminiscent of Jehovah. Mervis is further compared to Mandel'štam's perhaps ideal strong Jewish-Russian artist, the great actor and theater director Mikhoels, as he applies the epithet "*farforovyj*" (porcelain) to both of them.[19] But Mikhoels hails from and inhabits the flat spaces of shtetls and the rural roads of Belorussia; Mervis is a Petersburg Jewish creator. In his article "Mikhoels" [2: 106–10], Mandel'štam depicts the great rabbinical figure of the powerful actor-director sauntering

---

[16] Baxtin, *Problems of Dostoevsky's Poetics*, 211–21 and 224–27.

[17] Mandel'štam, *The Egyptian Stamp*, 137.

[18] Ibid., 156.

[19] Marat Grinberg, University of Chicago Slavic Forum, 11 April 2002.

though Belorussia, dominating the space all around him like a shtetl version of Walt Whitman. We could say that the overall message and semantic tendency of *The Egyptian Stamp*, which ends sadly even for Mervis, who is tearful in his final depiction in the novel, is to proclaim that a strong Jewish artist may have to kill off the Parnok tendencies in himself, an injustice against which Mandel'štam rants and raves in "Fourth Prose." However old-world Petersburgian, European, civilized, and wonderful the Parnoks of the world may have been, if the strong Jewish artist does not get rid of this part of himself, he will, like Parnok, collapse into nothing and fail to survive as a creative self, or as any self at all. Petersburg, and what the space/place has become in *The Egyptian Stamp* is not nurturing for the artist. Parnok, associated with the Biblical Joseph in Egypt (as is Mandel'štam himself by virtue of his first name), spatially connects himself with the pre-revolutionary Egyptian Bridge over the Fontanka, a bridge that totally collapsed before 1912![20] One artist with whose fate Parnok's is clearly connected in the tale is the nineteenth-century opera diva Angiolina Bosio, who died in the capital in 1859 from Petersburg-induced sickness, as recorded in Nekrasov's *About the Weather*.[21]

In *The Egyptian Stamp*, the Petersburg madness, delirium, and sickness that led to Goljadkin's schizophrenia and caused Hippolyte's tuberculosis are re-evoked by the direct comparison of Parnok to these characters by name and by the presentation of Parnok as a writer living out their sad fates in a more modern age. In *The Egyptian Stamp*, *The Defense of Lužin*, and in a more complex way still in *Poem without a Hero*, as we shall see in our final chapter, the combination of sickness and health that comprises human life and the life of the artist-genius is revisited in no uncertain terms. Parnok seems to have an elevated temperature, and like Hippolyte and Bosio, to be delirious and dying (living out the last days of his life) throughout the text. The temperature of Petersburg itself during this age ("when the temperature of the age shot up to 37.3"[22]) is that of a human fever.

In *The Egyptian Stamp* the tragedy of the pre-revolutionary artist who cannot fully realize himself—and survive—is strong. Mandel'štam's narrator chides Mervis for stealing Parnok's soul from his collapsing house ("Oh, Mervis, Mervis, what have you done? Why have you deprived Parnok of his earthly raiment, why parted him from his beloved sister?"[23]), but then himself betrays poor Parnok, whom he begs God to differentiate from him (the

---

[20] This is pointed out by Georgij Lukomskij in *Staryj Peterburg* (St. Petersburg, 1912).

[21] See p. 9, n. 16.

[22] Mandel'štam, *The Egyptian Stamp*, 137.

[23] Ibid., 134.

narrator) before allowing Mervis to go on and destroy him. Mervis shows no more mercy towards Parnok than Dostoevskij does towards many of his "little men," Goljadkin and Hippolyte especially. Mervis, associated with Dostoevskij, is a "cruel talent"[24] with epic Dostoevskian sweep and greatness. Admittedly, after Mervis does away with Parnok, who melts down, the character who gets Parnok's soul (*vizitka*) and has already taken his shirts from the laundry—Kržižanovskij, the other half of his doubled identity—does not seem to survive very long either. He drinks the "cemetery-earth-laced coffee" of Anna Karenina in Klin (the train stop where she met Vronskij and her fate was sealed), and he ends up himself "melting down" in the window of a hotel where Čeka agents stayed while working at the Lubjanka. The very name Kržižanovskij was clearly Bolševik-tinged, as we indicated earlier; it was the surname of the head of Gosplan in the mid-1920s.[25] We know from *Anna Karenina* that for a Petersburg man (Kržižanovskij), to take that train and go to Moscow is not portentous of his survival, and, as it had been for Anna, this railroad-riding is the beginning of his end.

What Nabokov does in *The Defense of Lužin* is even more tragic. When Nabokov says in his autobiography, "after I had bestowed on the characters of my novels some treasured item of my past, it would pine away in the artificial world where I had so abruptly placed it,"[26] he is admitting some autobiographical communality between himself and his characters, although he explicitly denies it in the same statement and on the same page. His characters emanate from the same Petersburg world; his supposedly genuine self has lent important parts of itself to his fictional world. When he goes on to admit that he had "lent" his French governess (Mademoiselle) "to a boy in one of my books," and that her memory "is engulfed in the description of a childhood entirely unrelated to my own," the reader recognizes that the child who borrowed Mademoiselle was Aleksandr Lužin. The reader knows, more importantly, that Lužin's childhood is not totally unrelated to Nabokov's own. Nabokov has "lent" Lužin entirely too much of his autobiography, and his childhood relates to Nabokov's childhood negatively as the nightmare turn that Nabokov's life might have taken. Lužin's life stands to Nabokov's autobi-

---

[24] Nikolaj Mixailovskij famously described Dostoevskij as having a "cruel talent" (*žestokij talant*).

[25] There are two Kržižanovskijs who were Mandel'štam's contemporaries. By far the best known one was the head of Gosplan in the mid-twenties. The other was a minor Russian writer of Polish origin active in Russia in the 1920s and 1930s, who wrote in Russian, and about whom little is known.

[26] Nabokov, *Speak, Memory*, 95.

ographical narrative in the same negative relationship that Parnok's stands to Mandel'štam's cheerful autobiography.

That Lužin is the nightmare double of the happy boy and young adult Nabokov is borne out by more than the fact that they had the same fat French governess and the same hydraulically-run elevator at home. Lužin's childhood, like Nabokov's, included vacations on the Adriatic and Biarritz and the identically-described nighttime visions in the Nord-Express traveling from Europe to Russia. The name of Lužin's school (Balaševskoe) in both its sound and its atmosphere reminds one of Teniševskoe; the teacher's dissatisfactions with the young student who was a loner and teased by his classmates is yet another parallel. Some of the childhood details of young Nabokov's life are given to the adult—but reinfantilized—Lužin, such as their common fondness for drawing cubes and geometric shapes. The reading list Lužina plans for her husband to keep him from returning to chess dovetails neatly with the books that made a strong impression on Nabokov the child. More importantly, Nabokov had his own "mania" as a child, lepidoptery, which gave him the same irresistible aesthetic pleasure that chess gave Lužin and with which Nabokov remained obsessed over time no less than Lužin. Even the tendency to view the world in terms of chess combinations, assaults, and defenses, is not reserved for Lužin alone but "lent to," in turn, the autobiographical self. When Nabokov learns from mocking school boys (just as Lužin's father had been mocked by the boy's classmates) that his father has been called out to a duel, he fears losing the friend and bulwark that his father has been to him—in this situation, the diametric opposite to Lužin's destructive real father as well as his "chess father," Valentinov. Nabokov presents that frightening Petersburg day and the actual assassination of his father in Berlin in 1922 as moves on a chessboard life, just like Lužin's. On the day when the elder Nabokov's duel was called off, the "*Endspiel*" was still ahead: "no shadow was cast by that future event upon the bright stairs of our St. Petersburg house; the large, cool hand resting on my head did not quaver, and several lines of play in a difficult chess composition were not blended yet on the board."[27] Nabokov's own great interest in chess and chess problems (many of whose solutions he published, just as Lužin's were published), is further complemented by the fact that both have grandfathers or great-grandfathers who were noted composers.

Parnok's collapse, as indicated, is presented in terms of high fever and illness; the shots of clock time (a military cuckoo clock with a marksman appearing on the hour) into his family living room; the flight of his family furniture down the stairs; the loss, confusion, and chaotic disarray of beloved objects that had made up the happy hearth; and the death-blow of the theft of his

---

[27] Ibid., 193.

morning coat-soul by Mervis. The novella, viewed as the story of the final day or two of Parnok's life (a unity of place and time) spent in high fever and delirium, gives a psychological motivation to the excessively beautiful poetic prose, compared by some to Surrealist imagery. Nabokov's attachment to the objects and furniture of his childhood is equally strong and equally disturbed when the family is forced to emigrate.

In *The Egyptian Stamp* allusions to climate and place-related sickness extending back into early childhood are clearly marked out but slightly less prominent than in Nabokov's novel. The sickness seems to be associated with time and worsened by the apocalyptic acceleration of time, by the fact that the novel is set temporally "at the end of" the life of imperial Petersburg and of Parnok—of the so-called Old World. That the sickness may have always threatened Parnok is clear in statements such as the following definition of his life and that of the Petersburger in general: "It is terrifying to think that our life is a tale without plot or hero, made up out of desolation and glass, out of the feverish babble [*lepet*, or childish speech] of constant digressions, out of the delirium of the Petersburg influenza."[28] This Petersburg threat is confirmed by the overprotectiveness towards the boy exhibited by his mother and grandmother: "Don't go in there—the dormer window—whispered mother and grandmother. But even into the keyhole it forced its way—the forbidden chill, the miraculous guest from diptherial [Petersburg] space."[29] Outdoors Petersburg, for all its danger, is the exciting space of inspiration and creativity.

The threat of a dangerous and sick Petersburg childhood lurks in the background for Parnok, as well as the delirium he suffers in the work's narrated present, and he seems to be delirious and dying in the day that transpires in the text's present. The Petersburg childhood of Lužin is likewise punctuated with illness. It is disastrous physically and psychologically. His illnesses (mental ones causing fevers and nervous breakdowns) seem to emanate in part from the absence of the wonderful parenting and idyllically supportive childhood Nabokov characterizes as his own. Out of vanity, Lužin's father wanted a *Wunderkind* son, but wanted him to fit his own conception of such; Lužin senior is a second-rate author of children's moral tales featuring a trite teenager named Antoša. In short, the elder Lužin was a frustrated, envious non-artist. His planned, but never written, fictionalization of his son's life is a last attempt, one among many, to control and refashion that life, and it includes killing off his protagonist (his son) at a very young age. Nobody wants to parent Lužin except his aunt, whose access to him is limited. His mother, who was fond of him as a baby, ceases to love him as the older *Wunderkind*.

---

[28] Mandel'štam, *The Egyptian Stamp*, 161.
[29] Ibid., 150.

Almost simultaneously with Lužin's discovery of his chess/artistic calling and his truancy from school, his mother withdraws her love and classes him with his father as a "deceiver." The aunt who first teaches him chess and supports his gift is the only relative Lužin considers as such, but she is also his father's mistress and therefore a source of shame and guilt for the boy. His relations with his father are cold and quite the opposite of Nabokov's with his.

Lužin's very supportive and protective wife repeats the role of his aunt at the end of Lužin's life, a role whose first purpose is to support and encourage him virtually to the level of champion of the world, and then to keep him away from chess as it comes to threaten his very physical survival. Nabokov once (and Lužin constantly) spatializes his life as a chessboard. For Lužin his town house, his country estate, his school, and his aunt's house in Petersburg are visualized as a chess board upon which he moves as the immobile "king," and others make strong and quiet moves against his existence, which he must counter with defenses. This is unquestionably an example of spatialization of one's identity as Petersburg—and a highly stylized one. The contents of the novel deal with his sick/sad and happy Petersburg memories—how he was insufficiently loved and how he found his true artistic vocation in chess. The beginning of his life is envisioned as a chess game, and its *Endspiel* is occurring in the ongoing present narrated in the novel. The "moves" and the "pieces" at the beginning and the end are largely the same, and the combinations seem to be repeating. Looming large is the threat that this is what life is going to be unless Lužin concocts a defense of his individuality that enables an exit from this evil infinity. To do this he must out-play Turati, his only real opponent and the force behind the current assaulting chess combination, which manifests itself throughout the novel. For example, as a teenager Lužin had been at the same resort where he meets his wife. He had been taken there to be cured of his obsession with chess, a Petersburg illness, only to discover that there was a chess tournament going on there. The repeated combinations at the end of his life have not only destructive but salvational elements. The appearance of a protective woman who especially guards his gift and admires him as a genius-artist coincides with his comeback to the level of world champion for most of the course of the Berlin tournament. Lužina is an exaggerated version of the loving aunt, and his first strong defensive move is to try to marry her and make her his "queen" immediately. The dark element against this defense is the reappearance of Valentinov. Valentinov, to whose influence and tutelage his father had ceded his son, had used and abused him, exhibiting Lužin like a freak while his great talents waned. Keeping his life entirely dominated by chess and making money out of him, Valentinov had then abandoned him, paying him off like a discarded mistress. One fully expects this "firing" of

Lužin to be as destructive to his existence and identity as the theft of Parnok's morning coat was to him, but Lužin has reserves of strength that Parnok lacks.

First of all, Lužin is already a genius-artist chess *Wunderkind* as a child, known for his daring combinations and moves. During his period touring with Valentinov in Europe, he falls into a slump, growing less daring, and at the point when we find him, Turati, an Italian player of the daring type Lužin had been as a child, has risen to international prominence. Valentinov is now casting his lot with the Italian, as Mervis had cast his with Kržižanovskij. But the most important thing in the question of Lužin's existence as an artist is that Turati has usurped the Lužin prerogative, has out-Lužined Lužin. Lužin must therefore defend against and defeat Turati in order to reassert himself as himself. This is made patently clear in a passage as much about early success in any artistic endeavor as it is about chess, which itself is obviously an art for Nabokov:

> Luzhin's game, which in his early youth had so astounded the experts with its unprecedented boldness and disregard for the basic, as it seemed, rules of chess, now appeared just a little old-fashioned compared with the glittering extremism of Turati. Luzhin's present plight was that of a writer or composer who, having assimilated the latest things in art at the beginning of his active career and caused a temporary sensation with the originality of his devices, all at once notices that a change has imperceptibly taken place around him, that others, sprung from goodness knows where, have left him behind in the very devices where he recently led the way, and then he feels himself robbed, sees only ungrateful imitators in the bold artists who have overtaken him, and seldom understands that he himself is to blame, he was petrified in his art which was once new but has not advanced since then.[30]

This is undoubtedly how Lužin feels, and in the course of the tournament he is returning, both in memory and in his present life, to his past, to a Russian family and family home (albeit in Berlin), to his native language, and to a protective Russian womanly presence, his queen Lužina. As he creeps up on Turati and forms a defense against the latter's daring, it becomes clear that the Italian Turati (whose very name is associated with one of the Russian words for the rook, *tura*, the others being *lad'ja* or, colloquially, *puška*, cannon) is a strong player who, it is noted in the text, does not castle often.[31] Cannons were

---

[30] Nabokov, *The Defense*, 97.

[31] It is said of Turati in the text that he rarely used the castle (*tura*), the chess figure that is associated with his name. This means that Turati uses his rooks aggressively from the beginning

very much feared by Lužin in his early childhood, and in particular, the cannon at the Peter and Paul Fortress near where he took morning walks regularly with his father and governesses. The fear of Turati stems from Turati's status as a more successful pseudo-Lužin who has usurped something of Lužin's identity as a unique chess artist in the same way Goljadkin junior has usurped the essential being of Goljadkin senior in Dostoevskij's *The Double*. To beat Turati, to find a defense again his daring, is in a real sense to become the whole Lužin again. This curing or taking the full self back from the usurping other is the real purpose of his *Endspiel*, and is far more important than being champion of the world. According to the newspapers, Lužin is well on his way to doing so until he becomes ill during the finale of the tournament.

SPATIALIZATION AS THE DENIAL OF HISTORY

The spatialization of a sequence of events—"folding up the magic carpet" so that one pattern can be superimposed upon another for Nabokov, closing the Bergsonian "fan" or "rolling up the manuscripts" for Mandel'štam—means that all events that were sequential can be presented on one temporal plane simultaneously. It is a way of denying time's flow, or at the least, its meaningful effect on individual life. It is in this sense that, in his autobiography, Nabokov superimposes his Russia on the snowy New England road where he stands as sixty years crumble into flakes in his hands.[32] Mandel'štam explicitly wants to reverse time. Parnok's last dash back to Malinov is an attempt to return to childhood, to catch up (*naverstat'*), to achieve a return in time. He fails, and he disappears on virtually the next page. Parnok, who fails to re-achieve his Petersburg in his "life," is compensated through his book: "'That evening Parnok did not return home to have dinner.... He listened to the sputter of the blowtorches as they approached the streetcar tracks with their blindingly white, shaggy roses. He received back all the streets and squares of Petersburg in the form of rough galley proofs, he composed the prospects, stitched the gardens."[33] Here Parnok gets back in art—as a book—the very streets and prospects that comprise Mandel'štam's spatialization of self in *The Noise of Time*. Parnok re-achieves himself in art—as a writer—just before he disappears in time as a biographical person. Lužin, as we shall see, disappears

---

of each game, as castling cannot be done once the rook has moved from its initial position on the board.

[32] See chap. 5, p. 196.

[33] Mandel'štam, *The Egyptian Stamp*, 158.

into his art in a similar way. They are both, as Mandel'štam predicted in "The End of the Novel," "plucked out of their biographies" [2: 269].

The image of the city as a huge book whose covers are drawbridges, whose content is the gaping Neva, and whose pages are the streets and flat prospects is an interesting variation on the closed fan. The narrator emphasizes the city's "bookishness": "It is more and more difficult to turn the pages of the frozen book, bound in axes by the light of gas lanterns. You, wood yards—black libraries of the city—we shall yet read, we shall still have a look."[34] Though Parnok was the victim of "preconceived notions of how a novel should go," his life in art, his Petersburg (artistic) identity is encompassed and immortalized in a book that will repeatedly be gazed upon and read. The destruction wrought on Petersburg by accelerated apocalyptic time will be stopped in this book, a moment immortalized in art. Anna Karenina, the character who bears her train-related sickness in her from her first meeting with Vronskij at the train station (mentioned on the last page of *The Egyptian Stamp*) was also a victim of her preconceived notions of how a romance (the other meaning of *roman*) should transpire. She wanted life to imitate the English novel she was reading in the train on that fateful trip to Moscow.[35] Both Anna and Parnok are victims in life but immortalized in art. Mandel'štam's attempt to deny that the revolution or civil war could kill his Petersburg self or art is seen in his constant reassertion of his sick childhood self in his late poems (quoted above), and his denial of the triumph of death in those poems; as Auden would say of Yeats, "the death of the poet was kept from his poems."[36] Parnok's death and Petersburg's sickness are presented as unrelated to the revolution. The Petersburg sickness has been with Parnok always, and he is still that Petersburg child.

This is even more dramatically, clearly, and tragically the case with Nabokov's Lužin. Though Nabokov begrudgingly admits that the revolution caused his own departure from Russia and at least "tried" to break his life in two by making the spaces of memory inaccessible to him, he is hidebound to deny that the First World War, the revolution, or any of the historical events of the early twentieth century caused Lužin's departure, death, or the disruption of his art. He makes this completely explicit in the novel in the thoughts of Lužin's novelist father. As the elder Lužin contemplates writing a novel about his *Wunderkind* son, he rants against the fact that one cannot present a

---

[34] Ibid., 156.

[35] In the train in pt. 1 of *Anna Karenina*, Anna is reading an English novel about the life of an English noble family in the country, a life that is uncannily repeated in her life with Vronskij on his estate Vozdviženskoe later in the novel.

[36] W. H. Auden, "On the Death of W. B. Yeats," 52–54.

Russian protagonist in fiction in the present time (the 1920s) without dwelling on the formative or deformative effects of the World War and the Russian Revolution on that main character. Lužin senior never actually writes his novel, but his conception of it is told in considerable detail for the reader. Nabokov, on the other hand, does write Lužin's story, and Nabokov's de-emphasis on the effects of historical events on Lužin could not be more dramatic. Before August 1914, Lužin was abroad, quite unaware of what changes the war and revolution portended, and when he is briefly in Petersburg during the actual revolution, his fear of the shooting in the streets is almost identical to his attitude as a child toward the daily cannon fire in the Peter and Paul fortress. He is totally oblivious to actual events. After the revolution, the differences in pre-revolutionary Russia and Soviet Russia, so painfully clear to his wife Lužina, her émigré parents, and their milieu, are totally beyond Lužin's ken. For him it is as easy for the couple to take a trip to the new Russia as to the Italian Riviera. For Lužin the only time that exists is his personal chess-time, that is to say, the time of his own individual life in art. This is especially clear in the close repetition of his first boyhood chess "illness," when he used to wrap himself in a blanket and imagine himself to be the "king" in a chess game on the floor of the room. In the present of the novel, which represents the last few months of Lužin's life—his *Endspiel*—there are frightening repetitions of the events of his youthful crisis. He is in the same place, there is a tournament, he is back in a Russian milieu speaking his native language. He has a strong force protective of his chess genius in the person of his young Russian fiancée and then wife. The engagement party scene in the novel, an interesting reprise of the introduction of Prince Myškin to the Epanchin's friends in Dostoevskij's Petersburg novel *The Idiot*, has the markedly different result that his fiancée does not disclaim him, however little he fits in. She does not succumb to social rules, but continues to make strong protective moves and does marry him. When "the enemy" makes what for him is the frightening move of placing in his way a school companion, Petriščev, who used to be cruel to Lužin, Lužin attempts the quiet move of confusing Petriščev so that Petriščev is unsure whether or not this is the same Lužin. Lužina, in turn, makes the strong move of taking her husband away from the society ball where he was so frightened and distressed. That this is a repeat of Lužin's childhood traumas and that he is back in Petersburg in his mind for better or worse is clear when he feels such happiness in his fiancée's parents' house on Russian Easter. Despite the fact that the author belittles this excessively Russian interior as in worse taste than the kind of noble homes and spaces in which Lužin and his wife were nurtured in erstwhile Petersburg, Lužin is truly happy in the house. The Easter celebration and his marriage in a Russian

Orthodox church call forth happy childhood memories in him of Orthodox Easters, memories of a type that are few and far between in this novel.

For Lužin it is clear that every European city is the same chess cafe, the same taxis and railroad stations. Petersburg is the only city that has any distinctive character in his mind, and at the end of his life he is back in the struggle-chess-game of that Petersburg again. The Berlin in which he walks has Petersburgian characteristics, snows, Russian language, and people; he has fallen into the émigré reconstruction of Petersburg and cannot distinguish it from his childhood home. Nabokov makes this very obvious:

> From the sanatorium he moved into a small, gaily papered room that had been rented on the second floor of his fiancée's building, and when he moved in he had exactly the same feeling as in childhood when he had moved from country to town. It was always strange, this settling into town. You went to bed and everything was so new: in the silence of the night the wooden pavement would come to life for several seconds of slow clip-clop, the windows were curtained more heavily and more sumptuously than at the manor; in darkness slightly relieved by the bright line of the incompletely closed door, the objects stopped expectantly, still not fully warmed up, still not having completely renewed their acquaintanceship after the long summer interval. And when you woke up, there was sober, gray light outside the windows and the sun slipped through a milky haze in the sky, looking like the moon, and suddenly in the distance—a burst of military music: it approached in orange waves, was interrupted by the hurried beat of a drum, and soon everything died down, and in place of the puffed-out sounds of trumpets there came again the imperturbable clopping of hoofs and the subdued rattling of a St. Petersburg morning.[37]

He believes that he can go outdoors and dig up the chessboard and pieces he buried on the family's Petersburg property as a boy. His reality in the last days, when he is secretly obsessed with chess again, is clearly Petersburg. Thus we see here a negative version of the power of the creator to change and superimpose spaces that we saw in chapter 8; the appearance of Petersburg in Berlin is taken by Lužin as the evil manipulation of some formidable chess opponent who imposes familiar "combinations" upon him. After his breakdown, when he is supposed to be kept away from chess as the source of his illness, a guest comes from the same "Petersburg," a Leningrad woman who knew his wife's

---

[37] Nabokov, *The Defense*, 170–71.

family and who socialized with his "chess aunt." Lužina sees that this could be dangerous and asks the guest not to talk about chess to Lužin, trying to pretend she doesn't know which aunt is at issue. Lužin, who feels he must be on guard for attacks "every minute of his life," does not fail to see the ominousness of this "strong move," and even sees the woman's morose little son as a double of his own childish self. Trying to perform a magic trick that had once been shown to him at one of his less-than-successful birthday parties, he pulls out a small chess game that has remained buried in his pocket and tries to teach the little boy chess, as his aunt had once done with him. He obsessively sets up his endgame with Turati on the board. At this time the guests from Russia act as a diversion and his wife's defense falls down. This is made clear in chess terms: «Ферзь стоял один» ("The queen stood alone"). Still, when a more ominous Petersburg personage, his evil chess tutor Valentinov, appears, Lužina makes a clear attempt to parry and prevent Lužin's knowing or seeing him. A few days later Lužina fails to prevent Valentinov from forcing Lužin into a cab on the street near their apartment and taking him to his movie studio, "Veritas." There it becomes clear that in his supposed "movie" Valentinov plans to force Lužin and Turati (as actors playing themselves) to play out the last tournament game which is set up on a chessboard on the movie set. Here Lužin begins his final defense of self, bolting from the set onto a tram and back to his apartment. In his final madness, which his wife senses, he has come to the conclusion that these repeating combinations are going to beset him ceaselessly, that his life is a chess game, an evil infinity of such repeating patterns. His final rejection of Lužina's help as he rushes to the bathroom, locking himself in, is his realization that life is going to be just such a bad infinity unless he, as king, makes a very daring move himself. Thus he jumps to his death, winning the game of his life-in-art, by cutting short his earthly existence. This ending cannot but remind us of Mandel'štam's notion in "Puškin and Skrjabin" that an artist's/poet's death is his last creative act, through which his entire creative life is illuminated: "it seems to me that the death of an artist should not be excluded from the chain of his creative achievements, rather it should be viewed as the final conclusive link in that chain" [2: 313].

The protagonist's two hostile fathers, Lužin senior, who planned to cut his life short in a novel, and Valentinov, who wishes to have him routed in cinematographic art and in the world chess championship, failed to kill Lužin the artist. Lužin's last days during the tournament and his night wanderings in Berlin have an uncanny resemblance to another Petersburg poem, where this type of life is as if predicted—the second poem in Blok's cycle *Danse macabre*:

> Ночь, улица, фонарь, аптека,
> Бессмысленый и тусклый свет.
> Живи еще хоть четверть века—
> Все будет так. Исхода нет.
>
> Умрешь—начнешь опять сначала,
> И повторится все, как встарь:
> Ночь, ледяная рябь канала,
> Аптека, улица, фонарь.[38]

> Night, the street, the streetlight, the druggist's shop.
> Senseless and dim light.
> Live another quarter century—
> Everything will be the same. There is no exit.
>
> Years will pass and begin again from the beginning,
> And repeat exactly as of old:
> Night, the icy rings in the canal,
> The druggist's shop, the street, and the streetlight.

It is obvious that Lužin's life-game has become just such a series of Petersburg combinations that Blok had proclaimed as inescapable in his famous poem. At one point Lužin thinks he has figured out the combinations, that he has found a key to the direction of the game, and his pleasure is compared to that of any artist: "During these first minutes he had still only had time to feel the keen delight of being a chess player, and pride, and relief, and that physiological sensation of harmony which is so well known to artists."[39] But this triumph is short-lived as he soon realizes the greater threat of his opponent's assault and its unrelenting repetitiveness:

> And as soon as his initial delight in having established the actual fact of the repetition had passed, as soon as he began to go carefully over his discovery, Luzhin shuddered. With vague admiration and vague horror he observed how awesomely, how elegantly and how flexibly, move by move, the images of his childhood had been repeated (country house … town … school … aunt).…[40]

Then he divines the striking device he must undertake to escape:

---

[38] Blok, "Noc', ulica, fonar', apteka," 172.
[39] Nabokov, *The Defense*, 213.
[40] Ibid., 214.

> Already ... he had thought of an interesting device, a device with which he could, perhaps, foil the designs of his mysterious opponent. The device consisted in voluntarily committing some absurd unexpected act that would be outside the systematic order of life, thus confusing the sequence of moves planned by his opponent.[41]

That absurdly daring move is the jump from his window into the outside Petersburg which gave birth to him. In this aspect the daring move has a parallel in Parnok's fearless move to drink the influenza-filled water of the northern capital shortly before he melts and blends into that which "alone held him together." Of course, Parnok's mad dash into a pharmacy shortly before his death reminds us of the druggist's shop of Blok's "Danse Macabre" poem. In Parnok's Petersburg the night, streets, lanterns, and druggist's shop are likewise extremely prominent.

The Dostoevskian, primary Petersburg sickness of the Petersburg creature reappears in Axmatova's diagnosis of the illness of the intelligentsia to which she belongs. Her *Poem Without a Hero*—whose acronym in Russian is Petersburg's own, PBG—clearly reprises the same crises of her creative Petersburg generation that Mandel'štam poses in *The Egyptian Stamp*. Not only is Mandel'štam-Knjazev not a great poet-hero in Soviet Russia, but the reasons for his failure to be are partly inherent in the Petersburg space that gave birth to him, in a Petersburg itself cast as a sick, even dying child in *The Egyptian Stamp*. Petersburg as a dying child, a dying or consumptive young girl, or as a dying great opera singer (Bosio): all of these images of Petersburg are like Parnok himself—not realized or not fully realized.

In the autobiographies of Mandel'štam and Nabokov, *however actually different their respective childhoods*, Petersburg was the source of self-integration; it braced them with memory which guaranteed their survival in art, as in Mandel'štam's image of the function of the Egyptian ship of the dead:

> ... and the stream will carry the fragile ship of the human word out to the wide sea of the future. How can one outfit this ship for its distant journey without supplying everything needed for such an alien and dear reader? Once again I shall compare poetic work to the Egyptian ship of the dead. Everything for life is laid in its stores; nothing is forgotten in this ship. [2: 258–9]

Alas, Mandel'štam's and Nabokov's *fictionalized* treatments of artists very much like themselves were much darker and more tragic than the citation above would imply, as predictions of the fate of the Petersburg writer in the

---

[41] Ibid., 242.

"real twentieth century" were borne out in the actual lives of many of their Russian contemporaries.

10

POEM WITHOUT A HERO: THE COMPLEXITY OF THE CREATIVE SELF IN TWENTIETH-CENTURY RUSSIA

In the foregoing chapters we have traced numerous and varied representations of self as space in the modern Russian tradition. We have seen how the lyric ego or the protagonist—modern creative man—is identified with the edifices, monuments, and the interior, exterior, and open spaces of the Northern capital. In consonance with the elegiac, subjective mode of the works considered (outlined in detail in chapter 2 above), time in these treatments of space is understood to be psychological time, both when its forward movement is destructive to the integrity of self, and when it fosters change and development of the self. This time is what Georges Poulet has termed *le temps humain*[1]— time experienced and refracted through a human prism, not *sub specie aeternitatis*, but rather *sub specie personae*. The possible escape from such time via artistic creation represents a vertical transcendence in the midst of advancing historical tragedy, an escape of and by the self from the "vortex of phenomena, their ceaseless flow." It is the removal of the self, the human personality, from time's fleeting, ephemeral quality to a state of greater permanence, quiescence, and stillness (*pokoj*), in the most positive sense. In this aspect all of our poets, with the notable exception of Brodskij, who particularly vacillates on this point,[2] subscribe to Berdjaev's view of man's experience and the meaning of the creative act as an ascent into eternal being.[3] Such a view of the artist and his work is tantamount to a religion of artistic creation, a kind of divine-human activity, as first laid out in Berdjaev's seminal 1916 work *The Philosophy of the Creative Act*. In this optimistic view of time, *le temps humain*, however tragic, is not a totally inescapable vicious circle, but can be triumphed over in human creativity. Of time Berdjaev writes, "Just as the entrance of the eternal into time [for example, Christ into human history] is possible, so also is an irruption in the closedness of time and the exit of time into eternity."[4]

---

[1] Poulet, see chap. 4, n. 1.

[2] See chap. 6. See also Day, *Memory as Space* and Aaron Beaver, *Time in the Poetry of Joseph Brodsky* (Ph.D. diss., University of Chicago, 2003).

[3] Nicholas Berdiaev, *Slavery and Freedom*, trans. R. M. French (New York: Scribner's, 1944). See 255–68 for the famous passage on the three kinds of time in which man participates.

[4] Ibid., 400.

The exit from the temporal, from man's human psychological experience of time and self, into the eternal means vertical transcendence. It implies that time itself, as a category of human perception like space (as held by Leibnitz and Kant) is something *a priori* implicated in the divine, in the bosom of eternity—like man himself. This means that not only does our earthly time, with its historical or biographical linear processes, exist, but that it is implicated in and can ascend to eternal non-temporal states. The possible achievement of superhuman experience and the transcendence of biographical and historical time is subscribed to by Blok, Mandel'štam, Belyj, Xodasevič, by Axmatova most certainly, and by Nabokov and Brodskij, though less consistently and directly.

We have shown throughout our study how space becomes temporalized and humanized, subjectivized, as Epštejn said of space in elegies (see chapter 3 above). Both the transcendence of this human time and the failure of attempts to transcend are experienced by Petersburg spaces, which correspond to moments and periods of the creator's life or the "out of time" creative idyll. What we have termed here attempts to deny the effect of history on the city self (in chapters 6–8), be it the projection of a permanent, abiding self onto Hermitage walls, or an eternal presence by the archway on Galernaja street, is a species of exit from history for the poet-self and the larger city-self. This exit is very clearly illustrated in Axmatova's poem to Mandel'štam "О, как пряно дыхание гвоздики" ("Oh, how pungent the breathing of the carnations"):

Там, где кружатся Эвридики,
Бык Европу ведет по волнам:
Там, где наши проносятся тени,
Над Невой, над Невой, над Невой;
Там, где плещет Нева о ступени,—
Это пропуск в бессмертие твой.   [1: 256]

There where Eurydices encircle,
And the bull leads Europe across the waves:
There where our shades pass by,
Above the Neva, above the Neva, above the Neva,
There where the Neva splashes against the steps—
That is your passage into Eternity.[5]

---

[5] Glück's opera, which Axmatova and Mandel'štam attended in 1910, differs from other versions of the legend in that despite the backward look, Eurydice does return to the upper world.

In chapter 9 we saw a felicitous Petersburg space as self in the autobiographies of Mandel'štam and Nabokov, but destroyed and battered in the suffering fictionalized selves of Parnok and Lužin. In the greatest modern work of the Petersburg tradition, *Poem without a Hero* (1940–66) we have both types of space as self in a single work, both the tragic failures and the victories (*podvigi*) of the martyred city culture and city-self. Hence *PWH* is a compendium and a culmination of all the simpler types of projection of self that we have presented heretofore in our chapter-by-chapter typology. The major differentiating factor we saw was the extent to which time's ravaging effect prevails or is acknowledged. In chapters 3–5 the tragic history of Petersburg-Russia from 1900 is destructive, emptying Petersburg and the Petersburger out. Movement forward in time in that model implied a progressive loss of what was conceived to be the true or basic self. History's headlong movement was seen as the accompaniment to and the cause of the *dédoublement*, the collapse of personality, of the divided Russian psyche, of rifts in character, of "double think," and of the gradual dismemberment and dispersal of the city's body and the components of the self. Such discontinuity in the life trajectory of the city and the self produced a suffering, strife-torn poetry. Places and people were what Brodskij called "embattled spirits."

It has often been observed that more and more as the twentieth century wore on, high culture in Russia came to take on the functions of traditional religion. After 1917 the creators of imperial culture, those who did not conform to the dictates of revolutionary art, were increasingly persecuted for the very nature of their art, and came to view themselves as long-suffering, no longer strictly secular martyrs.[6] *PWH* has much in common as a cultural document with T. S. Eliot's "Wasteland," chronicling as it does the fate of Petersburg art and culture at what Axmatova considered their tragic, even agonizing end (from 1914 through the 1960s). It is her agonic lament for Petersburg, as Cassandra had cried of Troy, "Oh my beloved city, dragged to uttermost death!"

As a recapitulation of all the types of identification with space in this book, *PWH* is more than the sum of those parts. It presents an even more complex layering of spaces, which work to thwart each other. City space is closely associated with the selves who, for Axmatova, were the last great Petersburg poets, and with Mandel'štam in the first instance; he was always her closest poetic ally, especially after his poem "Preserve My Speech" was dedicated to her in 1931. Together they are two closely-linked suffering selves,

---

[6] Discussed at length in Sarah Krive, *Appropriating the Early Akhmatova* (Ph.D. diss., University of Chicago, 2002).

one still present (alive) and one missing—yet in the logic of "negative tangibility," perhaps more palpable for the fact that he is missing.

Petersburg in 1940 is not altogether recognizable as itself given its losses, including the defection of its would-be poet-hero, but it is not solely a victim of vicious historical vengeance. It retains its past, though not everyone can access it. The *poèma* which assaults Axmatova as a rush of involuntary memory stops time and the emptying process to a remarkable degree—reconfiguring what has defected, what has been lost, sundered, evacuated forever; replacing it is a large part of what the poem achieves. As we saw in the ahistorical examples in chapters 6–8, the *poèma*'s incursion into her life gives her back a lost part of herself. Of the depicted Petersburgian spaces in the *poèma*, one could say there is a Blokovian space in which the tragic biography of Petersburg culture is symbolized in the set of poetic "doubles" introduced here (Knjazev, Sudejkina, Blok), and then there is the post-Blokovian space of Axmatova's present, constricted life. Blok himself reappears in this latter part not only in a style reminiscent of Blokovian Symbolism—as Nadežda Mandel'štam has pointed out—but in the role he plays as the man/epoch in the threesome.

The tragic biographies of Axmatova and of Mandel'štam—the missing hero just recently deceased, two years to the day before her writing began (27–28 December 1938)—are the impulse behind Axmatova's attempt to continue the Petersburg space and struggle of the self-as-Petersburg space that we observed in Mandel'štam's *The Egyptian Stamp*, from which her title doubtless derives: "our life is a tale without a plot or hero, made up out of desolation and glass, out of the feverish babble of constant digressions, out of the delirium of the Petersburg influenza."[7] The disappearance of Parnok in *The Egyptian Stamp* is discussed above as an evil representation of Mandel'štam's autobiography turned inside out, as a nightmare vision that later bore some resemblance to Mandel'štam's actual life. Before returning to the spatial poetics of *PWH*, which we will discuss as a continuation of Mandel'štam's text "I write on your manuscript," let us look at how Axmatova depicts the emptying of self in her several *Northern Elegies*.

HISTORICAL AND ANTI-HISTORICAL ORIENTATIONS IN AXMATOVA'S *NORTHERN ELEGIES (LENINGRAD ELEGIES)*

To understand the degree to which *PWH* accommodates the paradox of demolishing-rebuilding formally and thematically and stands as an amazing development in the tradition of the Petersburg Tale in general and the tradition of the poet's identification with Petersburg spaces, let us briefly consider several other complex works, written in the same period, where the poet deals

---

[7] Mandel'štam, *The Egyptian Stamp*, 161.

with the problems of history. We have in mind, of course, the *Northern Elegies*: they present considerable complexity in their treatment of the self and Petersburg, but are resolved with far less paradox and ambiguity than *PWH*. In the elegies, the problems of the Petersburg poet are projected onto the urban space. As we have seen, in the "Third Elegy" the question of a devastating epoch is raised, and the poet images herself as the river Neva "made totally other," which in its disorientation does not recognize the city it flows through: "And I do not recognize my own shores." Here loss of the speaker's sense of self, depicted in part as the river's confusion, is treated pessimistically, but not irreparably; after all, the poet knows "one city in this world," and she can find it even without the power of sight ("I will find it, groping, in my sleep") [2: 311–12]. This possibility notwithstanding, the reader does not feel that the lyric ego finds her true city or true self in this poem. It is resolved in the historical mode, in which the individual ends up divided, damaged, and even perhaps supplanted by an impostor. The negative results of inner conflicts occasioned by time are the same in the "Fourth Elegy" ("Reminiscence has three epochs"), as we observed in chapter 6 above.

Yet it is the "Second Elegy" ("So, there it is, that autumn landscape") in which the historical and antihistorical modes of projecting time upon space are most dramatically present and in conflict. This elegy again presents a multi-layered self, as does *PWH*, but unlike the *poèma*, in it history's destructive effects are emphasized instead of the ability of the poet-individual to withstand history's onslaught. Because it shows a divided and dispersed personal and artistic life in space and the "Leningradization" of Petersburg and of the heroine—both present also in *PWH*, but with a different resolution of the conflicting tendencies—we cite the elegy here in its entirety:

Вторая

Так вот он—тот осенний пейзаж,
Которого я так всю жизнь боялась:
И небо—как пылающая бездна,
И звуки города—как с того света
Услышанные, чуждые навеки,
Как будто все, с чем я внутри себя
Всю жизнь боролась, получило жизнь
Отдельную и воплотилось в эти
Слепые стены, в этот черный сад...
А в ту минуту за плечом моим
Мой бывший дом еще следил за мною
Прищуренным, неблагосклонным оком,

Тем навсегда мне памятным окном.
Пятнадцать лет—пятнадцатью веками
Гранитными как будто притворились,
Но и сама была я как гранит:
Теперь моли, терзайся, называй
Морской царевной. Все равно. Не надо…
Но надо было мне себя уверить,
Что это все случалось много раз,
И не со мной одной—с другими тоже,
И даже хуже. Нет, не хуже—лучше.
И голос мой—и это, верно, было
Всего страшней—сказал из темноты:
«Пятнадцать лет назад какой ты песней
Встречала этот день, ты небеса,
И хоры звезд, и хоры вод молила
Приветствовать торжественную встречу
С тем, от кого сегодня ты ушла…

Так вот твоя серебряная свадьба:
Зови ж гостей, красуйся, торжествуй!»   [1: 310]

Second (Northern Elegy)

So there it is, that autumn landscape
Which I have so feared all my life:
And the sky is like a flaming abyss,
And the sounds of the city, as if
Heard from the other world, are alien forever,
As if everything against which I
Struggled inside myself took on a life
Of its own and was incarnated in these
Blind walls, in this black garden…
But at that moment [when this happened], behind
My back my former house was still following me
With its squinting, unfavorable eye,
With that window I'll never forget.
Fifteen years pretended like they were
Fifteen granite centuries,
But I myself was like granite too:
Now plead, torture me, call me
A sea princess. It's all the same. No need…
But I needed to convince myself

That all this had happened many times before,
And not just to me—to others too,
And even worse. No, not worse—better.
And my voice—and this, truly, was the most
Terrifying thing—spoke out of the darkness:
"Fifteen years ago, with such a song
You greeted this day, you entreated the skies,
The choruses of stars, and the choruses of water
To greet your triumphant meeting
With the one whom today you left…

So there's your silver wedding anniversary:
Summon your guests, be beautiful, exult!"

Though the elegy (despite its date of 1942) most likely refers to Axmatova's separation from art historian Nikolaj Punin, the division into several mutually antagonistic selves in time projected onto the Leningrad-Petersburg river embankment and the wider city is what interests us here. We see the co-existence of several selves in one place, familiar from Dostoevskij's *The Double*, where two Goljadkins coexist in a single apartment, or from *The Egyptian Stamp*, where the Goljadkin-like doubles, Parnok and Kržižanovskij, are both attached to Kamenoostrovskij Prospect. In the "Second Northern Elegy" several selves are associated with different loci of the Petersburg cityscape and presented as if they were in very close proximity to each other, having been gathered mentally by the author whose inner life they comprise. Identification of a present tragic life with a tragically debunked and bleak city in this poem is more complicated and requires close scrutiny. Although the words "as if" (*budto, kak budto*) keep the actual images similes rather than metaphors, the symbolic significance of space is not weakened thereby. What is psychological or mental here is extremely "infelicitous space," to invert Bachelard's phrase.[8]

Gazing on autumnal Leningrad, the lyric persona is frightened by the sunset and the city. They are what she had always feared was in store for her, what she and her city might turn into—a fate realized over time. The sounds of the true city—the deeper, idyllic past, here a submerged Petersburg—are inaccessible in the poem's present, "forever alien."[9] The external world is the self she

---

[8] Bachelard, *The Poetics of Space*, xxxv.

[9] The more obvious interpretation of these lines is that in her upset state, the sounds of the present city are alien to her. This, though possible, is unlikely. That the present-day Leningrad is alien to her is clear from the first line and not to be lamented mid-poem. The exclamation that the sounds of the "true city" seem to be from the world of the dead make it more probable that

did not want to become. Its objective quality reflects her high degree of identification with it. We recall the lines from "The Sentence" in *Requiem*: "I long ago had a premonition of this bright day and emptied house" [1: 366]. In the "Second Elegy" the inner "house" is extended outward to cover a large cityscape. The virtually Tsvetaevan frequency of enjambment in this poem far exceeds Axmatova's usual use of this device, and has a semantic function: to reinforce the speaker's sense of disjunction between deeper self and place, a sense of not fitting into this place or this self.

In lines 6–9 she realizes that the wall upon which she gazes and the dark garden are objective correlatives, spatial equivalents of her most unwanted inner states. Concomitant with this realization, it becomes clear that the former house contains her recent past, the time spent with the man from whom she has just separated. In the line "My former house was still following me," the verb *sledil* may imply static contemplation (watching) or, by association with the verb *sledovat'*, movement behind or pursuit. It, of course, does not necessarily imply movement, but in either case it imputes intentionality and dynamism to the "former house" with which she has just broken. Moreover, a causal connection can easily be inferred, that is, that she is in her present predicament because she broke with that house. The house or former self, is, at any rate, breathing down her neck; an animated monument, like the Bronze Horseman, it is a source of the anxiety that permeates the poem. It may well be made of granite, and she, in her stubborn resistance to its pursuit, portrays herself as being granite also, as if she has turned into a stone building or statue. This is a later and altered reprise of her early self-image as Lot's wife turned into a pillar of salt. Existence is associated here with solidity and spatiality; as Dostoevskij had said in *The Possessed*, "stone structures" give people "something to hold onto."[10]

It is clear as the poem proceeds that originally—before the period of the "former house"—she was not "granite-like," and the city (as well as her life in which she began the affair) was far from the present frightening one. Proust pointed out repeatedly that places are as changeable, "as fugitive as the years," and this mutability is dramatically borne out here. In her resolve not to return to the pursuing house, she herself becomes a different, "hard and fast," opposing granite structure. These two "houses" are not from the same time period, as were, for instance, the yellow house representing Senator Ableuxov and the factories of Vasil'evskij Island standing in for Dudkin in Belyj's *Petersburg* (see chapter 4).

---

these are the sounds of the Petersburg of the past and not of 1944 Leningrad. Moreover, a similar expression occurs in a similar, but less ambiguous context, in *PWH*.

[10] See p. 3, n. 5.

Here we have a confrontation of diachronically distinct but nevertheless concomitantly presented spaces, two conflicting past periods of the poet's biography having a stand-off. It is witnessed by a third self, the one of the poem's present, who observes the exteriorization of her inner conflict in a space which she, too, inhabits. The quoted speech in lines 17 and 18 represents that self addressing itself, perhaps borrowing the words from her dialogue with the man who inhabited the "former house." It means "just try to entice me back to my past; it is futile." In the *Northern Elegies*, as in *Requiem*, Axmatova rejects the possibility of meaningful return to the past and its places ("My last link with the past is sundered"). She feels she can never more be her "sea princess" self, and the self "of granite" here affirms the impossibility of return. As Blok had been for Axmatova a granite monument to his troubled epoch, so she has become a granite monument to her own.[11]

In lines 19–22 the building tension of the elegy is temporarily broken, or softened, by the generalizing of her situation to many Petersbugers and Petersburg "houses." It ends with the observing, narrating self being surprised or shocked by its "own" voice, a very ironic voice "out of the darkness" or *de profundis*, which expresses the irony and tragedy of the biography with a sharpness and deeper understanding than the other "selves" seem to possess. We see that the city was still closer to being its original self, fully Petersburg, when the people shown as parting here met and came together; it was still Mandel'štam's 1914 "*vode i nebu brat*" ("brother to earth and sky"): "You entreated ... the choruses of stars and the choruses of water." It was a Tjutčevan city, with references to his Romantic poems about love and lost love set on the same embankments (see chapter 4). There is especial reference to Tjutčev's poem after Denis'eva's death, "Once more I stand above the Neva." Axmatova, however, compresses not only several meetings with the same person (as Tjutčev does) but several disparate temporal periods of her life into a single poem-space. Yet the Petersburg of the beginning of her love relationship has disappeared from view, become alien. The sky that once contained "choruses of stars" is now a "flaming abyss," and we are faced at the end of the relationship with the total annulment of "that Petersburg," the non-Petersburg which is the scene of this poem.

---

[11] It will be recalled that Axmatova thought of a literal monument to herself being constructed posthumously, and alludes to the place of its construction in *Requiem*, where she concluded that the prison "the Crosses" would be the proper site. In 1999 such a statue was in fact erected there.

Thus the elegy, quite simple on its face, maps spatial references to four temporal selves:

- a) the self of the remote Petersburg past («хоры звезд и хоры вод»)
- b) the self of the recent house («мой бывший дом»)
- c) the self of the present tragedy («тот осенний пейзаж»)
- d) the reflexive self, conscious of the other three.

In addition there are

- e) the present narrator of the poem, a self framing the other four; and
- f) the deeper self, perhaps equivalent to Proust's or Bergson's "*le moi profond*," a self seemingly conscious of the others, but surprising to them when it speaks up, and not immediately recognized as "self."

We see then the deep burial, verging on total loss, of the lyric persona's original positive self and of the original city. With all this, where is the true city of the "Third Elegy," the one identified with the self to such an extent that it can be found "in [one's] sleep"? In the "Second Elegy," the sounds of that city arrive "as if heard from the other world, alien forever." Of course, there is a paradox in their being heard at all, and in the contact with the deeper self which bursts in like involuntary memory beyond rational control. Though it is well nigh impossible to hear them, they are still heard. Something similar, but which is presented more sanguinely, is found in *PWH* when Axmatova hears the music of the lost Petersburg in the «музыка дикого мэтра, ленинградского дикого ветра» [2: 115] ("the music of a wild maestro, of the wild Leningrad wind"). This music, as she remarks in the prose to *PWH*, may be described as a note not actually played, but heard belatedly in the combination of sounds after a chord is struck. This is what Axmatova called the "second step" of the arrival of a sound or message. In the "Second Northern Elegy" the self, like Petersburg, is dispersed in space and time, disjunctive even with its present self as a result of history/time. The frightening realization of a once dreaded fate is now manifest.

The problems in the "Second Northern Elegy"—of Petersburg, the city and its culture, and of the poet Axmatova—are presented again in *PWH*, albeit on a much vaster canvas and with still greater complexity. In *PWH* the posing of these problems is so ambiguous that we can speak confidently not of a resolution, but of a tendency towards resolution. The historical and ahistorical, the resistant forces acting in Petersburg and the Petersburg poet in the *poèma* are both forcefully represented, constantly intertwined, and almost equivalent in strength.

PWH has been the subject of many excellent scholarly studies and much effort has gone into defining the work's general characteristics and the deciphering of the abstruse cultural, historical, and biographical allusions in the work. Yet, no one has yet attempted to treat the work as the culmination of the tradition of the poet's self-identification with Petersburg space from Blok to Brodskij. In *Axmatova's Petersburg* Sharon Leiter does treat it as the culmination of Axmatova's life-long relationship with the city, and in some aspects her project most closely approximates what we undertake here. Leiter's very valuable narrative, which includes materials from the overall tradition, is more firmly focused on Axmatova. Ours, while it coincides with Leiter's in some small measure, focuses rather on the work's membership in a discrete tradition of the poetics of Petersburg space, as discussed and demonstrated in the foregoing chapters of this book. The treatment of space as self and as the product of the self's regenerative (writing) activity in the work of many Petersburg poets has led us to focus more narrowly on Axmatova's contributions to that specific tradition. We per force highlight different aspects of PWH and its themes and structures than does Leiter, telling a story that complements her contribution to the study of Petersburg poetry.

"Devastation Undone"

In the "Second Northern Elegy" the space of Petersburg is excessively layered, and the presentation of Axmatova's self is complex and dismembered. The sounds of the true city—associated with the deepest layer of authentic selfhood—are "heard as if from the other world" and said to be alien to the present self forever. An emptying process, one of impoverishment of self brought on by the destructive forces of historical time, is afoot, marching through the city. Confronting what her city-space has become confirms the poet's worst fears of what she herself would and has become.

While Axmatova cannot and does not deny the devastating effects of time upon her city and self in *PWH*, these effects are much more powerful in the "Second," "Third," and "Fourth Northern Elegies" just analyzed, which were written concomitantly with the beginning and much of the subsequent writing of *PWH* in the early 1940s. In the elegies there is very limited resistance to the emptying and the forgetfulness of self caused by historical and biographical time. A completely different, almost balanced, treatment of historical devastation and of the ability to resist it is the achievement of her most complex work, *PWH*. While *Requiem* is and has been called by critics "an elegy for

Russia,"¹² *PWH* is what may be termed a "sanguine elegy," a curative elegy, if you will. This type of elegy resolves, or dramatically reduces, the motifs of its own sadness, and is somewhat rare in the annals of the Russian elegy. It makes a sad, even tragic loss, event, or absence a source of consolation or solace, self-understanding, or renewed hope. It makes of such loss the kind of thing Angela Brintlinger refers to as a "usable past"¹³—not the crippling or ossification which Nietzsche decries in "On the Uses and Disadvantages of History for Life," but the revitalizing, reinforcing lessons of even a tragic past.¹⁴

One of the most striking examples of such a sanguine elegy was written by Evgenij Baratynskij, whom, according to N. Ja. Mandel'štam, Axmatova was re-reading in the late 1930s.¹⁵ Baratynskij's "Devastation" ("Zapustenie," 1834), a great favorite of Iosif Brodskij, represents a structure close to that of the much longer and internally reticulating *PWH*.¹⁶ It presents the return of the poet to his past, but offers instead a striking inversion of the type of failed return we studied in chapter 5: here time's victory is denied. Unlike Axmatova's *Northern Elegies*, in which a loss of self and change of Petersburg are cases of true "devastation elegies," Baratynskij's elegy "Devastation" subverts its own title. Returning to his family estate Mara, the scene of his childhood and a place totally associated by him with his father, who lived there with him and who loved and designed the estate gardens, Baratynskij arrives to find his homestead utterly destroyed. All its fullness has been emptied out, and failure to find himself, as in Tjutčev's return to Ovstug (see page 146 above), seems inevitable. The first half of the elegy is the litany of a lost self, of the loss of his father—the devastation of a place and its former sense of fullness. The catalogue of spatial images of Mara is long, and everything there is falling apart or "othered" beyond recognition. In mid-elegy the lyric ego reaches a high point of dismay, claiming that his return home has been in vain: «Вотще!.... Ни в чем знакомого мой взор не обретал» ("In vain! In nothing did my gaze find anything familiar"). This dismayed cry is obviously echoed in Tjutčev's «Не здесь ... не здесь» ("Not here ... not here"); in

---

¹² See chap. 2, n. 1.

¹³ Angela Brintlinger, *Writing a Usable Past: Russian Literary Culture, 1917–1937* (Evanston, IL: Northwestern University Press, 2000).

¹⁴ Friedrich Nietzsche, "On the Uses and Disadvantages of History for Life," *Untimely Meditations*, trans. R. J. Hollingdale (Cambridge: Cambridge University Press, 1983), 57–123.

¹⁵ Nadezhda Mandelshtam, *Hope Abandoned*, trans. Max Hayward (New York: Atheneum, 1974). See her discussion of the poem on 433–39 and 442–43. See also Lydia Chukovskaya, *The Akhmatova Journals*, vol. I, 1939–41 (London: Harvill, 1989), 105–07, 130.

¹⁶ Baratynskij, "Zapustenie," *Stixotvorenija, poèmy, proza, pis'ma* (Moscow: Xudožestvennaja literatura, 1951), 264–66. Brodskij recites this poem very lovingly in the film *Brodskij v Venecii* (1990).

Axmatova's "Third Northern Elegy" («я своих не знаю берегов» ["I do not recognize my own shores"]; and in Annenskij's «Неужто ж точно … я здесь любил, я здесь был молод, и … домой пришел я в этот лунный холод?» ("Can it possibly be true … that it was here that I loved and here I was young … that I have come home to this moonlit coldness?").

Yet Baratynskij does not conclude on a note of lostness and despair; he refuses to let the work become an elegy of devastation. Rather, he presses on down a path created by his father, figuratively and literally, as his father had taken a hand in the landscaping of the place. He keeps losing the path, which itself falls downward at one point into a ravine. The images of devastation only grow stronger, but he perseveres:

> Иду я: где беседка тлеет
> И в прахе перед ней лежат ее столпы,
> Где остов мостика дряхлеет.
> И ты, величественный грот,
> Тяжело-каменный, постигнут разрушеньем
> И угрожаешь уж паденьем.

> I walk by where the gazebo is rotting,
> Where its columns lie in dust at my feet,
> And the skeleton of the little bridge is becoming decrepit.
> And you, grandiose grotto,
> Hewn of hard stone, have also been destroyed,
> And are threatening to fall asunder

As the physical destruction and loss grows more extreme, the poet protests his love for these ruins:

> Что ж? Пусть минувшее минуло сном летучим!
> Еще прекрасен ты, заглохший Элизей,
> И обаянием могучим
> Исполнен для души моей.
> Тот не был мыслию, тот не был сердцем хладен,
> Кто, безымянной неги жаден,
> Их своенравный бег тропам сим указал,
> Кто, преклоняя слух к таинственному шуму
> Сих кленов, сих дубов, в душе своей питал
> Ему сочувственную думу.

> So what? Let the past be gone like a fleeting dream!
> You are beautiful yet, ruined Elysium,

> And full of powerful charm for my soul.
> He was cold neither in thought nor in heart,
> The man who, eager for unnameable pleasure,
> Showed these paths their flight,
> Who lent his ear to the mysterious sound
> Of these maples and these oaks, and nourished in his soul
> A thought in tune with that sound.

Here we have the full subjectivization of space *as the father*, the one, the landscaper, who poured himself and his life spirit into it. Though he has been lost and is now the missing hero of these spaces, he has remained himself in/as the space in exactly the way Mandel'štam hovers eternally over the Neva in Axmatova's "Oh, how pungent the breathing of the carnations," as we saw above. Baratynskij continues:

> Давно кругом меня о нем умолкнул слух,
> Приняла прах его далекая могила,
> Мне память образа его не сохранила,
> Но здесь еще живет его доступный дух;
> Здесь, друг мечтанья и природы,
> Я познаю его вполне;
> Он вдохновением волнуется во мне

> For a long time there has been no talk of him around me,
> A distant grave has received his dust,
> My memory has not preserved his image for me,
> But here his still accessible spirit lives;
> Here he, the friend of reveries and nature, lives,
> I will recognize him wholly;
> As inspiration he lives in me

His link with his father is restored and he is made whole, recuperating the part of himself left in this space.

Something quite similar happens in Baratynskij's final and wistfully elegiac poem "To my Italian Tutor,"[17] where his tutor, the Neapolitan Giacinto Borghese, makes Russia his own and dies there, buried at Mara. Baratynskij, meanwhile, achieves Giacinto's "Italy" as his own formative or mentoring space, which he describes as «благодать нерусского надзора» ("the blessing of a non-Russian [early Italian] upbringing"). As he comes to Naples, "Giacinto's Italy," an "Italy" always a part of his childhood self, is what he achieves. And actually dying suddenly in Giacinto's native Naples, he fulfills so

---

[17] Baratynskij, "D'jadke ital'jancu," 317–18.

ironically the chiasmus, the changing of places between Giacinto and himself set up in the poem, that one almost suspects he had a premonition of death, though his last letters to Putjata show no signs of it.[18]

In "Devastation," this powerful identity with place is especially associated with the creative activity and spirit of his father, who is alive in the poet's own inspiration; in "To My Italian Tutor" it is conveyed by his finding the outer Naples so consonant with the inner Naples his tutor had imprinted upon him from childhood. His embracing of his native place in its devastation and his recognition of Naples as his in a kind of anagnorisis both effectively bring him back the Proustian wholeness he seeks.

A twentieth-century example of a Petersburg émigré's sanguine elegy, with similar connections between poetic creativity and the poet's father, can be found in Nabokov's 1932 poem «Вечер на пустыре»[19] ("Evening in a Vacant Lot"), written in Berlin ten years after the death of Vladimir Dmitrievič Nabokov. The poet, overcome with weariness and grief, finds himself wandering through a deserted and overgrown lot:

> Вдохновенье, розовое небо.
> Черный дом с одним окном
> огненным. О, это небо,
> выпитое огненным окном!
> Загородный сор пустынный,
> сорная былинка со слезой,
> череп счастья, тонкий, длинный,
> вроде черепа борзой.
> Что со мной? Себя теряю,
> растворяясь в воздухе, в заре;
> бормочу и обмираю
> на вечернем пустыре.
> Никогда так плакать не хотелось.

> Inspiration, a rosy sky.
> A black house with one fiery
> window. Oh, that sky,
> drunk up by the fiery window!
> Deserted rubbish outside of town,
> A withered weed with a tear,
> the skull of happiness, delicate and long
> like the skull of a borzoi.

---

[18] Baratynskij, "Pis'mo k N.V. Putjate," 538.
[19] Nabokov, *Vsemirnaja biblioteka poèta*, 281–83.

> What's wrong with me? I'm losing myself,
> dissolving in the air, in the sunset;
> I mutter and grow faint
> in the evening desert.
> I've never wanted to cry so much.

The vacant lot, and especially the black house and the skull thereon, become the spatial equivalents of the poet's emptiness. Unaccountably, however, he is visited with poetic inspiration, faint at first but then growing stronger. The "withered weed" on the field becomes a catalyst to coax out the poem:

Выходи, мое прелестное,	Come on out, my lovely one [poem],
зацепись за стебелек,	catch on to this little stalk,
за окно, еще небесное,	catch on to the window, still heavenly,
иль за первый огонек.	or its first little light.

As he begins to yield to the inspiration that has been incipient in him ever since the first line of the poem, the sense of "dissolving" that had come with his sadness is transmuted into the beginnings of a creative superimposition of the type we saw in chapter 8. The pitiful weed and the fiery window of the black house become the analogues of his family estate of childhood, evoked here in loving and beautiful garden-like detail. The activity of verse-making is the crucial connection that allows the poet to cross time and space in this way; the burgeoning poem on the vacant lot in Berlin parallels his early experiments in writing, which are in turn associated by him with the very particular pastoral spaces of his childhood:

> Когда-то было легче, проще:
> две рифмы—и раскрыл тетрадь.
> ....
> над рекой—изумление ночи,
> отраженное полностью в ней;
> и сиреневый цвет, бледный баловень
> этих первых неопытных стоп,
> освещенный луной небывалой
> в полутрауре парковых троп

> It used to be easier, simpler:
> two rhymes, and I opened my notebook.
> ....
> over the river was the amazed night,
> completely reflected in it;
> and the color of lilac, pale pet

of these first inexperienced [metrical] feet,
lit by an unprecedented moon
in the half-mourning of the park lanes

Even as a youth, the poet is able to "amaze" the spaces of his nighttime reveries with his poetry, and as he stands in the overgrown field in Berlin, he is similarly able to "master" that space by the force of his poetic creativity. In typical Proustian fashion, the lushness of the "place past" is evoked with a vividness that not only changes his present surroundings, but even surpasses the original experience:

и теперь увеличенный памятью,
и прочнее, и краше вдвойне,
старый дом, и бессмертное пламя
керосиновой лампы в окне

and now, enlarged by memory,
more stable and twice as beautiful
is the old house and the immortal flame
of the kerosene lamp in the window

Thus the faded stalk of grass in the poet's present becomes the green garden of his poetic home, and the fiery window in the "black house" becomes the original house of his creative self, with its ever-burning flame. The overwhelming grief that had earlier nearly brought him to tears is now replaced by a firm belief in the irrelevance of time, its inability to deprive him of anything:

все, что время как будто и отняло,
а глядишь—засквозило опять,
оттого что закрыто неплотно,
и уже невозможно отнять...

everything that time seems to have taken away,
you look, and it shows through again,
because [the window] wasn't closed fully,
and now it can't be taken away...

For Nabokov, the logic of this reasoning indeed extends to the most important of the "things" that "that time seems to have taken away" and that which is most intimately connected here to his own creative power. This sanguine elegy works not only to restore lost places, but, as for Baratynskij, the poet's lost father as well. In the poem's last lines a ghostly and seemingly lost dog makes an appearance on the same vacant lot where the poet stands. The dog "appears to have gotten lost" («должно быть, потерялся»), reminding us not only of the dog's skull seen by the poet earlier but of the speaker himself ("I'm losing myself" [«себя теряю»]). This is, however, not the case:

> … Но вдали
> уж слышен свист настойчивый и нежный.
> И человек навстречу мне сквозь сумерки
> идет, зовет. Я узнаю
> походку бодрую твою.
> Не изменился ты с тех пор, как умер.

> … But in the distance
> an insistent and tender whistle can already be heard.
> And a man comes toward me through the twilight,
> calling. I recognize
> your energetic gait.
> You haven't changed since you died.

Through a clear association between poetic creativity and "amazed" space, the first and last lines of the poem are linked, and the living bond between the speaker, his native spaces, and his father is restored such that "it can't be taken away": "Inspiration, a rosy sky.… You haven't changed since you died." The black house and empty skull are transformed into an open window and a re-claimed dog. The poet's sense of self has been repaired and re-filled.

Admittedly, *PWH* is conceived on a much vaster scale than Baratynskij's and Nabokov's sanguine elegies, but in like manner it is not only an elegy for Petersburg's and the lyric persona's own losses, but a celebratory lyrical statement of their common recovered greatness. It is one that seeks to understand the role of Axmatova's generation and of the young Axmatova herself (whom she says she rejects until Judgment Day) in what befell their city, its culture, and themselves. In *PWH* there is elegiac commemoration of loss amidst which much that has been lost is re-evoked and reclaimed. It variously emphasizes that the city is devoid of its great poet-hero, that it lost him in a temporal process set on a historical path that began in 1914, and that Aleksandr Blok, the poet-hero of the previous generation, still managed to leave his defining "territorial marks" on the space. And despite this historical process, in the "Epilogue" to *PWH* the poet expresses the wish, "May time stop permanently on the watch you gave me" [2: 130]. In this very different kind of elegy, the destructive movement of time beginning in 1940 is stopped and slowed by memory embodied in art.

Thus *PWH* is constructed on the model of the sanguine elegy, in which the tension between loss and reclamation is great but ultimately resolved in the direction of reclamation and strength, despite the fact that the years 1940–62 were in their way as devastating as the preceding decade and just as terrible for Axmatova personally. In this work and in *Requiem* she finds her mature voice of resistance in art. *PWH* commemorates the resistance of Osip Mandel'štam, the now-"missing" man Axmatova felt should have dominated Petersburg poetry in the twentieth century, and whom she variously described as the greatest poet of her era, as a great martyr, and as a self who resisted being "othered," Sovietized. The glory, guilt, and sins of her generation—the one that brought about the current lack of heroes and the physical loss of Mandel'štam, something in which she admits her unconscious complicity—in the *poèma* are deflected onto the "young Axmatova," her intimate friend and erstwhile apartment mate Ol'ga Sudejkina, and Vsevolod Knjazev. The tragic Petersburg tale of 1913 is alluded to multiple times, and fully recounted twice in the first four parts of the *poèma*, including the intermedia, "Across the Landing," a time-space *ploščadka*. Having set the tale on a threshold of times, at New Year's Eve 1913–14, the poet is taken out of biographical time (1940, as she waits for the New Year 1941); there is an interstitial time-space in which another time, 1914, sneaks in and repeats cyclically thrice.

SPATIAL POETICS: SELF AS SPACE IN *POEM WITHOUT A HERO*

Since *PWH* is probably the most complex example of spatialization of self as Petersburg and represents a convenient culminating point of the tradition we have traced in this book, our detailed discussion of the work will be accompanied by descriptions of the spatial figures Axmatova uses.

In the Introduction (*Vstuplenie*) and chapter 1, Axmatova images herself as the Fontanka House (the former Šeremet'ev Palace), a building in which she lived off and on for 40 years. In the *poèma* there are two major chronotopes. In the first, the mature Axmatova is pinned to the time of writing and subsequent years (27 December 1940 to 1962 at least), a time represented by her room on the third floor of the palace where the Axmatova Museum is now housed, the maple outside the window, and her paltry furniture—taken together, a small part of the entire building. The second chronotope is that of the youthful Axmatova, fixed at New Year's Eve 1913 and the subsequent years of World War I, the revolutions, and her biography in the early postrevolutionary period. This chronotope is represented as the huge ballroom of the Šeremet'ev Palace, with its famous Hall of Mirrors. Axmatova's whole life up to 1940, a crisis point in her biography, is represented by the whole Fontanka House in these sections of the poem.

New Year's Eve of 1941 is represented spatially as a threshold, literally the threshold of the heroine's room: "I stand on the threshold and the New Year's bells still do not chime." A different time, her youth, then insinuates itself by appearing on that threshold. Confronted with this much richer time, her room in the Seremet'ev palace—a small, constricted space representing her present life and that of the true Petersburg in 1940—witnesses the expansion of its walls, while its ceiling rises cupola-like to accommodate the greater, fuller Petersburg life of that past time. It becomes the ballroom of the same palace, a room with much history, upon which the events of the past are projected: the balls and loves of the Seremet'evs; the serf ballerina Paraša, who became the wife of one of the princes; and the visit of Klara and Robert Schumann to the building in 1844. The motto etched on the Fontanka House, "*Deus omnia conservat*," is made into one of the poem's epigraphs. The maple branch outside the window of her room, personified as an extension of her room and her body; the coldness on her windowpane; and the old Seremet'ev grotto and oak are all points in her space that contain and conserve the past, and on this night they yield it forth, in a rush of involuntary memory, in an event that she calls the *poèma*. The narration of the love triangle between Knjazev, Sudejkina, and Blok (a fiction summarizing that generation of Petersburg poets, not a real occurrence in their lives) recurs like a broken record. The guilt of Knjazev for committing suicide before the "real tests" that the twentieth century had in store for the poet came (presumably in the 1930s) is a theme interpreted variously in each repetition. Sudejkina is variously chided for shallowness, her infidelity, and her fickleness, and praised for her blinding beauty in dance. Blok takes Knjazev's Muse (Sudejkina's role here), and indeed, the style of the Petersburg tale is very Blokovian, with allusions to Blok poems of the period (especially "Steps of the Commendatore," in which the Commendatore and the Don Juan figure are both seen by Axmatova as sides of Blok,[20] as well as the Demon and Tamara scene, which represents the great poet incorporating his Muse). Needless to say, Knjazev's love poems to Sudejkina showed no confidence that he would or could make her definitively his Muse or "his own" in any sense.[21] The accursed house of Blok's poem becomes in *PWH* the house where Ol'ga lived and where the young poet killed himself. When Knjazev becomes certain of her infidelity and sees his doom, it is spatially imaged: "Buildings crumbled!" [1: 120].

---

[20] That Axmatova views both Don Juan and the Commendatore as sides of Blok is clear from her ballet libretto for the poem, described in "Primečanija" (*Stixotvorenija*, 519–20).

[21] Vsevolod Knjazev's several poems to Ol'ga Afanas'evna Glebova-Sudejkina express a tragic tone of anticipated loss.

We recall from Axmatova's own scholarship on the Don Juan theme that she sees Puškin as associating the Don Juan role with a poet;[22] of course Blok, for Axmatova the consummate Petersburg poet of his age, brings the Don Juan legend into the twentieth century and modern Petersburg in "Steps of the Commendatore" with images such as automobile lights. This Blokovian space is present in *PWH* in several passages. Later Blok's "stormy landscape" of wind and snow of *The Twelve* and the wartime revolutionary marching-forward of history enter the *poèma*, but not until line 405—that is to say, very late in the work. The past, presented as the narrator's obsession, "that theme," replaces and fills the present and repeats itself. This effects a major retardation of catastrophe in the narrative structure—art (the poem) effectively stops time at the end of 1940 and for a good three-fourths of the work. Even when the young Axmatova chronotope (the past of 1913) begins to move forward internally to 1914, 1915, 1916, and towards the revolution as the ambulatory "real twentieth century," the biographical time of the mature Axmatova chronotope remains stilled at 1940, not reaching 1941. In this sense the work is like a clock, a part of whose inner mechanism is moving, but which is still stopped. This metaphor is entirely justified by the above-cited line, "May time stop permanently on the watch you gave me." Axmatova's life and its productive moving-forward in time need the repair that would come about by reintegrating her past fully into her present, and this is precisely the point of the work. Two spatially-imaged temporal levels clash with or invade each other, as in the famous lines «Как в прошедшем грядущее зреет, / Так в грядущем прошлое тлеет» ("As in the past the future ripens, / So in the future the past decomposes"). This key chiasmus is vitally important for the *poèma*, but at this point only the first part is being fulfilled. The poet is trying to make sense of how such a "present" grew out of her past. She is letting the relationship of the past—hers and Petersburg's—to any future "ripen" in her self/space. Later, when the poem moves on into 1941–42 and the remainder of Axmatova's creative life, the spaces of 1913, 1914, etc. will evaporate away, and Axmatova's self will extend horizontally and vertically to encompass not only all of Petersburg, but vast portions of Russia as a whole.

This horizontal and vertical visit to the past occurs on the second anniversary of Osip Mandel'štam's death, which was almost simultaneous with Axmatova's learning of the certainty and the date of his death. The mature Axmatova chronotope moves forward from December 28th to December 31st, as "Donna Anna" is invaded with memories and dreams in line 65. In Blok's

---

[22] Axmatova, "Kamennyj gost'," 2: 257–74. See also Anna Lisa Crone, "Blok as Don Juan in *Poema bez geroja*," *RLJ* (1981): 145–52; and V. N. Toporov, *Axmatova i Blok: k probleme postroenija poètičeskogo dialoga* (Berkeley: Berkeley Slavic Specialties, 1981).

poem, we recall, "Donna Anna has dreams," and it is clear that Donna Anna will arise at Don Juan's hour of death. One must then assume that starting the poem at the death anniversary of Mandel'štam makes him an important candidate for the "missing poet," the one the meal is set for, and that she has arisen precisely at a moment related to his death in order to have her "unearthly dreams." Since Don Juan is the hero alluded to in the epigraph from Byron, Blok was the Don Juan of Sudejkina in the 1913 chronotope, and Mandel'štam is the missing Don Juan whose death allowed this mature Anna to arise in the 1940 chronotope: «Анна в смертный час твой встанет, / Анна встанет в смертный час» ("Anna will arise at the hour of your death, / Anna will arise at the hour of death").[23]

Anna does arise and has unearthly dreams as in Blok's poem, which is clearly engrained into *PWH* in numerous places, as previous scholarship has shown.[24] Also imprinted on the *poèma* are the poetic texts of Blok at the time of the so-called crumbling of Symbolism (1910 and later) and the rise of Acmeism: "Steps of the Commendatore," as already mentioned; "In the Restaurant," with the black rose sent by Blok to Sudejkina in this *poèma*; and "The Demon," with Blok as the Demon incorporating Tamara.[25] Dramatic works are likewise reflected strongly in the parts of the text that refer to 1913–14. These include Blok's *Balagančik* (*The Puppet Theater*—in Mejerxol'd's staging) and Lermontov's *Maskarad* (*Masquerade*) with its frightening, destructive "stranger in a Venetian mask"—a play which Mejerxol'd was directing at the imperial theaters just as the 1917 revolution was raging in the Petersburg streets.[26] Petersburgers in the imperial theater watching *Masquerade* in 1917 felt that they were seeing the fall of the empire, and that the theatrical production reflected the essence of what was historically unfolding out of doors. Such an identification between art and history reflects the Silver Age doctrine of "theatricalization of life," and *PWH* itself can similarly be interpreted as a work in the vein of "theater of the self."[27] The ominous figure in Lermontov's play who brings doom upon Arbenin, causing his tragic homicidal steps, is repeated in the "superfluous uninvited shade" of *PWH*, and he is also alluded to in the Venetian setting and the Venetian half-mask (*bauta*) which was Mejerxol'd's chosen costume for that figure according to

---

[23] Blok, "Šagi Komandora," 184.
[24] Crone, "Blok as Don Juan," passim.
[25] Blok, "Demon," 179–80.
[26] See Anna Lisa Crone, "'Balaganchik,' 'Maskarad' and *Poèma bez geroja*: Mejerxol'dian Expressions of the Artist's Crisis in Twentieth-Century Russia," *Canadian Slavonic Papers* 36: 3–4 (1994): 317–32.
[27] Ibid.

descriptions of the play from the period. Knjazev, like Arbenin, makes a tragic and wrong choice under pressure from a stranger; both choices lead to destruction of the self.

The presentation of Blok and the poet-speaker in these sections is heavily influenced further by Blok's "Pljaski smerti" ("Danses macabres"), yet Blok's line, «Как страшно мертвецу среди людей» ("How hard it is for a dead man among the living") is inverted. The poet, instead, keeps asking, "How can it be that I alone am alive?" thus implying, "how terrible it is for a living person among the dead." People reflected in mirrors is also a constant image in Blok's poetry of 1910–14. Nadežda Mandel′štam is correct when she relates the bulk of the 1913–14 sections of the *poèma* to Symbolism, and Blokovian Symbolism in the first instance. The Petersburg of that period as a space is that of a Blok who had already proclaimed himself spiritually dead («с мертвым сердцем и мертвым взором» ["with a dead gaze and a dead heart," 2: 114]), who had said, spatializing himself as a damned house, «К чему спускать на окнах шторы? День догорел в душе давно» ("Why lower the shades on the windows? The day burnt out in my soul long ago").[28] Yet he triumphs over the challenger-poet Knjazev in a suicide tale that is told twice and strongly prefigured beforehand.

Significantly, however, the living Axmatova, who is present in the dedications and the first 65 lines of the poem, is not Blok's Axmatova, but Mandel′štam's. His overwhelming presence in the first lines of the poem has been traced.[29] The Axmatova we meet on this evening in 1940, "who arises at Don Juan's death," is Mandel′štam's Axmatova—a classic, sad Rochelle as attested in his poem "V poloborota, o pečal′" ("At a half turn, oh sadness") [1: 128], that is to say, the Acmeist Axmatova as Racine's Phaedra. First she says, as she stands on the threshold of times, «Каменею, стыну, горю… / И, как будто припомнив что-то, / Повернувшись вполоборота» [2: 105] ("I am turning to stone, I grow cold, I burn… / And as if recalling something, I made a half-turn"). Clearly, up to this point in the *poèma* she is speaking as Mandel′štam's Axmatova of 1914. She is not wearing Blok's "Spanish shawl" of his poem of the same year, but rather the shawl of Mandel′štam's poem, the one that has turned to stone («окаменела неоклассическая шаль» ["the neoclassical shawl turned to stone"]). She presents herself as Mandel′štam's "indignant Phaedra," not as Blok's "terrible beauty."[30] She crosses the threshold of times to join the lower level, the earlier period, by descending to

---

[28] Blok, "Vesennij den′ prošel bez dela," 183.

[29] Rory Childers and Anna Lisa Crone, "The Mandel′štam Presence in the Dedications to *Poema bez geroja*," *Russian Literature* 15: 1 (1984): 51–82.

[30] Blok, "Krasota strašna," 199.

it. Here she presents her self-life vertically, "as if from a tower," as an upper story from which she can gaze down.

Earlier in the poem, the threshold had been the temporal crossroads that allowed the expansion of her room-self. Then the landing of 1913–14 Petersburg introduced verticality into the presentation of the same crisis event, and it rejoins the Introduction ("From 1940, I look on everything as from a tower," 2: 103) which precedes the entire "Petersburg Tale." The past which invades her is represented by the enlarged ballroom and the phantasmagoric masquerade of all the leading Petersburg cultural figures of that period—almost all now dead and in costume, as if the coming revolution is a kind of masquerade "feast during the plague."

1940 was a time when the creative intelligentsia, especially Petersburgers (including Mejerxol'd, Mandel'štam, and Blok), had been purged, written out of cultural history, physically killed, or had died from being unable to live and create in a choking atmosphere.[31] Axmatova becomes obsessed with the "how and why" of this cultural devastation. At a time when the intelligentsia, Axmatova included, was being forced to participate in the Majakovskij celebration, the political goal of which was to remake the Futurist poet as a great Soviet hero (Soviet man), Axmatova flew in the face of this requirement, offering only "Majakovskij v 1913-om godu" [1: 241] ("Majakovskij in 1913"). It was as if even persecution would not jolt her out of the general mood of reconsideration of her life and generation, as if the certainty of Mandel'štam's death jolted her into a large-scale review of her life as a whole and that of her city-culture in the "real twentieth century." At the end of chapter 1 there is a brief return to the present, signaled spatially by the shrinking down of the ballroom to her own small room she inhabits in 1940. When the masqueraders run away, fearing "the hero" who has been summoned to center stage, Axmatova is left alone:

Что ж вы все убегаете вместе,
....
Оставляя с глазу на глаз
Меня в сумраке с черной рамой,
Из которой глядит тот самый,
Ставший наигорчайшей драмой
И еще не оплаканный час?   [2: 108–09]

Why do you all run away together
....
Leaving me face to face

---

[31] Blok, "O naznačenii poèta," 492–95.

> In the twilight with that black frame
> Out of which peers that very one
> Who has become the bitterest drama,
> And the hour still unmourned?

This repeated motif of fleeing some confrontation is attested in various contexts in the 1913 chronotope. Important here is that "lovers and love problems," rather than a more serious facing-up-to-history, are emphasized in each case. This is demonstrative because Axmatova will not flee in that way or treat any departure as fearful flight in the mature chronotope. That this running away of the masqueraders returns her to the time-space of 1940 is clear, as the stage directions indicate: "the torches go out, the ceiling lowers, the white hall of mirrors becomes once more the author's bedroom." This dismal future, the position of Axmatova and Petersburg culture in 1940, is the ripened fruit of that mistaken early flight and the suicides.

The italicized section ending in the line "I am ready for death" is interpreted by Carlo Riccio and Vitalij Vilenkin as having central reference to Mandel'štam.[32] These two scholars call Knjazev and Sudejkina the pseudo-hero and pseudo-heroine of the poem, tacitly assuming thereby that Mandel'štam and Axmatova are the real hero and heroine. The fact that on her evening with Isaiah Berlin in 1946 (according to his memoirs, first published in 1980) Axmatova read from the *poèma* and spent a great deal of the evening reminiscing sadly about Osip Mandel'štam makes it more likely that he is the "still-unmourned" figure. Her words to Isaiah Berlin, "verses like these and better than these were written by the greatest poet of our time, whom I loved and who loved me,"[33] strengthen this view, as does the fact that «Я к смерти готов» ("I am ready for death") was what Mandel'štam said to her on Gogol' Boulevard in Moscow, according to her memoir about him. Thus, chapter 1 ends in a brief return to the present of the writing, 1940, but continues as an expansion of the self beyond the room as stairs and a landing—a vertical presentation of a type we discussed here in chapter 5 in the poem "The Cellar of Memory."

"Across the Landing" spatially implies the stairs of the Fontanka House, and descending them leads one to the world outside, to the Petersburg of Axmatova's youth in 1913 and subsequent years. St. Isaac's Square and the Stray Dog cabaret as meeting places are mentioned. Leaving the palace for a

---

[32] Carlo Riccio, *Materiali per un'edizione critica di Poema bez geroja di Anna Achmatova* (Macerata, Italy: Universitá di Macerata, 2000), passim, and Vitalij Vilenkin, *V sto pervom zerkale* (Moscow: Sovetskij pisatel', 1987), 212–16.

[33] Isaiah Berlin, *Personal Impressions*, 189–208; also described in great detail in Gyorgy Dalos, *The Guest from the Future: Anna Achmatova and Isaiah Berlin* (London: John Murray, 1998).

more spatially-extended version of the self is implied in the question and answer "Where are you going from here? / —God knows!" But an answer is promptly given: "out of the Fontanka House ... through transparent gates." The dancing Ol'ga who was at the ball in chapter 1 reappears here on the streets. The Petersburg spaces here refer to a time of no later than 1915, when the Stray Dog closed. In this "Intermedia" it becomes clear for the first time that Knjazev commits suicide.

Chapter 2 reverts briefly to Axmatova's bedroom, but it is clear that the self has expanded to the old "Piter" of 1913, with horses and carriages in the streets, the Marinskij theater, the corridors of the Petrine Collegia, St. Petersburg University, where she attended the Bestužev courses for young noblewomen and where Punin taught, and the Summer Garden. These spaces as represented here smack of Blokovian Petersburg. This time-space continues and increases the extension of the city-space in "Across the Landing," and it includes the neighborhood of the Adamini Mansion, where in this work Knjazev witnesses Ol'ga's return home with Aleksandr Blok. That mansion, where Axmatova and Ol'ga lived together, is the scene of Knjazev's suicide here, and is the "accursed house" into which Blok and Knjazev enter. Their horoscope is already clear. She has no need to mark the house as the place of death or sacrifice, as was done in the massacre of Huguenot Protestants on Bartholomew's Night. It is bound to happen.

What happens in the Petersburg space of 1913–14, here so brilliantly re-evoked and reclaimed in a time when its colorful and praiseful presentation were not allowed by censorship, is a kind of positive evocation of a lively cultural past. It will be recalled that the treatments of Majakovskij required from "on high" in 1940 were directed to de-emphasize or excise totally his Futurist period.[34] It is just that "second death of Majakovskij of which he was not guilty" (Pasternak's famous words)[35] that Axmatova would take no part in. Majakovskij is ensconced in the art and culture of the period that Axmatova resurrects; she places him in the time-space that obsesses her and her art, 1913. That period of brilliance and artistic achievement was on a course of doom and destruction; it had even been cursed by Peter's first wife, Evdokija, at its inception, and had a predetermined "horoscope." Nevertheless, "all deliria are resurrected and the chimes do not ring" [2: 105]. In other words, time stops, and that age of brilliance reclaims its enormous space. As indicated heretofore, the poet compares that Petersburg to "Venice of the Doges"— Venice at the height of the Republic, while the Petersburg of 1940, called in

---

[34] See Laura Urbaszewski, "Creating the First Classic Poet of Socialist Realism: Mayakovsky as a Subject of "Celebration Culture" (Ph.D. diss., University of Chicago, 2002), 125–37.

[35] Pasternak, 694.

Requiem "only an appendage of its prisons," she compares here to the provincial city of Luga. How has such a debunking, such a peripheralization of the center come about? How has she, once the darling of the Russian reader, come to such obscurity and come to be so reduced in circumstances? How is it that Petersburg and Mandel'štam have been consigned to oblivion? When, in his words, "will we gather again in [a fully restored] Petersburg?"

PWH brings all this world back in chapters 2 and 4, and each time it is shown to be on a dangerous historical course. The fourth and last chapter gives the fullest graphic representation of Knjazev's feelings and his suicide, as well as of Axmatova's judgment. The threshold of Ol'ga's colorful apartment, where Knjazev's bloodied body is sprawled, is not the heroic death site this generation, whom she construed as being born into "the Petersburg of Dostoevskij," was born for:

> Да простит тебя бог!
> (Сколько гибелей шло к поэту,
> Глупый мальчик: он выбрал эту,—
> Первых он не стерпел обид,
> Он не знал, на каком пороге
> Он стоит и какой дороги
> Перед ним откроется вид…) [2: 120]

> May God forgive you!
> (How many deaths awaited the poet,
> Stupid boy, he chose this one.
> He could not bear the first offenses of fate,
> He did not know on what threshold
> He stood and what [historical] path lay before him…)

This judgment of Knjazev's sin comes only after the retelling of his suicide. In chapter 3, lines 400–05, the other spatial presentation of the Blokovian theme of history—as a space walked over, trampled, or traversed in some manner—finally strikes, as historical vengeance.[36] Here future time is marching threateningly down the embankment towards its waiting victims, victims of the revolution in the first instance. Destructive time, somewhat suppressed as a theme until this point in the work, is finally joined.

Chapter 3 images an Axmatova-as-cityspace that is the same as that in chapter 2, but after the clock strikes, time begins marching forward to 1914, 1915, and towards the revolutions of 1917. The city-space, however, is not moving with marching time, but is set adrift and floating away from its past. It

---

[36] This is the theme of Blok's *The Twelve* and *Retribution*, discussed in detail in chap. 3 above.

is in retreat from the future and loosed from its past, lost in time, not unlike Gumilev's "The Tram That Lost Its Way." As the whole city retreats from the advancing shade of a Dostoevskian figure, within this space the small figure of Axmatova also runs away—to Carskoe Selo and the protective presence of her beloved Nikolaj Nedobrovo. The city is floating away from its graves, retreating into its own fog (an image familiar from Dostoevskij's and Belyj's Petersburg), and carriages are falling off its bridges (an image from Gogol' and later from Mandel'štam's *Egyptian Stamp*, and also one reminiscent of the falling of the old-world representatives in the first poem of Blok's *The Twelve*). The moon over the Silver Age is freezing, perhaps in mortal terror at the coming future—hardly a sanguine image. Axmatova gives the reason:

> Оттого, что по всем дорогам,
> Оттого, что ко всем порогам
> Приближалась медленно тень,
> Ветер рвал со стены афиши,
> Дым плясал вприсядку на крыше
> И кладбищем пахла сирень.
> И, царицей Авдотьей заклятый,
> Достоевский и бесноватый
> Город в свой уходил туман   [2: 117]

> Because along all roads,
> Because toward all thresholds
> A shade was coming slowly,
> The wind ripped posters from the walls,
> Smoke danced the hopak on roofs,
> And the lilac smelled of the graveyard.
> And cursed by Tsarina Avdot'ja [Evdokija],
> Dostoevskij-like [Dostoevskij] and bedeviled,
> The city was withdrawing into its own fog.

Here the "shade" coming down the canal embankments like the approaching twentieth century is Dostoevskij; this is a vision of the writer and the city before the staged executions of both ("As the drum rolled before the execution"). In the Silver Age the great poets and Petersburgers could hear the noise of the coming terrible age in Dostoevskij's novels and in Blok's poems:

> И всегда в духоте морозной,
> Предвоенной, блудной и грозной,
> Непонятный таился гул…
> Но тогда он был слышен глуше,

> Он почти не тревожил души,
> И в сугробах невских тонул.   [2: 117]

> And always in the freezing, pre-war,
> Corrupted and ominous stuffiness,
> There lived a certain rumbling of the future,
> But at that time it was only faintly audible,
> It caused almost no alarm to the soul,
> And was drowned out by the Neva's snowdrifts.

This characterization recalls Blok's prophetic poem to Gippius:

> Рожденные в года глухие
> Пути не помнят своего
> Мы—дети страшных лет России—
> Забыть не в силах ничего.[37]

> Those born in deafened years
> Have lost their path.
> We are the children of Russia's terrible years,
> We can forget nothing.

The last line has the sense of "we are paralyzed by our terrible memories." This is followed by an allusion to Blok's "mirror poems," where he does not want to recognize the self he sees (1910–13). It may also contain a reference to Vjačeslav Ivanov's poem addressed to a self lost in the depths of many mirrors, "Where am I? Where am I? / I hungered to find myself ... I am at the bottom of my mirrors."[38] Yet the "real twentieth century" is marching forth. The section ends with the flight of the youthful Axmatova.

Knjazev's sin of retreat through suicide over love comes on the next page. But this and the treatment of Ol'ga in chapter 2 ("Forgive me, darling, I am punishing not you, but myself") refer equally to the lack of seriousness of Axmatova's own youth and youthful verse. At that time her sadness was motivated by personal, not national reasons, and her city-self spatialized a lovelorn private self and private tragedy oblivious to larger issues, like Knjazev and Ol'ga, whom she castigates. Lidija Čukovskaja's *Axmatova Journals* for the early part of 1940, when projected re-publication of some of Axmatova's earlier poetry was forcing her to face it, documents Axmatova's growing dislike of her youthful self. In *PWH* she rejects that youthful self, refusing to meet her at

---

[37] Blok, "Roždennye v goda gluxie," 232.
[38] Vjačeslav Ivanov, "Fio, ergo non sum," *Polnoe sobranie sočinenij*, ed. D. Ivanov and O. Deschertes (Brussels: Foyer Chrétien Oriental, 1971), 1: 740–41.

the masquerade, and in Čukovskaja's diary we read the poet's own words: "You know, at last I've understood why I can't stand my early poems.... Now I see them perfectly for what they are: unkind in their attitude towards the protagonist, unwise, naive and shameless."[39]

Chapter 4 ends the youthful Axmatova chronotope, presenting the self extended in the Champs de Mars and the Adamini House, with the bells of the nearby Church of the Spilled Blood, built on the spot of Tsar Aleksandr II's assassination. It includes both outside and indoor spaces. From outside, Knjazev sees Ol'ga's perfidious return with Blok, and, realizing he has been betrayed, enters the house, rings her bell, and shoots himself, sprawling across Ol'ga's threshold. The clear parallel with the past ghosts ringing Axmatova's doorbell and appearing on her threshold in chapter 1 serves to conflate Axmatova and Ol'ga and to relate her to Ol'ga's guilt, about which she wrote in the poem "The Voice of Memory" (here used as an epigraph). Despite Ol'ga's and her own complicity in the premature death and disappearance of the younger poet, his own responsibility for his "stupid" act is not diminished. His act was wrong, and this threshold was not the proper site for the poet's death in the twentieth century. Its consequences for the Poet's fate are shown to be great for all poets and for Petersburg culture.

After the fourth and last chapter the *poèma* is presented as lying complete, with crossed hands, the way the dead lie in their coffins, and the way Donna Anna in Blok's poem lies in the "accursed house." The vision is one of a silent *poèma*, where the dead are no longer lively, having been returned to the great silent epoch whence they had come. This is followed by an intermezzo, set once again in the present of 1940, and Axmatova makes a humorous imagined commentary on what she has written from the point of view of a contemporary Soviet editor. The scene is set in Leningrad before the siege (5 January 1941), which means that only five days of biographical time have elapsed in the mature Axmatova chronotope in the work. The proof that the visitors had been there is seen in the smoke remaining from the torches, the flowers on the floor of her room, and dropped religious souvenirs. The incursion from the past is treated as a celebration and a funeral procession at once, but either way the bestrewn objects on the floor attest to its reality. As she justifies what she has written in the "Intermezzo" added to the *poèma* proper, the chrysanthemum flowers on the floor come to represent the theme and the co-presence of the past in the space of her room (her present life):

Но была для меня та тема,
Как раздавленная хризантема

---

[39] Lidija Čukovskaja reports this conversation with Axmatova in her *Zapiski*, 1: 83–86.

На полу, когда гроб несут.
Между «помнить» и «вспомнить», други,
Расстояние—как от Луги
До страны атласных баут.   [2: 98]

But that theme was for me
Like a crushed chrysanthemum
On the floor as a coffin is carried out.
Between not forgetting and strong remembrance, friends,
There is a distance as great as that from Luga
To the land of the satin half-masks.

She had said of "that theme" earlier that it could burst in and fill her life at any time: «А вдруг как вырвется тема, / Кулаком в окно застучит» ("But at any time the theme can suddenly burst in, and beat with its fist on the window"). The window is the window of Axmatova's room, her mind or consciousness. This "distance" is her mental and emotional inner life—once Venice, now Luga, a cultural wasteland.

The Epilogue has two epigraphs referring to an emptiness all but accomplished, a city almost dead. One is Annenskij's ("deserts of silent squares, where they executed people before dawn") and the other is Tsarina Evdokija's motto, which we have referred to repeatedly in these pages. Though the central conceit of part 2, "Tails," is that the Soviet editor and reader will understand nothing of *PWH*, in this section the poet makes some telling statements about what they won't comprehend, that is, about what *PWH* means in her creative life. In fact, Susan Amert, in her study of the later Axmatova, draws her entire discussion of its overall meaning from a detailed reading of "Tails."[40] Of signal importance, and a repeated theme in this section, is her ironic dislike for her early poetry that her readers "love so much," echoed in her complaint to Viktor Žirmunskij: "Why have they walled me up in the 1910s?"

It is in "Tails," too, that she first speaks of having found the right path, the right road for a Petersburg poet in the "real twentieth century":

И другой мне дорогу нету—
Чудом я набрела на эту
И расстаться с ней не спешу.

---

[40] Susan Amert, *In a Shattered Mirror: The Later Poetry of Anna Akhmatova* (Palo Alto, CA: Stanford University Press, 1992).

And there is no other road for me,
I found this one by a miracle
And I'm in no hurry to part with it [depart from it].

Finding the right road, the complex understanding which the young Axmatova lacked when she fled the future in 1914, is accomplished only in 1940, after she had let the past back into her life and entered it again. In doing this she was a harsh judge of her younger self:

С той, которой была когда-то
До долины Иософаата
Снова встретиться не хочу   [2: 106]

With the person I once was
I do not want to meet again
'Til the Valley of Jehosaphat [the Last Judgment)

As wrong as Knjazev in 1913, now, after the reintegration of her past into the present described in *PWH*, she finally finds the right path of resistance for her city and herself. She now knows "on what threshold she stands and what road lies before her."

Axmatova's most ambitious *poèma*, her art, has forced time to stand still; in it she has reconsidered her own and cultural Petersburg's past greatness and errors of judgment as well as misfortunes brought on both by fate. In a love triangle emblematic of the relations of poetic generations and the fate of the Great Poet in the twentieth century, she speaks of herself as having learned from that symbolic past the right path or future for herself. Only by extending or expanding herself (her space) and Petersburg's self-space can Petersburg begin to move down the necessary path for its salvation and Russia's. If in the *poèma* she expanded from the room to the ballroom and then to the streets outside, in the "Epilogue" she grows into the vastest expanses of the Russian territory. This expansion repeats the figure we studied in chapter 9, the one who dominates and amazes spaces. Petersburg, which was always only a small space at the edge of Russia, executes exactly the same figure as the poet. All of Petersburg goes with her, and yet remains at the same time. Though emptied, bombed out, and appearing dead, Petersburg is its fullest self as it moves into Siberia, Tashkent, and the future.

Lopuxina's original curse, "May this place be emptied out," was uttered, according to different versions of the legend, as she was actually being banished or as a prayer in the nunnery in Suzdal', where she lived out her days. At this point in Petersburg's history, her curse seemed to have been fulfilled. The scene of a destroyed and emptied siege-period Leningrad seems to have reached the limit of emptying: "The city is in ruins. From the harbor to Smol'ny everything is empty as on the palm of one's hand." Axmatova herself is represented as her empty third-floor room, with its bombed-out window and black emptiness inside. Yet her voice is heard from 7,000 kilometers away, speaking to her city. We learn that she has been evacuated by plane to Tashkent. This epilogue to her city, an emptied shell at the highest point of its suffering and dispersion, is one in which Axmatova attempts to spread herself and Petersburg over all of suffering Russia, including Siberia, Tashkent, and Moscow.

Not only does her voice speak across the whole Siberian territory to evacuated Petersburg, she must walk the same funereal path that Petersburg, her own son, and Mandel'štam had traversed. Not having died, she leaves the city as her empty grave; *her departure is the opposite of Evdoxija Lopuxina's*. The one who said about Petersburg in *Requiem*, "I was not under foreign skies, I was not under the protection of foreign wings, I was there with my people, there where they unfortunately were [Petersburg/Leningrad, 1: 361]" here unwillingly leaves the actual space—her own body, as it were.

The spoken text depicts her house not yet left (a future-as-past), the time before she had to leave, anticipating an evacuation for salvation. Emphasizing that this is a positive form of emptying, she stresses that her separation from her city-self is only apparent, not real, that she is embedded in its walls, in its canals, in the Hermitage halls, in Volkovo Pole (the older cemetery). All those places are her body and her home. This image of leaving to come back more fully oneself takes on religious overtones. She meets Christ on her path, as St. Peter did when he left Rome as it was being burned by Nero; "Quo vadis?" is clearly a quotation, only askable by Christ of Saint Peter. This makes explicit the parallel between Axmatova's departure from a Petersburg persecuted by Stalin and the German Army, and St. Peter and Christians being persecuted in Nero's burning Rome. As Peter will return and rebuild his Church from its ashes, so Axmatova will return to rebuild her city culture.

There are further implications in this departure that make it the obverse of the departure of Evdokija. Called "half-nun, half-whore" by Ždanov, who used references to her as a nun by Čukovskij and Vinogradov's description of her as a person-oxymoron, Axmatova presents herself as undoing the curse of total devastation Lopuxina laid upon the city. She executes the opposite figure in space. Evdokija had laid her curse on a Petrine capital and project in its infancy, against a city that she hated and opposed She was banished to a nunnery never to return. Axmatova sets her poem at what appears to be the end of the city's life, at what appears to be the height of its tragedy of devastation, the greatest fulfillment to date of Lopuxina's curse as seen in the German siege, bombing, burning, death, illness, and evacuation. At the moment of greatest tragedy, Axmatova in *PWH* stops the movement of time and confronts her former self and her generation of Petersburg artistic intelligentsia. If she judges them, she judges herself, admitting the sins of insufficient foresight and moral preparation to withstand a tragic fate: "Fate is standing on the threshold."

This stoppage of time in art allows the author to return herself and Petersburg to a temporal crossroads, 1913–14, a threshold of times. Once more there, when she and her generation were still free to take different actions, she confronts head-on the inadequate decisions, judgments, and actions committed by her personally and by all concerned. And it is there that she "by a miracle stumbled onto this—a better path." In so doing she regains a certain control in art over her personal past, a resolve not to repeat the mistakes of that past. And Petersburg receives back its cultural heritage. This control revivifies both; it is a gesture of fortification. There is an admission in the line "It is not you, but myself that I punish" [2: 112] that to have been able to withstand the assaults of the "real twentieth century" she would have to have been stronger and taken responsibility for the foibles and great creative strengths of her generation in 1913. She had been an ineffective and flawed Cassandra.

Focusing on the loss of Mandel′štam that she and her generation did not prevent, she re-fortifies herself for the task he asked her to perform in "Save My Speech" (1931): to keep alive, at least in art, "our" Petersburg. Early in *PWH* she emphasizes that she is stronger than the generation of her youth ("I am more iron than they," 2: 106) and insists that she is no longer the early pre-revolutionary Axmatova, not the young girl from the seaside. Nor is she the young woman who, seeing the "real twentieth century" approach down the embankment, fled to the safety of the Cameron Gallery and to Nedobrovo, expecting him to explain life. Nor is she a woman who would mourn over lost love. As that flight occurred, Petersburg itself was moving away from its graveyards and disappearing into its own fog—self-annihilating retreats, as it turned out.

The change in her voice becomes very clear in the way she treats the romantic break with her beloved Vsevolod Garšin, which occurred when she returned from Tashkent in 1944. This is no longer the personal, private Axmatova who mourned lost love, as Knjazev does in *PWH*, and as the young Axmatova had done in so many early verses. Here is the voice of suprapersonal, all-national, not personal tragedy. The epilogue initially bore the double dedication "*Gorodu i drugu*" ("To my city and my friend") as two non-melded entities. When her relationship with Garšin ended, she left the epilogue intact, and the friend and the city become one. Everything said with reference to Garšin now refers to the whole city-self: "It seemed that you chased after me [also a reference to the Bronze Horseman], / You who stayed behind to perish there." Initially this passage referred to Garšin; here it is not deleted but redirected. Axmatova leaves it with the ambiguous meaning of "the chasing Bronze Horseman," the city's embodied spirit, its *genius loci*, turning herself into a species of latter-day Evgenij.

As Petersburg's embodied spirit, she finally must leave. Hers is a departure to return and save. The path of departure, the funereal road to Siberia, is the ritual one traversed by Bojarinja Morozova and by the Maiden Fevronija going back to Kitež (a monastic pre-Petrine image embodied in the 1940 poem «Путем всея земли,» "The Way of All Earth"). It is also the way of Petersburgers such as the Decembrists' wives and of her son Lev Gumilev—a path forged by Petersburgian and Russian, particularly Old Believer, martyrdom and heroism. Taking this path across Siberia, she represents a composite image of all-Russian suffering, and the movement into evacuation is followed by its reverse: "Russia was marching to save Moscow."

While this latter line undoubtedly refers to the Soviet army defending the capital, it also speaks to the healing of the antagonism between Moscow and Petersburg asserted in *The Bronze Horseman*, the first of the genre of "Petersburg tales" of which *PWH* is slated as the last:

И перед младшей столицей	And before the younger capital
Померкла старая Москва,	Old Moscow faded,
Как перед новой царицей	As a royal widow fades
Порфироносная вдова.	Before a new queen.

Significant here is the image of Petersburg and Moscow as women, as queens.

In *PWH* Moscow is saved by Petersburg's/Russia's resistance. Axmatova, by her salvific evacuation and return, intends her spatial self to encompass vast expanses of Russia and to erase or neutralize the old antagonism between Petersburg and Moscow, healing the old wounds and lifting Evdokija's curse. After stopping time to recuperate her full Petersburg self, as she does in *PWH*, she can go forward in time for future daring feats. No longer the pining voice of love's sadness, she lets the whole of Petersburg stand in for her estranged, beloved Garšin. She becomes what she is in *Requiem*, the wife and mother of a suffering Petersburg/Russia, the truly indignant Phaedra she should in fact have been in 1914 and throughout her whole life. "The Way of All Earth," written in the same period as *PWH*, projects her as such a figure in pre-Petrine Orthodox dress, and *Requiem* places her in the position of the wives of the *strel'cy*, a position very sympathetic to Evdokija, no doubt. She leaves her city for Siberia, the East, bearing all these Russian and Petersburg misfortunes and strengthened by her pan-Russian suffering. It is as this Petersburg self that she can be the feminine Petersburg which she describes, exactly as she had described herself so often in her early poetry. The image of herself as young (*molodaja*) and with clenched teeth (*sžimaja rot*) is a clear repetition of the frequent self-description "*sžatyj rot*" of her early, more personal poetry: «Долгу верная, молодая, сжимая рот, ломая руки, / Шла Россия спасать Москву» ("True to her duty, young and clenching her teeth, / Russia was marching to save Moscow"). This is the Petersburger Axmatova, the "young capital" turned into a tower of non-violent resistance, but still retaining recognizable marks of her/its youthful self. *Poèma bez geroja* is the work in which she shows how she reintegrated herself and her Petersburg for this sacred national task.

11   Conclusion: The Russification of Petersburg

A Note on Theory

This book is conceived as an example of practical criticism in the area of spatial poetics, and as such leans of necessity on the available theories of this approach. We have elaborated a detailed typology of Petersburgian spatial metaphors or synecdoches for modern Russian man in general and the modern creative self as projected in Russian letters in particular, with emphasis on the period from 1890 to the 1970s. Thus far we have left aside the vexed question of whether synecdochic usages (the part for the whole) are figures of contiguity (metonymic) or figures of substitution/replacement (metaphoric). Whether there is grafting or attachment of a part of one's biography onto a space (which would appear metonymic), or simple standing-in of a building or room for a person (which would appear metaphoric), the strong identification by the poet with the spaces of Petersburg makes the *metaphorical* (the element of substitution) dominant in virtually all our examples. This is so even when the specific use of spaces seems metonymic, and even when a simile occurs, as, e.g., when Sof'ja Petrovna in Belyj's *Petersburg* feels that "her life [was] like a road that was crumbling as she traversed it." Moreover, the compound and complex multi-partite modelings of self as space we have seen—from the simple and static "empty house" to the dynamic presentation of a self developing, changing, and being destroyed over time (in part 2) and the models of stalwart, at times almost fanciful resistance to time's deleterious effects by remembering and writing Petersburg and the self back together again (part 3)—provide a wealth of examples in praxis for those who wish to carry out chronotopic analysis, examples that flesh out what is only abstract and potential in the schematic typologies of Gaston Bachelard and Mixail Baxtin.

    Bachelard, whose magisterial mid-20th-century study *La poétique de l'espace* focuses on spatial imagery in European, mainly French, lyric poetry and is perhaps little used by Slavicists, treats all the same issues as the Russian theoretical works in spatial poetics, including those by Baxtin, Epštejn, and Toporov. Bachelard's strong emphasis on spatial structures in lyric poetry have made his work an excellent complement to Baxtin's work on the chronotope, with its focus on prose and especially on the development of the European novel.

On the face of it, the phenomenological theory of a scholar interested in Jungian archetypes (images from dreams and reverie that surface in unique forms in the poetic imagination) as used together with Baxtin's very historical treatment of time-space unities embodied in a series of sequential (that is, mainly prose genres) may appear to be a combination of incompatible approaches. The theoretical introduction of Bachelard's study, after all, is blatantly ahistorical": If [one] wants to study the problems posed by the poetic imagination ... the cultural past doesn't count."[1] Bachelard does relate new poetic images (spatial ones) to archetypes "lying dormant" in the depths of the human unconscious. According to him, a new poetic image is not *caused* by these dormant archetypes, but is independent of all causality: "The poet does not confer the past of his image upon me, and yet his image immediately takes root in me."[2] What stance could seem more rooted in an amnesiac present, where history is forgotten and cannot be viewed as causal or even antecedent? What theoretical basis could seem to fly more in the face of intertextual studies, which ours is to a large degree, in which every new image or utterance is in dialogue with an antecedent presentation of self and space?

Very few; nevertheless, the value of Bachelard for practical analyses such as ours lies in his direct readings of categories such as the house, immensity, nooks and crannies, and ins and outs—i.e., spatial structures. He found these structures in French poetry and prose. Be their provenance archetypal or the heritage of cultural and literary tradition, they recur in the same or very close variations in the Petersburg poetry and prose we treat. In Bachelard's readings, closer, more detailed treatments of actual texts are, despite his qualifications, spaces saturated with time in the same way our Petersburg spaces are. Bachelard, after all, says that he wants to examine "the quite simple images of *felicitous spaces*," "the space we love."[3] He begins with images of intimacy and the problem of the poetics of the house. In his topoanalysis (his term for spatial poetics), "the house image would appear to have become the topography of our intimate being."[4]

This approach resonated with our thinking, as it seemed to be a theoretical formulation of our notion of the Petersburg writer's identification with space. Petersburg spaces and Petersburg itself, as a big house, would seem to be the "topography" of all our writers' "intimate beings." On the practical level, there is very little that Bachelard describes in his first chapter that does not find concrete and specific instantiation in our Petersburg text. And his

---

[1] Bachelard, *The Poetics of Space*, xv.
[2] Ibid., xvii.
[3] Ibid., xxxv.
[4] Ibid., xxxvi.

house, like our city spaces, is not devoid of a past or multiple pasts; not only archetypes lurk in it, but the personal past of the individual poet. Bachelard comes very close to our formulation of identification when he speaks of "the passionate liaison of our bodies, which do not forget, with an unforgettable house."[5] Bachelard's idea that a great part of one's personal past is one's dreams and reveries in or of a certain space—one's poetic imagination as it inhabited the place—also contributes to our approach. We, too, assume not necessarily realistic or even correct evocations of Petersburg space, but mental, imaginary spaces.

Bachelard's conception of the house, of the earliest, even pre-sentient, childhood as the non-geographical locus of *real being* was very useful to us in part 3, where we discussed an ahistorical (history-denying) idyll within a non-idyllic space. In general his de-emphasis on time/history is not borne out in his treatments of spatial forms because of human memory and recollection. He wants to abstract himself from cultural history, and does to a large extent, but cannot and does not eliminate time from the mind and imagination of the human individual/poet.

Baxtin, by contrast, is firmly fixed within the diachronic dialogue of cultural history and the sequential treatment of time-space unities in the novel. Indeed, he subtitles his chronotopic study "Notes toward a Historical Poetics." The historical poetic framework Baxtin provides was necessary for our study. After all, we envision the chronotopes of Petersburg space as self as deriving from the time-space relations in two types of Romantic elegy: one in which history has destructive effects on the self, and one which exists out of historical time, where history cannot destroy the self. Our demonstration that such time-saturated, time-torn, or time-free chronotopes came from types of the Romantic elegy and migrated to a conflicted Petersburg urban space is clearly a project of historical poetics. It sees dialogue, intertextual interaction, and gains and losses (as Tynjanov defines it) over the period of eighty years it covers, and Baxtin's theoretical framework fortified by Bachelard's examples was adapted by us as an organizing tool. Additionally, many of Baxtin's observations on nineteenth-century prose, on the idyll and elegy, as well as on migratory personages and motifs had direct explanatory value for what we had observed in poetic texts.

Having based ourselves in texts before theory, we do not emerge in our study as orthodox Bachelardian phenomenologists, nor do we provide an orthodox Baxtinian poetics. Yet our debt to Bachelard and his individual close readings and to Baxtin in the tracing of elegy and elegiac elements over time is very considerable.

---

[5] Ibid., 15.

❦ ❧

As mentioned, we have divided our models of space as self into two master chronotopes corresponding to opposite types of psychologization of space in the Romantic elegy. The first chronotope presupposes the dominance of time/history and the preponderance of biographical time in its incessant flow, as in the elegy of loss or absence (for example, the loss of youth, of the past, of love, of self). In the poetic practice of our Petersburg writers, as we have seen, this chronotope is expressed in a history-riven, destroyed, emptied, and compromised space-as-self, whose variations form the subject of part 2 above (chapters 4–6).

The second chronotope involves a space that is dominant over time, and represents a resistance of history and of passing biographical time, whether in the subjunctive (out of real time) or in the mode of the wish-fulfillment elegy. In it we observe the protective encapsulation of time-spaces abstracted from the temporal flow in artistic products that may leave or halt linear time. We saw these attempts to recover or recompense lost Petersburg or lost selves in part 3 (chapters 7–9).

Part 4, where the most complex of mixed models were treated, first within the *oeuvres* of the same author (chapter 10) and finally, in the same work (Axmatova's *Poem without a Hero*, chapter 11), demonstrates the essential interdependence and perennial dialogue between the two chronotopes and the two types of elegiac speakers/selves: the integral, whole self who effectively resists time's ravages, and the self divided by time. Whether the elegiac speaker expresses the fact of loss or the possibility of self-maintenance, self-healing, and self-recovery, either stance or response to man's existential condition exists in dialogue with its opposite.

Baxtin was aware of the eighteenth-century focus on time, its passage, and its poetic expression in elegies as an undermining of the idyllic chronotope. He speaks of the "elegy of the meditative type with a strong idyllic component" in referring to both Gray's rural graveyard elegies and Žukovskij's translations and derivations in this genre (for example, in his poem "Evening").[6] Since Baxtin's entire discussion of the idyllic chronotope is focused on its destruction in the novel genre, where "the real organic time of idyllic life is opposed to the frivolous, fragmented time of city life or even to historical time,"[7] he overlooks the fact that the elegy, not only the novel, becomes urban in Russian Modernism. When he speaks of modern and Modernist novels being affected by the presence of personages "of idyllic

---

[6] Baxtin, *The Dialogic Imagination*, 228.
[7] Ibid.

provenance" who wander to the city, he seems to forget that the elegy itself comes to Petersburg, and that Petersburg cityscapes and its built environment undergo the idyllic identification and subjectivization that was reserved for rural spaces in an earlier age. Of course, the dynamic modern metropolis is hardly suitable for an idyllic unity of place where an entire life can thrive or easily be preserved—yet it remains a *desideratum* for the city-born lyric ego, who wishes to be stably "at home" in his spaces just as much as his rural ancestors did in theirs. The Petersburger experiences his wholeness and unity of self-space as a desire, a dream, a wish fulfillment no less, and perhaps even more than, his pastoral counterpart.

The destruction of the wholeness of idyllic life proclaimed by Baxtin as a fact of Russian literature in the second half of the nineteenth century is not a process passively accepted as inevitable, either in the Russian novel (Petersburg prose) or in poetry (elegiac or otherwise), and it seems to be more forcefully resisted as the twentieth century wears on. There is an equal and opposite tendency to proclaim the same wholeness, the same groundedness and integrity of place that we find in the idyllic genre. The idyll is undoubtedly challenged, but by no means given up for lost, even though its spaces be urban, constricted, and conflicted. Baxtin divines an identification of self/hero with space in the Balzacian novel in a manner very close to our concept here:

> Balzac's ability to "*see*" time in space was extraordinary. We need mention only Balzac's marvelous depiction of houses as materialized history and his description of streets, cities, rural landscapes at the level where they are being worked upon by time and history.[8]

However, Baxtin observes these chronotopic phenomena in the novel and overlooks them in urban and/or Petersburg poetry. And what he terms "materialized history" we see rather as humanized, subjectivized space. Treated from the point of view of the creative artist/poet, this is not materialized time, but de-materialized matter or space, even spiritualized space.

Thus our typology of models of space as self involve complexities and strategies that Baxtin and Bachelard, with their more abstracted typologies, do not describe or foresee. Our poetry-derived models have a dynamism Baxtin's typology reserves for the so-called chronotope of the threshold, the chronotope of crisis and breaks in life.[9] The Baxtinian concepts of the destruction of the idyllic chronotope and the more dynamic chronotope of the threshold, as we have shown on these pages, are not by any means limited to the modern novel, but are vitally present as well in modern poetry. What is more, these

---

[8] Ibid., 247.
[9] Ibid., 248.

two models give rise to their opposite—a chronotope of resistance to crises-thresholds and to the destruction of the idyll. This chronotope we call the *reintegrative or regenerative chronotope*, one that attempts, not totally to escape, but to undermine the destructive processes Baxtin describes. To repair, to reconnect, or rebridge the breaks, to neutralize the threshold sense, and to reconstruct the idyll: this is the chronotope of the reintegrated, reconnected, and regenerated self, and it implies a reunified, serene, once-more-idyllic space-time.

The movement toward this reintegrative chronotope emerges in the preceding chapters as the undoing and repair of temporal destruction to the self and to Petersburg. It is finally and fully exemplified in *Poem without a Hero*. No solipsistic denial of the existence of linear historical/biographical time, as some of the treatments in part 3 can be viewed, it accepts and admits the breaks at the same time that it undertakes their relentless repair and mending. This reconstructive treatment of Petersburg space-time results in the domestication and integration of Petersburg and the Petersburg creative individual to the rest of Orthodox Russia.

THE RUSSIFICATION OF PETERSBURG

> Ведь просто быть не может двух Россий
> Как быть и двух Ахматовых не может[10]

> There simply can't be two Russias
> Like there can't be two Axmatovas

Since the Petrine Reformation, the national consciousness of Russians was, as Belyj eloquently put it, "torn in twain," and few were the Russian writers oblivious to or unaffected by this rift. Aleksandr Benois' extreme strategy, to consider Petersburg alone to be his motherland, is the defensive posture of a highly Europeanized Russian that only bears witness to the depth of the split in the national psyche, and hardly resolves the dilemma.

This disunity has been conceptualized variously by succeeding generations: as the Slavophile-Westernizer controversy in the first half of the nineteenth century; as the oft-decried antagonism of the Folk and the intelligentsia by Apollon Grigor'ev (the *počvenniki*) and the Populists; and as the tension between vertical culture (Petersburg, imperial, Westernized) and horizontal culture (folk-based, Orthodox). These intellectual constructs express the two paths of the unique Russian national character and destiny—two straight lines that, it appears, will never meet.

---

[10] Evtušenko, 246–48.

Though our Petersburg writers and poets, in their fierce self-identification with the spaces and places of the Northern capital, may at times appear to have made the same partisan choice as Benois, in fact, over some sixty years, this identification led to a non-partisan and reconciliatory Russification of Petersburg. At the time of the heated Slavophile-Westernizer debates, Petersburg was still viewed as un-Russian or non-sufficiently Russian and non-national (*narodnyj*). Gogol′, a Slavophile and Orthodox thinker and an imperial citizen of Ukrainian ethnicity, made no bones about the spiritual defects of Petersburg and Petersburgers. In his humorous "Petersburg Notes for 1836," Gogol′ contrasts Moscow and St. Petersburg in his inimitable style. His folksy narrator is clearly pro-Muscovite in his sympathies, envisioning Moscow as a maternal figure:

> … what a wilderness between mama and her dear boy! What views, what sort of nature is this! Air shot through with fog; burnt tree stumps and pines on pale gray-green earth….[11]

From its natural surroundings to its architectural image, to its spiritual nature and populace, for Gogol′ Petersburg is the antithesis of Moscow. It is a non-Russian, a foreign city, *ausländisch* and outlandish at the same time. In the speaker's view, it is even questionable whether it is located in Russia at all:

> … where was the Russian capital hurled to—the ends of the earth!… Imagine, running seven hundred versts away from mama! Oh, what a fleet-footed one he is![12]

Gogol′ emphasizes Petersburg's foreignness repeatedly:

> She [Moscow] is still a Russian beard, but he [Petersburg] is already a fastidious German. How you have extended and spread yourself, old Moscow![13]

Here Gogol′ echoes, in reference to Moscow, the opening lines of a well-known folk song about the Volga, mother of Russian rivers.[14] Petersburg, on the other hand, is styled as a male fop with no ear for music but rather an eye for the latest styles:

> … how that dandy Petersburg pulls himself up straight as a rod…. And there are so many mirrors before him. Here the Neva, there the

---

[11] Gogol′, "Peterburgskie zapiski 1836-ogo goda," 7: 481.

[12] Ibid.

[13] Ibid.

[14] The song is "Oh, thou, Volga, how broadly thou hast unleashed thy waters."

Finnish Gulf ... and he strolls on the boundary, preening before Europe, which he sees but does not hear.[15]

The collective personification of Petersburg is that of a foreign dandy, eating French bread, clad in foreign finery, and completely lacking in hospitality, generosity, and the inner qualities usually associated with the Russian character and "soul." Consumed with the superficial, secular aspects of life, this unsympathetic figure struts about, aping Europe in its external forms, but without "hearing" in any meaningful way the deeper "words" Europe has pronounced to the world.

More than one hundred years separate the negative, Slavophile characterization of the capital that Gogol' penned in Petersburg and the many versions of Axmatova's *PWH*. During that time, processes gradually took place that changed the image of Petersburg in the national consciousness greatly. Anciferov, as we noted in chapter 2, writes of a darkening of the image of Petersburg in Russian culture occurring in the wake of the Decembrist uprising in the late 1820s and continuing beyond the reign of Nicholas I. Beginning in the 1890s he observes a renewal of interest and pride in Petersburg and a positive attitude towards it in the *fin-de-siècle* generation of Petersburg writers, poets, art historians, architects, and artists. It is this positive attitude toward Petersburg that developed into the intimate identification with the capital and its spaces that we have treated in such detail here. In the period of the decline of the empire of which Petersburg was the head, a period of apocalyptic forebodings that seemed to be confirmed daily by the events we have spoken of, the threatened city becomes emotionally and creatively associated as never before with the frail and threatened human subject.

The historical and social processes Anciferov speaks of and traces in Russian literature can be said to occur within the framework of overarching chiasmata which explain St. Petersburg's trajectory. They are present in the literary mythology and in the tradition of folk sayings and dicta associated with the Northern capital. The first, pessimistic, chiasmus expresses the negative *kenosis* of the city ("Petersburg will be emptied out"):

Nothing (*Bronze Horseman*) — Creation of Petersburg
Emptying of Petersburg (*PWH*) — Return to Nothing

The second chiasmus, seen and upheld in *PWH*, is far more positive, and represents the resistance of Petersburg to the first chiasmus, to its tragic debunkment and humiliation:

---

[15] Ibid.

The first two terms represent the destructive role of history, and the second two, the victory over history affirmed in powerful Petersburg art. We saw this more positive treatment in chapters 7, 8, and 9, as well as in *PWH*, where the poet immortalizes all the beauty and complexity that went with her down the road of "emptying-out." This is a beauty of self and of Petersburg culture that existed and was removed, but nevertheless has its great moment in a resurrection, a return accomplished through the true *kenosis* of a sacrificial complicity in the emptying-out process. The immortalization of these movements, artists, and their works, the fixing in art of great and inspiring moments, includes both chronicling and lamentations, but does so in a way that new life is instilled into what is remembered. The 19th-century Underground Man's Petersburg is "the most abstract and premeditated city in the world," («самый отвлеченный и самый умышленный город на всем земном шаре»), where "the only purpose of any intelligent person is chatter, that is, the deliberate pouring-out of emptiness into emptiness" («единственное назначение всякого умного человека есть болтовня, то есть умышленное пересыпанье из пустого в порожнее»). The words of the twentieth-century Petersburg self, in its dialogic identification with city space, are no longer mere chatter; and the creative return to Petersburg through art is not a futile and absurd exchange of emptiness. Pouring out one's inner Petersburg onto the outer space and accessing the secret content of memory-laden architecture and streets refutes the belief that the city would continue unleashing its inner void upon its spaces and selves, that it would "stand empty."

The debunkment of Petersburg in terms of power and political prestige is represented by the following chiasmus:

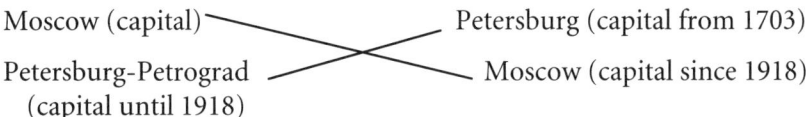

The changes in the name of the Northern capital itself have reflected the peripatetics of the betrayal of Peter's project.

The Latinate German universalist sound of the original name reflected Russia's purpose of joining Europe and the Western world in all spheres of endeavor. The Slavic "Petrograd" already signaled a falling-away from the internationalist aspirations of Peter and the unity of great European interests. With "Leningrad," the name of the founder was supplanted with that of a Bolševik who openly disliked the city, and who "beheaded it" in favor of Moscow. The Leningrad period was the one when "Piter" was most humiliated, debunked, punished, altered, and provincialized. It contributed like no other to the city's tragedy and martyrdom. Petersburg in this period perhaps suffered more than any other Russian city, except in the area of architecture, where Moscow suffered more. The systematic dismantling of Russian culture and achievements affected all Russian cities, but Petersburg symbolized what was being attacked, and frankly possessed much more to be destroyed. The exceptional harshness of the Ežovščina and the Purges in Leningrad, as well as the 900-day Blockade by the Germans in World War II only intensified Petersburg's tragedy and its punishment, making Axmatova seem to cry out like Cassandra, "Oh, my city, dragged to uttermost death!" All these tragedies finally made "Piter" more Russian than any other place in Russia; Petersburg, in all that it stood for, including the aspirations of Peter and its great pre-revolutionary culture, achieved the status of a Russian martyr once and for all. "Mentally this city is still the capital," wrote Petersburg patriot Brodskij in 1978,[16] meaning that it was the capital of Russian letters and culture. This is the minority view sustained and put forth in Axmatova's *PWH*. By collapsing and compressing a glorious cultural history into a small space and constricted time and by making it simultaneous through the unity of time in a world of art, Axmatova destroys the sense that it is dead. Art has a powerful reanimating and resuscitating effect. After works like *PWH*, Petersburg is utterly changed.

ଓ ଞ

In Berlin, near Checkpoint Charlie and within sight of the former Berlin Wall, architect Peter Eisenmann erected a residential building whose external character was so unfinished that the observer felt it was still in progress. Most importantly, the casual observer would be hard put to say whether it was in a state of construction or demolition. So many Germans felt this building to be symbolic of the divided city and divided Germany after the war that the Bundesrepublik issued a postage stamp with Eisenmann's building on its face. Now that the wall has been removed, the building near the wall stands as a constant reminder of the invisible divisions and differences still preventing Germany's national reconciliation.

Given the Stalinist tendencies in architecture in the Soviet period and the fortunate preservation of much of Petersburg's historical center, Petersburg

---

[16] Brodskij, "A Guide to a Renamed City," 93.

has no such symbolic structure in stone, brick, or wood. Brodskij often hailed the signs of dilapidation and duress on the façades of old buildings, their valiant struggle with the winds of a bad climate and an unfriendly history. Yet it is not a building, but Axmatova's *PWH* that is the Russian equivalent of Eisenmann's building. Often criticized for the same unfinished quality as is the German edifice, the *poèma* in its creative tensions is in a constant state of building, demolishing, displacing, replacing, killing, resuscitating, dying, and resurrecting Petersburg and the creative self identified with it. Elegiac fragmentation and loss of self alternates with an idyllic mode in which a coherent self is enabled to stop time, to commune with its kindred poets, or to burst forth, projecting the whole, inner self and Petersburg onto the amazed exterior space. Such a dynamic tension between creation and destruction, appropriately enough, had always been a feature of the classic "unified Petersburg text" as described by Toporov and others, but, it is only in the works we have described herein, and especially in *PWH*, that this uneasy balance becomes a mark of Petersburg's Russification. The *voluntary*, kenotic emptying of the self on the part of Petersburg poets—their projection of creative power and compassion onto city spaces—has replaced Petersburg's perverse negative *kenosis*. Axmatova's truly polyphonic work resonates with her city's great cultural past, provoking a dialogue with Petersburg's dead in each new reader. The inner symphony thus evoked is unending; it heals those readers of their cultural amnesia and ignorance, confronting them directly with the sights and sounds of their own past.

Nothing was more destructive of Silver Age Petersburg than official Soviet ideology. The twentieth-century Petersburg tradition treated here opposes it, and within that tradition *PWH* does so more effectively and cogently than any other, answering the call of Osip Mandel'štam, "We will gather again in St. Petersburg." Anna Axmatova lived long enough to see some of the fruits of her cultural project for her city-self. Her biography did achieve a certain level of reintegration before her death, some restitution of her erstwhile fame and validation of her cultural role and Mandel'štam's. But she would have had to live another "quarter of a century" to see her city's original name restored in 1991.

The tragic chiasmata of the Petersburg tradition which inform the works dealt with here are biblical in type. There is another, unspoken one which friends of Russian culture hope will be fulfilled. This is the paradox of life and death from the Orthodox Easter liturgy:

| Христос воскрес из мертвых, | Christ is risen from the dead, |
| Смертью смерть поправ | Having trampled death with death |

In *PWH* this process is begun, but far from completed, and it is threatened with sabotage at every turn. In the "Epilogue," Axmatova writes, "And my city stands enshrouded." The creative and intellectual community must gather again and actively pray for art and culture, for the "blessed, senseless word" (the Puškinian spirit) that should have been buried in Petersburg, to aid the future rising of the night sun.

Axmatova began the process of raising the buried sun. Communing with and reuniting living and dead artists of Petersburg in 1940, she carried out this almost Fedorovian project—the resurrecting of the ancestors by the sons—until her death in 1966.[17] This process has proceeded by fits and starts ever since, accelerated somewhat in the Gorbačev era, and it continues today. True to the nature of the Petersburg text, since *PWH* this resurrection has been accompanied, not so much by destruction as by deconstruction, especially in Andrej Bitov's monumental novel *Puškin House* (1968). This deconstruction, however, is one that cannot occur without the implicit assumption of the identification between self and Petersburg city-text. For better or for worse, Petersburg selves continue to be "held together" by their city.[18]

In recent years, city projects and events such as the Petersburg carnivals (including parades and vignettes of Petersburgers in "architectural" costume), the City Day festivities in May, the long-awaited Puškin anniversary celebrations in 1999, and the Interior Theater (a museum/theater dedicated to the preservation of Petersburg spaces and architecture) have proven the ongoing success of the kenotic endeavor by Axmatova and the other writers we have discussed. So much has Petersburg been Russified, in fact, that in this its 300th anniversary year, it is enterprising, bustling Moscow that is associated with foreign influence, economic dominance, a bureaucratic flavor, and a non-Russian superficiality.[19] The modes of elegiac identification we have traced here have effected in Petersburg's mental architecture and imaginative spaces a newly Russian sense of *self*.

---

[17] Nikolaj Fedorov's philosophical project of resurrecting the deceased former generations is expounded in his major work *Filosofija obščego dela* (Moscow: Izdatel'stvo "Mysl'," 1982).)

[18] "My God! My God, what a city! What a cold brilliant joke! Unbearable! But I belong to it ... all of me" (Andrei Bitov, *Puškin House*, trans. Susan Brownsberger [Ann Arbor: Ardis, 1990], 336).

[19] See Krivulin chap. 4. Sidney Monas also noted as early as 1983 that "the spiritual capital and the seat of power have changed places" ("St. Petersburg and Moscow as Cultural Symbols," *Art and Culture in Nineteenth-Century Russia*, ed. Theofanis George Stavrou [Bloomington, IN: Indiana University Press, 1983], 38).

INDEX OF NAMES

Aeschylus, 128
Aksenov, Vasilij, 174
Alcaeus, 106
Alexander I: see Romanov, Aleksandr Pavlovič
Alexander II: see Romanov, Aleksandr Nikolaevič
Alexander III: see Romanov, Aleksandr Aleksandrovič
Aleksin, Aleksandr (chess grand master), 307
Amert, Susan, 353
Anciferov, Nikolaj, 5, 8, 11, 304
Annenskij, Innokentij, 3, 4, 9, 29, 109, 127, 147–53, 167, 253, 259ff., 281n, 353
Auden, W.H., 165
Axmatova, Anna, 3, 12, 29, 36, 54–55, 63, 64, 85–89, 98, 115–18, 119–20, 126–27, 132–37, 151–58, 161, 162, 164, 172, 197, 204, 216–18, 219, 221, 236–38, 240, 245, 252, 259–66, 296n, 321, 323–58, 362, 369–70
Bachelard, Gaston, 1, 101, 114–15, 151, 210, 306n, 359–64
Balzac, Honoré de, 363
Baxtin, Mixail, 10, 36, 55, 204–05, 246, 253, 308n, 359–64
Baratynskij, Evgenij, 42, 108, 111–12, 334–37
Batjuškov, Konstantin, 39, 41–44, 109, 204

Baudelaire, Charles, 23
Beaver, Aaron, 323n
Beljak, Nikolaj, 1n
Belyj, Andrej (Bugaev, Boris), 4, 9, 28–29, 45ff., 52, 53, 63–75, 102, 103ff., 140, 166, 225, 229, 269–70, 279, 80, 283–87, 298, 324, 330
Benois, Aleksandr, 8, 46, 52, 53, 245, 274
Berdjaev, Nikolaj, 46, 323
Bergson, Henri, 305, 332
Berlin, Sir Isaiah, 155n, 347
Bernštejn, Sergej , 205n
Bethea, David, 239n, 272n, 273
Bitov, Andrej, 3, 370
Blok, Aleksandr, 3, 9, 14–17, 27, 29, 37, 45, 58–59, 63, 65, 69–70, 73–74, 75–85, 88, 101, 162, 207, 215, 223, 239, 298, 320, 324, 343ff., 345–46, 350–52
Bogdanovič, Ippolit, 14
Borges, Jorge Luis, 271
Bornštejn, Mark, 1n
Bosio, Angiolina, 9n, 39, 140
Boym, Svetlana, 5, 274n, 276n
Brodskij, Iosif, 3, 5, 17, 20–21, 29, 37, 46, 98, 54–55, 145, 158–90, 204, 206, 217, 218–38, 240, 246, 271, 275–76, 279, 285, 297–98, 300, 304, 324, 325
Brojde, Inna, 277n
Brjusov, Valerij, 62
Čaadaev, Petr, 2, 16, 70, 136

Cain, 6
Chagall, Marc, 273
Childers, Rory W., 345n
Churchill, Sir Winston, 73
Cioran, E. M., 2
Clark, Katerina, 5, 52–54
Crone, Anna Lisa, 18n, 48n, 54n, 102n, 145n, 253n, 344n, 345n
Čukovskaja, Lidija , 151, 156ff., 351–52
Dalos, Gyorgy, 347n
Dante, 53
Day, Jennifer Jean, 44n, 145n, 252n, 323n
Del'vig, Anton, 253, 54, 258
Denis'eva, Elena, 110, 331
Deržavin, Gavrila , 14, 107, 135, 253–54, 258
Dobužinskij, Mstislav, 52
Dolgopolov, Leonid, 5, 11n, 283
Dostoevskij, Fedor, 2, 3, 23, 36, 47, 48, 52, 65, 82–83, 85, 100, 114, 128–29, 175, 226, 280, 304, 308, 315, 317, 330, 350
Dreyfus, Alfred 307
Driver, Sam, 85–86
Eisenmann, Peter, 368–69
Eliade, Mircea, 244
Eliot, T. S., 188, 325
Emerson, Caryl, 36n
Èpštejn, Mixail, 37–41, 44–45, 324ff.
Escher, Max, 218
Ètkind, Efim, 34n
Evtušenko, Evgenij, 55, 133–34, 216, 364n
Falconet, Etienne, 16, 67
Fedorov, Nikolaj, 370
Filippov, Boris, 18n, 54n
Forš, Ol'ga, 101
Freidin, Grigorij, 284n, 288
Frizman, Leonid, 39

Garšin, Vsevolod, 356
Gippius, Vladimir, 302
Gippius, Zinaida, 220, 351
Glück, Christoph 126, 286, 324n
Gogol', Nikolaj, 3, 4, 62, 79–80, 125–26, 128, 141, 201, 221, 304, 365
Goncourt, Jules, 91–92
Gordin, Jakov, 244
Gor'kij, Maksim, 273
Grabar', Igor', 8
Gray, Thomas, 362
Grinberg, Marat, 308n
Gul', Roman, 259, 303
Gumilev, Nikolaj, 3, 46, 69, 166–67, 259, 274, 280, 295, 350
Hackel, Sergej, 73–4, 83, 84n
Harris, Jane G., 138n
Heine, Heinrich, 108
Herzen, Aleksandr, 274
Homer, 123
Isaiah (Biblical prophet), 188
Isenburg, Charles, 95n
Ivanov, Georgij, 3, 29, 93–94, 124–26, 161, 274, 298
Ivanov, Vjačeslav, 123, 170, 286n, 295, 351
Ivask, George, 63n
Jaanus, Marie, 179n, 266n
Jakobson, Roman, 210n
Jesus Christ, 7, 71, 83–85, 355
Jung, Carl G., 114–15
Kandinskij, Vasilij, 273
Kant, Immanuel, 324
Kireevskij, Ivan, 53
Kjuxel'beker, Vil'gelm, 254–56, 259
Ključevskij, Vasilij, 19n
Kol'cov, Nikolaj, 26, 62
Könönen, Maija, 248n
Koteliansky, S., 73
Krive, Sarah, 325n
Krivulin,Viktor, 3, 5, 370n

Kušner, Aleksandr, 3
Lachmann, Renate, 5, 211, 253
Leblond, Jean-Baptiste Alexandre, 50, 212
Leibnitz, Gottfried von, 324
Leiter, Sharon, 239–40, 262–63
Leont′ev, Konstantin, 63n, 302, 307
Lermontov, Mixail, 10, 41, 344
Link, Constance, 138n
Livšic, Benedikt, 30–36
Lo Gatto, Ettore, 5, 11n
Lukomskij, Georgij, 53, 309n
Lopuxina, Evdokija, Tsarina, 7, 100, 348, 354ff.
Lotman, Jurij, 5
Maderno, Carlo, 32
Majakovskij, Vladimir, 24–30, 28–30, 346, 348
Mallarmé, Stéphane 260
Mandel′štam, Nadežda, 334
Mandel′štam, Osip, 3, 9, 17–22, 26, 30ff., 46, 47, 54, 58, 59, 64, 94, 98, 106–07, 112–14, 119–27, 131, 135, 137, 138, 139, 140, 153, 155, 157, 161–62, 170–71, 174–78, 184, 205, 207, 213–18, 219, 225, 242–45, 250–51, 253, 266–67, 269–70, 279, 286, 287–88, 290–92, 295, 296, 298, 300–22, 324, 341, 343, 345, 346, 347, 349, 369–70
Markov, Vladimir, 34n
Merežkovskij, Dmitrij, 3, 14–16, 185, 220, 292
Mejerxol′d, Vsevolod, 344ff.
Mickiewicz, Adam, 83
Mixailovskij, Nikolaj, 310n
Mikhoels, Solomon, 308
Monas, Sidney, 370n
Montaigne, Michel, 92, 159n
Murav′ev, Mixail, 14n

Nabokov, Vladimir (father of novelist), 337–40
Nabokov, Vladimir, 3, 29, 94ff., 98, 140, 179, 190–202, 234, 245, 273–74, 300–22, 324
Nedobrovo, Nikolaj, 256ff.
Nekrasov, Nikolaj, 9, 39, 298
Nerval, Gérard de, 179, 198
Nicholas I: see Romanov, Nikolaj Pavlovič
Nietzsche, Friedrich, 47, 114, 334
Nikitenko, A.V., 118–19
Orpheus, 126, 287, 289
Ostroumova-Lebedeva, Anna, 52
Otradin, M.V., 27n
Ovid, 298
Pasternak, Boris, 57–59, 271–77, 287–88, 292–96, 301
Paul: see Romanov, Pavel Petrovič
Perlina, Nina, 205n
Peter I (Peter the Great): see Romanov, Petr Alekseevič
Pike, Burton, 6
Poe, Edgar Allan, 92
Polonskij, Jakov, 117
Poulet, Georges, 91ff., 149, 151n, 159n, 323n
Proust, Marcel 2, 95–97
Punin, Nikolaj, 329
Puškin, Aleksandr, 4, 8, 13–14, 16–17, 23, 28, 38–39, 41, 62, 101, 118ff., 146–47, 166, 179, 184, 197n, 207, 243, 253–58, 262–66, 281, 286, 289–96
Racine, Jean, 345
Reeder, Roberta, 253, 261
Rejn, Evgenij, 3
Riccio, Carlo, 347
Romanov, Aleksandr Aleksandrovič (Aleksandr III), 11

Romanov, Aleksandr Nikolaevič (Aleksandr II), 11
Romanov, Aleksandr Pavlovič (Aleksandr I), 118
Romanov, Nikolaj Pavlovič (Nikolaj I), 11, 98, 118
Romanov, Pavel Petrovič, 67
Romanov, Petr Alekseevič (Petr I, Peter the Great), 6–7, 12, 19–20, 21, 50, 106–09, 188, 209, 281, 290–92, 295, 368
Romanovskij, V., 27
Rosslyn, Wendy, 261n
Rozanov, Vasilij, 47, 73, 92, 100, 124, 215, 218, 281, 298
Rudnickij, Il'ja, 53
Sagatov, Bogdan, 86n
Saint Aleksandr Nevskij, 209
Saints Boris and Gleb, 7, 209
Saint Peter, 7
Samigullin, Fuat, 1n
Schumann, Robert 342
Šklovskij, Viktor, 243
Solov'ev, Vladimir, 45, 69–70, 283
Sosnora, Viktor, 3
Struve, Gleb, 18n, 54n
Tarkovskij, Andrej, 271
Tibullus, 192n
Timenčik, Roman, 228

Tjutčev, Fedor, 44, 47, 108–14, 146–49, 151, 162, 164, 166–69, 176, 206–07, 242, 253, 331, 335
Tolstoj, Lev, 124, 126
Toporov, Vladimir, 4–5, 40, 232, 343n, 359
Tred'jakovskij, Vasilij, 14
Tynjanov, Jurij, 361
Urbaszewski, Laura, 348n
Vaginov, Konstantin, 3, 101, 245
Verhaeren, Emil, 23
Vilenkin, Vitalij, 156, 347
Virgil, 204
Volkov, Solomon, 5
Voronixin, Andrej, 33ff., 54
Vroon, Ronald, 34n
Wells, H.G., 274
Wolfe, Thomas, 146
Woolf, Virginia, 279
Xlebnikov, Velimir, 30
Xodasevič, Vladislav, 4, 29, 98–99, 119, 175, 215, 239n, 240–42, 244, 246–47, 250, 271–73, 281, 283–88, 298
Yeats, William B., 6, 50n, 165
Zamjatin, Evgenij, 129–31, 171
Ždanov, Andrej, 57, 354
Žirmunskij, Viktor, 353
Zoščenko, Mixail, 57
Žukovskij, Vasilij, 40, 253, 259

INDEX OF SUBJECTS

Ahistorical treatment of space: see space, ahistorical treatment of
Antigone complex (Axmatova), 120ff.
Alternative time in wish-fulfillment elegy: see elegy, wish-fulfillment
Carnival, 1ff.
Carskoe Selo
  as idyllic alternative to Petersburg, 252ff.
  as non-Petersburg, 252ff.
Elegiac cast (in other genres), 37ff., 208, 298ff.
Elegiac-despondent space, 39–41
Elegiac identification with space, 359–70
Elegiac returns, dehistoricized (in Nabokov), 190–203
Elegiac space, Epštejn's categorization of, 37–44
Elegy
  sanguine, 337ff.
  and space, 4–10, 37, 44, 324ff.
  urban, 10, 39–44
  wish-fulfillment, 43ff., 249ff., 211, 249ff., 270ff., 297
Exile in situ, 255
Exile myth, explosion of 249ff.
Historical time: see time, apocalyptic acceleration of
Historical space: see space, historical treatment of
Human condition (existentialism), indirect depiction of, 2–3, 6

Idyll, 4–10, 39–44, 94, 204, 247, 249ff., 251–52, 261, 266–67
  anti-idyll, 204, 240ff.
  evil urbanism in, 6
  and historical time, 205
  urban, 94, 204, 247
  writer's, 250
Idyllic chronotope (Baxtin), 204, 240ff., 253ff.
Imaginary returns, 254ff.
Kenosis
  negative, 7ff., 39, 58, 63–64, 70, 86, 103, 189, 297
  Orthodox / kenotic sainthood, 7ff., 189, 254 ff., 364–70
Negative tangibility, 258ff.
Ostranenie (making strange), 22ff.
Petersburg
  death of, 99
  disappearance of, chapter 3, 82ff.
  emptying out of, 10, chapter 3; see also Lopuxina, Evdokija in Index of Names
  foreignness of, 3–4, 7, 11, 365–66
  as illness, 303–22; see also Petersburg, death of
  mentality, 2ff.
  negative mythology of, 5–7
  positive mythology of, 5ff.
  re-ensavagement of (*odičanie*), 62–63, 240
  Russification of, 8ff., 364–70
  second (made of words), 29n, 206, 236

Sovietization of, 210
"Petersburg period" in Moscow writers, 4
Petersburgs, personal, 59ff
Petersburg writer (our definition), 3–4
"Russian" beauty, 8, 20
Self
  bursting out of, 279ff.
  demolishing-rebuilding model of, 326ff.
  integral (*cel'najaličnost'*), 221; see also Ivan Kireevskij
  loss of, as disintegration, 124ff., 125–27, 127–41
  loss of, in elegiac-tinged works, 7, 76, 92–96, 108ff., 129–31
  loss of, as emptying: see kenosis
  loss of, as loss of objects in space, 139–41
  reintegration of through writing, 221, 359–70
  reintegration of (recovery of self's wholeness), 333ff.
  spreading upon widening spaces, 279ff.; see also bursting out of
  sustaining of via support of solid space, 93, 95–97, 206, 211–21, 218–38
  withdrawal of into small enclosure, 279ff.
  See also: water-bound spatializations of self
Selves, co-presence (in same space) of selves from different periods of life, 132–41
Space
  ability to change, 270ff.
  ahistorical or anti-historical treatment of, 208ff. (part 3), 41ff., 45, 297
  dialogue with, 1, 29, 89
  domination over, 208–37
  empty or emptied, 101
  functions of in Petersburg texts,
    decorative (virtuoso), 12, 22–24
    encomiastic, 12–14
    historiosophic, 12, 14–17, 61–62, 65ff.
    metapoetic, 17–22
    neutral, 12
  historical treatment of, 9–10, part 2, 41ff., 45, 56–59, 298ff., 244, 297
  intimate identification with, 1, 6, 11ff., 22–35, 28ff., 34, 37, 39ff., 42ff., 214, 359–70
  mixed treatments of (within one work), 297–370; see also self, demolishing-rebuilding model of
  psychologization of in Belyj, 45–52, 64–75; see also the novel *Petersburg* in Works Cited Index
  as self, spatialization of self, 1–10, 27ff., 206, 297ff., 324, 341–64
  stormy, and Petersburg, 39–40, 44, 98
  and superimposition of inner visions, 270–77
Space-time, horizontal movement through, 61ff., 225
Spatialized selfhood: see self-as-Petersburg space
Text and reality (stones and words), chapters 3 and 4, 206, 210–11, 236, 297–98
Time, apocalyptic acceleration of, 64, 69ff., 12ff., 88, 141
Time-stoppage of eternal moment, 356
Water-bound spatializations of self in Petersburg, 106–14

Index of Titles (by Author)

Aeschylus,
  Agamemnon, 128
Aksenov, Vasilij,
  The Burn (*Ožog*), 174
Amert, Susan,
  In a Shattered Mirror: The Later Poetry of Anna Akhmatova, 353n
Anciferov, Nikolaj
  The Soul of Petersburg (*Duša Peterburga*), 5n, 8n, 11
  Unfathomable City (*Nepostižimyj gorod*), 5n
Annenskij, Innokentij,
  "Before Sunset" ("Pered zakatom"), 147–49
  "Nox vitae," 149–50
  "Petersburg" ("Peterburg"), 9, 109
  "To L. I. Mikulič" ("L.I . Mikulič"), 265–66
Apollon, 52
Auden, W. H.,
  "On the Death of W. B. Yeats," 165, 316n
Axmatova, Anna,
  "And there my marble double" ("A tam moj mramornyj dvojnik"), 265
  "Carskoe Selo Statue" ("Carskosel′skaja statuja"), 265
  "The Cellar of Memory" ("Podval pamjati"), 115–17, 126–27
  "First Northern Elegy" ("Pervaja severnaja èlegija"), 132–33, 296n, 298
  "Fourth Northern Elegy" ("Četvertaja severnaja èlegija"), 333
  "He is right, again the streetlight and the druggist′s shop" ("On prav, opjat′ fonar′, apteka"), 54
  "The Nevsky Shore" ("Nevskoe vzmor′e"), 119
  "Night" ("Nox"), 265
  "Majakovskij in 1913" ("Majakovskij v 1913-om godu"), 346
  "My heart beats evenly, measuredly" ("Serdce b′etsja rovno, merno"), 263
  "Oh, how pungent the breathing of the carnations" ("O, kak prjano dyxanie gvozdiki"), 324
  "Oh, woe is me! They have burned you down" ("O, gore mne! Oni tebja sožgli!"), 217–18
  "Petrograd in 1919" ("Petrograd v 1919-om godu"), 236
  Poem without a Hero (*Poèma bez geroja*), 85–89, 117–18, 127, 135, 197, 288–89, 298, 323–58, 362, 366–70
  Pro domo mea, 157
  "Quietly flows the quiet Don" ("Tixo l′etsja tixij Don"), 102
  Requiem (*Rekviem*), 102, 131, 260, 331n, 357
  "Second Northern Elegy" ("Vtoraja severnaja èlegija"), 111–12, 327–33

"The Sentence" ("Prigovor") 102
"The Stone Guest" ("Kamennyj gost'"), 343n
"Summer Garden" ("Letnij sad"), 261–62, 264–65
"There my shade remains and is melancholy" ("Tam ten' moja ostalas' i toskuet"), 157
"Third Northern Elegy" ("Tret'ja severnaja èlegija"), 113–14, 131, 136–38, 327, 333, 335
"The unburied ones, I buried them all" ("Nepogrebennyx vsex ja xoronila ix"), 120
"The Voice of Memory" ("Golos pamjati"), 352
"The way of all earth" ("Putem vseja zemli"), 357
"We forgot forever" ("I my zabyli navsegda"), 236–37
"White Nights" ("Belye noči"), 265

Bachelard, Gaston
  La poétique de l'espace, 1, 114n, 306n, 359-364
Baratynskij, Evgenij,
  "Devastation" ("Zapustenie"), 334–37
  "Elegy" ("Èlegija"), 108
  "To My Italian Tutor" ("K djad'ke-ital'jancu"), 336–37
Batjuškov, Konstantin,
  "To Daškov" ("K Daškovu"), 39, 40, 41, 42
  "Separation" ("Razluka"), 40
  "Tauris" ("Tavrida"), 43–44, 109, 204
Baxtin, Mikhail,
  The Dialogic Imagination, 362n
  "Forms of Time and Chronotope in the Novel," 55n, 246n
  Problems of Dostoevsky's Poetics, 36n, 308n
Beaver Aaron,
  Time in the Poetry of Joseph Brodsky, 323n
Belyj, Andrej (Boris Bugaev),
  Petersburg (Peterburg), 9, 28, 45–49, 64–75, 102–06, 140–41, 166, 211–13, 223, 281–83, 285, 287
  "Symbolism as a Worldview" ("Simvolizm kak mirovozzrenie"), 65
  The Symphonies, 65
Berdjaev, Nikolaj,
  Slavery and Freedom, 323n
Berlin, Isaiah,
  Personal Impressions, 155, 347n
Bethea, David,
  Khosadevich: His Life and Art, 239n, 272n, 273
Blok, Aleksandr,
  "Beauty is frightening" ("Krasota strašna"), 345n
  "Danses macabres," 319ff., 345
  "Dear brother—evening has begun" ("Milyj brat—zavečerelo"), 239n
  "The Demon" ("Demon"), 344n
  "Hanging over the universal city" ("Visja nad gorodom vsemirnym"), 27
  "On the Calling of the Poet" ("O naznačenii poèta"), 346n
  On Kulikovo Field (*Na pole kulikovom*), 69
  "On the Islands" ("Na ostrovax"), 223
  "Peter" ("Petr"), 17
  The Puppet Theater (*Balagančik*), 88, 344

"To Puškin House" ("Puškinskomu domu"), 101
Retribution (*Vozmezdie*), 61, 70, 75–82, 86, 109
"The Snow Maiden" ("Snežnaja deva"), 15–16
"The spring day passed in idleness" ("Vesennij den' prošel bez dela"), 345n
"Steps of the Commendatore" ("Šagi Komandora"), 243ff., 342ff., 344n
"Those born in deafened years" ("Roždennye v goda gluxie"), 74, 351
"To Jurij Verxovskij" ("Jurij Verxovskomu"), 38
The Twelve (*Dvenadcat'*), 9, 63, 73–74, 80ff., 172, 186
"The Unknown Lady" ("Neznakomka"), 280
Vladimir Solov'ev and the Present Day (*Vladimir Solov'ev i naši dni*), 69–70

Boym, Svetlana,
 The Future of Nostalgia, 5n, 243n, 274n, 276n
Brintlinger, Angela,
 Writing a Usable Past, 334
Brodskij, Iosif,
 "The Child of Civilization," 32n, 184–85
 "Conversations with Cvetaeva" ("Razgovory s Cvetaevoj"), 163n
 "Description of morning" ("Opisanie utra"), 235–36
 "Embroidering on Plato" ("Razvivaja Platona"), 247–52
 "Everything is strange for a house's new tenant" ("Vse čuzdo v dome novomu žil'cu"), 158–59
 "Flight from Byzantium," 246
 "Footnote to a Poem," 179n
 "Fourth (Winter) Eclogue" ("Četvertaja èkloga [zimnjaja]"), 229n
 "From the Outskirts to the Center" ("Ot okrainy k centru"), 50, 165–75, 177–78
 "The Guest" ("Gost'"), 224
 "A Guide to a Renamed City," 21n, 27, 29n, 45n, 98, 179n, 206 (226)n, 224n, 225n, 228n, 233n, 289n, 291n, 297n, 368n
 "A Halt in the Desert" ("Ostanovka v pustyne"), 165, 180–89
 "I embraced those shoulders" ("Ja obnjal èti pleči"), 159–61
 "I was born and grew up…" ("Ja rodilsja i vyros…"), 228–29
 "In a Room and a Half," 219
 "July Intermezzo" ("Ijul'skoe intermecco"), 161
 "The Keening Muse," 54n, 57, 204n, 206n
 "Less Than One," 145, 219–220, 227n, 230n, 231n, 292n
 "A Letter to Horace," 203, 224n
 "Midday in a Room" ("Polden' v komnate"), 145
 On Grief and Reason, 203n
 "On Via Giulia" ("Na via Džulija"), 230
 "Petersburg Novel" ("Peterburgskij roman"), 222–23
 "The Poet and Prose," 21n
 "You go back to your hometown" ("Vorotiš'sja na rodinu"), 161–64
 Watermark, 271n
Brojde, Inna,
 From Xodasevič to Nabokov (*Ot Xodaseviča do Nabokova*), 277n

Čaadaev, Petr,
  Philosophical Letters, 2, 16n
Cioran, E. M.
  The Temptation to Exist, 2n
Clark, Katerina,
  Petersburg: Crucible of Cultural Revolution, 5n, 51n, 53n
Crone, Anna Lisa,
  "Axmatova and the Passing of the Swans: Horatian Tradition and Carskoe Selo," 253n
  "Balagančik, Maskarad and Poèma bez geroja," 344n
  "Blok as Don Juan in Poèma bez geroja," 343n, 344n
  "The Mandel'stam Presence in the Dedications to Poèma bez geroja," 345n
  "Nietzschean, All Too Nietzschean," 48n
  "Wood and Trees" Mandel'štam's Use of Dante's *Inferno* in 'Preserve My Speech,'" 54n
Čukovskaja, Lidija,
  Notes on Anna Axmatova, 1952–62 (Zapiski ob Anne Axmatovoj, 1952–62), 151n
  The Deserted House, 103ff.
Cvetaeva, Marina,
  "Missing Home" ("Toska po rodine"), 163–64
Day, Jennifer,
  Memory as Space: The Created Petersburg of Vladimir Nabokov and Iosif Brodskij, 44n, 252n, 323n
Del'vig, Anton,
  "To Puškin" ("Puškinu"), 258
Deržavin, Gavrila,
  "The river of times in its flow" ("Reka vremen v svoem tečen'i"), 107, 135–36

"The Swan" ("Lebed'"), 258
Dolgopolov, L.,
  Andrej Belyj and His Novel Petersburg (Andrej Belyj i ego roman Peterburg), 5n
Dostoevskij, Fedor,
  Crime and Punishment (Prestuplenie i nakazanie), 9n, 128
  The Double (Dvojnik), 3, 9n, 128–29, 304, 308, 315
  The Idiot (Idiot), 85, 317
  Notes from Underground (Zapiski iz podpol'ja), 35n, 47, 48, 100n, 114, 211
  "Petersburg dreams in verses and prose" ("Peterburgskie snovidenija v stixax i v proze"), 82–83
  The Possessed (Besy), 3, 330
  "White Nights" ("Belye noči"), 3, 225–27
Driver, Sam,
  "Axmatova's *Poema bez geroja* i Blok's *Vozmezdie*," 86n
Eliade, Mircea,
  Myth and History, 244
Epštejn, Mixail,
  Nature, the World, the Mystery of the Universe (Priroda, mir, tajnik vselennoj), 37–41, 44–45
Evtušenko, Evgenij,
  "To A. A. Axmatova" ("A. A. Axmatovoj"), 55, 133–34, 216, 364
Fenomen Peterburga, 6n
Freidin, Gregory,
  A Coat of Many Colors, 284n
Frizman, Leonid,
  Russkaja èlegija XVIII–načala XX veka, 39n

Glück, Christoph
 Orfeo et Euridice, 126, 286, 324n
Gogol′, Nikolaj,
 Dead Souls (*Mertvye duši*), 62
 "Diary of a Madman" ("Zapiski sumasšedšego"), 126
 "The Nose" ("Nos"), 141
 "The Overcoat" ("Šinel′"), 201
 "Petersburg Notes for 1836" ("Peterburgskie zapiski 1836-ogo goda"), 365–66
 "A Terrible Vengeance" ("Strašnaja mest′"), 79–80
Gordin, Jakov,
 Calling in the dark: Joseph Brodsky and His Circle (*Pereklička vo mrake: Iosif Brodskij i ego sobesedniki*), 244n
Gumilev, Nikolaj,
 "The Tram That Lost Its Way" ("Zabludivšijsja tramvaj"), 46, 69, 166–67, 280–81, 350
Hackel, Sergei,
 The Poet and the Revolution:Alexander Blok's 'The Twelve,' " 74n
Isenburg, Charles,
 Substantial Proofs of Being, 95n
Ivanov, Georgij,
 "A quarter century has passed abroad" ("Četvert′ veka prošlo za granicej"), 93–94
 The Splitting of the Atom (*Raspad atoma*), 124–26
 "It's good there is no tsar" ("Xorošo, čto net carja"), 161
Ivanov, Vjačeslav,
 Dionis i pradionijstvo, 286n
 "Fio, ergo non sum," 351n
Jaanus, Marie,
 Literature and Negation, 179n, 266n

Jakobson, Roman,
 Pushkin and His Sculptural Myth, 210n
Jung, C. G.,
 Modern Man in Search of a Soul, 114–15
Könönen, Maija,
 Four Ways of Writing the City, 248n
Krive, Sarah,
 Appropriating the Early Akhmatova, 325n
Krivulin, Viktor,
 Hunting the Mammoth (*Oxota na mamonta*), 5n, 370n
Kjuxel′beker, Vil′gelm,
 "Carskoe Selo," 255–56
Lachmann, Renate,
 Memory and Literature, 5n, 211, 253
The Lay of the Host of Igor (*Slovo o polku Igoreve*), 123–24
Leiter, Sharon,
 Akhmatova's Petersburg, 240n
Leont′ev, Konstantin,
 "The Triune Process of Development," 63n
Lermontov, Mixail,
 "A lone sail whitens" ("Beleet parus odinokij"), 10, 39
 Masquerade (*Maskarad*), 344
 "When the yellowing cornfield stirs" ("Kogda volnuetsja želtejuščaja niva"), 41
Livšic, Benedikt,
 "Fontanka," 34–36
 From the Marshy Swamps (*Iz topkix bolot*), 34
 "Kazan Cathedral" ("Kazanskij sobor"), 31–34
 The Swamp Medusa (*Bolotnaja medusa*), 34

Lo Gatto, Ettore,
  Il Mito de San Pietroburgo, 5n
Lotman, Jurij,
  "The symbolics of Petersburg and problems of urban semiotics" ("Simvolika Peterburga i problemy semiotiki goroda"), 5n
Lukomskij, Georgij,
  Old Petersburg (*Staryj Peterburg*), 309n
Majakovskij, Vladimir,
  "Broadway" ("Brodvej"), 26
  "Brooklyn Bridge" ("Bruklinskij most"), 26
  "From street into street" ("Iz ulicy v ulicu"), 24–26
  "The Last Petersburg Tale" ("Poslednjaja peterburgskaja skazka"), 28
  "A Thing or Two About Petersburg" ("Koe-čto pro Peterburg"), 27
Mallarmé, Stéphane,
  "Virginal, vivacious, and beautiful today" ("Le vierge, le vivace, et le bel aujourd'hui"), 260n
Mandel'štam, Nadežda,
  Hope Abandoned, 334
Mandel'štam, Osip,
  "The Admiralty" ("Admiraltejstvo"), 18–22, 34, 290–92, 331
  "At a half turn, o sadness" ("V poloborota, o pečal'"), 345
  "Blue eyes and a burning forehead" ("Golubye glaza i gorjaščaja lobnaja kost'"), 269n
  "The Caucasian mountains shouted to him" ("Emu kavkazskie kričali gory"), 269n
  "Conversation about Dante" ("Razgovor o Dante"), 179
  "The courage of midnight maidens" ("Dev polunočnyx otvaga"), 305
  The Egyptian Stamp (*Egipetskaja marka*), 11, 19, 47, 65, 95, 114, 121–24, 127, 138–39, 141–43, 176ff., 229n, 298, 300, 302n, 308n, 306–22, 326
  "The End of the Novel" ("Konec romana"), 49, 58–59, 153, 170–71, 316
  "Fourth Prose" ("Četvertaja proza"), 309
  "From where was he brought? Who? Who has died?" ("Otkuda privezli? Kogo? Kotoryj umer?"), 269n
  "The ghost-like stage barely flickers" ("Čut' mercaet prizračnaja scena"), 95
  "He conducted the Caucasian mountains" ("On dirižiroval kavkazskimi gorami"), 269n
  "Help me, Lord, to live through this night" ("Pomogi, Gospod', ètu noč' perežit'"), 98, 176
  "I forgot the word" ("Ja slovo pozabyl"), 121–24, 127, 131, 286
  "In a crystal pool what steepness lies" ("V xrustal'nom omute kakaja krutizna"), 296n
  "Kazan Cathedral" ("Kazanskij sobor"), 30–34
  "The apartment is as quiet as paper" ("Kvartira tixa, kak bumaga") 287–88
  "Leningrad," 161, 174–76
  "Mixoel's," 308–09

"Morning of Acmeism" ("Utro akmeizma"), 65
The Noise of Time (*Šum vremeni*), 12, 19, 113ff., 139, 176–77, 298ff., 315
"On the Nature of the Word" ("O prirode slova"), 21
"Puškin and Skrjabin" ("Puškin i Skrjabin"), 119, 130, 195n, 304
"Preserve My Speech" ("Soxrani moju reč'"), 53–54, 325
"The Tenth of January, 1934" ("10-ogo janvarja 1934 g"), 269n
"Under arches of ancient quiet I love" ("Ljublju pod svodami sedyja tishiny"), 213–15
"Voronež," 26
"A wandering fire at a terrible height" ("Na strašnej vysote bluždajuščij ogon'"), 95
"We will die in transparent Petropolis" ("V Petropole prozračnom my umrem"), 120
"We will gather again in St. Petersburg" ("V Peterburge my sojdemsja snova"), 94, 118, 119, 126, 215–16, 239, 242, 243, 244, 250–51, 286, 369
"The Word and Culture," 267n
"Yes, I lie in the earth" ("Da, ja ležu v zemle"), 286

Merežkovskij, Dmitrij,
 Peter and Aleksej (*Petr i Aleksej*), 14
 Metaphysics of Petersburg (*Metafizika Peterburga*), 5n
Mickiewicz, Adam,
 Dziady, 83n
Mir iskusstva, 52n, 65n
Murav'ev, Mixail,
 "To the Goddess of the Neva" ("Bogine Nevy"), 14n

Nabokov, Vladimir,
 The Defense, 195, 200, 298, 306–22
 "Evening in a Vacant Lot" ("Večer na pustyre"), 337–40
 "The Firing Squad" ("Rasstrel"), 277
 "For nighttime wandering" ("Dlja stranstvija nočnogo"), 199–202
 The Gift (*Dar*), 196n, 273–74
 "The Ice Skater" ("Kon'kobežec"), 281
 "No matter what battle canvas" ("Kakim by polotnom batal'nym"), 277–78
 "Peterburg," 259
 "Sankt-Peterburg," 278
 Speak, Memory (*Drugie berega, Conclusive Evidence*), 94–98, 140, 190–98, 266, 298, 306–22
 "A Visit to a Museum" ("Poseščenija muzeja"), 275–77, 288
Nekrasov, Nikolaj,
 "About the Weather" ("O pogode") 9, 39
Nerval, Gérard de,
 "El Desdichado," 179, 198
Nietzsche, Friedrich,
 The Antichrist, 114
 The Birth of Tragedy, 47
 On the Uses and Disadvantages of History, 334n
Otradin, Mixail,
 Peterburg v russkoj poezii XVIII-načala XX veka, 27n
Ovid,
 Tristia, 298
Pasternak, Boris,
 "To A. A. Axmatova" ("A. A.Axmatovoj"), 271n

"Isn't it time for birds to sing?" ("Ne vremja l' pticam pet'?"), 56n
"Paul Marie Verlaine," 58–59
"Theme and Variations" ("Temy i variacii"), 292–96
Pike, Burton,
 The Image of the City in Modern Literature, 6n
Poe, Edgar Allan,
 "Lenore," 92
Polonskij, Jakov,
 "Miazma," 117
Poulet, Georges,
 Studies in Human Time, 91n, 95n, 96n, 97n, 151n, 197n
Puškin, Aleksandr,
 The Bronze Horseman (Mednyj vsadnik), 4, 8, 13–14, 16–17, 20, 23, 38–39, 41, 108–09, 123, 125, 252–53, 290, 292, 295, 357–58, 366
 "Carskoe selo," 256–58, 264–65
 Eugene Onegin (Evgenij Onegin), 42–43, 101, 292–94
 "Exegi monumentum," 17–18
 "I have visited again" ("Vnov' ja posetil"), 166
 "Memories in Carskoe Selo" ("Vospominanija v Carskom Sele"), 264–65
 "October 19" ("19 oktjabrja"), 256
 "The Poet" ("Poèt"), 289, 295
 Poltava, 290
 "The Prophet" ("Prorok"), 242, 246
 Ruslan i Ljudmila, 293
 "The Town" ("Gorodok"), 263
Reeder, Roberta,
 "Tsarskoe Selo in the Poetry of Anna Akhmatova: The Eternal Return," 261n

Riccio, Carlo,
 Materiali per un'edizione critica di Poema bez geroja di Anna Achmatova, 347n
Rozanov, Vasilij,
 Apocalypse of Our Time (Apokalipsis našego vremeni), 47, 72–73, 92, 100, 215
 Fallen Leaves (Opavšie list'ja), 124, 281n
 Solitaria, 124
Šklovskij, Viktor,
 The Knight's Move (Xod konja), 243n
Solov'ev, Vladimir,
 "Valentinian and Valentinianism" ("Valentin i Valentinianstvo"), 283n
Timenčik, Roman,
 "Poètika Sankt-Peterburga epoxi simvolizma," 229n
Tjutčev, Fedor,
 "And so I have met you again" ("Itak, opjat' uvidelsja ja s Vami"), 146–48, 167–69
 "The blue-gray shadows have merged" ("Teni sizye smešilis'"), 44
 "Day and night" ("Den' i noc'"), 47
 "The east grew white" ("Vostok belel"), 110
 "The Greeting of the Spirit" ("Privetstvie duxa"), 108
 "Oh, how bright the moon sometimes" ("Kak poroju svetlyj mesjac"), 108
 "On the Neva" ("Na Neve"), 112
 "Once more I stand above the Neva" ("Opjat' stoju ja nad Nevoj"), 110–11, 331

"Shipwreck" ("Korablekrušenie"), 108
"Standing above the Neva I gazed" ("Gljadel ja, stoja nad Nevoj"), 109–10
Tolstoj, Lev N.,
  Anna Karenina, 124–27, 298, 310, 316n
  What is Art? (*Čto takoe iskusstvo?*), 126
Toporov, Vladimir,
  Axmatova and Blok (*Axmatova i Blok*), 343n
  "Petersburg and the Petersburg Text in Russian Literature" ("Peterburg i peterburgskij tekst russkoj literatury"), 5n, 232n
Urbaszewski, Laura,
  Creating the First Classical Poet of Socialist Realism: Mayakovsky as a Subject of Celebration Culture, 348n
Vaginov, Konstantin,
  Goat Song (*Kozlinaja pesn'*), 245
Vilenkin, Vitalij,
  In the One Hundred and First Mirror (*V sto pervom zerkale*), 347n

Volkov, Solomon,
  Petersburg: A Cultural History, 5n
Vroon, Ronald,
  "The Citadel of the Revolutionary Word," 34n
Wolfe, Thomas,
  You Can't Go Home Again, 146
Xodasevič, Vladislav,
  "Ballad" ("Ballada"), 239n, 283–88
  Necropolis (*Nekropol'*), 99, 175, 284
  "Petersburg" ("Peterburg"), 240–42, 246
  The Shaken Tripod (*Koleblemyj trenožnik*), 119n, 284
  "Sorrento Photographs" ("Sorrentinskie fotografii"), 271–73
  The Way of the Grain (*Putem zerna*), 283
Yeats, W. B.,
  "The Second Coming," 50n
Zamjatin, Evgenij,
  "The Cave" ("Peščera"), 129–131, 171
Žukovskij, Vasilij,
  "The Swan of Carskoe Selo" ("Carskosel'skaja lebed'"), 258–59